THE
LITERARY WORKS OF
Matthew Prior

My noble, lovely, little Peggy,
Let this my first Epistle beg ye
At dawn of Morn and close of Even
To lift Your Heart and Hands to Heaven.
In double Beauty say your Prayer
Our Father first, then Nôtre Pere:
And, Dearest Child, along the Day,
In every thing You do or say
Obey and please my Lord and Lady,
So God shall love, and Angels aid ye.

If to these precepts you attend,
No second letter need I send:
And so I rest, Your constant Friend
                    Matthew Prior.

Wimple March 29.
        1720

A Letter to the Honorable Lady Mrs: Margaret Candish Harley
From Prior's autograph at Longleat

THE
LITERARY WORKS OF
Matthew Prior

EDITED BY

H. BUNKER WRIGHT

AND

MONROE K. SPEARS

Volume II

OXFORD

AT THE CLARENDON PRESS

1959

Oxford University Press, Amen House, London E.C.4

GLASGOW   NEW YORK   TORONTO   MELBOURNE   WELLINGTON
BOMBAY   CALCUTTA   MADRAS   KARACHI   KUALA LUMPUR
CAPE TOWN   IBADAN   NAIROBI   ACCRA

PRINTED IN GREAT BRITAIN
AT THE UNIVERSITY PRESS, OXFORD
BY VIVIAN RIDLER
PRINTER TO THE UNIVERSITY

CONTENTS

VOLUME II

Prior's signed autograph of 'A Letter to the Honorable Lady Mrs: Margaret Candish Harley' (1720), from the Prior MSS. at Longleat, vol. i, fol. 64. Reproduced by kind permission of the Marquis of Bath   *Frontispiece*

LATIN WORKS

Edited with the assistance of A. Brandon Conron

Edited with the assistance of A. Brandon Conron

1683

On the Marriage of George Prince of Denmark, and the Lady Anne.

CONJUNCTUM *Veneri Martem, Danosque Britannis*
    Dum canit altisonis docta caterva modis,
Affero sincerum culto pro carmine votum,
    Quod minus ingenii, plus pietatis habet.
Vivant Ambo diu, vivant fœliciter, opto;   5
    Diligat hic Sponsam, diligat illa Virum;
Junctos perpetuâ teneas *Hymenæe* catenâ;
    Junctos, *Juno*, die protege, nocte, *Venus*.
Exultent simili felices prole Parentes,
    Ut petat hinc multos Natio bina duces.   10
Cúmque senes pariter cupiant valedicere terris,
    Ne Mors augustum dividat atra jugum;
Sed qualis raptum transvexit currus *Elijam*,
    Transvehat ad superas talis utrúmque domos.

Ad Decanum Westmonasteriensem Carmen Pastorale.

Thyrsis, Tityrus.

THYRSIS.

TITYRE vicinos volitavit fama per agros
    Illius enarrans nomen, titulosque recentes
Quem mihi, dum patulis recubavimus ambo sub ulmis
Dicere tu toties, toties laudare solebas.
Granta triumphali testatur gaudia plausu   5

On the Marriage. Title: Supplied by 1781

Et sonat omne nemus Pastoris arundine læti
Tu tamen, ut fueris pars hujus nulla Triumphi
Hic inter densas Corylos umbracula quæris
Et mala sopitis exerces otia musis.

TITYRUS.

Audivi famam de Præsule magna loquentem   10
Atque avida voces lætissimus aure recepi,
Audivi pueros de Præsule magna canentes
Ast ægra voces has invidus aure recepi,
Invidus illorum tentavi vincere plausus,
Et paulo majore tuba celebrare patronum   15
Sylvestres decies repetivi sedulus umbras
Pierides decies in Carmina læta vocavi;
At toties frustra non audivêre vocantem
Nam sedes fugere Sacras solitosque recessus
Mutantes Notum Thamesis pro littore Camum   20
Illic (ante quidem meminissem læva fuisset
Ni mihi mens) habitant pastores me meliores
Et Calamos inflare leves, et dicere versus.
Horum Thyrsi (fatebor enim nec turpe fateri)
Fistula si mea sit facundis juncta Choreis   25
Dulcia turbarem rauco modulamina cantu
Tam bene se Cygnis jungat morientibus Anser
Tam bene Cecropias offendat Pica querelas.

THYRSIS.

Si tamen, ut dixti, præsul te semper amavit
Si bonus est facilisque, Deoque simillimus illi   30
Quem colimus pecoris custodes, incipe Carmen,
Hoc capiet vultu quo pristina dona sereno.

TITYRUS.

O! si nostra alios superaret fistula cantus
Qualiter ante humiles curas, vulgusque Clientum
Devinctum facilis præsul me semper amavit   35
Invida tum nostræ vicinia tota Camænæ

---

14 vincere *edd.*: vinceræ *L 28*   17 vocavi *edd.*: vocani *L 28*   21 læva *edd.*:
lava *L 28*   28 querelas. *edd.*: querelas *L 28*   30 Si bonus ... simillimus *edd.*:
Sibonus ... simillimis *L 28*

Cederet Idæis quantum viburna cupressis
Sed modo quod totam penetrabant gaudia mentem
Gaudia quæ solum poteram narrare silendo
Velox et tacitus puerosque Chorosque reliqui   40
Spretaque vicinâ jam pendet ab ilice Avena.

1684

Ad Comitem Dorcestriæ in Annum ineuntem 84.

Ad Ianum.

SIC tua perpetuis fument altaria donis
   Plurima sic flammæ pabula mittat Arabs
Sic dum Sacra novis redimuntur tempora sertis,
   Nestoreos poscant fæmina virque dies.
Casside depositâ placide sic nuncia Pacis   5
   Ianua sopito cardine limen amet.
Candida procedant festiuo tempora motu
   Et faveat Domino quælibet hora meo
Publica conciliis gravibus seu commoda tractet,
   Seu vacuum pectus mollior urat amor.   10
Seu pia Mordaci meditetur Vulnera chartâ
   (Vulnera quæ tali sola levantur ope)
Seu legat oblito facilis mea Carmina fastu,
   O! bene carminibus consule, Diue, meis.
Iane fave, Domini veniet Natalis ad aras   15
   O Superis ipsis sacra sit Illa dies,
Sacra sit Illa dies, niveoque notata Lapillo,
   Qua tulit illustris nobile Mater onus
Qua Mihi Patronum gestit, gentique Quiritem
   Artificique Deo pene dedisse Parem.   20

Title: 84] 1684 *1740*   3 sertis, *1740*: sertio *L 28*

In XXIX Diem Maij Carmen Pastorale.

Lycidas canit Natalitia, Melibæus reditum Regis.

LYCIDAS.

Hic densas inter Salices et flumina nota
Conjuncti patulâ residebimus ambo sub Umbrâ
Tu Melibæe canes, ego respondebo canenti
Quos festiva dies, quos Carolus exigit Hymnos.

MELIBÆUS.

Ante strepens dulces imitabitur Anser Olores,   5
Raucaque Cecropias superabit pica querellas
Quam mea Præ Lycidæ conabitur ire Camæna;
Incipe Tu Lycida, Phæbeos incipe cantus,
Fac modo vestra loquantur et haud mea fila tacebunt.

LYCIDAS.

Nascitur Angliacis, Pastores nascitur oris   10
Chara Deo soboles magni Patris incrementum
Gloria præsentis secli, columenque futuri;
Ferte Rosas juvenes, Colocasia ferte Puellæ,
Ridentes uariis spolientur honoribus Agri
Ut puero texam primo de flore Coronam.   15

MELIBÆUS.

Rursus ad Angliacas, Pastores, venit ad oras
Unica cura Deum, miseræ spes unica gentis
Præsidium secli præsentis, lausque futuri.
Tollite mista rosis Colocasia, tollite flores,
Et Jovis et Caroli lacerentur ab arbore rami   20
Ut reduci texam meritâ de fronde Coronam.

LYCIDAS.

Ite celebrentur Sacro natalia plausu,
Salua coronatis requiescant rura juvencis
Et sonet omne nemus pastoris arundine læti;
Ferte decus frugum pressique coagula lactis,   25

Titl *Regis edd.*: requis *L 28*   6 querellas *edd.*: quereolos *L 28*   7 Camæna *edd.*:
Carmæna *L 28*   16 venit ad *edd.*: veritur *L 28*   18 futuri. *edd.*: futuri *L 28*

Et parco gratam pertingite melle placentam;
Mystica dum gaudens meditatur verba Sacerdos,
Et multo faciles gaudent libamine Diui
Qui dant cum Carolo pietatem visere terras.

MELIBÆUS.

Ite triumphali reditum celebrate Choræâ,   30
Gaudia communes regnent effusa per Agros.
Et cadat e pleno memorabile Munus Ovili
Chio solvite Vinc'la cado, proferte Falernum.
Lætitiam reduci longos optate per Annos,
Audivisse Deos dum læva tonitrua dicunt,   35
Et redit e cælis geminatæ vocis imago;
Ebria dum multo saturantur Numina Baccho
Quæ dant has Carolum, pacémque revisere terras.

LYCIDAS.

Blande puer, tibi prima dabit Munuscula tellus
Florentes Violas, et odoriferos hyacinthos,   40
Pulchræ grata ferent Calathis tibi Lilia plenis
Naïdes, et molli spargent Cunabula Musco;
Tu puer, innocuis transcurres tutus in agris
Dum flos illæsus placido sub pondere surgat,
Calcarique petat Tua sub vestigia gramen: 45
Dum fera divini mirabitur oris Honorem
Et sacra mansueti cumbent ad Crura leones
Te colet omnis ager, montes te, Carole, regem
Te fluviusque loquax strepitansque fatebitur Arbos
Concedet Pan sceptra tibi, Thyrsumque Lyæus   50
Tu lætus curabis oues oviumque magistros,
Gaudentesque reges justo moderamine Sylvas.

MELIBÆUS.

Maxime vir, tibi mille dabunt discrimina Diui
Intrepidoque feres animo discrimina mille,
Victrix causa Deis, tibi Carole, victa placebit   55
Usque fatigatus donec Divum atque hominum Rex

31 Gaudia *edd.*: Gaudie *L 28*   33 Vinc'la cado *edd.*: Vin'cla eado *L 28*   45 Tua *edd.*:
Tua, *L 28*   47 sacra *edd.*: sacre *L 28*   50 Pan *edd.*: pan *L 28*   52 moderamine
Sylvas *edd.*: mederamine Syloas *L 28*   54 discrimina *edd.*: discriminia *L 28*   56 donec
edd.: doneo *L 28*

Heroem agnoscit, fatumque errasse fatetur.
Posthæc incipient magni procedere Menses,
Ætas felici revocabitur aurea Mundo
Nec lupus insidias pecori, pecorisve magistris   60
Latro struet, raptos iterum nec flebimus Agros.
Tu pacemque tuis longam, Cereremque reduces
Tu junges stabili bellantes fædere gentes
Incolumes longa solves formidine fluctus;
Eximiisque reges placidum virtutibus orbem.   65

LYCIDAS.

Te Venerande Redux, seri pastoris arundo
Te celebrabit adhuc inamatæ virginis hymnus.

MELIBÆUS.

Cumque tuis olim Pani miscebimus aras
Sylva canet Carolum Carolumque remugiet Eccho.

Ad Franc: Episc: Eliensem.

CUM virtutes tuas unusquisque collaudet et honores gratuletur nostræ V R audaciæ ignoscat tua benignitas si minimâ pollens eloquentiâ ardentissimo tamen studio accensus ad communem Populi Chorum adjungens vocem cum Virum optimum tum benignissimum celebret Patronum qui tuis maximè devinctus beneficiis summoperè 5 conatur merito vocari

Favoris tui Studiosissimus
M. Pr:

Reverendo in Christo Patri Thomæ (Sprat) Episcopo Roffensi &ca:

Εὐδαιμονεῖν.

VICIMUS, exultans fausto crepat omine Daphnis
Testaturque bonos nuncia fibra Deos,
Grandius eloquium meditare Thalia, patronum
Quem modo laudasti nunc venerare Patrem

---

62 longam *edd.*: longuam *L 28*   67 inamatæ *edd.*: inimatæ *L 28*
Ad Franc: Episc: Eliensem. 2 nostræ *1740*: nostra *L 28*

Quis putet incertis volvi subtemina parcis?   5
  Quis meritos æquum destituisse Iovem?
Cum virtute tuum crescit decus, Aucte Sacerdos,
  Impatiensque breves spernit utrumque modos
Qualiter Elæo fælix in pulvere Victor
  Cui semel ornatas lambit Oliva comas   10
Suspirans partas queritur marcescere frondes
  Et parat elapsas ad nova bella rotas
Sic tibi major honos veteres protudit honores,
  Metaque præteritæ laudis origo novæ est;
Phæbææ Iuvenile caput cinxere corollæ,   15
  Palma Viri decuit tempora, Mitra Senis.

Epistola eodem tempore Missa.

CUM voluntas regia, Optimatum consensus, bonorumque omnium
studia infulam merenti concesserint, ignoscas pater Reverende
quod inter communem populi plausum Cliens eo Minus ad enarrandum
sufficiens quo beneficiis plus fuerim devinctus et tuos in Ecclesiâ
honores et Ecclesiæ a tuis honoribus fælicitatem festinet gratulari,   5
Favoris tui Studiosissimus
M. Pr.

1685

Supposito Hobbæano statu naturæ non datur jus omnium ad omnia.

(*Feb: 28th: 1684/5.*)

SUFFICIT ut cedam ruptæ de vulnere quercus
  Fato mortales exiliisse pari
Non tamen ut strictos fatear nascentibus enses
  Et nece Cognatâ triste madere nemus

---

10 Oliva *1740* : Olivia *L 28*   *After l. 16, 1740 adds* M.P.
  4 Ecclesiâ *1740* : Ecclesiam *L 28*   5 gratulari, *1740* : gratulari. *L 28*   6 Studiosissimus *1740* : Studiosissimus. *L 28*
  1 quercus *edd.* : quereus *L 28*

Diua sagax per quam generatim secla propagent 5
 Indulget curæ pacis avara suæ,
Intima communi fovit præcordia flammâ
 Vt quos disjungant commoda, jungat amor.
Rerum mitis Amor concordi pace ligavit
 Semina, & æternam jussit habere fidem. 10
Cum bene floruerant a flavo dicta metallo
 Tempora, nobilior nemo nec hostis erat.
Viderunt Primas argentea Sæcula lites
 Cum fuit imperium cædis origo nouæ
Supprime inæquales fluctus maris ira recumbet 15
 Et pax sopitas alta tenebit aquas,
Plurima gemmatum cum stella coronat Olympum
 Et par contiguo spargit ab axe jubar
Lumine quæque tamen proprio contenta refulget.
 Nec furit in socias ambitiosa faces. 20
Tityre Phæbeas justo pone ordine laurus
 Quas rivo parili nutriat æquus Amor
Florescunt inter sese Socialibus umbris,
 Nec malè vicinis invidet ulla comis.
    Ergo 25
Mutua sorte pari junctas concordia servet,
 Dum quisque incolumis quod tueatur, habet.

Ad Regios Fratres.

QUALITÈR exornant *Geminâ* qui *lampade* cœlum,
 Si simul eniteant, non feret axis onus:
Sic cœlo quod abest, nè Numine terra fruatur,
 Alternâ decorat Vos diadema vice.
Sydera Tu calca, Tu protege serior orbem; 5
 Nam Deus è vobis alter es, alter eris.

---

8 amor. *edd.*: amor *L 28*   10 fidem. *edd.*: fidem *L 28*   11 floruerant *edd.*: flouerant *L 28* 12 erat. *edd.*: erat *L 28* 16] Horrida nec raties [rabies?] nec grave murmur erit *Alt. MS. reading* aquas, *edd.*: aquas *L 28* 24 comis. *edd.*: comis *L 28*

Theme.

Scribimus indocti doctique poemata passim.

VERA me Hercule res est notatuque dignissima, versus qualescunque
possumus, omnes, temerarie, passim conscribimus: cum Virgiliis
Mævi cum pupillis Doctores cum cygnis anseres concinunt, aut
aspirante aut, irato Deo tum optimi tum Pessimi Poetæ mæstissimos ac
lætissimos affectus promunt turbatur Helicon multitudine bibentium 5
vexatus fatiscit Apollo ingemiscit prælum laborat e dolore Academia
mater paritura Poematum vere Fasciculum, monstrosam progeniem,
populi natam ipsamque sui dissimillimam: quam quod nemo agnoscet
suam Scombrorum invidiam aut Oxonien. non injuria metuens regi
ante Januam educenda apponitur. 10

Nobis Deus otia fecit.

Written in 1685.

ERGO perpetuis oneratas floribus aras
Sentiat, innumeris precibus, flammaque perenni
Exorandus ovet, quisquis fuit ille Deorum
Qui primus sortes hominum miseratus iniquas
Afflictos animosque catenatosque dolores 5
Grata fatigatis concesserit Otia terris.
Otia, spes operum, longique corona laboris
Votorum finis, solatia flebilis *Esse*;
Nauta quid intrepidus patriamque Deosque relinquit,
Barbariem terræ Peregrino sole calentis 10
Vimque ferens Thetydos, variique incommoda cæli?
Quid Jovis invidiam, tenebrasque hostisque furores,
Miles dissimulat? nocturnis vigil armis
Friget, et ex galeâ concretas ebibit vndas?
Scilicet emeritos exoptat uterque recessus, 15
Longa ubi præcipitis memorantem damna juventæ

---

2 temerarie *edd.*: temeraris *L 28*   4–5 mæstissimos ac lætissimos *edd.*: matissimas ac
lætissimas *L 28*
11 variique *edd.*: variisque *L 28*   cæli? *edd.*: cæli *L 28*   15 recessus *edd.*: re-
cessons *L 28*

Ingenti platanus ramorum protegat umbrâ:
Seráque Pensetis dubios, Vos, Otia, casus.
Vos rogat ad tepidas Rhetor cum dixerit aras,
Grande sophos temnens, et fessæ præmia linguæ.　　　　　20
Vos fortunatâ gladiator anhelus arenâ,
Insanæque vagis lassus clamoribus vrbis.
Ardet et applausus dederit qui munera consul
Laudibus ipse suis oppressus, siqua darentur
Otia, sublimi non posthabuisse Curiali　　　　　　　　　25
Curtatum dubitabit equum Prochytamque Suburæ.
Otia, vos hominum Sincera Deûmque voluptas,
Fluctusque terrasque ipsumque beastis Olympum,
Nam simul ac rapidum multâ vi presserit æquor
Neptunus, nubesque cavas hyememque fugârit　　　　　30
In gremium pulchræ se rejicit Amphitrites,
Et thalamo gaudens et longæ pacis avarus.
Post iter emensum Phæbus post prælia Mavors
Muneris hoc avidos sese petiisse fatentur,
Ipseque Rex superum sacros cum torserit ignes　　　　35
Armaque jam ponit tempestatesque serenat
Otia dia colit trepido quæ reddidit orbi,
Fratris sola Quiete carent horrenda profundi
Regna, loci miseris, sedesque doloribus aptæ,
Hic labor æternus vexatum Sisyphon vrget,　　　　　40
Hic rota Continuos hic exigit vrna labores
Et suprema manet pæna hic quia nil datur Oti.

---

18 dubios, *edd.*: dubios *L 28*　　　　20 linguæ. *edd.*: lingua *L 28*　　　23 et applausus
dederit] purpureusque dedit *Alt. MS. reading*　　　　25 Curiali *edd.*: Curali *L 28*
26 Suburæ *edd.*: suburræ *L 28*　　　28 beastis *edd.*: beatis *L 28*　　　33 prælia *edd.*:
pralia *L 28*　　　42 Oti *edd.*: Ori *L 28*

1687.

Fuit justum et injustum ante Leges Civiles.
Prim Comitijs 1686/7.

ANTE datas tabulis leges positumque tribunal
   Ante coercentes merita formidine fasces
Cum nondum torva quem majestate timeres
Nec prece nec pretio revocandam quasserat urnam
Æacus, et sortes signatâ morte minaces   5
Cum Numa juridicæ non constituisset amicæ
Nec sacra servassent memores decreta columnæ.

Jus erat et Judex, hominesque quid utile quid non
Cum bene cognôrint, et ab æquo cernere iniquum
Non oculis aliena malis confinia visi   10
Inspicere, insomnesve sub alta nocte latrones
Surgere ad insidias, non ausi sanguine ferrum
Polluere innocuum non aurum implere veneno
Et mixtam cyathis fallacibus addere mortem.

Nam quam cura dedit custodi serior æri   15
Humano potior sub pectore lex latitabat
Dum quid vitandum dicebat quidve petendum
Conscia quæ recti quæ non ignara mali mens
Externæque sagax Ratio nihil indiga legit.

Non erat artifici qui mugiit ære Perillus   20
Non rota vexatum præceps Ixiona torsit
Non Tityon cruciabat avis non Belidas urna.
Sed violare fidem, sed testes temnere Divos
Ausus et a rigido quâcunque abscedere honesto
Has, se damnato, patitur, se judice, pœnas   25
Nam quoties meminit quoties meminisse recusat
Quæ lugenda manent animo tortore reposta
Urna sibi est sibi vultur edax, et ahenea moles.

---

3 torva *edd.*: tarva *L 28*   7 columnæ *edd.*: columna *L 28*   13 innocuum *edd.*:
innocus *L 28*   14 mortem. *edd.*: mortem *L 28*   16 potior *edd.*: portior *L 28*
17 petendum *edd.*: pretendum *L 28*   19 legit. *edd.*: legit *L 28*   22 Belidas
urna. *edd.*: Bolidas urna *L 28*   25 patitur *edd.*: partitur *L 28*   judice, pœnas *edd.*:
judice; penas *L 28*   27 reposta *edd.*: reposto *L 28*

Tunc etiam Jove sub puero cæloque recenti
Non monstris Hobbæe tuis perterritus orbis   30
Impia vis avidum nunquam caput ostendebat
Non lites paritura graves neve horrida bella;
Incolumis certa populus sub lege vigebat
Omnis erat Judex, et in omni mente tribunal.

1688

For an Exhibition.

C UR ad tuos pedes me projecerim requiras? quod ad aras afflicti:
cur plura hodie expeterem beneficia? quod dudum plurima ex-
ceperim: si adveniendo quidem impudens, petendo autem importunus
videar, culpetur isthæc divina Tua munificentia quæ exoranda quotidie
nunquam fatiganda et accedendi mihi audaciam et exorandi spem in- 5
jecerit: nudam itaque ad Te V P R ærumnarum mearum narrationem
afero, misericordiam Tuam si non et opem meriturus: Scholæ West-
monasteriensi nondum valedixeram cum pater meus et inopiâ coactus et
ære alieno oppressus secessit, languebat, mortuus est: ibi tum Illustris-
simæ Ducissæ beneficio fretus Academiam advenio, egenus, tristis, 10
orbus nec quos ipse norim nec qui me norint habens Tu me benevolus
accepisti, acceptum vigilans curasti beneficiis, effecisti ut ex damnis
ditior evaserim, præceptisque effecisti ut et Magistrum celeberrimum
et Patrem mitissimum commutarem potius quam amiserim; ablato
demum ducissæ munere Fundatricis sub te reservasti; periturum Me 15
fovisti, Tuo Patrocinio imo etiam Alieno adscripsisti; lubenti liceat
veracique dicere

       Quod spiro et placeo (si placeo) Tuum est.

Eo tamen angustiâ redactus sum (pudet dicere sed tacere piget) ut
nec collata a Te beneficia absque conferendis retinere amplius potero: 20
Te itaque (V R) per illustrem Tuam benignitatem quæ velit cupiat,
gaudeat bene facere, per Nostras quæ gravissimæ sunt et maximæ

1 projecerim *edd.*: projecerem *L 28*   5 et exorandi *edd.*: ex exorandi *L 28*   6 itaque
edd.: itque *L 28*   ærumnarum *edd.*: ærumenarum *L 28*   9 oppressus *edd.*: oppresseus
L 28   14 mitissimum *edd.*: mitissirnum *L 28*   amiserim; *edd.*: amiserim *L 28*
15 reservasti *edd.*: reservati *L 28*   19 angustiâ *edd.*: angustiæ *L 28*   22 gravissimæ ... maximæ *edd.*: gravissime ... maxime *L 28*

necessitates oro obtestorque ut qui Discipulatum dederis exhibitionem
aliquam adjicias; ut qui a Te benevole admissus libere eductus fuerim,
affluenter demum nutritus Beneficiorum Tuorum quasi Filius ado- 25
lescam.

> Sic ubi flet Semeles perituræ languida proles
>   Et negat ultricem pallida Mater opem
> Jupiter innato properat Succurrere Baccho
>   Ipsaque quem prohibent vivere fata, jubet: 30
> Rumpe Lyæe femur, fæcundo e vulnere prodi,
>   Amissâ reperis dum Genitrice Deum.

Ad Socios Seniores.

April the 2d: 1688.

ID præcipit Natura id Virtus adhortatur ut vehementius expetamus
quæ clarissima sunt et maxima; faveas ideo desideriis nostris et indulgeas precibus si inter Eos cooptari efflagitem quos et liberiora studia
exornant et eximia pietas. id etiam pater meus moriens orbo ac egenti
Nato solum legavit, ut studio fideli ac honestâ ambitione provectus 5
colendos semper atque imitandos haberem Viros, doctos, bonos et
sanctos et Tui V P R quam simillimos; repetitis itaque precibus Te
tuamque notam indulgentiam oro obtestorque ut provinciam nactus
quam Tu dudum ornasti (Deusque concedat Te diu esse ornaturum)
Tuo usque vivam modo tuis inhæream vestigiis: nam eo felicior vitæ 10
nostræ ratio quo vestram magis exprimat. Te ego per nostram quæ
gravissima et maxima egestatem obnixe rogo illud muneris Me exorem
sinas quod sudanti pulchrum desiderium, lassato summum solatium
quod unica studiorum spes, quod ultimus votorum finis. Scio magnum
me petiisse ideoque dignum quod nostra eroget paupertas dignum 15
quod vestra concedat humanitas; quod ad Me attinet Rei literariæ
operam sedulo, dabo moribus exornandis diligentiam summam adhibebo. Curis laboribus vigiliis id efficere meditabor ut agnoscant omnes
undique in quam Societatem receptus sim, quales Patronos nactus,
quales viros imitatus.   20

1 vehementius expetamus *edd.*: vehementius Ex expetamus *L 28*   2 maxima; *edd.*:
maxima *L 28*   7 sanctos *edd.*: sanclos *L 28*   simillimos; *edd.*: simillimos *L 28*
8 obtestorque *edd.*: obtestosque *L 28*   11 per *edd.*: P *L 28*   13 quod *edd.*: q^d: *L 28*
14 quod unica *edd.*: q^d: unica *L 28*   quod *edd.*: q^d: *L 28*   16 quod ... humanitas;
edd.: q^d: ... humanitas *L 28*   quod *edd.*: q^d: *L 28*   17–18 adhibebo. Curis *edd.*:
adhibebo curis. *L 28*

Ad Magistrum eodem die Epistola.

QUOD solent ij qui hodiernum Munus expetunt aut Patroni laudare benevolentiam aut egestatem suam significare id a Me alienum duxi. nam quam ego beneficentiam narrem? tuamne? At tua erga Me singularia et maxima beneficia alta mente atque intimis sensibus firma manent et inscripta majora quam quæ dicendo complecti 5 & plura quam quæ numerando percensere possim; nam quas calamitates conquerar? pauperiem non citius circumstantem quam a Te repulsam sensi, imo non adhuc impendens malum tum prævideram cum Tu remedium invenisses. Patrem patruum & amicum ereptos vix hercle flere datum est, Tu orbo parentem, egenti Patronum, tristi amicum 10 reddidisti, Te ipsum V P R reddidisti. grandi vtique et incredibili beneficiorum serie effecisti ut nullas unquam miserias perpessus sim nullas passurus unquam modo plenissima tua erga Me indulgentia sit diuturna ac perpetua. Te itaque V P R per preces Nostras quas nunquam ad tua genua irritas infixi per præterita tua omnia beneficia 15 (futurorum uti sperem pignora) oro obtestorque ut petitioni nostræ ex consuetudine Bonitatis Tuæ indulgeas, ut hodie velis esse Tui quam simillimus et munera impertias digna quæ post tanta accedant digna quæ vel maxima confirment. Me V P R et res omnes meas Tibi hodie, notæque pietati credo, conferenda expeto beneficia et quoniam pro 20 collatis Magnis & innumerabilibus referre gratias non possim ad vota confugiendum est: quam meretur constans et invicta temperantia utaris sanitate; honores quos eximia ac Summa sibi vendicet doctrina vel invitus assequens affluentiam quæ benignissimi Patroni liberalitati respondeat longum Possideas; salute ac fælicitate Viri optimi moribus 25 et vitæ sanctissimique Xtiani Charitati promissâ æternum perfruaris.

6 possim; edd.: possim *L 28*   7 quam *edd.*: qua *L 28*   14 perpetua. *edd.*: perpetua *L 28*
preces *edd.*: preaes *L 28*   18 munera *edd.*: muneria *L 28*   19 confirment. *edd.*:
confirment *L 28*   22 est: *edd.*: est *L 28*   23 sanitate; *edd.*: sanitate *L 28*   24
assequens *edd.*: assequans *L 28*   25 Possideas; *edd.*: Possideas *L 28*

In Scholâ Westmr: May 14: 1688.

Mallem esse in Villâ Primus quam Romæ secundus.

CUM illud Natura suadeat illud virtus provocet ut ad primas quisque pro virili contendat favete, Patres, teneræ ambitioni, indulgete
honestæ cupidini si in quocunque statu secundos recusarim, si in
Villâ mallem esse dominus quam Romæ dominum pati. nam quis tam
patiens urbis ut ibi primo proximus esse dignetur ubi omnium oculi 5
animique ad primum studiose contendunt? ubi pauca recte effecisse
existimabitur quia nihil optime effecerit? si quando animus ad scriben-
dum appellat, vnus ille melior protinus emicat ad respondendum
Paratus, si rei studeat militari, audacior aliquis ad arma provocet; si
lites moveat callidior alius aut emptâ voce aut extortâ cadentem causa 10
fefellerit. in villâ plura mihi modo sint jugera et res feliciores si scribam
doctior si pugnem fortior si litigem victor facilime evadam. illic mihi
faveant plaudentium villicorum duræ manus et ora ferrea, illic plenos
indulgeant honores quos vel minimos in vrbe superior unus præripuerit.
illic imperem dominus non inglorius dum adversarius in turba secundus 15
feliciori invidet, idemque adulatur nobilis Gnatho et servus splendidus.
lentus Romæ Vrbicus parendo discat imperare; ruri meo primus ac
prædii Monarcha ad imperium non factus sum sed natus, eo fortius
imperaturus quo minus ad parendum doctus. Hoc animo Cæsar irato
senatu fruitur exulum superbe primus nec unquam Romam rediturus 20
nisi inter Quirites nulli secundus. Hoc animo Africanus invidiosos
respuit titulos in villâ primus regnare ultro cupiens ne quando fluctu-
ante aura Populari in vrbe cederet secundus. feliciores Idae dies trans-
egit Paris cum pecori pariter ac dominis jura diceret tanto famosissimus
quam cum aulam paternam repetens Hectori primas daret et bellis 25
minor et natu. Pan uberiori gaudet victimâ sylvarum dominus cui
frugum intactæ festinant primitiæ quam aut Bacchus aut Hercules
vrbana Numina quorum turpes arae ad nauseam onerantur neglectis
istis visceribus quæ deorum princeps delicatior contempserit.

---

3 cupidini edd.: capidini L 28   recusarim, edd.: recusarim. L 28   6 contendunt?
edd.: contendunt. L 28   7 effecerit? edd.: effecerit. L 28   animus edd.: animum L 28
17 imperare; edd.: imperare L 28   21 Quirites edd.: Quvites L 28   24 diceret
edd.: dicerit L 28   famosissimus edd.: famisissimus L 28   26 natu Pan uberiori
edd.: natu Pan oberiori L 28

Ad Magistrum.

GRATIAS Tibi animus meus quam multas habeat, quam plures debeat, cum nec vox exprimere nec cogitatio comprehendere potuerit hodierno velim silentio ignoscas, quid enim de te dicam, de quo omnia bona sunt dicenda, num optimum venerabor magistrum qui mores meos excolueris? at studiis arrisisti benignissimus Patronus 5 benignissimum itaque Patronum prædicabo? at alium mihi nactus es bonum ac facilem ac Tibi simillimum. Ideone magnum mihi et Memorabile beneficium contulisse Te fatebor? at nova novorum beneficiorum cumulatione locupletasti quotidie pergis locupletare. Isthæc omnia meritorum erga me Tuorum Specimina nec culpa ingenii deterere ausim 10 nec facundâ (si potuerim) garrulitate minuere. non epistolæ non Diei opus est repetitam Benignitatis Tuæ seriem commemorare, sed totius vitæ atque omnium cogitationum: Immo detur commemoranti Herculea alacritas adjiciatur ætas Nestorea. Isthoc tamen Injuriæ dedit, miranda vestra munificentia ut vivendum mihi sit et moriendum ingrato. 15

Epistola ad Magistrum.

From Burleigh.

COGITANTI mihi vir plurime Reverende dubium videtur an diuturnum silentium an scripturam hodiernam excusarem. nam quid ego ausim ad virum eximii acerrimique judicii rudis et impolitus tandem aliquando Scribere? ad Patronum vero singularis summæque benignitatis obligatus idem toties et devinctus antea scripsisse quid 5 non festinaveram? adeo res rediit V. P. colende ut petam veniam, duplicem; et exorabo, certe nam et Te novi et benevolentiam tuam. jam vero repetitas tibi gratias ago quotquot agi solent ad Virum optimum pro maximis beneficiis. Salutem tibi mitto plurimam idque merito propter Collegii præsidium, Academiæ decus rei publicæ literariæ et 10 Christianæ religionis tutamen et gloriam, atque (si minima maximis adjungere liceret) propter nostrum gaudium felicitatemque. quod ad me attinet ab Honoratissimo Comite Exonensi benigne acceptus sum

---

7 simillimum. *edd.*: simillimum *L 28*   9 locupletare. *edd.*: locupletare *L 28*   11
minuere. *edd.*: minuere *L 28*   14 Nestorea. *edd.*: Nestorea *L 28*
1–2 an diuturnum *edd.*: andiuturnum *L 28*   2 hodiernam *edd.*: hodierniam *L 28*
3 acerrimique *edd.*: acceriimique *L 28*   4 singularis *edd.*: singuloris *L 28*   12 felicitatemque. *edd.*: felicitatemque *L 28*

ideo ab uno illustri Viro non despectus quod missus ab altero filiis ejus
optimis meæ curæ traditis, mihique ipsi an ad Burleiam per Hyemem 15
manendum an ad Academiam adeundum an peregrinandum, omne id
incertum faciunt molesta hæcce et periculosa tempora. hoc solum in
animo mihi certum manet et æternum manebit quod in qualicunque
vitæ ratione, omnique rerum vicissitudine te summo colam studio te
plurima prosequar reverentiâ.   20

Ad illustrissimam Dm: Margaritam Coll: D. Jo: Fundatricem.

M AGNIFICAS propter sedes, murosque loquentes
   Divi perpetuos & Fundatricis honores,
Consita jucundos nectunt saliceta recessus,
Et fluit unda loquax, et Somnos suadet inire,
Illic dum peragit sopitis otia Damon   5
Cantibus haud memorans seræ decedere nocti
Lux nova miratum radiis cælestibus antrum
Complevit, noctisque fugatas reppulit umbras
Descendunt gravidæ divino pondere nubes,
Pulchraque cedentes monstratur Imago per auras.   10
Stat puer, incerto lacerantur pectora motu,
Et modo delectant miracula quæ modo terrent
Gaudia deinde jubent vanos oritura timores
Ponere, Matronamque pio sic ore profari.

O Decus elapsi venientis gloria sec'li,   15
O fælix Thalamis, sed felicissima partu,
Et dum vicinis carmen pietasque manebunt
Mænibus, o seris veneranda nepotibus umbra!
Tu mihi sis felix humili tu Musa Clienti
Annueris; cytharæ multam celebranda dedisti   20
Materièm, faciles addas in carmine vires,
Magnarum doceas exordia sumere rerum,
Ambagesque tuæ longas transcurrere laudis.

Title: Margaritam . . . Fundatricem edd.: Margattam . . . Fundatricens *L 28*   5
Illic *edd.*: Illie *L 28*   6 memorans *edd.*: inemorans *L 28*   14 pio *edd.*: pia *L 28*
20 Annueris; *edd.*: Annueris *L 28*   23 laudis. *edd.*: laudis *L 28*

Dicam cum longis tereretur cladibus ætas
Et peritura suas horreret Patria vires   25
Te laceras junxisse Rosas, te Pace Perenni
Languenti longos populo pensasse dolores,
Iam post pacatas acies servataque regna
Et lauro Martis contextas Pacis Olivas
Irrequieta moras discit contemnere Virtus   30
Maxima quod dudum vicit majoribus instans
Longaque quæ meritos reddant per secla triumphos
Tranquillis gaudet posuisse Cubilia Musis
Et reddent (dum plectra sibi vocesque supersint
Lampade dum pulchrâ fulgebis sydus amicum   35
Dum laudent homines muros, superique struentes)
Divi perpetuos et fundatricis honores.

Ad Dm: Gower, Coll: Magistrum, Epistola Deprecatoria.

NISI tuam jampridem benevolentiam et laudatam ab expertis audivissem et expertus ipse sæpissimè laudassem et pudor & tristitia conscio mihi silentium indixissent: atenim V R dum coram Patrono, Amico, Patre provolvor, te non dubitat impetrare audax dolor per accepta olim beneficia per effluentes lacrymas (et hæ mentiri 5 nesciunt) perque tuum isthunc celeberrimum candorem quem imprudens læsi, solicitus repeto ut non solum ad condiscipulorum mensam sed ad magistri gratiam restituatur

Favoris Tui Studiosissimus

M: P.   10

---

24 cladibus *edd.*: eladibus *L 28*   26 laceras *edd.*: loceras *L 28*   29 Martis *edd.*: martis *L 28*   33 posuisse *edd.*: possuisse *L 28*   36 struentes *edd.*: struente *L 28*   2 audivissem *1740*: audivisem *L 28*   3 indixissent: *1740*: indixissent *L 28*   7 ut non] ut peccanti ignoscas, & obliteres crimen, ut non *1740*   condiscipulorum *1740*: condisciplorum *L 28*   8 restituatur *1740*: restituatur. *L 28*   9 Studiosissimus *1740*: Studiosissimus. *L 28*

Carmen Deprecatorium ad eundem.

IRATAS acuit dum læsus Apollo sagittas
　　Neglectas renovat mæsta Thalia Preces
Qualescunque potest jejuno promere cantu;
　　Heu mihi non est res ingeniosa Fames!
Grana neges alacri languet vis ignea Gallo,　　　　　　5
　　Deme laboranti pabula languet equus.
Latrantis Stomachi sterilis nec pascis hiatum
　　Daphni, nec arentem castalis unda sitim.
Tum bene lassatur Flaccus cum dixerit ohe
　　Pieriasque merum nobilitavit aquas.　　　　　　10
Jejuni depressa jacet vel Musa Maronis,
　　Flet culicem esuriens qui satur arma canit.
O si! Mecænas major mihi riserit, O si
　　Fulgenti solitum regnet in ore jubar
Crimine purgato pie post jejunia, Musa　　　　　　15
　　Inciperet Præsul grandia Teque loqui.

Epistle to . . . .

NOBILIS et generosus avito sanguine cum sis
　　Nobilior pulchris virtutibus, optime Amice,
Magnis dignare a studiis paulisper abesse
Quæ patria expectat quæ nec mea Musa silebit;
Pone supercilium fronti quod grande Volumen　　　　　　5
Et lex addidit abdita, et æquâ mente hilarique
Notam ad amicitiam et tenues descende Camænas;
Quam mihi Dii dederint multam tibi mitto salutem
Et curas tepidas ne forsan auarus ad aras
Auditor sudore malo noceare per artus　　　　　　10
Frigore neu tacito vincenti membra veneno
Nocturnus lædare libros curans forenses
Cum te prospicient inter morientia cæli

Title: Carmen Deprecatorium *1740*: Carmen, Deprecatorum *L 28*　　4 Fames! *1740*:
Fames *L 28*　　6 equus. *1740*: equus *L 28*　　8 sitim. *1740*: sitim *L 28*　　9 lassatur
1740: lassat ebur *L 28*　　ohe] O! he, *1740*　　10 aquas. *1740*: aquas *L 28*　　11 vel
1740: nel *L 28*　　13 O si *1740*: osi *L 28*　　*After l. 16, 1740 adds* M.P.
　　4 silebit; *edd.*: silebit *L 28*　　7 Camænas; *edd.*: Camænas *L 28*　　9 curas *edd.*:
curos *L 28*　　11 vincenti] violanti *Alt. MS. reading*　　12 curans *edd.*: curaso *L 28*

Sydera, et assiduâ fuligo epota lucernâ.
Interea quid agam et quo calcem tramite vitæ   15
Sicut semper erat tibi mos bonus accipe lector:
Puro animo atque alacri divinas cultor ad aras
Matutinus eo, pro Me parvas et apertas
Fundo preces, veteris sed non oblitus amici.
Hinc lego seu quicquid divinus scripsit Homerus   20
Iram Peleidæ, duplicis seu tædia Ulyssei;
Hæc prosunt simul ac delectant, hunc ego vatem
Hunc amo nam tu mi Charissim semper amasti.
Sed nec negligo ridens quod sapienter Horati
Dixisti quod quid fugiendum quidve petendum   25
Fortius enarrat torvi quam Crantoris umbra
Aut Schola Chrysippi, me talibus ire paratum
Auxiliis studeo reclusus et usque studebo
Non tamen ut macies aut tristi pallor in ore
Insideat non ut curis Mens ægra senescat;   30
Nempe verecundi non nunquam pocula Bacchi
Parca tamen lectosque inter facilesque Sodales
Compotare libet non nunquam poscere Phæbum
Atque rudes quales tibi Mitto ludere Versus
O puer hæc charo committe fidelis amico.   35

Ad Doctorem Montague.

PHÆBE Pater, duplicis qui dignus honoribus artis
     Exhilaras Cithara mentem, medicamine corpus,
Annue, Te totum geminataque munera posco:
Munera si geminata neges, redeunte Patrono
Utilius spretæ plectrum præpono saluti.   5
Eia age! florentem doceas per tempora laurum
Serpere, da facili salientia carmina venâ;
Carmina quæ Pindi poterunt spondere favorem
Quæ fieri a Musis meruêre, darique Patrono.
Emicat en sperata dies! en fausta Camænis   10

14 lucernâ. *edd.*: lucernâ *L 28*   15 calcem *edd.*: colcem *L 28*   16 lector: *edd.*:
lector *L 28*   19 amici. *edd.*: amici *L 28*   21 Ulyssei; *edd.*: Ulyssei *L 28*   22
delectant, *edd.*: delectant *L 28*   23 amasti. *edd.*: amasti *L 28*   26 Fortius *edd.*:
Fortias *L 28*   30 senescat; *edd.*: senescat *L 28*
    3 totum geminataque *edd.*: totam geminátque *L 28*

Tempora volvuntur, lassantis dura Minervæ
Non ultra querimur studia, immanemque laborum
Longorum seriem, cum nox sit conscia curæ
Testis, et assiduâ fuligo epota lucernâ:
Nam venit et vigili compensat tædia Daphnis   15
Daphnis Grantæ solus amor, fidissimus aræ
Custos, deliciæ Musarum, æterna Lycæi
Gloria, Sacrorum columen, Geniusque Penatum,
Daphnis adest, reduci sertum properate capillo
Pierides, properate tamen ne dignior adstet   20
Merces, ne vestras præcedat Mitra corollas:
Gratior armato non stat Victoria regi
Desperata salus ægris, Hymenæus amanti,
Quam tu porticibus, Mæcenus optime, nostris,
Gratior haud Siculo prensis in gurgite stella   25
Optata dubiam confirmat lampade vitam
Gratior Ægypto non largior amnis hianti
Fæcundo gravidos immergit flumine campos
Gratior haud Patriæ Victor plaudentibus Anglis
Haud genitor tuus, asserti post tempora Ponti   30
Cum fluctus reduci Sulcasset classe Britannos
Lauris velatus, spoliisque decorus Iberis.
Gratior hoc solum placidos ut sera per Annos
Communem reditûs plausum præsentia firmet:
Dum tibi subjectas Venerabilis Arbiter ædes   35
Nobilitas, dignans Dominusque paterque vocari
Dum jubeas late nascentia surgere templa
Illis Tu muris opifex quibus incola Numen.

Theme.

Eheu fugaces Posthume, Posthume,
Labuntur anni.

MOTU tam celeri fluit ætas, et derepentè adeò ab infantiâ labimur in Canitiem ut non Annos vivere sed unius solummodo diei Ephemerides videamur, e carceribus semel effusi in medio morandi

---

16 Daphnis Grantæ *edd.*: Daphis grantæ *L 28*   18 Penatum *edd.*: Plenatum *L 28*
25 Siculo *edd.*: siculo *L 28*   28 gravidos *edd.*: gravidas *L 28*   34 plausum *edd.*: plausam *L 28*
    Title: Posthume, Posthume, *edd.*: Posthume posthume *L 28*   1 derepentè *edd.*: de repentè *L 28*   2 diei *edd.*: dici *L 28*

spem vix inchoamus quin citatis bigis rotisque ferventibus ad metam
rapimur temerarii: mirantes quid ipsi sumus, & quo fugimus, non ultra 5
sumus. Proh! vestram Dii immortales invidiam qui æternitatis adeo
avidi ut ne unam e millibus horam humano generi indulgeatis, Sol,
diurnum permensus iter, eo unde egreditur novus redit, flores ad
tempus solum moriuntur, vitamque propediem de integro ordiuntur,
nobis vero semel marcentibus futuri nihil conceditur, sed cum haud 10
dieculam viximus æterna nox est dormienda.

> Quin cita perpetuo volvantur Tempora motu,
> Maturetque suam quælibet hora fugam.
> Vos modo, vos hodie vultu fulgete sereno,
> Cras adsit Lethum non piget inde mori. 15

Theme.

————*Minuti*
Semper et infirmi est Animi exiguique voluptas
Ultio.

VINDICTAMNE efflagitas? ridiculum, quod dederit inimicus etiam
docebit malum? indignis actibus te dudum oneravit satis; pes-
simis etiam moribus inquinabit? et modo quod corpus læserit lædendi
animi copiam tribues? condonare velim discas contumelias et oblivisci,
venia mitis ingenii ultio Canini specimen, mulieribus una temerariis 5
altera viris fortibus, una feris stupidis, diis altera sapientibus nos reddit
simillimos: injuriam rependendo damnum compares, ferendo, gloriam;
fac itaque apud te ut sies contumeliasque virili animo sustinens
Aristidem exulem Phocionemve moriturum imitare; rideant invidi et
admirentur forti animo constantique non posse conjunctas hominum 10
vires nocere nec bello Loricam aut Clypeum firmius munimentum
quam bellanti gerere patientiam quâ tela fortis propulsas simul et
eludas.

6 invidiam *edd.*: in vidiam *L 28*
  2 satis; *edd.*: satis *L 28*   8 contumeliasque *edd.*: contumelisque *L 28*   9 imitare; *edd.*: imitare *L 28*   10 conjunctas *edd.*: conjuntas *L 28*

Dum bibimus ...
Obrepit non intellecta Senectus.

S ISTE mero bibulas effuso Temporis alas
    Hesternumve minax coge redire Diem;
Nil facis, usque volabit inexorabilis ætas,
    Canitiemque caput sentiet, atque rugas.
I brevis, et properans in Funus necte corollas,   5
    Mox conflagrando conde Falerna rogo.
Clepsydra Saturni tua nec Chrystallina distant,
    Dum motu parili vinum et arena fluunt.
Dum loquor Ecce! perit redimitæ gloria frontis,
    Dat rosa de sertis lapsa, Memento Mori.   10
Sed tibi, dum nôras nimis properare Puellas,
    Ut citius rumpat Stamina, Bacchus adest.
Destituit cæcum subito Sol ebrius orbem,
    Occasum tremulo narrat adesse Rubor.

Quicquid Vult, valdè Vult.

D UM Tingit Siculus Solis Cœlique meatus,
    Astra polosque tuos quos sibi condit habet.
Nil facit instantis mortis bellique tumultus;
    Usque sed egregium sedulus urget opus.
Non vacat exiguæ curas impendere vitæ;   5
    Sat sibi curarum conditor orbis habet.

Dulce Bellum inexpertis.

S ACRA coronatus scandit Capitolia Cæsar,
    Densaque spumantem turba fatigat equum;
Tunc ardens juvenis voto languescit anhelo,
    Invidet et meritis debita serta comis.

Dum bibimus. 2 Diem; *1740*: Diem *L 28*   4 rugas. *1740*: rugas *L 28*   5 brevis
1740: breois *L 28*   corollas *1740*: Carollas *L 28*   11 nimis *1740*: nimii *L 28*   *After*
l. 14, 1740 adds M.P.
    Dulce Bellum inexpertis. 2 Densaque *edd.*: Dersque *L 28*   equum; *edd.*: equum *L 28*

     Usque ego maternis inquit, tumulabor in ulnis?   5
        Usque reducta mihi signa videre satis?
     Quando ferar niveis pompæ pars ipse Quadrigis?
        Quando triumphales, Parthe, sequere rotas?
     Intempestivis indulgent fata querelis,
        Et decorat nutans horrida crista caput;   10
     Arma rapit litui resonant, gravis imminet hostis
        Qui fugat imberbem prosequiturque Virum;
     Saucius exclamat, tuti salvete Penates
        Castra petant alii, sit mihi Fama Domi.

Aliquando bonus dormitat Homerus.

    Μῆνιν ἄειδε Θεὰ bene te Scripsisse fatemur
       Dum matutinos jungis Homere Duces
    At cum cæcati nox opprimat atria cæli
       Sopitumque liget callida Juno Jovem
    Falleris, haud Patrem sed fugit Apollo Poetam   5
       Et te, non Superos οὖλος ὄνειρος ἔχει.

Tragædiæ comædiis præferantur.

NON is sum Stoicus Academici qui voluptates a me omnes alienas sentiam, qui ubi in Theatrum pedes intulerim cum Catone illico severus exirem; imo volens lubensque Roscium partes quaslibet agentem Ciceroni utcunque impar defendere non rubesco. cum vero non puerorum sed optimæ spei Iuvenum Stipatus fuerim frequentiâ quorum 5 animi non tam levibus demulcendi ineptiis quam gravi argumento oblectandi, habiturum me tot causæ fautores quot orationis auditores non possum mihi non polliceri; si autem varios vitæ status hominumque ordines Scena exprimat partes eas in fabulis tuendas arbitrer quas in Republicâ assumptas malim, tam infirmi autem abjectique animi vix 10 ullum reperimus qui Principum majestatem Plebeorum tenuitati, qui imperium servituti, purpuram pannis præferendam esse non fateatur.

---

7 Quadrigis? *edd.* : Qudrisis *L 28*   8 Parthe *edd.* : parthe *L 28*   11 imminet *edd.* :
imminent *L 28*   14 Castra *edd.* : Costra *L 28*
   6 οὖλος *edd.* : οὐλος *L 28*
   3 exirem; *edd.* : exirem *L 28*   volens *edd.* : solens *L 28*   8 polliceri; *edd.* : polliceri
L 28

Sternantur itaque aulæa, poscatur ad actus histrio, non pede nudus,
vestitu horridus, vultu distortus, de industriâ malus ac qui contemptum
potius pariat quam voluptatem alliciat sed lautus & illustris amictu 15
elegans, habitu corporis decorus, gressu magnificus, personæque quam
assumpserit exquisité par. sin loquatur quæ hominis facundia! qui
spiritus! quam grande Argumentum quam vere regium, sermo purus
& pressus & profluens res magnæ verbis electis graviter ornateque
dictatæ, orationis & gestus venustas quæ summæ ætatis, doctrinæ, loci 20
homines coire faciat et circumfundi coram ut plaudentes accipiant
affectus quoscunque Tragicus induerit; in hac Scæna quod virginum
aures oculique respuant inverecundi nihil, non qui pueros lædant
lascivi sales, non quæ viros offendant futiles ineptiæ, non gestus mimici
et invrbana scurrilitas quæ in fero transeuntes aut reprehendimus aut 25
cum fastidio fugimus, non hic ex alieno rubore plausus acquiritur, non
datur irridendus Socrates, neminis Errores in medio omnibus ponuntur,
neminis adaugentur culpæ, sin quis de populo bene promereatur, im-
præsentiarum cum dignitate exhibetur posterarum laudi commendabi-
tur. moveatur itaque loco errabundus grex qui tam sordidis quam tritis 30
nos dudum enecavit fabulis; non feramus cum perdito amore Pamphilum, dum liceat Oedipodis lugere infortunium. damnetur vix expressa
meretriculæ Lachrymula dum veros Jocastæ fletus intueri concedatur;
non stet vix irrepens e pistrino Davus dum ereptus e communi Trojæ
incendio Patrem Deosque protulerit Æneas nec sua secum incommoda; 35
Meditetur Chremes quod unicus se in nuptias parum felices natus con-
jecerit cum natos quinquaginta crudeli fato extinctos ploret superstes
Priamus. At Populo placent comædiæ, fatemur, cachinnum movent;
concedimus, vos autem Auditores populo quæ placeant didicistis contemnere vos ridiculum cum Aristotele partem turpitudinis agnoscetis, 40
cum Platone Sceleris Homerum incusabitis quod ridentes Deos intro-
duxerit, cum plerisque illustrioribus Philosophis indignos sapiente
indignos viro effusos risus judicabitis. Apagite itaque planipedes Anilibusque modo digniores fabulæ quarum materies plerumque ficta
semper jacens, quarum oratio tenuis & Scriptura Levis; Siqua vero 45
fama et laus est Sanctiori isti & augustiori tragædiarum eloquentiæ vt
iis insint personæ nobiles, eloquium grande Stylus sublimis vestrique

13 aulæa, *edd.*: aulæa *L 28*   21 coram *edd.*: corum *L 28*   22 induerit; *edd.*:
induerit, *L 28*   26 fugimus, *edd.*: fugimus *L 28*   27 Socrates, *edd.*: Socrates *L 28*
31 fabulis; *edd.*: fabulis *L 28*   31–32 Pamphilum *edd.*: pamphilum *L 28*   33
meretriculæ *edd.*: meritriculæ *L 28*   concedatur; *edd.*: concedatur *L 28*   35
incommoda; *edd.*: incommoda *L 28*   38 Priamus. At *edd.*: Priamus at *L 28*   movent;
edd.: movent *L 28*   43 Apagite *edd.*: A Pagite *L 28*   43–44 Anilibusque *edd.*:
Anilisbusque *L 28*

juvenes Simillimus non est ut jubeam vos heroas nostros leviter laudare
sed diligenter imitari, nec peractam Scenam cum Vulgo Plaudere sed
cum judicibus quales vos me nactum gaudeo, doctissimis, admirari.   50

Theme.
Paucos novit secura quies.

IMO certe vel paucissimos, quid enim res humanæ? molestiarum
vicissitudines. quid vita? malorum congeries. quid orbis universum?
plenus vario clamore locus & inextricabilis Curarum labyrinthus;
nascimur omnes eâ lege plurimis ut afficiamur incommodis, miserias
simul ac lucem sentit nascens infantulus circumstantes plorat molestias   5
quæ una cum ætate accrescent: accrescunt quidem & adolescens idem
quantillum tranquillitatis noscet dum ætas metus magister et Crambê et
ferula vexatum in otio considere prohibent; sin excedit ex ephebis quo-
tidianis angetur curis, catenatis doloribus vexabitur in pericla damna,
exilia; in nuptias demum conjicietur. nec minima Senem manet tran-   10
quillitas cum ætas decrepita morbo ipsumque vivere oneri sit: nullus
itaque dies tranquillitatem affert, nullus locus; urbem petes? enecabit
insanus clamor. rus ibis? terrebit triste silentium; perstrepit tumultu
terra, procellis mare; amoveantur autem omnia hæc vel siquid possint
ad vitæ tranquillitatem, efferant, nihil adeo agitur, intus habes quod   15
te cruciet, huc, illuc, ubique pervagantem equitabunt aut Cupidinum
insania, aut timorum sævitia, aut quia desit quod ames aut quia superest
dolebit, usque dum affectus intellexeris exuisse et ipse te vitare; hinc
uno ore clamitant omnes quietem te non comperîsse, hinc nec in castris
miles inventam nec in Foro causidicus agnoscet, audaces hinc Poetæ   20
divam contendunt jamjudum reliquisse terras, audaciores vero Philo-
sophi non omnino prospexisse.

Quod quisque vitet nunquam Homini satis Cautam est in Horas.

CUM nobis undique plurima impendeant mala gravissimaque impendeant pericula, cum vel acinum, crinem aerem exitio non nunquam fore necesse sit fateamur totque morbos nobis in quamlibet
horam imminere vt dum enumeremus hora abiit, quâ prudentiâ, quo

---

48 leviter *edd.*: leritor *L 28*
   2 universum *edd.*: universus *L 28*   3 labyrinthus; *edd.*: labyrinthus *L 28*   8
prohibent; *edd.*: prohibent *L 28*   10 conjicietur *edd.*: conjicietur *L 28*   12 locus;
edd.: locus *L 28*   13 silentium; *edd.*: silentium *L 28*   14 mare; *edd.*: mare, *L 28*
16 cruciet *edd.*: oruciet *L 28*   18 vitare; *edd.*: vitare *L 28*
   2 crinem *edd.*: erinem *L 28*

consilio dirigenda manet vitæ ratio? quid rei geretur quæ non secum 5
afferat molestias? quânam insistendum erit viâ quæ non ducat prorsus ad
Inferos? incendia, fures, lapsus tremebundus horreat Civis, arboris ictus
tempestatum vim, cæli ruinas palleat agricola; ideóne fugiendum demum
cum terris discrimina? nil agitur; tanta mare circumstrepunt pericula
ut illic inimicos soleamus devovere, quisnam igitur relictus est locus 10
ubi supervacuus fuerit infortunii metus ubi spes salutis confirmata?
cum ab hostibus, gladiis, furoribus, tutus rediisset Cæsar, a Romanis,
coram amicis, in senatu occidendus? cum Trojam, Hectorem Deosque
adversos superasset tandem Agamemnon in ipso vxoris amplexu peri-
turus? Æschylum denique reputemus? et in aere tela agnoscet recondita, 15
& ipsas Aves jaculari posse.

Forma Viros neglecta decet.
Ad occursum Cotili.

SALVE itaque omnium ornatissime resinatæ juventatis princeps,
homo mea, ah! vix tandem agnovi stolidus! at quid sibi hic vestitus
quærit? quid volsa tibi brachia specto? quid crines ordine digestos?
num inter fæminas (renouatâ Achillei historia) ignavus delituisti? num
(inversâ Cænei fabulâ) in fæminam mutatus metamorphosi gratularis? 5
at Masculini ad huc generis te fateris, per Junonem (Divam tuam) aut
exuendus est ornatus istic, aut fides verbis deneganda; horrida per
corpora setæ promitterent militem, mentita fuerit barba Philosophum;
emanans negligenter sudor oluerit Virum. At mollem, delicatulum,
perunctum quis aspiciens animal ejusdem cum Curio speciei crediderit? 10
Juvenalem itaque an Catonem assimilem objurgem an arrideam incertum est. Mutatio pellucens! capillas dealbatus! (Dii boni) quam
impar Viro es? quam malum Tui simulacrum? quam (ante sepulturam)
pulvis & Umbra? quin desinas tandem miser ineptire neglecta cute
curetur Anima, ne nitidum te ac bellum hominem sed constantem & 15
bonum civem præbeas, ne mollibus Eunuchis et tibi similibus mulier-
culis sed viris sapientibus imo Dijs immortalibus gratum aut si adhuc
ornari velis et conspici non Othonis speculum sed Abantis clypeus
gestamini sit, exutis tandem Bombycinis ære coruscus fulgeas, mendaci-
que sepositâ Cæsarie Equinâ caput decoretur Cauda.   20

6 molestias? *edd.*: molestias *L 28*

   2 stolidus! at quid *edd.*: stolidus at at quid *L 28*   7 ornatus *edd.*: ornati *L 28*   9
oluerit Virum. At *edd.*: oleriat Virum at *L 28*   10 perunctum *edd.*: peronctum *L 28*
crediderit? *edd.*: crediderit. *L 28*   12 est. Mutatio *edd.*: est mutitia *L 28*   13
simulacrum *edd.*: simulaerum *L 28*   18 Abantis *edd.*: abantis *L 28*

Non bene ibi imperatur ubi Vulgus ducit Regem.

IN ea Civitate res pessime geruntur ubi Libertas in vitium excesserit, ubi infimi ordines agunt feruntque cuncta, atque imperandi imperant; silent enim leges inter vulgus dum suo more vivat quisque suisque studiis obsequatur non quod Res publica postulet sed quid usui domestico suppetat, non quid omnibus prosit sed quid singulis 5 requiritur: rapinas, incendia, cædes moliuntur invidi, Stupro & Luxuriæ se tradunt libidinosi otio ventrique indulgeant ignavi et quanta hominum tanta scelerum varietas; non officiis fungebantur Dii minores cum sese Jupiter devinctum permisserit, non recta insistebant via equi Cælestes ubi lora regiminis negligenter fluerent, nec Stetisset 10 Angliæ res si chartulis suppliciter rebellibus importunè benignus annuisset Rex.

Declamation.
Poetæ exulent e re-publica Platonis.

CUM multa divinitus a Sancto Legislatore ad feliciorem Rei Publicæ statum inventa atque instituta sint tum nihil præclarius Judices quam quod pro singulari quâ summa fuit prudentia mendicos, mimos balatrones ejecerit, nec satis tandem ad Patriæ commodum a se provisum crediderit nisi perniciosæ hujus pestis principia et causas radici- 5 tus extirparet; ad Poetas itaque deventum est infimos profecto homines sed pertinaces qui divino Platonis nostri decreto refragantes vobis se & nugas suas audent obtrudere vestro ore dijudicandi, nec nisi vestra exigendi sententiâ, quamobrem ut vobis hodie audiantur, damnentur, emittantur Poetæ si minus permisserit vel sanctiorum ratio studiorum, 10 vel ipsius rei levitas; vos agat & impellat Judices integerrimos sordidorum hominum confidentia, vos viros sapientes Platonis Decretum, vos cives optimos Patriæ cura et publicæ vtilitatis conservatio: quis ideo iis locus est in civitate quam nec consilio nec re juverint, qui cum Angustâ includantur Cellâ nec res Politicas experti sint nec apud malos 15

6 requiritur: *edd.*: requiritur *L 28*   8 hominum *edd.*: homini *L 28*   varietas; *edd.*: varietas *L 28*
    1 Rei Publicæ *edd.*: R Pæ *L 28*   6 extirparet; *edd.*: extirparet, *L 28*   11 levitas; *edd.*: leritas, *L 28*   12 viros *edd.*: viro *L 28*

quibus inhiant libros unquam invenerint? num quis est qui con-
scribendos milites aut acies instruendas meditabitur horum consilio
fretus qui de Dijs obsessis & rixantibus Centauris puerilia, absurda,
contraria cecinerunt? num quis de pacis Stabiliendæ modis justitiæque
conditionibus illos consulet qui fortunatum Scelus excusarunt sæpius, 20
imo palam aliquando celebrarunt, qui Tyrannos evexerunt ad heroas,
qui legum contortores et in cælis collocandos et precibus colendos
docuerunt? de religione vero ac rebus divinis quis illorum suffragio
assentietur qui de cælicolis suis indigna Viris fabulati fuerint qui et ira
inflammatos, & libidine furentes induxerunt Deos, qui Jovem Op: 25
Max: insimularunt Scelerum quæ Pueri Vos Audivistis & Auditorum ad
huc memoriam perhorrescitis? nec certe consilii locum habent neque
auxilii copiam nam eorum Penatibus tam deest substantia quam verbis
fides; ab Homero principe paupertatem æque ac figmenta derivant, in
Vrbe potius sunt quam vivunt, Deorum convivia Jejuni canunt, et 30
aquam bibunt (post cantatum Nectar) suo Pegaso immo Canibus
suburbanis communem, adeo Rei Publicæ non adjumento ut sint
prorsus Oneri et nisi optatâ sustentandi sportula vel in ipsis Triviis
famelici morientur. cui bono interim Auditores, est, si in Theatro
metricis edoctus et instructus Artibus vrbanè loquatur Achilles aut 35
Ajax diserte nisi eadem Pollentes facundia Magistri apud forum aut
Senatum reos defendere, et excitare afflictos, et se ipsos in civitate
retinere cognoscant? quid prosit inutilis Citharæ eloquentia quid jacta-
bunda Amphionis aut Orphei recordatio dum hodierna Musica (quam
dissimilis priori) adeo nec Trabes possit colligere nec Muros convocare, 40
ut ipsis cantatoribus domicilia vix supersint? Adsint itaque lictores,
pateant portæ, exulent Poetæ, non illud nobis factum Deorum quis-
quam vituperabit quod alere nolimus homines edaces et Improbos,
cum publicâ pascendos benevolentiâ, insanos et fatuos è cælis ipsi
dimiserint; nec habebit ipse suus quod succenseat Apollo qui sat 45
spectatam erga se religionem nostram fatebitur quod alterum ejus
Gregem Medicos retineamus; ausim contendere illum ipsum Deum e
re publica cælesti excludendum fore, nisi aliis artibus quam Musicis
operam impenderet, nisi iter Diurnum carminibus nocturnis adjungere-
tur, & Poetæ desidiam Aurigæ labor perabunde compensaret. at si 50
prudentes quot fuerint Legislatores id sibi negotii datum crediderint

16 invenerint *edd.*: invererint *L 28*   18 obsessis *edd.*: oblessis *L 28*   28 eorum
edd.: eroum *L 28*   29 fides; *edd.*: fides *L 28*   32 Rei Publicæ *edd.*: R Pᵃᵉ: *L 28*
34 morientur *edd.*: morienter *L 28*   39 hodierna *edd.*: hodiurna *L 28*   41 supersint? Adsint *edd.*: supersint adsint *L 28*   42 pateant *edd.*: pateant, *L 28*   48 re
publica *edd.*: repa *L 28*   51 quot fuerint *edd.*: quot quot fuerint *L 28*

ut Civium libertate et legum præsidio nullatenus fruerentur ij qui Rem
Publicam vicissim non adjutarint, quid illis faciendum Judices, qui
damnum dederint et malum, quorum vulnerat acumen corrumpunt
lenocinia et ipsa nocet suavitas in exitium usque dulcis? omnem enim 55
rempoeticam malam esse ineptiarum fabricam et splendidam mendaci-
orum seriem, omnesque ejus partes credulitatem Plebis inquinare,
Nobilium gravitatem offendere, toti populo vitium indulgere, nemo
tam insanus tam Poetæ similis qui inficias ire non erubescat; inducit
Ebrietatem Lyricorum Jucunditas libidinem excitat Elegorum lascivia 60
serit discordias Iamborum amaritudo, veritati oppugnant fictitia he-
roicorum commenta et quanta datur Carminum tanta Scelerum diversitas. quinam sub personâ Mercurii servorum fidem corrumpunt? Poetæ.
quinam per Danaes vitium amoribus virginum lenocinantur? Poetæ:
quinam ad exemplum Junonis vxorum linguas acuunt? Poetæ: quinam 65
sacram Magistratuum auctoritatem omnium quicquid est hominum
fidem Deorum immortalium Religionem irritam faciunt et contem-
ptam? iidem Poetæ. amoveatur itaque ignavum Pecus Exhauriatur Rei
Publicæ sentina, Extinguantur Seditionis faces. Abeant et supellectilis
siquid habent secum auferant properantes aquas et amænos recessus 70
quibus tantum delectantur exquirant aut Anticyram navigantes aut
novam Rem Publicam ad Delon Posituri.

Error Proprie et immediate dependet ab Operationibus Intellectus.

D IVA potens Veri cur latius imperat Error?
Spissas per tenebras passim, tristesque latebras,
Cur miseras mentes, incertaque pectora cogit?
Duplex Vis Animæ bene præsidet; Intellectus
Solers & Pollens varias expendere rerum, 5
Expensasque Voluntati deducere Formas,
Quid Verum, atque Bonum, quid turpe, quid Utile narrat.
Inde alto in solio sublimis sacra Voluntas

52 Civium *edd.*: Cevium *L 28*   52–53 Rem Publicam *edd.*: R Pam: *L 28*   53 faciendum *edd.*: faciend m: *L 28*   54 corrumpunt *edd.*: cornempunt *L 28*   56 malam *edd.*: malem *L 28*   fabricam *edd.*: frabricam *L 28*   57 Plebis *edd.*: Phebis *L 28*   60 Lyricorum *edd.*: Lyticorum *L 28*   63 Poetæ. *edd.*: Poetæ *L 28*   66 auctoritatem *edd.*: autoritatem *L 28*   68–69 Rei Publicæ *edd.*: R Pæ: *L 28*   69 faces. Abeant *edd.*: faces abeant *L 28*   71 Anticyram *edd.*: antyciram *L 28*   72 Rem Publicam *edd.*: R Pam: *L 28*   Posituri *edd.*: Postituri *L 28*
2 tristesque *edd.*: tristeque *L 28*

Effigies recipit teneras, multaque receptas
Majestate probans, nascentes trudit in Actus.   10

Unde ideo est, inquam quod pauci recta capessant,
Aut fugiant illis contraria, & unde laborant
Obductæ tantâ dubiæ caligine mentes?
Anne Voluntati culpæ est, quæ cæca facultas
Et Jovis arbitrio atque æternâ lege coacta,   15
Vis ubi percipiens ad Eam simulachra tulisset
Nec prava devitare potest, nec bona tenere?
An fallax Animæ, ut contendimus, altera Virtus
(Hoc magè credibile est:) non rectè Idola capessens
Sedula decipiet, solidi sub Imagine Veri   20
Oggerit Errores speciosos, pulchráque damna,
Et sociam eludit Virtutem, eluditur ipsa?

Sic est, apta Deo petiisset munera nusquam
Mortalis Phaethon, superas aptare Quadrigas,
Et frænare Diem, cognosset si sua Vota,   25
Ni mens a ratione recesserit avia rectâ.
Mollis Amatorem Semele voluisset inermem
Aut Cygnum formosum, aut stillans imbribus Aurum,
Armatum igne procum, flammaque nocenti minacem
Convenisse horrens, & aperto occurrere Divo.   30

Ergo supervacua hinc aut perniciosa rogarunt
Munera multi homines, quod non curâ atque labore
Perspexisse student, quæ perficienda requirant.
Intellectus enim quoties Simulachra dedisset
Fortius extracta & Studio compôstá fideli,   35
Impatiens Animus surgit, Vis emicat ardens,
Motus fertur avara, nec audit Fræna Voluntas:
At cum propositi non vivida datur Imago
Sed perfecta minûs cadit Ignis languidus, & mens
Refrænari eadem, retróque residere gaudet.   40

---

13 caligine *edd.*: caligne *L 28*   17 Nec prava . . . nec bona *edd.*: Nec bona . . . nec
prava *L 28*   21 speciosos *edd.*: specioses *L 28*   25 frænare *edd.*: frænate *L 28*
31 Ergo *edd.*: Ego *L 28*   37 avara *edd.*: avava *L 28*

1689

The Crest of the Arms of the Earl of Exeter a Wheatsheaf supported by Two Lyons.

DUM Tibi dat fortes Cybele veneranda Leones
  Flavaque collectas addit Eleusis opes
Invidiâ major, victoque potentior ævo
  I decus I nostrum, Ceciliana domus.
Sparge Inopi fruges, et pelle Leonibus Hostem   5
  Copia quid valet hinc quid tremor inde, refer.
Junctis muneribus Belli vel Pacis, habes quo
  Atque Homines vincas, atque imitêre Deos.

Sent to Constantinople. Sepr: 1689.

Roberto Grove Anglo, ex Agro Wiltoniensi oriundo Amicus summus & popularis Radulphus Lane Sepulchrale Saxum posuit.

LUGUBRE Marmor
Inscripto dicas Vulnere
In Morbi violentiam Iuventutis Robur
In Mortis Invidiam Fiducia humana
In Fati Decretum Morum Sanctitas   5
Quantillum prodest.
Nam Ille Quem custodis fuit,
(O Vox lugenda, Fuit!)
Inter Iuvenes flos & Decus,
Inter senes spes & Desiderium   1o
Ad omnes vbicunque Exemplar.

Title] An Epigram by Mr. Prior On the Crest ... Lyons. *Lansd*: In Comitis Exoniensis Cristam Tritici fascem a Leonibus Sustentatum. August 1. 1689. Lemma Sustentare et de bellare *L 28*: IN ... FASCEM LEONIBUS SUSTENTATUM. LEMMA ... DEBEL-LARE. *1740*   3 ævo] *L 28, 1740* æro *Lansd*   4 nostrum] *Lansd* nostra *L 28, 1740* 6 tremor] *Lansd* Timor *L 28, 1740*   7 Junctis] *Lansd* Pollens *L 28, 1740*   8 vincas] *Lansd* superes *L 28, 1740*   *After l. 8, 1740 adds* Scripsit Aug. 1. 1689.
Title] MISSA *CONSTANTINOPOLIN*, 1689. *1740*

Animi Magnitudine Viros superans,
Corporis Venustate Fæminas
Sexum Virtutibus Utrumque.

In Negotiis Summâ Iustitiâ providus,   15
Pari cum Modestiâ Hilaris in otio
Ad Peregrinos humanus, faciles ad suos
Ad Amicos sine promissis firmus,
Ad omnes sine dissimulatione benevolus;
Ad Deum sine superstitione Religiosus.   20
Ingenio florens, proposito sanctus, vitâ
Innocens, beatus Morte.

At Tu, fidele Saxum
Defuncto quod amico dedit
Amicus vix superstes: 25
Æterno sis Interpreti
Quod Virum Meliorem
Anglia nec genitum, nec Thracia deficientem
Aut vidit unquam aut videbit.
Charas corporis reliquias per longa tuêre sæcula   30
Divinas Animi virtutes seris Nepotibus commenda.

Anglia cui cunas dederit, dat Funera Thrace
Tam longum Virtus impigra tendit iter.
Quid fletis Gentes? hinc gaudeat vtraque tellus,
Quod dedit Vna Viris Munus, & vna Deo.   35

14 Utrumque. *edd.*: Utrumque *L 28*: utrumque. *1740*　　　15 Summâ Iustitiâ] summâ
cum Justitiâ *1740*　　　19 benevolus; *1740*: benevolentie *L 28*　　　27 Meliorem *edd.*:
Meliorem. *L 28*: meliorem *1740*

1690

Lamentatio Davidis super Saulum & Jonathanem.

I.

Eheu quam cecidere fortes!
Armaque quam periere Belli!
Viduata tristi Juda silentio
    Acerba ploret funera
Nec nimio malesana tumultu   5
Securis repetet damna doloribus
    Indulgensque querelis
    Lugubres vlulet sonos
Ne vaga Gilboicis habitans in montibus Eccho
    Tristem vocis imaginem   10
Crudelis tua Gath tua deferat Ascolon arva.
    Fortunæ crimen garrula fama tace
        Pæana ne canant impium
    Satiatæ nostro sanguine matres
Philistæque nurus male nostrâ in strage triumphent.   15
    Eheu! quam cecidere fortes!
    Armaque quam periere belli.

II.

Vobis Gilboici montes florescere passim
    Flebili discant aconita succo:
    Injuriosis callida poculis   20
        Mixtam condere mortem
Tristibus heu! talis convenit herba locis.
    Illic sub antris abditus horridis
    Spargat tristitiam terribilis draco;
Illic immanesque lupi fulvique leones   25
    Aptas inveniant domos
    Aut sacra sævorum progenies hominum
    Longe immanior illis:

15 triumphent. *edd.*: triumphent *L 28*

Gilboici montes Sterili vos culmine longum
   Rores expectate salubres;   30
Nullæ ibi discutiant prægnantia vellera nubes
   Et nullus aridum
      Irriget imber
   Prodigo qui non lacrymosa fletu
      Funera ploret.   35
     Crudele culmen! quo cecidit Pater
     Et notus melior Patre.
Caput Scelestum! quo jacet obrutus
   Squalletque plebeio cruore
   Quem populi petiere vota   40
Quem regio vnguento decorum
   Auctumque justis Numen honoribus
   Gentibus imperitare jussit.
   Eheu quam cecidere fortes!
   Armaque quam periere belli!   45

III.

Illic fugaces impiger hostium
Versare turmas Jonathan extulit
Arcum minacem: illic frequenti
   Morte quatît gravidam Pharetram.
   Inde pennatum bene doctus heros   50
     Mittere vulnus
   Et vacua inde redit Pharetra.
Illic Saul stetit arduus
Spectandus in certamine nobili
Vibravit illic victor Ensem   55
Hostili madidum sanguine Regius
   Et inde cæsis dextera Millibus
   Rettulit fælix meritos honores
Et satiata quidem nec dum lassata recessit.
   Eheu quam cecidere fortes!   60
   Armaque quam periere belli!

30 salubres; *edd.*: salubres *L 28*   36 cecidit *edd.*: cecidet *L 28*   43 jussit. *edd.*:
jussit *L 28*   45 periere *edd.*: perire *L 28*   47 Versare *edd.*: Verare *L 28*   49
Pharetram *edd.*: Pharetrum *L 28*   50 doctus *edd.*: doctos *L 28*   51 Mittere *edd.*:
mittere *L 28*   52 Pharetra. *edd.*: Pharetra *L 28*   58 Rettulit *edd.*: Rettulis *L 28*

IV.

Qualem fulminis alitem
Divi ministrum per liquidum æthera
    Penna volantem præpeti
Tremendumque avibus sæpe minoribus   65
    Vrget amor dapis atque pugnæ.
      Talis Jonathan agmina
    Dejecit acer fulmine et alite
      Ocyor ipse.

Qualisve Sylvæ dominus et terror Leo   70
Intrepidus late incedit spoliata per arva
    Mactatosque ovium greges
Prædam minorem morsibus vastis premens
    Talis per Medios globos
    Saulem corripuit furor   75
Et pulsos celer insequutus hostes
    Talis fatigavit ruina et
      Cæde gravi pepulit catervas.
    Eheu quam cecidere fortes!
    Armaque quam periere belli!   80

V.

O par beatum quos facili jugo
Natura junxit! quos melior brevi
Natura æterno fædere junxit amor!
O par nobile, quos nec separavit
    Nec fatum grave terruit   85
Devota morti pectora aut victoriæ.
    O par nobile! par beatum!
    Eheu quam cecidere fortes!
    Armaque quam periere belli!

VI.

Orbata flete turba Isâcidæ nurus   90
Ferite palmis pectora et planctus date
    Et justa Sauli facite.
Nam vos ornavit pretiosâ Syndone, Vobis

---

78 catervas. *edd.*: catervas *L 28*   86 victoriæ. *edd.*: victoriæ *L 28*   87 beatum!
edd.: beatum? *L 28*

Multo splendida Coccino
Vestimenta dedit; Tyros   95
Vobis littoribus peperit felicibus ostrum.
Vobis misit Ophir prodiga divites
Lectosque partus, Phæbus ipse
Vobis laboravitque vobis
Et tenerum properavit aurum: 100
Eheu quam cecidere fortes!
Armaque quam periere belli!

VII.

Te, te, Jonathan urgeo
Tristi Camæna et flebilibus modis
Mœrens ademptum Te mihi barbiton   105
Murmure te querulo requirit:
Non desiderio pari
Ereptum tepido flet puerum sinu
Orba Parens, similive planctu
Sponsa virum viduata quærit: 110
Te magis amissum ploro tibi Charior illis.
Eheu quam cecidere fortes!
Armaque quam periere belli!

Contra Astrologos.

Ex principiis Astrologicis nil potest
præcognosci de rebus humanis.

ABSIT Judices Academici ut in hoc literaturæ emporio ubi artes
liberalis florent et dominantur ubi multi Mathematicis operam
magnâ cum felicitate collocarunt nonnulli summa cum laude profitentur, ego Thracum Patronus contra artem tam divinam dicturus pro-
direm: eamque omnibus ideo esse spernendam quia paucis intellectam   5
contenderem: cum vero Scientia in præstigias Mathematicus in Astro-
logum evaserit ne cui vestrum mirum sit Judices si istos futurorum
institores, artis ignominiam, reipublicæ sentinam vobis dijudicandos
et damnandos proposuerim: homines profecto pertinacis audaciæ et

---

97 misit *edd.* : misset *L 28*   105 barbiton *edd.* : barbaton *L 28*   111 illis. *edd.* : illis
L 28
  5 spernendam *edd.* : spernenda *L 28*

ignorantis impudentiæ qui cum in Terris sint plebis fæces astris sese 10
dominari prædicant et eorum influxus regere quorum citius numerum
quam nomina recenserent; qui pro vario cæli aspectu, mores, animam,
casus cujusque et eventus fingi non tam putant quam tradunt et
Proinde ridiculam humanis actionibus necessitatem imputant imo Dijs
immortalibus peccatum: quamvis autem cum vulgo ea omnia pro veris 15
accipiamus quæ aut astrologorum jactantia asserit aut adversarii credu-
litas defendit: quam non sint adjumento imo quam sint incommodo
hujusmodi artificia vel ipsa evincet prædictio: quæ Siquid lætum pro-
mittat sperati magis boni expectatione quam amissi desiderio torque-
mur: dum spe longa atque avidâ laborantes ea gaudia contaminamus 20
quæ si insperantibus obtigissent Solidiores multo voluptates obtulis-
sent: sin mali aliquid minitetur ante præstitutum tempus cruciamur
infelices, miseriis heu nimium properantibus temere occurrimus et
ærumnas quas defugere malumus occupamus ultro et amplectimur:
sed quid laudem afferunt nobis Homines e cælo delapsi stellarum 25
domini assessores Deorum? nempe si pergat fluere imbrem futurum:
sin sol circumcingentibus nebulis gloriosum caput explicuerit, sudum
fore et serenum: Vere deinceps serendum, autumno metendum summa
cum gravitate admonent et doctâ Thermometrorum ope varias cæli
affectiones non tam prædicunt quam nunciant: at vnde viri Saturno suo 30
hebetiores, Mercurio etiam furaciores artis suæ præcepta mutuantur?
vnde recognitam promunt Scientiam? ab ijs scilicet qui mentiuntur
quidem sed magis ingenuè mentiri se profitentur quicquid ut oblecta-
ret otium lusit Aratus, id totum plebi ut imponeret labore verè im-
probo sed magis incomposito transcripsit Circulatorum antesignanus 35
Albertus; ex tuis tamen victum, fidem famam acquirunt Astrologi
Poetis (proh pudor) eorundem inventoribus egregie esurientibus: Quin
hodie tu declamas? obturbat aliquis Chaldeus, artemque ideo ab
omnibus contemnendam velis quoniam a paucis intellectam? annon
varia cælorum conditio varia aeri temperamenta impartit? annon ipse 40
aer vel turbatus vel Serenus sese insinuat in mortalium corpora ex ejus
deinde inflatu annon magis aut minus incitatus sanguis passiones animi
aut elatiores efficiat aut depressiores? annon demum ex diversitate
affectuum diversitas actionum elicitur? Probe narras, mi homo philo-

11 eorum *edd.*: eorem *L 28*   12 recenserent; *edd.*: recenserent *L 28*   18 hujusmodi *edd.*: hisjusmodi *L 28*   24 defugere *edd.*: de fugere *L 28*   25 delapsi *edd.*:
dælapsi *L 28*   26 Deorum *edd.*: Decrum *L 28*   27 explicuerit *edd.*: explicuerint *L 28*
30 nunciant *edd.*: nunciat *L 28*   viri *edd.*: viris *L 28*   34 otium *edd.*: otiam *L 28*
38 declamas? *edd.*: declamas *L 28*   42 incitatus *edd.*: ipcitatus *L 28*   · 43
depressiores? *edd.*: depressiones *L 28*   44 elicitur? Probe *edd.*: elicitus probe *L 28*

mathematice nam quid si non omne imperium syderibus negabimus? 45
quid si sub Venere ortos ad lubidinem proclives, sub Marte ad arma
promptos confiteamur? quid si demum hunc hilariorem fore tristiorem
illum quia vnum Jupiter Saturnus alterum vagitus primos edentem
exceperit, quamvis nascentium omnium quota portio est quæ vel
isthanc hypothesin confirmavit! Nam ego nec vitæ nec salutis nec quid 50
dignitatis prospiciam si nascenti dicta est quid me esse oporteat! nec
timerem Deos nec ambirem qui aut non possunt aut nolunt quid de
me Statutum est non ab illorum imperio sed influentiis syderum inflectere. Alia tamen mihi tecum res est. Sydera ista impellunt tantum
cur affirmas cogere? ea dicunt sic posse esse, dicis tu aliter esse non 55
Posse: cur ideo inter hos muros nos patimur concludi cur bonis litteris
matutini insurgimus, iisdemque adhæremus vigiles nisi ut malos istius-
modi affectus (a consuetudine an a Syderibus inditos non hodie dis-
putabitur) amoveamus prorsus et radicitus extirpemus? actum prorsus
esset de Omnigenâ morali disciplinâ si virtutes ad propitiam si vitia ad 60
infaustam referenda fuerint cælorum influentiam: actum de ipsâ Religione si a Deo ad astra a Creatore ad Creaturam transditum sit
humanarum rerum aut permutatio aut imperium. Pergant vero per me
licet nunc syderii fatum perscrutari circumscribere naturam, Jovem
dirigere: Crassum in Patriâ Cæsarem in militiâ Pompeium in lectulo 65
moriturum Pronuncient; dum modo Firmiano veteri non insaniunt nec
vrbium ac provinciarum natales dies repetant nec jus syderibus in-
ferant in cementa et lapides; dum modo cum Neotericis fatorum insti-
toribus totam Americam nullis cælorum plagis assignare negligant; his
vero et peractis et derisis mendacia et Astrologiam relinquas oro et 70
coactus tu voluntate concedes nil ex Principiis astrologicis de rebus
humanis præcognosci unquam Potuisse.

---

45 negabimus? *edd.*: negabimus *L 28*   46 Venere *edd.*: venore *L 28*   arma *edd.*:
armas *L 28*   47 confiteamur? *edd.*: confiteamur *L 28*   50 confirmavit! Nam *edd.*:
confirmavit nam *L 28*   salutis *edd.*: salusti *L 28*   51 dignitatis *edd.*: dignitati *L 28*
oporteat! *edd.*: oporteat,? *L 28*   52 non *edd.*: *om. L 28*   53–54 inflectere.
Alia *edd.*: inflectere alia *L 28*   57 matutini *edd.*: matutiui *L 28*   59 extirpemus?
edd.: extirpemus *L 28*   63 imperium. Pergant *edd.*: imperium pergant *L 28*   65
Cæsarem *edd.*: Cæbasem *L 28*   lectulo *edd.*: lectubo *L 28*   66 Firmiano *edd.*:
firmiano *L 28*   68 lapides; *edd.*: lapides *L 28*   Neotericis *edd.*: Nectericis *L 28*
69 Americam *edd.*: americam *L 28*   negligant; *edd.*: negligant *L 28*

1692

Ad Virum Doctissimum, & Amicum Dominum Samuelem Shaw,

dum Theses de Ictero pro Gradu Doctoratus defenderet.

Phæbe potens sævis vel Morbis lædere Gentes,
    Læsas solerti vel relevare manu
Aspice tu decus hoc nostrum, placidusque fatere
    Indomitus quantum prosit in Arte Labor.
Non Ictrûm posthac Pestemve minaberis Orbi,   5
    Fortius hic Juvenis dum Medicamen habet.
Mitte dehinc Iras, & Nato Carmina dona,
    Neglectum telum dejice, sume Lyram.

Carolo de Berkely dilecto Domino suo Matthæus Prior Sam: Pam: Dit:

Litteras tuas mi Charissime sorori tuæ dilectissimæ scriptas accepimus, atque perlegimus, quando nihil secreti iis inesse credibile esset. domesticæ nostræ res quomodo se habent, brevi accipias. Mater tua hic est, fraterculum pulcherrimum et tui simillimum ex Angliâ Sibi transportavit, soror tua natû maxima cum Avitâ 5 Nelson Angliam profecta est, ad recuperandam Sanitatem, quâ malâ profecto in Hollandia usa est: jam vero subirasci tibi debeo, nec injuriâ, quia Epistolas nobis nec Latine nec Gallicé Scriptas mandare curas: Incumbas studiis, oro, et fac ut videamus progressus, quos Te octodecim jam menses audientem præceptores optimos fecisse in 10 utraque linguâ oportet. Hoc Pater tuus hoc tuum postulat officium: Quod ad me attinet ea solummodo conditione Parentes tuos optimos

---

Title] Written for one that took his Degree at Leyden. *L 28*   1 lædere] ladere *L 28*
2 relevare] velevare *L 28*   manu *L 28*: manu. *1692*
    3 esset. *1740*: *om. L 28*   4 pulcherrimum *1740*: pucherrimum *L 28*   5 natû *1740*: natum *L 28*   6 recuperandam *1740*: recuperandum *L 28*   7 subirasci *1740*: subirasci *L 28*   debeo *1740*: debes *L 28*   9 videamus *1740*: videamg *L 28*
10 fecisse *1740*: fæcisse *L 28*   11 oportet. Hoc *1740*: oportat hoc *L 28*

exorandos conabor quo nos revises brevi, hoc quoque sibi scriptum
frater tuus credat. Præceptores tuos amicos mihi optimos meo
Nomine saluta, fac Me ames, Te æternum amabo, Vale.   15

Hagæ Comitum
Pridie Nonas Septembris.

1695

Inter Emblemata et Carmina quædam quæ composuit Monsr: de Vrigni ad decorandum tumulum Mariæ, Reginæ Angliæ Inscriptum voluit Author per Nobilem Gallum de Vrigni Iudicium Apollinis.

IN tumulum magnæ cum vidit Apollo Mariæ
Nobilis ut Gallus proprios junxisset honores,
Ede tuos titulos sed da tua carmina flammis
Agnosco procerem dixit sed damno Poetam.

1696

To Lord Woodstock.

20th: December 1696.

DICAS amabo, Nobilissime et Charissime Juvenis, An Orationes
et Epistolas Ciceronis nuperrime legisti quod tam eleganter
possis scribere, an eundem potius memoriâ tenes de Officijs et Amicitiâ
disserentem, quia tanta arte scias animos et benevolentiam Tibi con-
ciliare? in una Solummodo epistola scribendâ id hercle effecisti ut si   5
Te mirer potius an amem prorsus nescio: pulchrum autem exemplar

---

Inter Emblemata et Carmina. Title: quæ edd.: qui *L 28*   2 ut *edd.*: *om. L 28*   honores,
edd.: honores *L 28*   4 Agnosco *edd.*: Agnosceo *L 28*
To Lord Woodstock. 3–4 Amicitiâ disserentem *edd.*: amicitiâ disserim tem *L 28*

Tui erga me amoris epistolium custodiam inter res quas teneo pre-
ciosissimas, sed ut illud Ego corrigerem qui Musis Tibi Amicissimis
longo abhinc tempore ualedixi imo vero literas quas in posterum
scripserim Latinas tibi corrigendas Tradam Teque optimo ingenio 10
præditum et Politioribus studijs florentem summo usque colam
honore plurimaque prosequar reverentiâ: perge semper quo cœpisti
pede, et omnes Tibi omnia bona dicant. Vale.

Amicissimum nostrum Rapinum
meo nomine salutes oro   15
Die Jovis, hora 11ᵃ: matutina

1698

In adventum Cæsaris Mosci in Angliam.

INGENS fama Viri Te Nili a fontibus Olim
     Traxit ad Hebræos, Ethiopissa, Lares
Et Tu Nassaui titulis et nomine longo
     Inductus, nostrum, Sarmata, littus ades.
Par Munus retulistis, ab anteriore Subacta   5
     Afra loco, Cæsar posteriore redis.

1700

Preamble to Baron Halifax's Patent.

SI ab antiquissima Procerum Familia Splendorem derivare, Hone-
stum; Si rebus a se pulchré gestis inclarescere, Gloriosum censeatur;
Utroque hoc Nomine Singulari Nostræ æstimationi sese commendat
Prædilectus et perquam Fidelis Consiliarius Noster Carolus Montague
Armiger: Illa Domo Ortus, quæ et tres Comites, et Octo simul alterius 5
Ordinis Senatores, in Imperij Nostri Decus et Subsidium felici ubertate

---

11 colam *edd.*: eolam *L 28*
   1 fama *edd.*: famæ *L 28*
3 titulis et *edd.*: tituliset *L 28*
   Title: edd.: om. PRO

                        2 Hebræos, Ethiopissa, *edd.*: Hebræos Ethiopissæ *L 28*
                        4 nostrum, Sarmata, *edd.*: nostrum Sarmatu *L 28*

sufficit; Illis VIRTUTIBUS ornatus, quibus nullum Honoris Incrementum aut bonus Civis invideat, aut æquus Princeps non ultro offerat.
Ingenium ei ad res arduas formavit Natura, Excoluerunt Literæ, per-
fecêre et bene dicendi Usus, et gnaviter agendi Exercitatio. In tractan- 10
dis in Senatu Negotijs strenuum et disertum, In Concilio Sanctiori
fidum et prudentem, in Administrando Ærario habilem et incorruptum,
in Fisci causis dijudicandis integrum et perspicacem experti sumus.
Quod Nobis pro Libertate et Religione, pro Communi Europæ in-
columitate, per Novennium Militantibus Belli Subsidia haud defuerint, 15
Id Senatui omnino deberi gratê agnoscimus: Sed nec tacenda est Viri
egregij Solertia, qua cautum est, ne in Summa Nummorum inopiâ Fides
publica, fænore plus æquo debilitata concideret. Ejusdem quoque
fælicitati saltem tribuendum, Quod Ærario Nostro eo tempore præfuit
quo Monetam Sceleratorum Fraude Vitiatam et Imminutam, Consilio 20
non minus fausto quam Audaci, (quod Seculi Opus videbatur) intra
biennium recudi et redintegrari cum Admiratione vidimus. Et in-
gruentibus adhuc rei Pecuniariæ Angustijs, eo authore novam et
inusitatam inivimus rationem, quâ Chartæ Pretium arrogando, Divitias
Publicas ampliari curavimus. Ob hæc præstita Nobis Officia, Populo se 25
charum præbuit, Ob hæc collata in Populum Beneficia, Nostram facile
consequutus est gratiam; Qua igitur Animi propensione frequentibus
Subditorum Votis solemus respondere, Ea alacritate, Hunc Procerum
numero adscribi Volumus; Quem Senatus communi Suffragio, PROPTER
EGREGIA SUA IN NOS NOSTROSQUE MERITA, REGIO FAVORE DIGNUM 30
PRONUNCIAVIT.

1704

Epitaphium Joannis Comitis Exoniæ.

H.S.E.

JOHANNES CECIL, Baro de Burleigh, Exoniæ Comes, Magni Burleii
Abnepos haudquaquam degener Egregiam enim Indolem optimis
Moribus optimis Artibus excoluit. Humanioribus literis bene instructus
peregre plus vice simplici profectus est; et ab excultis Europæ regionibus 5
multam Antiquitatum Linguarum nec non et rerum Civilium scientiam reportavit. Cum nemo forte melius vel Aulam ornare vel curare

Title: *1740 : om. Mon, L 28*   2 Burleigh] *1740* Burley *Mon*   3 Indolem *Mon,
1740*: Inolem *L 28*   6 non *Mon, 1740*: not *L 28*   7 melius *Mon, 1740*: metius *L 28*
vel curare *Mon*: Vel *1740*: *om. L 28*

Res publicas posset, maluit tamen otium et Secessum. Itaque Ruri suo vixit, eleganter, sumptuosè, splendide; Liberalibus Studiisque oblectatus, Amicis comis et jucundus, Egenis largus; Legum et 10 Ecclesiæ Anglicanæ fortis semper propugnator. Suarum Virtutum, et Peregrinationum, imo ferè et scientiarum sociam habuit Uxorem, Annam, ex prænobili domo de Cavendish, Gulielmi Comitis Devoniæ Filiam; Corporis Formâ, et Animi Ingenio, et omnibus, quæ Fæminam decere possent, Dotibus insignem: E quâ quinque Liberos suscepit: 15 Fælix Conjuge, fælix et Prole. Sed inter omnia, vitam quæ faciunt beatiorem, mortalitatis haud immemor, dum apud Italos præcipuæ Artis Opera curiosus lustrabat, hoc Monumentum illic, ubi exquisitissimè fieri potuit sibi et Charissimæ Lecti sui et Itinerum et Curarum omnium Consorti   20

F. F.

Obijt Ille   Obijt Illa
Aug. 29: 1700   June. 18: 1703

1710

Epitaph.

H.S.E.

GEORGIUS CHURCHILL:
Winstonij Equitis Aurati
Ex agro Dorcestriensi
Filius natu Secundus   5
Invictissimi Ducis Marlburij
Frater non indignus.
A primâ juventute Militiæ nomen dedit,
et sub Regibus Carolo et Jacobo
terra marique   10
multa cum laude meruit.
Serenissimo Principi Georgio de Daniâ
Per Viginti plus Annos a Cubiculis

---

8 maluit *Mon, 1740*: maluet *L 28*   Secessum. *Mon, 1740*: Secessum *L 28*   Ruri *Mon, 1740*: Rurio *L 28*   10 oblectatus *Mon, 1740*: obtectatus *L 28*   13 prænobili *Mon, 1740*: prænobilis *L 28*   15 quinque *Mon*: Octo *1740*: *om. L 28*   17 apud *Mon, 1740*: apod *L 28*   19 fieri *Mon, 1740*: fiori *L 28*   22 Ille . . . Illa] *Mon* illa . . . ille *1740*
     3 Winstonij *Mon*: Winstanij *L 28*   4 Dorcestriensi *Mon*: Docestriensi *L 28*   9 Carolo *Mon*: Caroli *L 28*

fide, obsequio, moribus
Gratum se reddidit et Charum.   15
Regnante Gulielmo
Quo Die Classis Gallica ab Anglis
Ad oras Neustriæ fugata et combusta est
(Die semper memorabili)
Eo Animi vigore et fortitudine pugnavit   20
Quo ducem Anglum decuit.
Mox ab eodem Rege
Æquissimo meritorum Judice
Unus è Commissariis Admiralliæ constitutus
res Maritimas quarum erat peritissimus   25
Curavit diu et Ornavit.
Sub fælicissimo demum Annæ imperio
Instaurato iterum Bello contra Gallos
Infestissimos Hostes Britanni Nominis
ex Admirallis vnus   30
et Celsissimo Principi Daniæ
Magnæ totius Britanniæ Admirallo
Factus é Consilijs
Curarum omnium et laborum particeps
Domino suo   35
Fælicissimam navabat operam
Donec fractæ Gallorum vires
toto mari cesserant.
Inde Principis optimi lateri adhærens
ad Extremum vsque diem   40
Omnia Grati pijque animi officia
persolvit
Laboribus tandem et morbis confectus
Inter amplexus et lacrymas
Amicorum, Clientum et Servorum   45
Quos fidus ipse benignus et munificus
Dilectos gratos et fideles reddidit
Pius, tranquillus, animosus, cælebs
Obijt VIII. Maij 1710.
Æta: LVIII.   50

23 Æquissimo *Mon*: aquissimo *L 28*   41 pijque *Mon*: piisque *L 28*   46 ipse *edd.*:
ipsee *L 28*   46–47] Quos, Humanus, officiosus, liberalis, Gratos, devinctos et fideles
habuit, *Mon*   47 Dilectos *edd.*: Dilectes *L 28*   49 Maij 1710.] Maij. &c. *Mon*
50] Ætat. LVIII MDCCX. *Mon*

1719

Epitaph on Charles Lord Halifax.

M S

CAROLUS MONTAGUE

Honorabilis Georgii de Horton in agro Northantoniensi
Filius natu sextus,
Henrici Comitis de Manchester   5
Nepos.
Scholæ Regiæ Westmonasteriensis Alumnus
Collegii, SS. Trinitatis Cantabrigiensis Socius
Literas humaniores feliciter excoluit
Et in dispari laudis genere clarus   10
Inter Poetas pariter ac Oratores Anglos
Excelluit
Magna ingenii indole,
Bonarumque Artium disciplinis instructus
Ex Academiæ Umbraculis   15
In conspectum Hominum
Prodiit,
Literatorum decus et præsidium
Omni dehinc cogitatione
Communi bono promovendo   20
Incubuit
Brevique
Hunc Virum
Sua in Senatu Solertia
In concilio providentia   25
In utroque Iustitia Fides Auctoritas
Ad gerendam Ærarii curam
Evexit

Title] EPITAPHIUM CAROLI Comitis HALIFAXIÆ. *1740* : *om. Mon*   1–2] H.S.E.
CAROLUS MONTAGUE *Mon* : M. S. CAROLI MONTAGUE, *1740*   3 Georgii de]
1740 Georgij Mountague De *Mon*   4 natu sextus,] *1740 om. Mon*   7 Scholæ Regiæ
Westmonasteriensis] *1740* Qui Scholae Regiae apud hanc Ecclesiam *Mon*   8 SS.
Trinitatis Cantabrigiensis] *1740* Stae Trinitatis apud Cantabrigienses *Mon*   9 humaniores feliciter] *1740* humaniores tam feliciter *Mon*   10–13] *1740* Ut inter nostratium
primos Tum Poetas, tum Oratores, Disparilicet in studiorum genere, Pari tamen cum laude
floreret; *Mon*   16–22] *1740* In publicum prodiret, Literatorum jam dum Decus,
Mox et Praesidium. Brevi etenim *Mon*   24 Solertia] *1740* facundia, *Mon*   25
concilio *Mon*, *1740* : concilia *M*   26 Iustitia] *1740* solertia, *Mon*

Ubi laborantibus Fisci rebus
Opportunè Subveniens　　　30
Simul monetam Argenteam
Magno rei-publicæ detrimento imminutam
De novo cudi fecit
Et inter absolvendum tantæ molis opus
Flagrante etiam bello　　　35
Impressis Chartulis
Pecuniarum rationem pretiumque
Impertiit
His meritis
Et Patriæ et Principis gratiam consecutus　　　40
Familiam suam diu illustrem
Illustriorem reddidit
Baro scilicet, deinde Comes de Halifax
Creatus
Ad tres Montacutani nominis Proceres　　　45
Quartus accessit
Summo Denique Periscelidis honore
Ornatus
Publici commodi indefessus adhuc consultor
Media inter conamina　　　50
Otium cum dignitate
Quod desideravit & meruit
Vix tandem assecutus
Proh brevem humanarum rerum fiduciam
Omnibus bonis　　　55
Flebilis occidit
XIX die Maij: Anno Salutis MDCCXV
Ætatis suæ LIV
Patruo de se Optimè merenti
Et bonorum & honorum hæres　　　60
Georgius Comes de Halifax
P.

30 Opportunè *Mon, 1740* : Oppertunè *M*　　　31 Simul] *1740 om. Mon*　　　33–42]
1740 Valori pristino restituit; et tantae molis opus Cum, flagrante jam bello diutino, Et
aggrederetur, & absolveret, Ne subsidia Regi Regnoque necessaria Deessent interim, Ne Fides
aut privata, aut publica, Vacillaret uspiam, Sapienter cavit. His erga Patriam et Principem
meritis Utriusque Benevolentiam complexus, Avitum Stirpis suae splendorem Novis Titulis
auxit: *Mon*　　　45 Montacutani] *1740* Montaculiani *Mon*　　　48–62] *1740* Insignitus,
Dum promovendae saluti & utilitati publicae Omni mente incumberet, Medios inter conatus,
(Proh lubricam rerum humanarum sortem!) Cum bonorum omnium luctu Extinctus est, XIX
die Maij Aº. Dⁿⁱ. MDCCXV Aetatis suae LIV. *Mon*

1720

Preamble to the Duke of Dorsets Patent.

CUM Sackvillorum Gentem recolimus, qui Gulielmum Conque-
storem in Angliam comitati magnam etiam eo tempore inter
Normannos suos a generis antiquitate, majorem veró a virtutibus
vendicaverant Gloriam, cúmque Horum posteri, serie perpetuâ egregia
Majorum facta suis illustraverint, et Regijs nostris Antecessoribus　5
meritó et apprimé chari summâ cum laude summa regni munera ex-
pleverint; ideóque ex hoc sanguine oriundus Unus a Richardo primo
Baronis titulum accepit, postea veró Alter longo annorum intervallo
a Regina Elizabethâ, cui erat etiam consanguineus, Baro de Buckhurst
creatus est, vel potius in pristinum honorem revocatus; idemque post　10
paulo Dorsettiæ Comes factus est; Huic etiam Familiæ, satis jam suo
splendore illustri, novi ex matrimonio tituli, Baro scilicet de Cranfield,
et Comes Middlesexiæ, accesserunt; Hi omnes tot tantique tituli in
Carolo nupero Dorsettiæ Comiti collecti fulserunt, et cum hi omnes jam
ad illum Virum a Patre derivati fuerint, qui eos non modo digné　15
sustinuit, sed suis etiam virtutibus ampliavit, Ipsum ob multa in nos
præstita Officia Periscelidis honore dudum Ornavimus; Eundémque,
quem inter Comites pené primum invenimus, ad Superiorem Nobilitatis
gradum hodie evehimus; ne alios olim ad summum hunc Ordinem
promovendo Illius et locum et meritum oblivisci videamur, et illam　20
dignitatem quam suo quasi jure petere potuerit etiam non petenti ultro
concedimus.

Title: M: Preamble *Wh*: Proœm. Litt. Patent. LIONELLI Ducis Dorsettiæ, 1720.
1740: *om.* PRO　　5 nostris M, *PRO, 1740*: Nostriss *Wh*　　13 tantique] *PRO, 1740*
tantiq M　　14 Comiti] M, *PRO* comite *1740*　　19 alios] *PRO* alius M, *1740*

WORKS OF DOUBTFUL
AUTHENTICITY

1684

Out of the Greek of Menage.

WHILE here for the fair *Amarillis* I dye,
    She o're Rocks and o're Streams from my Passion does fly;
O! bring her, kind *Venus*, bring her here back again,
And the chief of my Herd unto thee shall be slain:
But if she's appeas'd, if to Love she encline,   5
Take all my whole Herd, my little Herd is all thine.

1693

Out of the Italian of Fulvio Testi.

*To Count Montecuccoli. Against Pride upon sudden
Advancement. Ruscelletto Orgoglioso, &c.*

I.

PROUD and foolish noisie Stream!
    Who to some muddy Plash thy *Birth* dost owe,
      Which casually a *Brook* became,
    Assisted by the Rain, and melting Snow:
      Tho' now thou boasts thy swelling Tide,
August will soon be here, and end thy *short-liv'd* Pride.   5

Out of the Greek. Title: 1693 : om. 1684   2 She *1693*: she *1684*   4 And *1693* : and
1684   chief ... be] best of my Heifars on thy *Altar* lies *1693*   6 Take *1693*: take *1684*

2.

The *Thames*, great King of Floods! the *Thames*
With peaceful Course hastes gently to the Main;
   Yet He upon his silent Streams
The tallest Vessels does with ease sustain: 10
   And while one Summer Thee devours,
His Flood shall ne're decrease, not Time contract his Shores.

3.

   Thou foam'st, and boil'st along the Plain,
The Flocks, and Shepherds threatning by the way;
   Through borrow'd Waters basely vain,   15
Lift'st up thy head, and do'st regardless stray,
   Troubled, Oblique, and this alone,
Thy noisie Pride is *All* which thou canst call Thy own.

4.

   I know, Sir, you may well admire,
To hear me Reason with a deaf'ning Stream,   20
   But thus the Muse oft strikes the Lyre,
When she'd most Lofty, and Majestick seem,
   And in Mysterious Numbers shroud
Deep Oracles, too deep, for the unthinking Croud.

5.

   While thus I spake, there did appear,   25
Phæbus the God of every tuneful Lay,
   A Lawrel crown'd his beamy Hair,
Which with a brighter Light improv'd the Day;
   And thus he, what I saw, apply'd,
Short is th'incertain Reign, and Pomp of Mortal Pride.   30

6.

   New turns, and changes every day,
Are of inconstant Chance the constant *Arts*,
   Soon she gives, soon takes away,
She comes, embraces, nauseates you, and parts;
   But if she stays, or if she goes,   35
The wise Man little Joy, or little Sorrow shows.

7.

Good is the Pilot, who preserves
His shatter'd Vessel on the Stormy Main;
But he no leass applause deserves,
Who fears the Flattery of the Watry Plain;   40
Who never trusts the fairest Gale,
But dreads to be o'reset, and spreads but little Sail.

8.

Of all the Heroes known of old,
I honour most *Agathocles*'s Name;
Who, tho' he made the sparkling Gold   45
In polish'd Goblets on his Table flame:
To temper, and rebate its Ray,
He mixt his Father's Trade, the good old Potter's Clay.

9.

While thus the Charming God went on,
And fixt in Wonder, and Delight I stood: 50
Behold! the Upstart Stream was gone,
No drop remain'd of its insulting Flood:
But the worst Cattle of the Plain,
Trod o're the thirsty Sand, and spurn'd it with disdain.

Catullus. Epig. 19.

Suffenus iste, Vare, quem probè nôsti.

*S*UFFENUS whom you know, the Witty,
    The Gay, the Talkative, and Pretty;
And, all his Wonders to rehearse,
The THING which makes a World of Verse,
I'm certain I shou'd not bely him,   5
To say he has several thousands by him,
Yet none deform'd with Critick blot,
Or wrote on Vellom to rub out.
Royal Paper! Scarlet Strings!
Gilded Backs; and such fine things!   10

But—When you read 'em, then the Witty,
The Gay *Suffenus*, and the Pretty:
Is the dullest, heaviest Clown,
So alter'd, he can scarce be known.
This is strange! that he who now
Cou'd so flatter, laugh, and bow,
So much Wit, such breeding show,
Shou'd be so ungenteel a Wight,
Whenever he attempts to write,
And yet the Wretch is ne're so pleas'd,
As when he's with this madness seiz'd.

Faith, Sir, w'are all deceiv'd alike,
All Labour in the same mistake,
Nor is the best of Men so clear
From every Folly, but somewhere
Still the *Suffenus* will appear.
Quickly we others Errors find,
But see not our own Load behind.

Invitation into the Country.

In Imitation of the 34th Epig. of Catullus.

Go—for I'm impatient grown,
Bid him leave the noisie Town,
Charge him he no longer stay,
But with haste devour the way.
Tho' a thousand times he's staid
By that fond, bewitching Maid:
Tho' she summon all her Charms,
Kiss him, press him in her Arms.
Let him not the *Syren* mind,
Tears are Water, Sighs are Wind.
Tell him how kind Nature here,
Dresses up the Youthful Year,
Strowing on the thoughtless Hours,
Opening *Buds*, and new-born Flow'rs;
Tell him underneath this Shade,
Innocence and Mirth are laid;

Not without forbidden Claret,
Books or Musick, if he'll hear it.
See the Lawrel, and the Vine,
Round about that *Arbour* twine,   20
So we Wit, and Pleasure joyn;
So *Horace*, and *Anacreon* meet
The Jolly God, within that Seat.
Thus from Noise and Care set free,
The snares of *Beauty* we defie.   25
Let him then no longer stay,
But with haste devour the way.

1700

On some Votes against the Lord S.

WHEN Envy does at *Athens* rise,
    And swells the Towns with murmurs loud,
Not *Aristides*, Just and Wise,
Can scape the moody factious Crowd.

Each Vote augments the common Cry,   5
While he that holds the fatal Shell,
Can give no Cause, or Reason why,
But being Great, and doing Well.

Prologue,

By Sir John Falstaff.

SEE *Britains*, see, one half before your Eyes,
    Of the Old *Falstaff*, lab'ring to arise:
Curse on the strait-lac'd Traps, and *French* Machines,
None but a Genius can ascend these Scenes.

26 then *edd.*: them *1693*
    Title] On the Report of my Ld. Somers being to be remov'd from his office of Ld. high Chancelour. *Bodl*   2 swells the Towns] fills the Town *Bodl*   3 Just] great *Bodl* 4 moody] busy *Bodl*   5] Each common Vote augments the Cry, *Bodl*   6 While] Nor *Bodl*   7 give no] see a *Bodl*
    Title] *Prologue for Sir* John Falstaff, *rising slowly to soft Musick. 1703*   3 the] these *1703*

Once more my *English* Air I breath again,   5
And smooth my double Ruff, and double Chin.
Now let me see what Beauties gild the Sphere;
Body o'me, the Ladies still are Fair;
The Boxes shine, and Galleries are full,
Such were our *Bona Roba's* at the *Bull*:   10
But Supream *Jove*! what washy Rogues are here!
Are these the Sons of Beef and *English* Beer?
Old *Pharaoh* never dream'd of Kine so Lean;
This comes of meagre Soop, and sowre Champeign.
Degenerate Race, let your old Sire advise,   ⎫   15
If you desire to fill the Fair one's Eyes,   ⎬
Drink Unctuous Sack, and emulate my Size.   ⎭
Your half-flown Strains aspire to humble Bliss,
And proudly aim no lower than a Kiss;
Till quite worn out with acting Beau's and Wits,   20
Your all sent crawling to the Gravel-pits;
Pretending Claps, there languishing you lie,
And like the Maids, of the Green-sickness die:
The Case was other when we rul'd the Roast,
We Robb'd and Ravish'd, but you Sigh and Toast.   25

But here I see a side-Box better lin'd,   ⎫
Where old plump *Jack* in Miniature I find,   ⎬
Tho they're but Turnspits of the Mastiff kind.   ⎭
Half-bred they seem, mark'd with the Mungrel Curse,
Oons, which amongst you dare attempt a Purse?   30
If you'd appear my Sons, defend my Cause,
And let my Wit and Humour, meet Applause:
Shew you disdain those nauseous Scenes to taste,   ⎫
Where *French* Buffoon's like honest *Switzer* drest, ⎬
Turns all good Fellowship to Farce and Jest.   ⎭   35
Banish such Apes, and save the sinking Stage,
Let Mimicks and squeaking Eunuchs feel your Rage;
On such let your descending Scourge be try'd;
Preserve plump *Jack*, and banish all beside.

---

23 like] let *1703*   29 Mungrel] Mungrel's *1703*   30 amongst you dare] among
you dares *1703*   32 meet] find *1703*   34 Buffoon's] Buffoon *1703*   35
Fellowship] politicks *1703*   37] Let mimes any squeaking Eunuchs fill you rage *1703*
38 Scourge] Curse *1703*

1703

An Epitaph.

HERE lyes little Lundy a yard deep or more
That never lay silent or quiet before
For her brain was still working, her tongue was still prating
And the pulse of her heart continually beating
To the utmost extreams of loving and hating.   5

Her reason and humour were always at strife
But yet She perform'd all the duties of life
For She was a true friend and a pretty good Wife.

So indulgent a Mother that no one could say
Whether Minty or Patty did rule or obey   10
For the government chang'd some ten times a day.

At the hour of her birth some lucky star gave her
Witt and beauty enough to have lasted for ever
But fortune still froward when Nature is kind
A Narrow estate maliciously joynd,   15
To a very great Genius and generous Mind.

Her body was made of that super fine clay
Which is apt to be brittle for want of allay
And when without show of outward decay
It began by degrees to moulder away,   20
Her Soul then too buisy on some forreign affair
Of its own pritty dwelling took so little care
That the tenement fell for want of repair.

Title: Harl, 1704: om. W   *Capitals supplied at beginning of ll. 3–8, 11, 12, 14–16,*
19, 21–25   1 Lundy] *Harl* ⸺ ⸺ *1704*   or] *Harl* and *1704*   2 silent or
quiet] *1704* quiet or silent *Harl*   3] *Harl* Her Head always working, her Tongue
always prating, *1704*   5 hating. *edd.*: hating *W*: Hating. *1704*: hateing *Harl*   6
Her] *1704* For her *Harl*   7 But] *Harl* And *1704*   8 For . . . true] *Harl* An excellent *1704*   Wife. *1704*: Wife *W*: wife *Harl*   9 Mother . . . one] *Harl* Lover, . . .
Man *1704*   10 Minty or Patty] *Harl* Patty or Minta *1704*   11 day. *1704*: day
W, Harl   14 froward] *1704* Frown'd *Harl*   16 very great . . . generous] *Harl*
vast . . . a noble *1704*   Mind. *1704*: Mind *W*: mind *Harl*   17 made] *Harl* built
1704   18 Which . . . be] *Harl* That . . . grow *1704*   19 of outward] *Harl* it was
apt to *1704*   20 away, *edd.*: away *W, Harl*: away. *1704*   23 repair. *edd.*: repair
W, Harl: Repair. *1704*

Far be from hence both the fool and the Knave
But let all who pretend to be witty or brave   25
Whether generous friend or Amorous Slave
Contribute Some tears to water her grave.

1704

Epigram.

Like a True Irish Marlin that Misses her Flight
Little Nanny sat Pensive and Sullen all Night;
The Jack Daw escap't Her, the Loss was not great,
She may yet take a Woodcock, and that's better Meat.

1709

The Mice. A Tale.

To Mr Adrian Drift.

Two Mice (dear boy) of genteel fashion,
And (what is more) good education,
Frolic and gay, in infant years,
Equally shar'd their parents cares.
The sire of these two babes (poor creature)
Paid his last debt to human nature;   5
A wealthy widow left behind,
Four babes, three male, one female kind.

24 and] *Harl* or *1704*   25 who] *Harl* that *1704*

    Title: L 29 (D): On Mrs: Roche *Lansd*: Mrs Anne Roche, when she Lost Sr John Daws *Harl*: A Prophecy by the E of Dorset found among his papers upon Mrs. Roch having been contracted in Ireland and the Match after broke off *Add*: *om.* L 29 (X)   1 True . . . Misses] L 29 (D), *Add* right . . . has lost *Lansd*: true . . . has lost *Harl*   2 Little Nanny sat . . . Sullen] L 29 (D) Poor Nancy lay . . . Sighing *Lansd*: Little Nacy sate mumping and sullen *Harl*: Little Nanny lies sullen and Peevish *Add*   3 The Jack Daw . . . was] L 29 (D) Tho' the Jack-Daws . . . is *Lansd*: Tho' the Jac Daw . . . is *Harl*: Tho the Jack-daw has scap't her the losse is *Add*   4 yet take] L 29 (D) catch *Lansd*: yet catch *Harl*, *Add*
    Title: Mice. edd.: MICE *1740*

The sire b'ing under ground, and bury'd,
'Twas thought his spouse would soon have marry'd;   10
Matches propos'd, and num'rous suitors,
Most tender husbands, careful tutors,
She modestly refus'd; and show'd
She'd be a mother to her brood.

    Mother, dear mother, that endearing thought,   15
Has thousand, and ten thousand, fancies brought;
Tell me, O! tell me (thou art now above)
How to describe thy true maternal love,
Thy early pangs, thy growing anxious cares,
Thy flatt'ring hopes, thy fervent pious pray'rs,   20
Thy doleful days, and melancholy nights,
Cloyster'd from common joys, and just delights:
How thou didst constantly in private mourn,
And wash with daily tears thy spouse's urn;
How it employ'd your thoughts, and lucid time,   25
That your young offspring might to honour climb;
How your first care by num'rous griefs opprest,
Under the burthen sunk, and went to rest;
How your dear darling, by consumption's waste,
Breath'd her last piety into your breast;   30
How you alas! tyr'd with your pilgrimage,
Bow'd down your head, and dy'd in good old age.
Tho' not inspir'd, O! may I never be
Forgetful of my pedigree, or thee,
Ungrateful howsoe'er, mayn't I forget   35
To pay this small, yet tributary debt,
And when we meet at God's tribunal throne,
Own me, I pray thee, for a pious son.

    But why all this? is this your fable?
Believe me MATT, it seems a bauble,   40
If you will let me know th'intent on't,
Go to your Mice, and make an end on't.

    Well then dear brother, ——
As sure as HUDI's sword could swaddle,
Two Mice were brought up in one cradle,   45

Well bred, I think, of equal port,
One for the gown, one for the court:
They parted, (did they so an't please you)
Yes, that they did (dear Sir) to ease you;
One went to Holland, where they huff folk,   50
T'other to vent his wares in Suffolk.
(That Mice have travell'd in old times,
HORACE and PRIOR tell in rhymes,
Those two great wonders of their ages,
(Superior far to all the sages.)   55
Many days past, and many a night,
E'er they could gain each other's sight;
At last in weather cold (not sultry)
They met at the Three-Cranes in Poultry.
After much buss, and great grimace,   60
(Usual you know in such a case)
Much chat arose, what had been done,
What might before next summer's sun;
Much said of France, of Suffolk's goodness,
The gentry's loyalty, mobbs rudeness,   65
That ended; o'er a charming bottle,
They enter'd on this tittle tattle.

    Quoth Suffolk, by preheminence
In years, tho' (God knows) not in sense;
All's gone dear brother, only we   70
Remain to raise posterity;
Marry you brother; I'll go down,
Sell nouns and verbs, and lie alone.
May you ne'er meet with feuds or babble,
May olive-branches crown your table,   75
Somewhat I'll save, and for this end,
To prove a brother, and a friend.
What I propose is just, I swear it,
Or may I perish by this claret.
The dice are thrown, chuse this or that,   80
('Tis all alike to honest MATT)
I'll take then the contrary part,
And propagate with all my heart.

After some thought, some Portugueze,
Some wine, the younger thus replies.   85

    Fair are your words, as fair your carr'age,
Let me be free, drudge you in marr'age,
Get me a boy call'd ADRIAN,
Trust me, I'll do for't what I can.
Home went well pleas'd the Suffolk tony,   90
Heart-free from care, as purse from money,
Resolving full to please his taudy,
He got a spouse, and jerk'd her body;
At last when teeming time was come,
Out came her burthen from her womb,   95
It prov'd a lusty squalling boy,
(Doubtless the dad's and mammy's joy.)
In short, to make things square and even,
ADRIAN he nam'd was by DICK, STEPHEN.
MATT's debt thus paid, he now enlarges,   100
And sends you in a bill of charges,
A cradle (brother) and a basket,
(Granted as soon as e'er I ask'd it)
A coat not of the smallest scantling,
Frocks, stockings, shoes, to grace the bantling,   105
These too were sent, (or I'm no drubber)
Nay add to these the fine gum-rubber;
Yet these wo'nt do, send t'other coat,
For (faith) the first e'nt worth a groat,
Dismally shrunk, as herrings shotten,   110
Suppos'd originally rotten.
Pray let the next be each way longer,
Of stuff more durable, and stronger;
Send it next week, if you are able,
By this time, Sir, you know the fable;   115
From this, and letters of the same make,
You'll find what 'tis to have a name-sake.

    Cold and hard times, Sir, here, (believe it)
I've lost my curate too, and grieve it,
At Easter, for what I can see,   120
(A time of ease and vacancy)

If things but alter, and not undone,
I'll kiss your hands, and visit London;
MOLLY sends greeting, so do I Sir,
Send a good coat, that's all, good b'ye Sir.   125
                              Your's entirely,
                                    MATTHEW.

Wednesday Night,
10 *o'Clock, Feb.* 16, 170⅜.

1712

A Fable of the Widow and her Cat.

I.

A WIDOW kept a Favourite Cat,
 At first a gentle Creature;
But when he was grown Sleek and Fat,
With many a Mouse, and many a Rat,
 He soon disclos'd his Nature.   5

II.

The *Fox* and He were Friends of old,
 Nor cou'd they now be parted;
They Nightly slunk to rob the Fold,
Devour'd the Lambs, the Fleeces sold,
 And Puss grew Lion-hearted.   10

III.

He scratch'd her Maid, he stole the Cream,
 He tore her best lac'd Pinner;
Nor Chanticleer upon the Beam,
Nor Chick, nor Duckling 'scapes, when *Grim*
 Invites the *Fox* to Dinner.   15

IV.

The Dame full wisely did Decree,
 For fear He shou'd dispatch more,
That the false Wretch shou'd worry'd be:
But in a sawcy manner He
 Thus Speech'd it like a *L——re.*   20

V.

"Must I, against all Right and Law,
  "Like Pole-Cat vile be treated?
"I! who so long with Tooth and Claw
"Have kept Domestick Mice in awe,
  "And Foreign Foes defeated!   25

VI.

"Your Golden Pippins, and your Pies,
  "How oft have I defended?
"'Tis true, the Pinner which you prize
"I tore in Frolick; to your Eyes
  "I never Harm intended.   30

VII.

"I am a Cat of Honour—Stay,
  Quo' She, no longer parly;
Whate'er you did in Battle slay,
By Law of Arms became your Prey,
  I hope you won it fairly.   35

VIII.

Of this, we'll grant you stand acquit.
  But not of your Outrages:
Tell me, Perfidious! Was it fit
To make my Cream a PERQUISITE,
  And Steal to mend your Wages?   40

IX.

So flagrant is Thy Insolence,
  So vile Thy Breach of Trust is;
That longer with Thee to Dispense,
Were want of Pow'r, or want of Sense:
  Here, *Towzer!*—Do Him Justice.   45

Epigram.

I STOOD, *Sir patient at your Feet*
    Before your Elbow-chair.
But make a Bishop's Throne your Seat,
    I'll kneel before you there.
One only Thing can keep you down,   5
    For your great Soul too mean;
You'd not, to mount a Bishop's Throne,
    Pay Homage to the Queen.

1714

Epigram.

To Richmond and Peterburgh Matt. gave his Letters,
    And thought they were safe in the Hands of his Betters.
How happen'd it then that the Packets were lost?
These were knights of the Garter, not Knights of the Post.

1715

'*Mais cette voix, et ces beaux yeux*'

MAIS cette voix, et ces beaux yeux,
    Font Cupidon trop dangereux,
Et je suis triste quand je crie
Bannissons la Melancolie.

Title: edd.: om. 1751
Title: Supplied by 1779
Title: edd.: om. 1781   1 cette *edd.*: celle *1781*

1716

Song in Prison.

THE Sergeant tapp'd me on the back,
   Then hie for Brownlow-street;
There to converse with witty Jack,
   And with his spouse so sweet:
Since a prisoner I must lie, must lie;   5
   Since a prisoner I must lie.

   ★   ★   ★   ★   ★   ★   ★   ★

We doze away the morn so bright,
   From noon on books we muse:
When home the Sergeant comes at night,
   Ads'bud he brings no news!   10
So a prisoner I must lie, must lie;
   So a prisoner I must lie.

No news! I cry! Why? What the pox,
   Must I stay here for ever?
Do let me go to Betty Cox,   15
   And wash grief from my liver,
Since a prisoner I must lie, must lie;
   Since a prisoner I must lie.

   ★   ★   ★   ★   ★   ★   ★   ★

   ★   ★   ★   ★   ★   ★   ★   ★

Here light the candles, Hetty,
   And, William, stir the fire: 20
Your servant, Mistress Betty:
   I am yours, Mr. Prior!
Tho' a prisoner you must lie, must lie;
   Tho' a prisoner you must lie.

Title: Supplied by 1892

When I attempt to ope the bar,   25
  My hat I humbly move.
With scorn she cries, "You come not here
  For money nor for love,"
Since a prisoner you must lie, must lie;
  Since a prisoner you must lie.   30

To make the bowl that cheers the heart
  The choicest drugs are chosen:
"Little lemons are most tart,"
  And eleven to the dozen!
Since a prisoner I must lie, must lie;   35
  Since a prisoner I must lie.

  *   *   *   *   *   *   *   *

Come, Betty, fill another bowl.
  "Lard, Sir! the watch is set!"
Nay! nay, I'll have it, by my soul!
  I have not drank *Nan* yet: 40
Since a prisoner I must lie, must lie;
  Since a prisoner I must lie.

So now the reck'ning must be paid,
  I must either *tick* or borrow.
"No matter, Sir," the Gypsey said,   45
  "I'll call on you to morrow!
Since a prisoner you must lie, must lie;
  Since a prisoner you must lie."

But tell me, pretty neighbour,
  At what o'clock you'll come?   50
"I cannot lose my labour,
  "You'll be all day *at home*,"
Since a prisoner you must lie, must lie;
  Since a prisoner you must lie.

1717

The Old Gentry, out of French.

THAT all from *Adam* first begun,
    Sure none (but *Wh—ston*) doubts;
And that his son, and his son's son
    Were plowmen, clowns and louts:
Here lies the only diff'rence now;   5
    Some shot off late, some soon,
Your sires ith' morning left their plow,
    And ours ith' afternoon.

1718

Upon Lady Katherine H—de's first appearing at the Play-House in Drury-Lane.

I.

THUS *Kitty*, beautiful and young,
    And mad as Colt untam'd;
Bespoke the Fair from whom She sprung,
    With little Rage enflam'd.

II.

Inflam'd with Rage at sad Restraint,   5
    Which wise *Mamma* ordains,
And sorely vex'd to play the Saint,
    Whilst humbler Beauty reigns.

Upon Lady Katherine H—de's first appearing. Title] The Female *PHAETON. N.D.*
2 mad] wild *N.D.*   6 ordains,] ordain'd; *N.D.*   8 humbler . . . reigns] Wit and
. . . reign'd *N.D.*

III.

Shall I thumb Holy Things confin'd,
    With *Abigails* forsaken!   10
Kitty's for something else design'd,
    Or I am much mistaken.

IV.

Must Lady *Jenny* frisk about,
    In Visits with her Cozens?
At Masques and Balls make all the Rout,   15
    And bring home Hearts by Dozens?

V.

What has She better, pray, than I?
    What hidden Charms to boast,
That all Mankind for her should die,
    Whilst I am scarce a Toast?   20

VI.

Dearest *Mamma*, for once let me,
    Unchain'd my Fortune try;
I'll have my *Earl* as well as She,
    Or know the Reason why.

VII.

I'll soon with *Jenny*'s Pride quit Score,   25
    Make all her Lovers fall;
They'll grieve I was not loose before,
    She, I was loos'd at all.

VIII.

The Mother's Fondness soon gave way,
    Kitty at Heart's Desire,   30
Obtain'd the Chariot for a Day,
    And set the World on Fire.

9 Things] Books, *N.D.*   11 something else] other Things *N.D.*   14 In Visits]
And Visit *N.D*   15 Masques and Balls] Balls must *She N.D.*   17 has She better]
better has She *N.D.*   26 Make all] And make *N.D.*   27 loose] loos'd *N.D.*
29 The . . . soon] Fondness prevaii'd, *Mamma N.D.*   31 Obtain'd] Obtains *N.D.*

1720

The Judgment of Venus.

I.

WHEN KNELLER's Works of various Grace,
  Were to fair VENUS shown,
The Goddess spy'd in every Face
  Some Features of Her own.

II.

Just so, (and pointing with her Hand)   5
  So shone, says she, my Eyes,
When from Two Goddesses I gain'd
  An Apple for a Prize.

III.

When in the Glass and River too,
  My Face I lately view'd,   10
Such was I, if the Glass be true,
  If true the Chrystal Flood,

IV.

In Colours of this glorious kind
  Apelles painted me;
My Hair thus flowing with the Wind,   15
  Sprung from my Native Sea.

V.

Like this, disorder'd, wild, forlorn,
  Big with ten Thousand Fears,
Thee, my *Adonis*, did I mourn,
  Ev'n Beautiful in Tears.   20

VI.

But viewing *Myra* plac'd apart,
  I fear, says she, I fear
Apelles, that Sir *Godfrey*'s Art
  Has far surpass'd thine here.

VII.

Or I a Goddess of the Skies   25
    By *Myra* am outdone,
And must resign to her the Prize,
    The Apple which I won.

VIII.

But as soon as she had MYRA seen
    Majestically fair,   30
The sparkling Eyes, the Look serene,
    The gay and easie Air.

IX.

With fiery Emulation fill'd,
    The wond'ring Goddess cry'd,
Apelles must to *Kneller* yield,   35
    Or *Venus* must to *HYDE.*

1721

Couplets.

I.

THIS drawn by Candlelight and hazard
    Was meant to shew Charles Christian's Mazzard.

2.

This Fizz, so well drawn, you may easily know
Was done by a Knight for one Tim with an O.

31 the *edd.*: rhe *1720*
    Title: Supplied by 1892   1 drawn] *1771* done *1793*   2 Was *1771* : was *B.M.* :
Is *1793*   Charles *1771* : Ch. *B.M.* : Kit *1793*   3 know] know; *1793*   4 Was
edd. : was *Morg* : It was *1793*   Knight *1793* : Kt. *Morg*   Tim] Tom *1793*

WORKS WRONGLY ATTRIBUTED
TO PRIOR

THIS list consists of attributions that are demonstrably wrong or are not supported by evidence. In the hope of clearing away some of the debris surrounding the Prior canon, we have included works that seem never to have been definitely attributed to Prior, but have been ascribed to him by suggestion or implication. For example, we include all the works listed by Waller in *1907* (p. 408) as attributed to Prior, although many of them had not—so far as we can discover—been previously attributed to him in print.

We do not usually give these works entire, but we include first and last lines of verse for purposes of identification. In some cases we have identified the true author, but we have not felt obliged to do this; our purpose is accomplished when we show that there is no valid reason for ascribing a work to Prior.

1644

On a F . . t let in the House of Commons.

Reader I was born, and cry'd,
I crack'd, I smelt, and so I dy'd.
Like Julius Cæsar's was my Death,
Who in the Senate lost his Breath.
Much alike entomb'd does lye
The noble Romulus and I;
And when I dy'd like Flora fair,
I left the common Wealth my Heir.

Although this poem was transcribed by Drift in *M*, 70 (from which we print the text above), and was published in *1740*, p. 74, it is certainly not Prior's. The first two lines, with the title *A fart's Epitaph*, occur in *Wits Recreations*, 1641 (Case 95–b), p. 24. The whole poem, with minor variants, is in *B.M. Sloane 1792*, 95, a manuscript book of verses compiled probably in 1644 for Robert Killigrew. (The date of the manuscript is established by A. Conway, 'A New Stanza to "You Meaner Beauties of the night" ', *Times Literary Supplement*, 4 Sept. 1924, p. 540. We are much indebted to Miss Frances Mayhew for calling our attention to this article and for rechecking the manuscript for us.)

Perhaps P copied the poem, as he did a few by Dorset (see commentary on *An Epitaph*, under Works of Doubtful Authenticity, 1703), and Drift mistakenly assumed that it was P's. The author is unknown.

792

1687

[*Epigram.*]

The Church of Rome on ours Reprisals makes,
For Turncoat Oates, she Turcoat Dryden takes.

Eves (pp. 33–34) attributes this epigram to Prior and Charles Montagu in collaboration, and dates it 1686. It occurs in a letter from Charles Montagu to George Stepney (*P.R.O., S.P. 105/82*), dated 'Apr. 14. Manchester House in Channell Row'; since the letter describes James II's attack on Cambridge ('The Vice Chancellor is summon'd to appear before the Commissioners on the 21 to Answer for such things as shall be objected to them on his Majestys behalf, and is to bring up whom the university shall chuse to Represent them . . .'), the year is clearly 1687. Montagu thanks Stepney for his verses, 'particularly that which you said of the new Converts, which I show'd my Ld Dorset, who upon that took notice of your Verses on the King, which he remember'd so long after. I have not time and leasure yet to set to an Epistle, but I will certainly clear that debt; in the Mean Time I will give you some of our Epigrams. For our Heads have layn much that way of late, and they may serve for some Recompense for those you sent us on the French King.' He then quotes this and three other epigrams. P is not mentioned in the letter, and there is nothing in it to suggest that he had been with Montagu or had had any part in composing the epigrams. Montagu seems to be saying that he and Dorset wrote them.

Love a Spirit.

I told Jacinta t'other day,

★   ★   ★

And I can feel him on your lips.

I. A. Williams in *London Mercury*, xi (1924–5), 525, suggested that this poem in Philip Ayres's *Lyric Poems* (1687) might be Prior's. This suggestion was based on the assumption that Ayres printed P's *To Cloe Weeping* in his *Emblems of Love*, 1683; but this assumption is incorrect: see commentary on *To Cloe Weeping* (1708).

1689

An Apology to a Lady, who told me, I cou'd not love her heartily, because I had lov'd others. In Imitation of Mr. Waller.

Fair *Sylvia*, cease to blame my Youth

★   ★   ★

And never settle more.

First attributed to Prior by John Nichols in *A Select Collection of Poems*, iv (1780), 47. Nichols says, 'By the manner in which this and the two following little pieces [*Against Modesty in Love* and *On a young Lady's going to Town*] are printed in the *Oxford and Cambridge Miscellany Poems* [1708], there is little doubt but they are the productions of the excellent poet to whom I have ascribed them. N.' These three poems were included, on Nichols's authority, in collected editions of P for more than a century. R. B. Johnson, in *1892*, I. xiii, pointed out that Nichols's argument from the arrangement of the *Oxford and Cambridge Miscellany* was not valid (the three poems 'come immediately after one of Prior's poems, but, as the other signed by him is in another part of the book, this affords no argument') and rejected the three poems from his edition. Waller, in *1907*, printed the three in his appendix of 'Poems Attributed to Prior'.

But Nichols himself, in vol. v (1782) of the *Select Collection*, printed *An Apology* as one of a collection taken from the manuscripts of Bishop Francis Atterbury, with the title, *Song, Taken from Bp. Atterbury's Own Hand-Writing* (pp. 4–5). Neither Nichols nor any subsequent editor seems to have noticed that this established Atterbury's authorship of the poem Nichols had two years before attributed to P.

An Apology was first published (without title or author) in *The Banquet of Music*, 1690—licensed Oct. 1689—(Day & Murrie, 105), Bk. IV, p. 4, with a setting by A. Damascene.

1693

A Paraphrase on the French.

In Gray-hair'd *Celia's* wither'd *Arms*

*   *   *

Te Deum sing in quiet.

First attributed to Prior by John Nichols (*Select Collection*, ii, 1780, 332), who says only, 'This poem has been ascribed to Mr. Prior. N.' Apparently Nichols's memory played him false (perhaps because of the similarity in theme to some of P's poems, such as *An English Ballad*, 1695), for the poem had never been ascribed to P. It was, on Nichols's authority, printed in collected editions of P until Waller, in *1907*, questioned it. Waller printed it in his appendix of 'Poems Attributed to Prior', noted that it was printed as Dorset's in *Johnson 1779*, and commented that it 'may be Dorset's'.

Of the three British Museum manuscripts, one (*Add. 21094*, 120ᵛ) attributes the poem to Dorset; the other two (*Stowe 305*, 203ᵛ; *Harl. 6947*, 167) leave it anonymous. The two earliest publications are without attribution: *Examen Poeticum*, 1693 (Case 172–3–a), p. 419; *P.O.A.S.*, 1698 (Case 215), p. 103. It is ascribed to Dorset in *Miscellaneous Works of . . . Rochester and Roscommon*, 1707 (Case 242), ii. 103; *Poems on Several Occasions by . . . Roscommon and Dorset*, 1714 (Case 278), p. 39; *Works of the . . . Minor Poets*, 1749 (Case 467–1–a), p. 137; and by Giles Jacob in *An Historical Account of . . . our most Considerable English Poets*, 1720, p. 175. Harris (*Dorset*, p. 235) accepts the poem as Dorset's. We are indebted to Mr. Harris for providing some of the references above.

The French poem of which this is a paraphrase is printed on facing pages in *Examen Poeticum*. It is by Henriette de Coligny, Comtesse de la Suze, and begins, 'La jeune Iris aux cheveux gris'.

1695

Song to the King, after the Taking of Namur.

Harmonious Strings, your Charms prepare,

*   *   *

The Praise of their Victorious King.

This poem was published only in *P.O.A.S.*, 1698 (Case 215), p. 277, where it is described as '*Written by Mr. Prior, and Sung before His Majesty at the* Hague'. It is fortunate that none of Prior's editors or commentators ever noticed this attribution, for the poem was written by Stepney. H. T. Swedenberg, Jr. ('George Stepney, My Lord Dorset's Boy', *Huntington Library Quarterly*, x, 1946–7, 29) quotes from *B.M. Add. 28897*, 319ᵛ, 323, a letter from Stepney to John Ellis, dated at The Hague, 1/11 Oct. 1695, enclosing the poem and describing it as 'a Song wch I was bidd to make for Abel'. (We are indebted to Mr. W. J. Cameron, Victoria University College, Wellington, New Zealand, for calling this article to our attention.)

1700

A Law against Cuckoldom: or, The Tryal of Adultery.

London: Printed in the Year 1700.

Too weak are *Laws*, and *Edicts* Vain,

*   *   *

She sav'd her self, and *Damn'd the Law.*

Waller (*1907*, p. 408) lists this among poems which 'have been attributed to Prior', though we have not found any such attribution. B. Boyce (*Tom Brown of Facetious Memory*, Cambridge, Mass., 1939, p. 198) lists it among Brown's works. In *Letters, Poems, and Tales*, 1718 (Case 307), p. 30, the title is changed to: *The Edict of Prato: or, Cuckoldom Defended. A Tale from Boccacce*; no author is given.

The Virtuous Wife. A Poem. In Answer to the Choice, That would have No Wife. Containing I. The Virtuous Wive's Character . . . VII. Her Conversation.

London: Printed, . . . by J. Nutt, . . . MDCC.

If *Heaven* would a greater *Blessing* give

*   *   *

He'd have a *Wife*, and wish to *live* like me.

Listed by Waller in *1907* among poems attributed to Prior, though we can find no earlier attribution. The poem, an innocuous reply to Pomfret's *The Choice*, is most unlike P's verse.

The Shoe-Maker Beyond his Last, or, A Satyr upon Scurrilous Poets. Especially Ned W——D, Author of a Poem intituled, A Journey to Hell: or, a Visit Paid to the Devil.

London, Printed for S. Cook, . . . 1700.

What private Sin hath fertile *England* Nurst,

★   ★   ★

And all at once to such dull *Poets* given.

Listed by Waller in *1907* among poems attributed to Prior, though we can find no earlier attribution. Possibly someone confused it with P's *Satyr on the Poets* (1687), to which it bears a faint resemblance, though much of it directly attacks Ned Ward. The author is identified as Richard Burridge in S. Halkett and J. Laing, *Dictionary of Anonymous and Pseudonymous English Literature* (ed. J. Kennedy, W. A. Smith, and A. F. Johnson, Edinburgh, 1926–34).

1701

Against Modesty in Love.

For many unsuccessful Years

★   ★   ★

Had foolishly deny'd.

See the discussion of *An Apology to a Lady*, above. First attributed to Prior by John Nichols in *1780*, and included in collected editions on his authority until R. B. Johnson rejected it in *1892*. In *1907*, Waller printed it in his appendix of attributed poems.

When Nichols ascribed this poem to P in *Select Collection*, iv. 48, he forgot that he had printed the same poem (with the title, *Advice to a Lover*) in iii. 168, as by Yalden. Thomas Yalden (1670–1736) was undoubtedly the author; the poem was attributed to him when first published in *A New Miscellany*, 1701 (Case 223), p. 237, and in later collections. Anderson, in *Works of the British Poets*, 1793 (vii. 774), and Chalmers, in *Works of the English Poets*, 1810 (xi. 85), repeat Nichols's blunder, printing *Advice to a Lover* as Yalden's and *Against Modesty in Love* as P's without noticing that they are the same poem.

Wedlock a Paradice; or, A Defence of Woman's Liberty Against Man's Tyranny. In Opposition To a Poem, Entitul'd, The Pleasures of a Single Life, &c.
London: Printed . . . by J. Nutt . . . 1701.

When Time had freed me from my Childish Years,

     ★   ★   ★

To be a Heav'nly Gift beyond the World's desert.

Listed by Waller in *1907* among poems attributed to Prior, though we have found no earlier attribution. The autobiographical sketch at the beginning identifies the author as a lawyer (ll. 19–30).

1702

The Lawyer Turn'd Butcher, and the Physician, Cook: or, Hungry Dogs Will Eat Dirty Pudding.
London: Printed in the Year, 1701.

One Night when that salubrious Cordial, Wine,

     ★   ★   ★

Thus hungry Dogs will dirty Pudding eat.

Listed by Waller in *1907* among poems attributed to Prior, though we have found no such attribution. The tale describes two friends who, being hungry late at night, cook and eat an old tomcat; it is vulgar and, unless there are concealed personal references, pointless. There is nothing to suggest a connexion with P.

The Character of a Covetous Citizen, or, A Ready Way to get Riches. A Poem.
London, Printed, . . . by the Booksellers . . . 1702.

The Man who dotes on Gold, how curs'd his Fate!

     ★   ★   ★

Thus leaves his ill-got Treasure, and dispairing dies.

Listed by Waller in *1907* among poems attributed to Prior, though we have found no earlier attribution. The poem tells the story of a typical Whig merchant, somewhat like Pope's 'Sir Balaam' (*Epistle to Bathurst*, ll. 341–402). There is nothing to suggest any connexion with P.

1704

Faction Display'd. A Poem.
London: Printed in the Year 1704.

Say, goddess Muse, for the All-searching Eyes

*   *   *

Retiring leaves their Hopes involv'd in endless Night.

This satire on the Whigs, including the Duke and Duchess of Marlborough, was almost certainly written by William Shippen (1673–1743); it is attributed to him by Giles Jacob (*Historical Account*, 1720, p. 306). Many contemporaries, however, believed Prior to be the author, and the Duchess of Marlborough's persistent enmity toward P seems to have arisen from her conviction that he wrote this poem. (See A. Rosenberg, 'Prior's Feud with the Duchess of Marlborough', *Journal of English and Germanic Philology*, lii, 1953, 27–30.) In a letter to Lord Godolphin, 28 April 1704, P strongly denied any connexion with the satire: 'But since yesterday I saw a Book called *Faction display'd answered Paragraph by Paragraph* The Prose part whereof is addressed to me as if I were the Author of that Libel, I take the Liberty to Repeat to your Lordship, that before God, Angels, and Men I neither did write that Book, or any Line in it, nor do I directly or indirectly know who wrote the whole or any part of it . . .' (*L 13*, 42–43).

1706

Ode for the Thanksgiving Day.
London: Printed for Jacob Tonson . . . 1706.

Begin, my Muse, and strike the Lyre!

*   *   *

She Chains th'Oppressor, and She Frees th'Opprest.

Attributed to Prior in the *Cambridge Bibliography of English Literature* (1944), probably through confusion with his *An Ode, Humbly Inscrib'd to the Queen . . . 1706*. There is nothing to support the attribution; if P had written this innocuous poem, praising Marlborough, Godolphin, and the Queen, he would have had no reason not to claim it. We have not identified the author.

An Epistle from the Elector of Bavaria to the French King, after the Battel of Ramillies.

London: Printed for Jacob Tonson . . . 1706.

If yet, great Sir, your heart can comfort know,

★　　★　　★

An unsuccessful, but a faithful friend.

Attributed to Prior by Waller, who prints it in his Appendix, and says, 'This also seems to me to be Prior's. Mr. Wise tells me that it was identified as Prior's by Birkbeck Hill' (*1907*, p. 407). T. J. Wise also ascribed it to P in his *Catalogue of the Ashley Library*, vol. iv, and his *Catalogue of the J. H. Wrenn Library* (Austin, Texas, 1920), vol. iii. R. W. Chapman, in 'A Poem Attributed to Prior', *R.E.S.*, i (1925), 92–93, points out that the Dedicatory Epistle printed with the poem makes it clear that the author was a lawyer, and describes a presentation copy in which the author is identified as Stephen Clay, a lawyer. Mr. Chapman's identification is confirmed by Oldmixon's note in *The Muses Mercury* for Jan. 1707: 'S—— C—— Esq; has also obliged the World with an Epistle in Verse, from the Elector of *Bavaria* to the French King, written after the Manner of *Ovid*, being a letter of Complaint . . .' (p. 22).

To the Duke of Marlborough.

Pardon, Great DUKE, if *Britain's* Stile delights;

★　　★　　★

Fill all the Loftiest Cedars of the Wood.

Published with the preceding (*An Epistle from the Elector of Bavaria*), and evidently by the same author, Stephen Clay. Waller prints it in the notes to *1907* (pp. 406–7).

To Mrs. S. F. on her poems.

Hail to Clarinda, dear Euterpe hail,

★　　★　　★

Strive all, ye thinking fair, to copy her.

M. P.

Attributed to Prior by 'J. N.' [John Nichols?] in *Gentleman's Magazine*, li (1781), 455. Nichols [?] says that the poem was first printed (as recommendatory verses) in Mrs. Sarah Fyge Egerton's *Collection of Poems on Several Occasions*, 1706. The poem was clearly written by a woman, perhaps Mary Pix.

1708

On a young Lady's going to Town in the Spring.

One Night unhappy *Celadon,*

*   *   *

Not satisfy'd with private Sway at home.

See discussion of *An Apology to a Lady,* above. First attributed by Nichols in *1780,* and included in collected editions of Prior on his authority until rejected by R. B. Johnson in *1892.* In *1907,* Waller prints it as 'attributed'.

Though we have not been able to identify the author or to find an earlier printing than the *Oxford and Cambridge Miscellany,* 1708 (Case 248), p. 36, there is no reason for assigning this poem to P. Nichols's argument from the order of poems in the *Oxford and Cambridge Miscellany* has no validity, and we have demonstrated the two other attributions he made on that basis to be erroneous.

Jack Frenchman's Lamentation. An Excellent New Song, To the Tune of I'll tell thee Dick, &c.
[Four broadside editions, 1708.]

Ye Commons and PEERS,

*   *   *

For Old Bully, thy Doctors are gone.

The authorship of this ballad has been extensively discussed; see Sir Harold Williams, ed., Swift's *Poems,* p. 1078. Williams cites an attribution to Prior on a contemporary manuscript copy in his possession, and calls this a 'more probable attribution' than that to Congreve, though he thinks that to Swift most likely. In a letter, he has kindly given us his present opinion: 'Although I still think it possible that Swift may have written Jack Frenchman's Lamentation I incline to doubt it. I think you might include a mention of it as a Prior possibility.' We have not, however, been able to find any evidence to support an attribution of the poem to P.

1709

'In pity to the empty'ng Town'

In pity to the empty'ng Town

*   *   *

Tho' he's a younger Brother.

Williams (Swift's *Poems,* p. 122) notes: 'Dr. Elrington Ball (*Notes and Queries,* 12 S. viii. 2) suggested that these verses may have been written by Prior; but he had never seen the original manuscript.' The poem is by Swift.

1710

Consolation to Mira Mourning. A Poem. Discovering a certain
Governor's Intreigue with a Lady at his Court.
Printed and Sold by the Booksellers of London and Westminster.
1710.

Why thus disguis'd? Ah! Why's thy lovely Face

★   ★   ★

My Love to Cherish, ever, and Admire.

F. C. Brown, in *Elkanah Settle: His Life and Works* (Chicago, 1910), p. 131, quotes T. J. Wise as saying that this poem has been ascribed to both Prior and Settle, but is now pretty generally accepted as Settle's. Brown (p. 37) thinks that it is probably Settle's.

The poem is extremely unlike P; if it was ever really ascribed to him, the ascription was completely absurd.

1711

On Mr. Harley's being Stab'd.

Weltring in blood, when Harley calls to mind

★   ★   ★

May all such wounds light rather here, than there.

Attributed to Prior by a careless transcriber in the *Thynne Papers* at Longleat, vol. lxxvi, f. 249. It is certain that P did not write the verses, for reasons explained in the commentary on *To Mr. Harley* (1711).

1712

When the Cat's away, The Mice may play. A Fable, Humbly
inscribd to Dr. Sw—t.
London: Printed for A. Baldwin, ... [N.D.; 1712].

A *Lady* once (so Stories say)

★   ★   ★

Least she again repent it.

Nichols (*Select Collection*, iv, 1780, 50) printed this as 'Probably by Mr. Prior', noting that it had also been ascribed to Swift. Subsequent collected editions of Prior included it, on Nichols's authority; Waller questioned it, but included it in *1907* in his appendix of attributed poems.

C. H. Firth, in 'Two Poems Attributed to Prior', *R.E.S.*, i (1925), 456–8, notes that the poem is a Whig reply to *A Fable of the Widow and Her Cat* (in Works of Doubtful Authenticity, 1712), and comments: 'It is absurd to attribute to Prior a poem written against the party of which he was a member and the policy which he was employed to carry out.' He suggests that the author may have been Arthur Maynwaring.

The Fable of the Lyon and the Fox.
London, Printed in the Year 1712. . . .

A Lyon by his valiant Deeds preferr'd,

★　　★　　★

If not, He's able to revenge the Deed.

Printed as 'Attributed to Prior' by Waller, who says, 'The above [*The Fable of the Lyon and the Fox* and *An Answer to the Curious Maid*] seem to me to be by Prior. Mr Wise informs me that he bought both as Prior's on the advice of Dr Garnett' (*1907*, p. 405). Ascribed to P also in Wise's *Catalogue of the Ashley Library*.

We have not found the author of this poem, which appears to be a defence of Harley (the fox) and a justification of the downfall of Marlborough (the lion). But there seems to be no reason whatever to attribute it to P.

The Perquisite-Monger: or the Rise and Fall of Ingratitude. Being One of the Stories, which the Monks of Godstow were formerly wont to divert Fair Rosamond with, and which may serve to clear up several Absurdities in the History of Prince Mirabel.
London: Printed and Sold by the Booksellers . . . 1712.

Listed by Waller in *1907* among poems attributed to Prior. The work is not a poem but a prose satire on Marlborough and a justification of his downfall. We have not found any earlier attribution to P, nor anything to suggest his authorship.

Palmyra: or, Poems on Several Subjects Never before Publish'd.
London: Printed and Sold by J. Morphew, . . . 1712.

This collection of nineteen poems and a verse introduction is obliquely attributed to Prior by T. J. Wise in the *Catalogue of the J. H. Wrenn Library*: 'There is no proof whatever that the book was the product of the pen of Matthew Prior. The poems are more in the manner of Prior than in that of any other Author by whom it is possible that they could have been written, but no external evidence whatsoever has as yet been adduced to fix them upon him.' This artful statement creates two completely false impressions: first, that the book had been previously attributed to P; second, that Wise was cautious in making attributions. For discussion of Wise's editing of the Wrenn catalogue, see J. W. Draper, 'Thomas J. Wise and the Wrenn *Catalogue*', *Modern Language Notes*, lxiii (1948), 135–9. Wise not only made irresponsible attributions wholesale in this catalogue and the catalogue of his own Ashley Library, but suggested others to scholars and editors such as Waller. Unfortunately, he was particularly fond of P, and it is probable that he was ultimately responsible for about half of the attributions in our list.

The University of Texas catalogue attributes *Palmyra* to Richard Palmer, as Miss Fannie Ratchford, Curator of Rare Books, kindly informs us. We are much indebted to Miss Ratchford for providing us with photographs of this and other books in the Wrenn collection at the University of Texas.

The Examiner, 1710–12.

Prior wrote No. 6 of *The Examiner* and a poem (*A Fable*, 1710) published in No. 3. There is no definite evidence for identifying as his any other contributions to the periodical.

Some of the Whigs believed that P wrote most of the early numbers and that he continued to contribute (Eves, pp. 224–9); in an effort to stop the consequent attacks on P, Swift stated in No. 27 (1 Feb. 1711) that P was not the author (see also *Journal to Stella*, ed. H. Williams, i. 185, 209). Addison in *Tatler*, No. 239 answered *Examiner*, No. 11 together with No. 6 as if he thought they were by the same author; but he may only have been maintaining the fiction that the Examiner was one person, and there is no other evidence for P's authorship. (G. A. Aitken, *Life of Steele*, 1889, i. 292, attributes No. 11 to Dr. William King.) L. M. Beattie, in *John Arbuthnot, Mathematician and Satirist* (Cambridge, Mass., 1935), pp. 166–8, suggests that P may have had something to do with *Examiner*, vol. ii, No. 24 (8–15 May 1712), which presents 'Sir Humphrey Polesworth' (cf. *1907*, p. 404); but he concludes—correctly—that there is not sufficient evidence to attribute it to P.

1713

Yarhell's Kitchen: or, the Dogs of Egypt. An Heroic Poem.
London: Printed for Bernard Lintott . . . MDCCXIII.

I Am the Bard; who whilom did rehearse

＊　　＊　　＊

Mixt with the fragrant Steam, which from the Stoves arose.

Listed by Waller in *1907* among poems attributed to Prior; but we have found no earlier attribution to P. G. C. Faber, in his edition of Gay (Oxford, 1926), pp. xxxii–iv, makes what he regards as a 'certain attribution' of the poem to P on four grounds: (1) the poem defends Harley (Yarhell) and attacks the Whig dogs Walpole, Godolphin, and Marlborough; (2) the beginning of the poem seems 'to allude to Prior's literary record, and in particular to his prose *Dialogues of the Dead* . . .'; (3) 'A modern hand has pencilled "By M. Prior" on the British Museum copy of *Yarhell*'; (4) the poem has a motto from *Hudibras*, which P imitated in *Alma*.

Of these arguments, only the second need be discussed. The lines in question are these:

> *I Am the Bard; who whilom did rehearse*
> *Pathetick Tales of Love in humble Verse:*
> *Who solemn Hymns compos'd for Raree Shows;*
> *And* Ghosts *and* Goblins *feign'd in tuneful Prose:*
> *Who oft have made judicious Mobs rejoice,*
> *Attentive to the Ragged* Siren's *Voice:*
> *Works grateful unto Hawking Dames.—*

The reference in l. 4 cannot be to P's *Dialogues of the Dead*, which were not written until much later (all indications are that they were composed 1718–21). The poet described here has written many ballads, broadsides, chapbooks, and similar pieces for the mob; his work has been 'non-literary'. This is not a description of P's literary career.

Mr. Faber's last two arguments are offered only as confirmation, and carry no weight alone; his first gives no ground for attributing the poem to P, for many other poets celebrated Harley's victory over the Whigs. There is, then, no reason whatever for assigning the poem to P; it is a coarse epic travesty and mock beast-fable, diffuse and quite unlike P's verse in style.

1714

A Tale of Midas the King. Dedicated to Ar——r Tariff, One of my Lords Footmen.
London: Printed for J. Baker . . . 1714.

Ye Sisters Nine, assist my Quill,

★   ★   ★

His throne, but by the Mob was Slain.

Attributed to Prior by W. T. Morgan, *A Bibliography of British History (1700–1715)*, vol. ii, 1937, Q 518, who describes it as an attack on George I and the Whigs for depriving P of his commissionership of customs. Morgan's attribution is based on his misreading of a bookseller's catalogues—Pickering and Chatto, Catalogue 247 (N.D.), No. 13475a; Catalogue 284 (1934), No. 252—which state that the poem is about P, not that he wrote it. The bookseller's catalogues are themselves wrong, however; 'MATTHEW PARIS' is cited in the postscript to the dedication as a 'fabulous' historian, and does not stand for P; in fact, the poem seems to have nothing whatever to do with P.

The dedication is signed by the author, T. Tomkins.

A Genuine Epistle from M——w P——r, Esq; at Paris, To the Reverend J——n S——t, D.D. at Windsor.

London: Anno Salutis M.DCC.XIV. [A second issue has the half-title: *A Farther Hue and Cry After Dr. Sw——t. Being a Collection of Curious Pieces Found Since his Departure.*]

Since you, Dear *Jon——an*, alone best know

★   ★   ★

To rail, impeach, and draw important Schemes,
To★ ★ ★

Multa desunt.

Attributed to Prior in the title and in numerous library catalogues. The piece is a Whig satire on P, Swift, and the other Tories, representing them as Jacobites.

1716

To His Grace the Duke of Argyle, upon his Arrival at Court, after the Defeat of the Northern Rebellion, March the 6th, 1715.

London: Printed for Jacob Tonson . . . MDCCXVI.

Eternal *Phoebus*! whose propitious Ray,

★   ★   ★

May shield our Freedom and protect our Land.

Waller in *1907* lists this among poems attributed to Prior, though we have found no earlier attribution. That P, while under confinement, should write a poem praising Argyle, a Whig and an enemy of Harley, seems inconceivable. There is nothing to suggest that he had any connexion with the poem. This may be the same poem listed by Giles Jacob (*Historical Account*, 1720, p. 130) as by Major Richardson Pack.

A Letter to the Knight of the Sable Shield.
London: Printed for Bernard Lintot . . . 1716.

Sir Knight, who know with equal Skill

★   ★   ★

When two such perilous WITS Combine?

Listed by Waller in *1907* among poems attributed to Prior; we have found no earlier attribution. The poem, a mild satire on Sir Richard Blackmore and Jacob Tonson, was apparently written by Elijah Fenton. It is printed as Fenton's in *Works of the English Poets*, ed. A. Chalmers, 1810, x. 401. There is nothing to connect it with P.

Colin's Complaint. A Song. To the Tune of 'Grim King of the Ghosts.'

Despairing beside a clear stream,

★　　★　　★

His ghost shall glide over the green.

A reviewer of the third volume of Warton's *History of English Poetry*, in *Gentleman's Magazine*, li (1781), 230, says: 'In p. 309, note *O* Mr. Warton mentions '*Prior's* Song, *Despairing beside a clear stream*'. This song was by Rowe. . . .' Johnson (*Lives*, ii. 111) says that it was written about Addison and the Countess of Warwick, whom he married in Aug. 1716. It appeared in *The Merry Musician*, 1716 (i. 159) and is printed as Rowe's in *Works of the British Poets*, ed. R. Anderson, 1793 (vii. 143) and *Works of the English Poets*, ed. A. Chalmers, 1810 (ix. 474).

1717

[Epitaph on William Ettricke.]

In the church of Wimborne Minster, Dorset, there is a mural monument on which is a Latin inscription 'said to be written by the famous Mathew Prior' (John Hutchins, *The History and Antiquities of the County of Dorset*, 1774, ii. 95–96). We cannot find any connexion between Prior and William Ettricke (1652 ?–1716), barrister and M.P.

We are much indebted to J. C. Page-Phillips, Esq., son of the present vicar of Wimborne Minster, for sending us a rubbing of the inscription, locating the reference in Hutchins, and informing us that there does not seem to be even a local tradition to support the attribution of this epitaph to P.

[Satire on Samuel Fiske.]

In times like these with wonders so adorned,

★　　★　　★

The perfect model of the doctor's head.

Attributed to Prior by Alfred Hills in *Essex Review*, 1935. Discussed in the commentary on *Engraven on a Column* (1717).

1718

Austin, and the Monks of Bangor.
London: Printed for J. Roberts, . . . MDCCXVIII.

When *Saxon* Princes *England's* Sceptres bore,

★   ★   ★

The Church with UNIFORMITY was Bless'd.

Listed by Waller in *1907* among poems attributed to Prior; we have found no earlier attribution. The poem is a defence of Hoadly and the Low Church side in the Bangorian controversy; this would be a very unlikely position for P to take, and there is nothing to connect him with the poem.

The Tickler Tickell'd: Being an Epistle To the Author of the Incomparable Ode, Call'd, A Voyage to France, &c.
London: Printed for J. Roberts . . . MDCCXVIII.

Well, *Tickell*! thou hast found it out;

★   ★   ★

To fire the World, by asking *Peace.*

Thomas Burnet wrote to George Duckett, 29 June 1718: 'You will find Tickell's performance is but a very poor silly empty thing, but the Letter upon it, is written in a true Hudibrastic Vein, and has a great deal of cutting Satyr, which I am informed Addison is damnably stung with. It is said by the Town to be Mat. Prior's' (D. Nichol Smith, ed., *The Letters of Thomas Burnet to George Duckett, 1712–22*, Oxford, Roxburghe Club, 1914, p. 153). Nichol Smith, however, shows (pp. 156, 158) that the poem was by Burnet himself.

1719

The Enjoyment, 1719.

Waller lists this in *1907* among poems attributed to Prior. We cannot find any poem which fits his description. In *The Annual Miscellany*, 1694 (Case 172–4–a), pp. 164–71, there are two poems called *The Enjoyment*, beginning, 'Ye Gods! the Raptures of that Night!' and 'Go, Love, thy Banners round the World display'; they are both anonymous. In *The Works of the Earls of Rochester, Roscommon, . . . &c.*, 1721 (Case 323–1–a), Pt. II, p. 75, there is *The Enjoyment By Mr. Otway*, beginning, 'Clasp'd in the Arms of her I love'. But none of these were published in 1719, or published separately at any time, as far as we can discover.

The only separately published poem with this title that we can find is *The Enjoyment*. London, Printed in the Year, 1679, which begins, 'Since now my

Silvia is as kinde as fair', and ends, 'This Childe of hers, which most deserves her care'. This poem, however, is generally accepted as Rochester's.

There is not the slightest ground for attributing to P any of the poems mentioned.

To the Right Honorable the Earl of Oxford & Mortimer.

My Lord,
      Your Daughter went to View the Muses Seat,

     ★   ★   ★

   Fill'd with the *Deity*, He thus began,

These lines, constituting a verse introduction to Prior's *Verses Spoke to the Lady Henrietta-Cavendish Holles Harley, in the Library of St. John's College, Cambridge* (1719), were first published (from a 'MS. in the Harleian Library') and attributed to P by an anonymous reviewer of *Johnson 1779* in *Gentleman's Magazine*, xlix (1779), 551. In 1930 Mr. F. R. D. Needham reported that he had found at Welbeck a manuscript in P's hand of these lines together with *Verses*, inserted loose in Lady Henrietta's copy of *1718*, and published them as P's in *Times Literary Supplement*, xxix, 318.

The authorship of the verses is established by *L 29, 32*, where there is a copy in an unidentified hand, clearly labelled as by 'Charles Caesar Esque.' (Mr. Needham kindly informs us that he was mistaken in identifying the hand in the Welbeck MS. as P's, and that he now believes Caesar to be the author, on the evidence of this attribution in the Longleat MSS.) Charles Caesar had been treasurer of the navy in Oxford's administration, and was a friend of both Oxford and Harley. P saw much of him from 1718 on, and mentions him frequently in his letters. In a letter to Lord Oxford, 21 Nov. 1719, P refers to these verses of Caesar's: 'As I just now spoke of poetry, Your Lordship will have heard that at St. John's some days since I was attacked with the old hydrophobia, but that is not all; the infection spread, Caesar got it, as in the height of the distemper himself has confessed to you . . .' (*H.M.C. Bath*, iii. 471).

The Dream.

   Within a Grove, the Muses calm Retreat,

     ★   ★   ★

   And with my Sleep the flatt'ring Vision fled.

Published (with the following poem) in a folio pamphlet, *Astraea: or, The Dream, and Composition.* London: Printed for Sam. Briscoe, and sold by J. Roberts, . . .

1719. Attributed to Prior in Wise's *Catalogue of the J. H. Wrenn Library* (Austin, Texas, 1920), vol. iii. There seems to be no basis whatever for this attribution.

The Composition.

Thou fair Fore-runner! of the Sun's Up-rise,

★   ★   ★

Then in the precious Case an Angel's Soul inshrin'd.

Published together with the preceding poem (*The Dream*) in 1719, and like it attributed to Prior in the Wrenn *Catalogue*. There is nothing to suggest any connexion with P.

The Old Woman and her Doctor.

Dame Briton of the Grange, once fam'd

★   ★   ★

Myself a Beggar & a Fool.

Thomas Hearne records on 14 Feb. 1719 that this was communicated to him by William Bromley of Christ Church, Oxford; he labels it 'A Fable thought to be wrote by Mr. Prior' (*Remarks and Collections*, vi. 296–7; *Oxford Hist. Soc. Publications*, xliii, 1902). It is extremely unlike Prior. A transcript of the poem, in an unidentified secretarial hand, and without signature or ascription, occurs in *B.M. Lansd. 852*, 255ᵛ–56. The same story is told in Yalden's *The Blind Woman and her Doctors* (in *Esop at Court*, 1702; *Works of the English Poets*, ed. A. Chalmers, 1810, xi. 88).

The Plebeian . . . Considerations upon the Reports Relating to the Peerage . . . By a member of the House of Commons.
London, Printed for S. Popping . . . 1719.

Hearne noted in his diary, 27 March 1719: 'Some say Mr. Prior is the Author, and that the E. of Oxford puts him upon it, on purpose to put a Stop to the Bill now on foot about the Peerage' (*Remarks and Collections*, vi. 323). This weekly paper (in prose) was also attributed at the time to William Benson, but is now generally accepted as Steele's (G. A. Aitken, *Life of Steele*, 1889, ii. 211).

1720

The Curious Maid, A Tale.

London: Sold by A. Dodd . . . T. Edlin . . . and J. Roberts [N.D.; 1720]; [Another edition:] Sold by A. Dodd . . . 1720.

Beauty's a gaudy Sign, no more,

★　　★　　★

Be HID to be REVER'D the more!

Attributed to Prior in Wise's *Catalogue of the Ashley Library* and elsewhere. Wise cites Chesterfield's letter to P of 25 Jan. 1721, which mentions the spirit and vivacity 'which shine through Mr. Prior's other writings, particularly his curious *Maid*, which was lately sent me as yours, and from a friend of yours' (*H.M.C. Bath*, iii. 495).

Chesterfield, however, was mistaken; the poem is by Hildebrand Jacob, and is printed in his *Works*, 1735, p. 74. It is obviously an imitation of P, and is so labelled in *New Collection 1725* and later miscellanies: 'The Curious Maid: A Tale. *In Imitation of Mr.* Prior. By Hildebrand Jacob, *Esq.*'

An Impossible Thing A Tale.

To thee, Dear *Dick*, this Tale I send,

★　　★　　★

Both you and all your whole Fraternity.

Published, with the following poem, by J. Roberts, 1720, as a quarto pamphlet. Attributed to Prior by Bickley (p. 260), by G. A. Aitken, who says it is 'attributed to Prior in a manuscript list in a volume of pamphlets acquired by Mr. Wise' ('Notes on the Bibliography of Matthew Prior', *Transactions of the Bibliographical Society*, xiv, 1915–17, 39–66), and by others.

This and the following poem are by Congreve, and were published in the third edition of his *Works*, 1720.

The Peasant in Search of his Heifer A Tale after M. De La Fontaine.

It so befell: a silly Swain

★　　★　　★

If do'st, pray be so kind to speak.

Published in 1720 with the preceding poem, and attributed to Prior by the same persons. By Congreve.

1721

An Answer to the Curious Maid. A Tale.

London: Sold by T. Bickerton at the Crown in Pater-Noster Row [N.D.; 1721].

Thy Muse, O Bard! that Wonders tell,

*   *   *

By *others* Females Conquest *gain.*

Waller prints this in *1907* as attributed to Prior; he remarks (p. 405) that it seems to him to be by P, and that Mr. Wise says he bought it as P's on the advice of Dr. Garnett. Wise attributes it to P in his *Catalogue of the Ashley Library*, on the evidence of Chesterfield's letter (see discussion of *The Curious Maid*, above).

We have not identified the author, but he was an imitator of Hildebrand Jacob, who was an imitator of P.

The Curious Maid, Continu'd. A Tale.

London: Printed: And Sold by J. Roberts . . . MDCCXXI.

And having, with a careless Lift,

*   *   *

Thrust her out by very Force.

Listed in Wise's *Catalogue of the Ashley Library* as attributed to Prior, though even Wise does not believe P to be the author.

The Peeper: Being a Sequel to the Curious Maid.

London: Printed for Thomas Edlin . . . 1721.

And is this all? No, Curious Maid,

*   *   *

And Men will love what Puss has seen.

Attributed to Prior in Wise's *Catalogue of the Ashley Library*. Like the preceding poem, this is a poor imitation of *The Curious Maid*.

1726

The Members to their Soveraign . . . By the author of The Curious Maid.

London: Printed in the Year. 1726 [Reprinted in 1729: *The Silent Flute, a Poem: Being the Members Speech to their Sovereign.*]

O Thou, design'd by Nature to controul,

* * *

And may you prove the Dildoe of the Town.

Listed by Waller in *1907* among poems attributed to Prior. As the title indicates, the author was Hildebrand Jacob; the poem is printed as Jacob's in the miscellany section of *1733*, p. 79.

1730

The Judgment of Tiresias. By the Author of the Curious Maid.

When willing *Nymphs*, and *Swains* unite

* * *

That *Party* best obtains its End.

Attributed to Prior in various library catalogues because of the title. Published separately (without imprint, 173–?), and in *A New Miscellany* (Case 361), 1730. By Hildebrand Jacob, and included in his *Works*, 1735, p. 77.

The Rape. An Epistolary Poem. Addressed to Colonel Francisco.
London: Printed by J. Read, . . . [N.D.; 1730?].

When, fir'd by Novelty, and Beauty's Eyes,

* * *

And will herself pursue the Counsel which she gave.

Listed by Waller in *1907* among poems attributed to Prior; Waller gives the date '1714', as does the *Catalogue of the Wrenn Library*. 'Colonel Francisco', however, is a pseudonym for Col. Francis Charteris (1675–1732), a notorious libertine, who was convicted of rape in Feb. 1730, and pardoned in May. (A broadside on this occasion, *To the Glory of Colonel Don Francisco . . .*, is described in the B.M. *Catalogue of Prints and Drawings*, ed. F. G. Stephens, ii, 1873, 712).

1731

Epigram on a Lady Stung by a Bee.

To heal the wound the Bee had made

★ ★ ★

The sting went thro' my heart.

Attributed to Prior in *Amaryllis: Consisting of such songs as are most esteemed for Composition and Delicacy and Sung at the Public Theatres or Gardens* (London, 1750 ?), ii. 63, and by Eves, p. 371. The poem, however, appeared first in *Gentleman's Magazine,* i (1731), 23, without attribution; it then appeared in *The Windsor Medley,* 1731 (Case 371), *The Choice,* 1733 (Case 353–2), and numerous other miscellanies and songbooks. In none of them is it ascribed to P. The attribution in *Amaryllis* is, then, without authority.

1733

Horace's Integer Vitae &c. Imitated (Or, rather, Burlesqu'd.).

The Man that is Drunk, is Void of all Care;

★ ★ ★

And when I'm Dead-Drunk, then I'll stagger away.

R. P. Bond (*English Burlesque Poetry 1700–1750,* Cambridge, Mass., 1932, pp. 368–9) thinks this is attributed to Prior in *1733,* and concludes, 'The probability of Prior's authorship seems remote'. Bond is mistaken: the poem is not attributed to P in *1733,* but occurs (p. 112) in the miscellany section of the volume. This section has a separate title-page, 'Original Poems by Several Hands', and the authors of most poems are given; there is no suggestion that any of these poems are by P.

Song.

Dear *Cloe,* while thus beyond Measure,

★ ★ ★

That decrepid Old-Age cannot *freeze.*

Printed as Prior's in a volume of selected *Poems by Matthew Prior* (Manchester: Printed by G. Nicholson & Co., 1795) with the title *Old Darby and Joan.* The error is like that in the case of the preceding poem, for this song had first appeared in the miscellany section of *1733* (p. 109). In the 1754 reprint of *1742* (p. 267), it is said to be 'By Mr. B****'.

1736

A Genuine Dialogue: Facetious, and Pathetic; Amorous, and Political . . . Written by the Author of the Curious Maid.
London: Printed for J. Roberts . . . MDCCXXXVI.

This prose dialogue is listed in Wise's *Catalogue of the Ashley Library* with the comment that it may, or may not, be Prior's. It is by Hildebrand Jacob.

1737

The Unequal Match: a Tale By the Author of the Curious Maid.
London. Printed for W. Lewis, . . . 1737.

Two against *one*, when well agreed,

★   ★   ★

Fall back in Time, and be deflower'd.

Attributed to Prior in the B.M. *Catalogue*, in S. Halkett and J. Laing, *Dict. of Anonymous and Pseudonymous Eng. Lit.* (Edinburgh, 1926–34), and elsewhere. As the title indicates, the author was Hildebrand Jacob.

1739

The Statues: or, the Trial of Constancy. A Tale for the Ladies.
London: Printed for T. Cooper . . . M.DCC.XXXIX.

In a fair island, in the southern main,

★   ★   ★

Wou'd prove, no doubt, as CONSTANT as before.

Listed by Waller in *1907* among poems attributed to Prior. Probably by Laetitia Pilkington (1712–50); it is printed as hers in *Poems by Eminent Ladies* (London, R. Baldwin, 1755), ii. 239.

1741

The History of the Life and Death of David, with Moral Reflections. A Translation from the French. Found among the Papers of his late Excellency Matthew Prior, Esq; in the Custody of Mr. Adrian Drift, his Executor.

London: Printed for the Editor. MDCCXLI.

Never seriously attributed to Prior, but, because of the ambiguity of the title-page, frequently catalogued under his name. This prose translation of the *Histoire de la Vie de David* by François Timoléon, Abbé de Choisy, was possibly the work of Adrian Drift; the *Philosophical Essay Concerning Love and Friendship* published with it is addressed to him by his nephew, Adrian Drift, Jr.

COMMENTARY

1685

(1)   *On the Coronation*

MSS.   L *28*, 16 (D).
Pub.   [Title as in text.] . . . By a Young Gentleman. London, Printed for,
          and are to be sold by Randal Taylor near Stationers Hall, Anno
          Domini, 1685.
          Collected: *1907*, p. 279.
Text.   *1685*. Collated: *L 28*.

   This poem was not included among Prior's works until *1907* printed it
from the Longleat manuscript. The anonymous publication of 1685 has not
previously been noticed. Before this, his first English poem to be printed,
P had published only two Latin poems in collections of Cambridge verse
addressed to the royal family, *On the Marriage* (1683) and *Ad Regios Fratres*
(1685). In addition to his obvious motives for writing on this occasion, P was
seeking the favour of Francis Turner, Bishop of Ely, a former chaplain to the
new king and preacher of the coronation sermon. P had addressed Latin
verses to the bishop (*Ad Franc: Episc: Eliensem*) upon his translation from
Rochester to Ely in 1684, and later in 1685 he presented two English poems
to him.

   13–28. The traditional cavalcade through the city from the Tower to
Westminster was omitted at the coronation of James, depriving the citizens
of London of the spectacle which had been a feature of all previous corona-
tions. Making the best of the situation, P describes the progress of the king
and queen by water from Whitehall to Westminster, rather than the short
procession from Westminster Hall to the Abbey. According to Francis Sand-
ford's authoritative *History of the Coronation* (1687), the king 'passed through
St. *James's Park* to *Whitehal*; where the *Royal Barge* attending at the *Privy
Stairs*, He came therein privately by Water to *Westminster*, about Ten of the
Clock in the Morning, and Landed at the *Parliament-Stairs* . . .'. The queen,
however, did not in fact make the trip by water at all, but 'came privately
in Her Chair to *Whitehal*, and thence through the *Privy Garden* into *Chanel-
Row*, and so cross the *New Palace-Yard* up *Westminster-Hall* . . .' (pp. 57–58).

   25. asserted. In *Threnodia Augustalis* (March 1685) Dryden similarly paid
homage to James's reputation as a naval commander: 'Th' asserted Ocean
rears his reverend Head; | To view and recognize his ancient Lord again'
(ll. 514–15).

   50–53. See 1 Sam. ix–x.

58. *Prelate.* Archbishop Sancroft.

62. Cf. Dryden, *Threnodia Augustalis,* l. 431: 'Long may he keep, tho he obtains it late.'

(3)   *To the E of D.*

MSS. *L 28,* 22 (D; emend. by Pope?); *M,* 6 (A; ll. 48–84 only).
Pub. *1907,* p. 283.
Text. *L 28* [D]. Collated: *M.*

Prior's first patron, Charles Sackville, sixth Earl of Dorset, married Lady Mary Compton in June 1685 (Harris, *Dorset,* p. 96; Harris shows that the date of 7 March 1685 given by other authorities is erroneous). The earl's marriage (his second) to the young heiress was also celebrated by Robert Gould (*On my Lord of Dorset's Marriage with the Lady Mary Compton*) and by Aphra Behn, whose *Pastoral Pindarick* is in the same form as P's poem. P's ultimate models are Virgil's eclogues, especially the third and seventh.

1. Dogstar. Cf. Horace, *Odes,* III. xiii. 9.
13. Cf. *Paradise Lost,* iii. 1: 'Hail holy Light, offspring of Heav'n first-born.'
22. Cf. *Paradise Lost,* v. 19, where Adam calls Eve 'Heav'ns last best gift'.
53. hasty. Probably Drift's error in copying, influenced by l. 51. The opposite sense is required; perhaps *tardy.*
56. Drift was evidently unable to decipher P's original at this point; it may have read, 'May Daphnis' wound here find a Cure'.

(7)   *To the Countess of D....t*

MSS. *L 28,* 20 (D); *M,* 8 (D).
Pub. *1907,* p. 282.
Text. *L 28.* Collated: *M.*

Since the poem celebrates Prior's first sight of the Countess of Dorset in the garden of her new home, it was probably written soon after the marriage.

2. place. Probably Copt Hall rather than Knole, Dorset's other country seat. See *Journey to Copt-Hall* (1688), and Harris, *Dorset,* pp. 11–12, 195.

(8)   *Advice to the Painter*

MSS. *Bodl. Rawl. Poet. 19,* 26 (P); *L 28,* 31 (D); *B.M. Sloane 655,* 26 (X); *B.M. Add. 29497,* 15 (X); *Bodl. Wood 417,* No. 141 (X); *Bodl. Firth c. 15,* 184 (X); *Bodl. Firth c. 16,* 57 (X); *U. Nott. Portland 1661,* i. 257 (X).

Pub. *P.O.A.S.* ii, 1703 (Case 211–2–a), p. 148; *New Collection*, 1705 (Case 237), p. 346.
Collected: *1907*, p. 289.

Text. *Rawl.* Collated: *L 28*, *Sloane*, *Wood*, *1703*, *Firth 15*, *Firth 16*.

Rawl. is a holograph, probably sent to Bishop Turner in 1685 (see Prior's poems to him later in this year). It is unlikely that P was responsible for the variants in any of the other manuscripts, but they have as much authority as the variants in *1703*. *L 28* is marked as a transcript of *1703*.

Monmouth was executed on 15 July 1685. Shortly after his installation as Chancellor of the University of Cambridge in Sept. 1674 he had presented to the Vice-Chancellor a full-length portrait of himself by Lely. In April 1682 he was deposed as Chancellor, and succeeded by the Duke of Albemarle. 'On the 3rd of July [1685], by a grace of the Senate, it was ordered that the picture of the Duke of Monmouth (which had been taken down from the Convocation House on his being deprived of his Chancellorship) should be burnt by the yeomen bedel, and on the 11th of the same month another grace passed directing that his name should be taken out of all catalogues of University officers' (C. H. Cooper, *Annals of Cambridge*, Cambridge, 1842–52, iii. 611). Apparently the Vice-Chancellor was cautious enough to wait until Monmouth was captured (8 July) before carrying out the authorized burning. P's friend George Stepney ridiculed this caution and the servility of the university in *On the University of Cambridge's burning the D. of Monmouth's Picture, 1685* (*P.O.A.S.* ii, 1703, pp. 189–90).

P's poem belongs to the genre established by Waller's *Instructions To A Painter, For the Drawing of the Posture and Progress of His Majesties Forces at Sea, Under the command of His Highness Royal. Together with the Battel & Victory Obtained over the Dutch, June 3, 1665*. Waller's poem was a serious panegyric on the Duke of York, but it was shortly followed by four satirical *Advices*, variously ascribed to Denham and Marvell, but probably by neither. (See H. M. Margoliouth, ed., *Poems and Letters of Andrew Marvell*, Oxford, 1927, i. 268–70; T. H. Banks, ed., *Poetical Works of Sir John Denham*, New Haven, 1928, pp. 327–31.) Poems in the genre were very numerous, before and after P's; see Mary T. Osborne, *Advice-to-a-Painter Poems 1635–1856: An Annotated Finding List* (Austin, Texas, 1949).

[Motto.] Horace, *Ars Poetica*, ll. 9–10.

1. guilty Piece. 'The Duke of Monmouths picture burnt at Cambridge' (*Rawl.*).

2. thy. Sir Peter Lely, painter of the burned portrait, was Dutch by birth, and had died in 1680. However, the line can hardly be intended to apply literally to Lely, who had painted James II as Duke of York, as well as Charles II and most of his court. Presumably a fictional painter is addressed.

4. LYME. Monmouth landed at Lyme, in Dorset, on 11 June 1685.

6. Land. 'Holland' (*Rawl.*). Monmouth sailed from Holland, and the Dutch authorities had connived at, and possibly assisted, his expedition.

15. Julian. Samuel Johnson (1649–1703), called 'Julian' Johnson, published in 1682 a Whig attack on the Duke of York called *Julian the Apostate*, for which he was convicted of seditious libel and imprisoned.

16. Achitophel. Throughout the poem, P uses names from Dryden's *Absalom and Achitophel* (1681), and it is apparent that he is imitating Dryden's style.

18. tempting Woman. 'The Lady H: Wentworth' (*Rawl.*). Lady Henrietta Wentworth had been Monmouth's mistress probably since 1680, and is said to have joined Ferguson and Grey in urging Monmouth on to the rebellion.

25. Parricide. P assumes Monmouth's complicity in the Rye House Plot to murder Charles II.

30. Town. 'Taunton' (*Rawl.*). An earlier pretender, Perkin Warbeck, had been taken near Taunton and confessed there after his attempted invasion in 1497. During the Civil War the town was a Puritan stronghold, and afterwards 'their stubborn attachment to the old cause had excited so much fear and resentment at Whitehall that, by a royal order, their moat had been filled up, and their wall demolished to the foundation' (Macaulay, p. 575). Monmouth entered Taunton on 18 June; on the 19th the 'Maids of Taunton' presented him with flags, a sword, and a Bible; on the next day he proclaimed himself king.

42. enemy. 'Ferguson' (*Rawl.*). Robert Ferguson, the 'Plotter', one of the chief instigators of the rebellion. He had been a dissenting minister and was chaplain to Monmouth's army.

43. Arguile. Archibald Campbell, ninth Earl of Argyle, unsuccessfully attempted to rally Scotland to Monmouth's standard in May, and was taken prisoner on 18 June. He was executed on 1 July.

44. Oates. Titus Oates, fabricator of the Popish Plot in 1678, had been a clergyman of the Church of England until disgraced for misconduct; then he became ostensibly a Roman Catholic.

47. Long-ear'd rout. Cf. *Hudibras*, I. i. 9–10: 'When *Gospel-Trumpeter*, surrounded | With long-ear'd Rout, to Battle sounded.'

50. Gray. Forde Grey, Baron Grey of Werk, later Earl of Tankerville; he and Ferguson were Monmouth's evil geniuses. Grey's incompetence and cowardice as commander of the Horse at Sedgemoor played a large part in Monmouth's defeat. Afterwards, he turned witness against the other rebels and was pardoned. According to gossip, Monmouth earlier had seduced his wife.

59. Cf. Dryden, *The State of Innocence*, I. i. 5–6: 'In Liquid Burnings, or on Dry to dwell, | Is all the sad variety of Hell.'

61. Brennus. The Celtic Gaul who in 390 B.C. sacked Rome. He is said to have thrown his sword into the scale in which the ransom was being weighed, with the comment, 'Vae victis'.

63. Temples. 'The Rebells unleaded the Cathedral of Bath to make Bulletts' (*Rawl.*). At Wells on 30 June the rebels took lead from the cathedral roof to make bullets, and defaced and desecrated the building, stealing the silver vessels.

65–70. On Sunday, 5 July, Ferguson, as chaplain, and other Puritan ministers held forth to the rebels. At the battle of Sedgemoor, the next morning, their army was routed.

73. Grove. After the battle, Monmouth and Grey fled to the New Forest, where Charles II had taken refuge after Worcester.

81. 'D of Monmouth taken in a Ditch' (*Rawl.*).

83. Corah. See Num. xvi. 32.

97. sacred Prelate. 'The Bishop of Ely' (*Rawl.*), Francis Turner.

100–1. In spite of the efforts of Bishop Turner, Thomas Ken, Bishop of Bath and Wells, Dr. George Hooper, Rector of Lambeth, and Dr. Thomas Tenison, Vicar of St. Martin's, Monmouth refused to confess that his union with Lady Henrietta Wentworth was sinful or to acknowledge the doctrine of non-resistance. He was therefore refused the Eucharist.

102. Asaph. One of David's chief musicians; a number of the Psalms are attributed to him. Probably a complimentary reference to Dryden is also intended, since Nahum Tate, in the second part of *Absalom and Achitophel* (ll. 1037–64), praised Dryden as *Asaph*. Cf. note to l. 16 above.

108. Annabel. 'Dutchess of Monmouth' (*Rawl.*). Anna, Duchess of Monmouth; she had married Monmouth in 1663, and they had a daughter and two sons. The duchess had no part in the rebellion and was in favour with James II and succeeding monarchs; she married again in 1688.

(12)   *To the Bishop of Rochester*

MSS. *L 28*, 35 (D).

Pub. Aphra Behn's *Lycidus*, 1688 (Case 184), p. 120 of the 'Miscellany of New Poems. By Several Hands.'
   Collected: *1907*, p. 293.

Text. *1688*. Collated: *L 28*.

The Bishop of Rochester was Thomas Sprat (author of the *History of the Royal Society*), to whom Prior had addressed two Latin poems, the first, *Ad Decanum Westmonasteriensem*, soon after he became Dean of Westminster in 1683, and the second, *Reverendo in Christo Patri Thomae*, congratulating him on his elevation to the bishopric in 1684. In May 1685 appeared *A True Account and Declaration of the Horrid Conspiracy against the Late King, His Present Majesty, and the Government: As it was Order'd to be Published by His Late Majesty* (In the Savoy: Printed by Thomas Newcomb, One of His Majesties Printers. 1685). Bishop Sprat was known to be the author, though his name did not appear. The preface, signed by King James, states that Charles II gave the bishop special orders to prepare this account, full access to all records, and directions as to method; it was ready for the press at Charles's death, and is published now because 'the same Hellish Plot is not entirely extinguished'. The book is an account of the Rye House Plot of 1683.

P's opening lines suggest that he sent his *Advice to the Painter* to Bishop Sprat with this poem. Writing to Sprat in 1706 (*L 13*, 76), P says: 'I think you taught me the way to Parnassus, and the Infection of Your Plague of Athens gave me the first Symptoms of the Distemper.'

(13)   *Not Writing to K. P.*

MSS.   *L 28*, 18 (D).
Pub.   *1907*, p. 281.
Text.   *L 28*.

Prior sent this poem with a letter to Mrs. Katharine Prior, dated 11 Aug. 1685:

> My neglect, Madam, is but a new occasion for you to exercise your goodness on. You, like heaven, can as often return a pardon as I give up my repentance; the truth of which, Madam, be pleased to accept as well in honest prose as in bad verse: though, Madam, this afflicts my zeal, that the oracle never answers. My religion depends much upon faith, and I can tell no more news from my heaven than the astrologers from theirs, unless like them I fairly guess at it. . . .
>   (*H.M.C. Bath*, iii. 1–2; from *L 10*, e)

P's biographers have assumed that the lady addressed in this letter and poem, as well as in *To Madam K: P.*, was his aunt, the wife of Arthur Prior, keeper of the Rhenish Wine Tavern (Bickley, pp. 22–23; Wickham Legg, p. 7; Eves, p. 32). There are, however, two unpublished letters in *L 10* (a, b), both dated 29 June 1685, which suggest that the lady may have been P's cousin Katharine, daughter of Arthur and Katharine Prior. One of these is labelled 'To My Aunt Prior'; the other, labelled 'To Mrs. Katharine Prior', is unquestionably addressed to his cousin and is similar in tone and content to the present letter. After the death of his father (1675?), P had been brought up in the family of his uncle Arthur; his cousin Katharine was only two years older than he, and he remained on close terms with her throughout his life. See H. B. Wright, 'Matthew Prior's "Welbeloved and Dear Cossen" ', *R.E.S.* xv (1939), 318–23.

(14)   *To the Bishop of Ely. On his departure*

MSS.   *Bodl. Rawl. D. 739*, 84 (P; the MS. sent to Bishop Turner); *L 28*, 36* (D).
Pub.   *The Christian's Magazine, or a Treasury of Divine Knowledge*, ii (June 1761), 279.
      Collected: *Evans 1779*, ii. 103.

Text. *Rawl.* Collated: *L 28.* (*1761* prints from *Rawl.*, and *Evans 1779* from *1761.*)

Prior had congratulated Francis Turner in a Latin epistle when he became Bishop of Ely in July 1684, and had flattered him in later poems. Bishop Turner was an influential man, in high favour with the new king. He had been Master of St. John's from 1670 to 1679, and was Visitor to the college and to the Somerset Scholars there, of whom P was one of the first group.

The title of the poem probably refers to Bishop Turner's departure from Cambridge after one of his visitations. There is no clue to the exact date, but it is safe to assume that P would have been presented to the bishop by 1685. P's ultimate model was Virgil's fifth eclogue; but he was heavily influenced by Richard Duke's *Floriana, A Pastoral upon the Death of her Grace the Dutchess of Southampton,* which begins:

> Tell me my *Thyrsis,* tell thy Damon, why
> Do's my lov'd Swain in this sad posture lie?
> What mean these streams still falling from thine Eyes,
> Fast as those sighs from thy swoln bosom rise?
> Has the fierce Wolf broke thro' the fenced ground?
> Have thy Lambs stray'd? or has *Dorinda* frown'd?
>   (*Miscellany Poems,* 1684 [Case 172–1–a], p. 301)

Cf. ll. 1–2, 7–8, 13–14 of P's poem. P may well have been acquainted with Duke (1658–1711), who had attended Westminster and was at the time a Fellow of Trinity College, Cambridge. He certainly knew him later, for Swift notes that P attended Duke's funeral (*Journal to Stella,* 16 Feb. 1711).

8. Joanna. St. John's College.
    Shepheard. Dr. Humphrey Gower, Master of St. John's.
30. Wealth. 'my Lords blessing' (*Rawl.*).

(16)   *To Madam K: P.*

MSS. *L 28,* 5 (D).
Pub. *1907,* p. 272.
Text. *L 28.*

'K: P.' is Katharine Prior, probably the cousin rather than the aunt (see commentary on *Not Writing to K. P.*). The tone of exaggerated gallantry is in keeping with Prior's letters to his cousin. The poem is merely a copy of *To the Bishop of Ely. On his departure,* with some additions and revisions to fit the new occasion. Probably it was written soon after that poem.

43. fair Celinda's Shrine. Presumably Katharine Prior's home, where P had lived after his father's death. The occasion of the poem may have been P's return to Cambridge after a visit to Katharine and her family.

(18)   *To the Bishop of Ely*

MSS. *Bodl. Rawl. D. 739*, 86 (P; the MS. sent to Bishop Turner); *L 28*, 36 (D).
Pub.   *The Christian's Magazine, or a Treasury of Divine Knowledge*, ii (May 1761), 230.
       Collected: *Evans 1779*, ii. 101.
Text. *Rawl.* Collated: *L 28*. (*1761* prints from *Rawl.*, and *Evans 1779* from *1761.*)

Evidently written after *To the Bishop of Ely. On his departure*, and, if the title in *L 28* —'To My Lord of Ely at Christmas'—is correct, probably at Christmas 1685. Bishop Turner's literary works were first printed in *The Christian's Magazine* in 1761 and subsequent years; the editors had obtained access to his papers (which now constitute a part of the Rawlinson MSS. in the Bodleian) and published his *Life of Nicholas Ferrar* and numerous translations and odes.

5–6. Cf. the beginning of *To the Bishop of Rochester*.
25–26. 'We imagine from hence, that the bishop had recommended to the young student (Mr. Prior) the translation of Prudentius: but this being omitted, and leisure enough for poetry being granted him, at the close of his life, the bishop himself translated the author; the whole of which is in our hands' (*1761*). *Evans 1779* gave the poem a title based on this conjecture— 'To the Rev. Dr. Francis Turner, Bishop of Ely Who Had Advised a Translation of Prudentius'—which has been followed by all subsequent editions.

(19)   *A Satyr on the modern Translators*

MSS. *B.M. Sloane 655*, 10 (X); *Bodl. Firth c. 16*, 61 (X); *U. Nott. Portland 1661*, ii. 121 (X). (Index to *M*.) (The printed sheets from *1722* are included in *L 28*, 101.)
Pub.   *P.O.A.S.*, 1697 (Case 211–1–a), p. 205; *Pecuniae obediunt Omnia*, 1698 (Case 214–b), p. 117; *New Collection*, 1705 (Case 237), p. 144.
       Collected: *1707*, p. 1; *1892*, ii. 355.
Text. *1697*. Collated: *Sloane*.

The authenticity of this long-disputed poem is established by the letter, dated '1685', which Prior sent with a copy of the poem to Dr. Humphrey Gower, Master of St. John's (*H.M.C. Bath*, iii. 2; from *L 10*, f). Even before the question was settled by the publication of this letter in 1908, most scholars considered the poem to be genuine; see the discussions by Dobson (*1889*, pp. 219–27), R. B. Johnson (*1892*, ii. 353–67), and Waller (*1907*, pp. vii, 388–9). It was attributed to 'Mr. P—r' in all the early printings (except the first two issues of *P.O.A.S.*, 1697, where there was no attribution), but when Curll printed it and *Satyr on the Poets* (1687) in *1707*, P disowned both satires (see *Preface*, 1708, and notes). His chief reason for doing so undoubtedly was that both contained bitter attacks upon John Sheffield, Earl of Mulgrave, a powerful man who later (as Duke of Buckingham) became P's friend.

The satire was provoked by three miscellanies edited by Dryden: (1) *Ovid's Epistles*, 1680 (Case 165); a second edition appeared in 1681 and a third in 1683. The volume contains a preface by Dryden, who translated two epistles himself and a third in collaboration with Lord Mulgrave. Among the other translators were Tate, Mrs. Behn, Rymer, Settle, Otway, and Duke. (2) *Miscellany Poems*, 1684 (Case 172–1–a), which consists largely of translations, notably of Ovid's *Elegies* by Creech, Scrope, Rymer, Stepney, Tate, and others. (3) *Sylvae*, 1685 (Case 172–2–a), again consisting mostly of translations, many of them by Dryden, and with a preface by him. In his letter to Dr. Gower, P states the intention of his satire:

> . . . let our translators know that Rome and Athens are our territories; that our Laureate might in good manners have left the version of Latin authors to those who had the happiness to understand them; that we accuse not others, but defend ourselves, and would only shew that these corruptions of our tongue proceed from him and his tribe, which he unjustly casts upon the clergy. Thus, Sir, I humbly throw this trifle at your feet, hoping the product of my vacant hours may prove the diversion of yours. . . .

The poem was written after *Sylvae* appeared in Jan. 1685. The date '1684' is given in the Index to all editions of *P.O.A.S.* containing the poem; this may mean that it was written before 25 March 1685, though dates in these miscellanies have little authority.

[Motto.] Adapted from Horace, *Epistles*, I. xix. 19.

1–4. The two theatrical companies were united in 1682 and remained so until 1695. George Powell, in the Preface to *The Treacherous Brothers: A Tragedy* (1690), remarked: '*The time was, upon the uniting of the two* Theatres, *that the reviveing of the old stock of Plays, so ingrost the study of the House, that the Poets lay dorment; and a new Play cou'd hardly get admittance, amongst the more precious pieces of Antiquity* . . .' (quoted from ed. of 1696). The union left Thomas Betterton (1635?–1710), actor, manager, and playwright, supreme in the theatrical world.

5. *Rider.* John Rider (1562–1632), Bishop of Killaloe, compiler of a Latin–English dictionary. 'The line apparently means that, since all poets were turning translators, they needed only a classical and a rhyming dictionary' (*1892*).

8. The profits of the third performance were given customarily to the playwright.

13. *Sternhold.* Thomas Sternhold (d. 1549), author, with John Hopkins, of a metrical version of the Psalms.

25. John Sheffield, Earl of Mulgrave, collaborated with Dryden in translating 'Helen to Paris' (*Ovid's Epistles*, p. 153).

30. *T—e.* Nahum Tate translated three of Ovid's epistles in the 1680 volume, more than any other contributor.

35–36. *Hudibras*, I. i. 453–6.

42. *Bibulus.* Marcus Calpurnius Bibulus was consul with Julius Caesar in 59 B.C. His opposition to Caesar was so ineffective that he took no part in public business during the latter part of his consulship, which was humorously termed the consulship of Julius and Caesar.

49. *Bayes.* Dryden's derisive nickname since *The Rehearsal*, 1670.

Rose Alley Ambuscade. Mulgrave's *Essay on Satyr*, when first circulated in 1679, was believed to be the work of Dryden; P clearly attributes it to Dryden alone. 'The Rose-Alley Satire, as it came to be called, led to the notorious assault on Dryden on the night of 18 December 1679, instigated, it has generally been believed since Malone, by Rochester, though it may have been the work of the Duchess of Portsmouth' (Macdonald, pp. 217–18).

54. Referring to Dryden's translations from Virgil in the 1684 and 1685 miscellanies.

55. In the Preface to *Sylvae*, Dryden is particularly concerned to justify his translation of Lucretius on the Nature of Love.

57–58. Dryden's translation from Lucretius, Book IV, describing the extravagance of lovers: '*Assyrian* Oyntment from their temples flows, | And Diamond Buckles sparkle at their shooes' (*Sylvae*, p. 86).

60–61. Dryden translated 'Canace to Macareus' (*Ovid's Epistles*, p. 8). Canace's father is Aeolus, god of the winds. She writes to her brother Macareus before killing herself, lamenting their incestuous union.

62–64. *Almanzor*, hero of *Almanzor and Almahide: or, The Conquest of Granada*; *Maximin*, the tyrant, and St. *Katharine*, the martyr, in *Tyrannick Love, or The Royal Martyr*.

65–68. In the *Epilogue* to the Second Part of *Almanzor and Almahide: or, The Conquest of Granada*, and the prose *Defence of the Epilogue* (1672). It was in the *Defence* that Dryden made the charges to which P refers in his letter to Dr. Gower, that the clergy 'are commonly the first corrupters of eloquence, and the last reformed from vicious oratory'.

69–72. Referring to Dryden's adaptations of Shakespeare, and specifically to the *Prologue* to *Troilus and Cressida* (1679), 'Spoken by Mr. *Betterton*, Representing the Ghost of *Shakespear*'.

78. *Behn.* Aphra Behn (the 'Female Wit' of the next line) contributed 'A Paraphrase on Oenone to Paris' to *Ovid's Epistles* (p. 97). In the Preface, Dryden remarks that this is the only translation in the volume that follows the method of Imitation, and adds: '*I was desir'd to say that the Authour who is of the* Fair Sex, *understood not* Latine. . . .' Evidently he felt somewhat

uncomfortable about this situation, since in the second and later editions a translation of the same epistle by 'Mr. Cooper' precedes Mrs. Behn's.

80. *Sand's*. George Sandys did not translate Ovid's epistles; P presumably means that Mrs. Behn imitated the verse and style of Sandys's translation of the *Metamorphoses* (1626).

84. In the Preface, Dryden had praised Ovid for his closeness to nature in representing 'low' characters such as Oenone; P suggests that Mrs. Behn has failed to render this quality.

86. *her own*. *Love-letters between a Nobleman and his Sister*, 1684. Mrs. Behn's *Love-Letters to a Gentleman* was not published until 1696, but P may have known it in manuscript.

88. *Rover*. Referring to Mrs. Behn's play, *The Rover, or, The Banish'd Cavaliers*, 1677 (Second Part, 1680).

92. *R—mer*. Thomas Rymer (1641–1713), critic, historian, and poet.

96–100. Rymer's critical reputation was established by his *Tragedies of the last Age Consider'd and Examin'd by the Practice of the Ancients, and by the Common sense of all Ages*, 1678.

104. In Rymer's translation of Ovid's 'Elegy the Sixth. To a River, as he was going to his Mistress', occurs the following passage:

> Not my Love-tales can make thee stay thy course,
> Thou—Zounds, thou art a—River for a horse.
> Thou hadst no Fountain, but from Bears wer't pist. . . .
>   (*Miscellany Poems*, 1684, p. 153)

In *Ovid's Epistles* he translated 'Penelope to Ulysses' (p. 169).

105. *Pemberton*. Sir Francis Pemberton (1625–97) was removed as Lord Chief Justice of the King's Bench in 1683, probably because of insufficient zeal against Lord Russell when he was tried for his part in the Rye House Plot. He then returned to his practice as a barrister.

111. *Creech*. Thomas Creech (1659–1700) had produced verse translations of Lucretius (1682), Horace (1684), and Theocritus (1684); to the 1684 *Miscellany Poems* he contributed translations of five of Ovid's elegies, two eclogues of Virgil, and an episode from Ovid's *Fasti*.

122–7. Creech's translation of Lucretius was greeted with high acclaim; the second edition (1683) contains commendatory verses by Evelyn, Tate, Otway, Mrs. Behn, Duke, Tonson, and others. In the Preface to *Sylvae* Dryden called him '*the ingenious and learned translator of Lucretius*'. Though Creech was at pains to confute Lucretius in the notes to his translation, he was popularly supposed to have been led by him into atheism.

134. Creech's translation of 'The Story of Lucretia out of Ovid de Fastis. Book II', in *Miscellany Poems*, 1684, p. 180.

139. *Ogilby*. John Ogilby (1600–76), author of verse translations of Virgil, Aesop, and Homer, published with elaborate plates.

151. In the Preface to *Sylvae*, Dryden says of Virgil: '*In short they who have*

call'd him the torture of Grammarians, might also have call'd him the plague of Trans-
latours; for he seems to have studied not to be Translated.'

169. P may have in mind Roscommon's *Essay on Translated Verse* (1684):

> *Theocritus* does now to *Us* belong;
> And *Albion's Rocks* repeat his *Rural Song* . . .
> But hear, oh hear, in what exalted Strains
> *Sicilian Muses* through these happy Plains,
> Proclaim *Saturnian* Times, our own *Apollo* reigns.
>
> (Roscommon's *Works*, 1717, pp. 5–7)

Dryden published commendatory verses both with this poem and in *Miscellany Poems*.

172. As Louis's policy toward them became more severe, increasing numbers of French Huguenots sought refuge in England; after the Revocation of the Edict of Nantes in Oct. 1685, they flocked into England.

177. *Crown.* John Crowne (1640?–1712) had been writing plays since 1671. *Sir Courtly Nice; or, It Cannot Be* (May, 1685) was his most successful comedy.

178. *D'urfey.* Thomas D'Urfey (1654–1723) had written ten plays by 1685 as well as numerous songs and poems. Neither he nor Crowne had participated in the vogue for translation, and neither had contributed to Dryden's miscellanies.

1686

(24)   *A Hymn to the Spring*

MSS. *L 28*, 45 (D); *M*, 17 (A); *B.M. Add. 30303*, 6ᵛ (X; ll. 1–10 only).
Pub. *1907*, p. 298.
Text. *L 28.* Collated: *M, B.M.*

Dated in *L 28*, 'April 30: 1686', with the added note, 'Set by Mr. Turner'. 'Mr. Turner' is presumably William Turner (1651–1740), who wrote the music for songs and poems by D'Urfey, Tate, and others, as well as much church music. His setting apparently has not survived.

26. Cf. l. 19 of *To the E of D.* (1685).

1687

(25)   *To the E of D.*

MSS. *L 28*, 42 (D).
Pub. *1907*, p. 295.
Text. *L 28.*

Dorset's son, Lionel Cranfield Sackville, was born on 18 Jan. 1687 (Harris,

Dorset, p. 105; *D.N.B.* and other sources give the date, erroneously, as 1688).
Prior dedicated *1718* to him. P's chief model is Virgil's fourth eclogue.

(28) *Satyr on the Poets*

MSS. *L 28*, 128 (D; ll. 202–18 only, following the printed sheets from *1722*). (*Index to M.*)

Pub. *Chorus Poetarum*, 1694 (Case 202), p. 115; *P.O.A.S.*, Part III, 1698 (Case 215), p. 48; *P.O.A.S.* ii, 1703 (Case 211–2–a), p. 138; *New Collection*, 1705 (Case 237), p. 341. The continuation in *L 28* was first published in *1907*, pp. 389–90.
Collected: *1707*, p. 13; *1892*, ii. 368.

Text. *1698*; ll. 202–18 from *L 28*. Collated: *1694*, *1703*.

The signed continuation in *L 28* (which we print as ll. 202–18) establishes the authenticity of this poem, which Prior disowned with *A Satyr on the modern Translators* and for the same reason. Confirmation is provided by a note in Drift's hand (*L 29*, 91) that mentions a manuscript of the poem in the lost 'Smal Folio' and indicates that Drift, Pope, and P's other friends intended to publish it as P's in the posthumous collection they were preparing (see Introduction, section II). Drift further demonstrated his confidence in the genuineness of the satires by taking printed sheets of both from *1722* for inclusion in *L 28* while excluding the two poems of doubtful authenticity that were printed in that volume: *Upon Lady Katherine H—de's first appearing* and *The Judgment of Venus*.

The poem was probably written after Buckingham's death on 16 April 1687 (see l. 188 and note) and before the publication of Dryden's *The Hind and the Panther* about 27 May of the same year. Neither of these limits is certain, but numerous references in the poem indicate this as the approximate time of composition. P had taken his B.A. at Cambridge on 9 Feb. 1687, and was presumably living in London. The patron addressed in the opening and closing lines is almost certainly Dorset, as is suggested by the subtitle in *1694*: '*In a Letter to the Lord D.——.*'

The poem belongs to the genre known as the 'Imitation', for which see H. F. Brooks, 'The "Imitation" in English Poetry, Especially in Formal Satire, before the Age of Pope', *R.E.S.* xxv (1949), 124–40. The title given in Drift's note—'An Imitation of the First part of Juvenal VII Satyr'—is more accurate than any of the printed ones, since P follows only the first ninety-seven lines of Juvenal's satire, and freely adapts even these. As Mr. Brooks points out, P in several passages shows the influence of John Oldham's imitation, published in 1683, of the same satire of Juvenal: *A Satyr. The Person of Spencer is brought in. . . .*

Although *1694* is the earliest publication, we do not use it as our text because it represents a revision made certainly after 1689 (Shadwell is referred to as Laureate) and probably after 1692, and emasculated by deleting the personal references to Dryden, Mulgrave, and others. The revision may well have been the work of Charles Gildon, editor of *1694*; it is extremely unlikely that P had any part in it.

As in the case of *A Satyr on the modern Translators*, we are much indebted to R. B. Johnson's excellent notes in *1892*.

6. *Bayes.* Dryden wrote little verse after his conversion (probably late 1685; see Macdonald, p. 44) until *The Hind and the Panther*, which evidently had not appeared when P wrote.

10. *Shadwell.* From about 1683 to the production of his *Squire of Alsatia* in May 1688, Shadwell was in financial straits because there was no market for plays (see note to *A Satyr on the modern Translators*, ll. 1–4). During the reign of James II 'he seems to have subsisted mainly on the bounty of Dorset and Sir Charles Sedley' (Harris, *Dorset*, p. 124). His enforced silence is mentioned again at l. 182. Shadwell later claimed that his loyalty to his Whig principles had been responsible for his difficulties.

Tate. Nahum Tate suffered also from the lack of demand for plays; see notes to l. 183 below and to *A Satyr on the modern Translators*, l. 30.

11. Cf. *Absalom and Achitophel*, i. 99: 'For Priests of all Religions are the same.'

12. *Settle.* Elkanah Settle had been an ardent propagandist for Shaftesbury and the Whigs, and had organized elaborate pope-burning processions on Queen Elizabeth's birthday (see l. 56 below). In 1683 he recanted publicly in *A Narrative*; in this and later works he exposed Oates, attacked Shaftesbury and the other Whigs, and praised the Tories. But his change of allegiance apparently did him little good. He had probably begun writing for Bartholomew Fair, at Smithfield (l. 13), before 1683 (F. C. Brown, *Elkanah Settle*, Chicago, 1910, p. 35). Stourbridge Fair, near Cambridge, was an important market, but its entertainments were poorer than those of Smithfield.

18. *Newhall.* Seat of Christopher Monck, second Duke of Albemarle, one of Thomas D'Urfey's patrons. 'Jocky Muse' (l. 19) probably refers to D'Urfey's famous racing song, 'To Horse, brave boys of *Newmarket*, to Horse' (*Songs of D'Urfey*, ed. C. L. Day, Cambridge, Mass., 1933, p. 132). See note to *A Satyr on the modern Translators*, l. 178.

29–30. Cf. Oldham, *Satyr . . . Spencer*: 'Take heed betimes, repent, and learn of me | To shun the dang'rous Rocks of Poetry.'

32. *John Saul.* 'The Cambridge *Bellman, a Poetaster*' (*1694*).

35. *Baxter*'s Salve for Souls. Richard Baxter (1615–91), puritan divine; 'Salve for Souls' seems to be a descriptive phrase rather than the title of any of his works.

37. *Care.* Henry Care (1646–88), turncoat journalist, had been an ardent dissenter and had edited 1678–83 a weekly paper attacking the Church of England as papistical. In the reign of James II he wrote in the interest of the

king and the Roman Catholics, and edited another weekly paper in 1688 defending their policies. An *Epitaph on Harry Care* in *P.O.A.S.*, 1703 (i. 153) describes him thus:

> Thence, *Settle*-like, he to recanting fell
> Of all he wrote, or fanci'd to be well;
> Thus purg'd from good; and thus prepar'd by evil,
> He fac'd to *Rome*, and marcht off to the Devil.

Ketch. Jack Ketch (d. 1686), executioner.

Oates. See note to *Advice to the Painter*, l. 44. Oates was convicted of perjury soon after the accession of King James, and was whipped, pilloried, and imprisoned during his reign.

52. *George Croom*. Printer 1671–1707 of broadsides, periodicals, trials, and the like (H. R. Plomer, *Dictionary of Printers and Booksellers 1668–1725*, Oxford, 1922, p. 87).

60. *free-cost*. It was possible, and fashionable among the wits, to see the first act of a play without paying (Allardyce Nicoll, *Restoration Drama*, Cambridge, 1928, pp. 12–13).

61–62. Cf. Oldham, *Satyr . . . Spencer*: '*But is it nought* (thou'lt say) *in Front to stand*, | *With Lawrel crown'd by* White, *or* Loggan's *hand?*'

67. *Jony Armstrong . . . the Prodigal*. Broadside ballads, with woodcuts. See *Bibliotheca Lindesiana* (Aberdeen, 1890), Nos. 547, 701.

95. *Essay on Poetry*. By Mulgrave, 1682.

100. *Manly*. Hero of Wycherley's *The Plain-Dealer*, 1676.

113. Mulgrave was Lord Chamberlain 1685–9. His conceit, haughtiness, and stinginess were notorious, and he had satirized Dorset and Rochester in his *Essay on Satyr* (1679?). See commentary on *A Satyr on the modern Translators*.

116. *Graves-end*. On the Thames; the last stop for ships outward bound from London.

123. *T. R. 1892* quotes Chamberlayne's *State of England* (4th ed., 1670, p. 75): 'In all such felonies where the benefit of clergy is allowed (as it is in many), there the criminal is to be markt with a hot iron with a T or an M, for thief or manslayer, on the left hand, and wandering rogues are to be burnt on the shoulder with an R.'

137–8. From Oldham's *An Ode of Anacreon, Paraphras'd. The Cup* (1683): 'Make me a Bowl, a mighty Bowl, | Large as my capacious Soul.'

145–6. Cf. Oldham, *Satyr . . . Spencer*: '*Sidley* indeed may be content with Fame, | Nor care should an ill judging Audience damn: | But *Settle*, and the rest, that write for Pence. . . .'

152. *Snuff*. Dryden 'was so great a taker of snuff, that . . . no box, however capacious, could serve him: he therefore carried a copious supply of snuff loose in his waistcoat-pocket' (E. Malone, *Prose Works of John Dryden*, 1800, I. i. 518–19).

155. *Otway*. Thomas Otway lived in poverty after 1682, and died, after

a long period of slow starvation, on 14 April 1685 (R. G. Ham, *Otway and Lee*, New Haven, 1931, pp. 201–18). For the union of the theatres which deprived playwrights of a market, see note to *A Satyr on the modern Translators*, ll. 1–4.

158. *Castalio*. 'In the Orphan' (*1698*), acted in 1680.

159. Soldier. *The Souldiers Fortune*, 1680, a comedy.

160. *Jaffier*. In *Venice Preserv'd*, 1682.

166–8. Betterton and others are said to have provided Otway with money to retire into the country and write another tragedy, which is supposed to have been lost at his death; Betterton offered a reward for the recovery of this lost play in *The Observator* of 29 Nov. 1686 (Ham, *Otway and Lee*, pp. 215–17).

171. *Carlile*. James Carlisle (d. 1691) and William Mountfort (1664?–92) were, according to Downes, the two good actors who had matured before the union of the theatres in 1682 (*Roscius Anglicanus*, ed. M. Summers, 1928, p. 39). Carlisle left the stage in 1685 and became a soldier; he was commissioned ensign in the Duke of Norfolk's regiment of foot on 20 June 1685 and ensign in another regiment in 1686, was promoted to lieutenant and then to captain, and was killed at Limerick (A. S. Borgman, *The Life and Death of William Mountfort*, Cambridge, Mass., 1935, p. 23 n.).

172–4. Mountfort was a friend of Judge Jeffreys, the Lord Chancellor, and apparently withdrew from the stage for some time in 1686 to live with him. Sir John Reresby thus describes a dinner with Jeffreys on 18 Jan. 1686: 'After dinner the Chancellor, having drunke smartly at dinner (which was his custome), called for one Monfort, a gentleman of his that had been a comedian, an excellent mimick, and to divert the company, as he called it, made him give us a caus, that is plead before him in a feigned action, wher he acted all the principal lawyers of the age, in their tone of voice, and action or gesture of body, and thus ridiculed not only the lawyers but the law itselfe. This I confess was very diverting, but not soe prudent as I thought for soe eminent a man in soe great a station of the lawe . . .' (*Memoirs*, ed. A. Browning, Glasgow, 1936, p. 408).

Sir *Courtly*. In May 1685 Mountfort had played the title role in Crowne's *Sir Courtly Nice*, with great success.

Jack Daw. Sir John Daw in Ben Jonson's *Epicoene, or the Silent Woman*; Mountfort took this role probably in Jan. 1685.

175. See note to l. 113 above.

183. Tate's only recent plays had been two farces, both adaptations of earlier plays: *A Duke and No Duke*, Nov. 1684; *Cuckold's Haven*, Sept. (?) 1685.

187. *King's-Bench*. 'The Debtors' Prison, where one would naturally look for poets' (*1892*). It was near the Mint, in Southwark.

Bethlem Friend. Nathaniel Lee was confined to Bedlam from about Sept. 1684 to 1689.

188–93. George Villiers, second Duke of Buckingham (1628–87)—the

'Zimri' of *Absalom and Achitophel*—was Cowley's patron, but treated him with characteristic fickleness. Cowley died in 1667, and Buckingham was reluctant to pay for his monument in Westminster Abbey, which was not erected until 1675. At the same time Buckingham was spending vast sums in building Cliveden, one of the most splendid houses in England.

194-7. P implies a contrast between two earls of Pembroke. The first couplet describes William Herbert, third earl (1580-1630), patron of play-wrights and poets, 'the greatest Maecenas to learned men of any peer of his time or since' (Aubrey, quoted in *D.N.B.*). The second couplet applies to Philip Herbert, seventh earl (1653-83), a drunkard and murderer, to whom Lee dedicated his *Caesar Borgia* (1679). Lee 'at one time had partaken so heavily of the bounty of the Earl of Pembroke and had lingered at his house so long that "the butler feared he would empty the cellar" ' (Ham, *Otway and Lee*, p. 58). Lee dedicated plays to Rochester, the Duchess of Portsmouth, Mulgrave, the Duchess of Richmond, and Dorset, as well as to Pembroke.

198-9. A reference to the '*Rose Alley* Ambuscade' of Dryden in 1679; see note to *A Satyr on the modern Translators*, l. 49.

(35)   *The Hind and the Panther Transvers'd*

MSS. None.
Pub. [Title as in text.] London: Printed for W. Davis, MDCLXXXVII; [Title as in text.] Printed in the Year, MDCLXXXVII (a Dublin piracy; Macdonald, p. 254); *P.O.A.S.* (*State-Poems; Continued*), 1697 (Case 211-1-c), p. 65; [Title as in text.] London: Printed and Sold by H. Hills . . . 1709.
Collected: *1707*, p. 48 (verse only); *New Collection 1725*, Append.; *1892*, ii. 311.
Text. *1687* [London].

Dryden's *The Hind and the Panther* appeared probably on 27 May 1687, and the parody was published by 19 July of the same year (Macdonald, pp. 46, 254 n.). Although the parody was unsigned, Charles Montagu and Prior were known to be the authors. Sir James Montagu, brother of Charles and lifelong friend of P's, describes its composition in a manuscript volume preserved at Longleat, *Memorandums Concerning the late Celebrated Poet & Statesman Mr Matthew Prior Copy'd from a MSS of Sir James Montagu Ld Chief Baron of the Exchequer*:

The Hind and Panther being at that time in every bodys hands Mr Prior accidently came one morning to make Mr Montagu a visit at his Brothers Chambers in the middle Temple London where the said Mr Montagu lodged when he was in London and the poem lying upon the table Mr Montagu took it up and read the four first lines in the Poem of the Hind and Panther . . . where stopping he took notice how foolish it was to commend a four footed beast for not being guilty of sin and said the best way of answering that Poem wou'd be to ridicule it by telling Horace's fable of the City mouse and Country mouse in the same manner which being agreed to Mr Prior took the book out of Mr Montagu's hands and in a short time after repeated the 4 first lines which were after printed in the City mouse and Country mouse. . . . The repeating these lines set the Company in Laughter and Mr Montagu took up the pen by him and wrote on a loose peice of paper and both of them making several Essays to transverse in like manner other parts of the Poem gave beginning to that work which was afterwards published to the great Satisfaction of many people, and tho' no name was set to the book yet it was quickly known who were the Authors of it, and as the reputation Mr Montagu got thereby was the foundation of his being taken notice of, so it Contributed not less to the Credit of Mr Prior who became thereby reconciled to his first Patron the Earl of Dorset. . . .' (fols. 15–19; first printed by Dobson, *1889*, pp. 213–15)

Sir James Montagu's *Memorandums* was apparently written after P's death in 1721, but not long after, since Montagu died in 1723. Though it contains some slips of memory, it is generally reliable, and certainly so for this event in which Sir James was personally concerned.

P himself explained the occasion and plan of the burlesque in a letter written some years after it to an unidentified person (perhaps a patron or the child of a patron). Drift's transcript, labelled 'Copy from the Original in Mr Priors own hand', is preserved in *L 28*, 1–4 (first printed by Waller in *1907*, pp. 385–6):

> The Occasion of writing the Country-Mouse, and the
> City-Mouse. In a Letter To . . . .

Mr: Dryden turning R: C: wrote a Poem which he called the H. and the P. By the H. he means the Church of R: and the C. of E: by the P. The Argument of the whole Work is that the P: walking abroad one Evening was met by the H. and invited to her Cell, and there entertained with aboundance of Civility. They talk together of the Plot and the Test, real presence in the Sacrament, Infallibility in matters of Faith. Tell one another two long Stories in which they allude to the State each C: has of late been under, and is in at present, and so bid each other good Night.

When People expected a great deal from so famous a Man on so fine a subject, Out comes this Poem applauded by the Pa: and at first a little dreaded by the Protestants: but the noise it made (like that of the Log in Æsop's Fable) was only terrible at first, like the Log to[o] the Poem was found lumpish and rediculous, & so soon trampled and insulted on by every One. The main Objection against it was that the matter of it was false and inviduous, and the way of its writing ungentile & rayling; but Billingsgate Manners in better Language, and Far below even the dignity of Satyr, for which the Author has formerly been beaten. For it affirms that the Reformation took its Original from the Lust of K. H. VIII, and the luxury and incontinence of Martin Luther, that the C. of E. sides with the Phanatics against the K. that her Doctrines continue or change just as the State pleases with many other indignities as malicious as any Jesuit could invent, & yet so very absurd as hardly an Irishman would repeat 'em.

The second Objection was that this piece contradicted the known rules of Poetry and even common Sense, for the whole being a Fable, the Beasts who speak should have reference to the Characters of the Persons they represent; thus by a Lion, a Wolf or a Fox, we mean a fierce, a rapacious, or a designing Man because the Nature of these Creatures and the Inclinations of such Men bear something of resemblance and proportion. Now, by his two Beasts how can we Understand the Two Churches? The C: of R: is no more like a Hind than 'tis like an Elephant, & the Rhinoceros is as good a representation of the C. of E. as the Panther.

Then the Beasts should keep such Company as tis likely they may love, as tis probable they should know, or else 'tis not a Fable. A Hind, who is so quiet and innocent a beast would not in all probability be much delighted in the Conversation of so fierce & Cruel a Creature as a Panther, or if She was, they would discourse rather of Woods and Shades and Streams than of St Paul to the Corinthians and the Council of Trent. The Hind, I fancy would not run over the Fathers, or repeat the Canon Law and the Code, and if She did the Panther would scarse be able to tell her where she quoted false or when She argued foul.

Amongst Authors who have written a Fable, Correct and well Horace has told the common Tale of the City M: and the C: M: in Latin, and Mr: Cowley has Translated it into English. This Fable we have rediculed and told in the same way Mr Dryden does his H: and P: it being really as probable and Natural that two Mice should take a Coach, go to the Tavern, get drunk, break windows and be taken by the Constable, as that a Hind and a Panther should sit up all Night together a talking; One proving Oates and Bedlow were Villains, and desiring the Penal Laws may be Repealed, and t'other defending the Doctrines of Non resistance and Passive Obedience.

To make the thing yet more rediculous we took the same humour the D: of B: had some years since in his play, the Rehearsal; that is we Bring in B: by whom we mean D: defending (as his way is) the foolishest things in his Poem, and Smith & Johnson by whom we mean any two Gentlemen of Tolerable Sense and judgment finding those faults which are most Obvious, and urging B. to be rediculous.

Thus M: I have given your Honor an Account of the Original of this Trifle, the Credit it happened to gain at L. was indifferent to me till my L: of Ex: was pleased not to discommend it at Burleigh, and what ever was said of it before I had no reason to sit down contented with the Value of it, or of any thing I ever writ, till Your Honor thought it not unworthy Your Acceptance.

> So tho we chance to have some smal Estate
> And few dispise and some approve our Fate
> Repining stil we view our little Store
> Judge the World errs, and think our Selves but poor
> But when we offer to the Pow'rs above
> When they are kind, when they our Gifts approve
> Then our own Happiness we justly prize
> And bless the Stores that gave the Sacrifice.

I beg Your Honors pardon for making Similies, a Young Poet can no more write without them, than a Parson preach without a Text.

To these two accounts little need be added. According to the *Works and Life of . . . Halifax* (Curll, 1715, p. 11), Montagu wrote the Preface, and a recently discovered poem by him (H. M. Hooker, 'Charles Montagu's Reply to *The Hind and the Panther*', *E.L.H.* viii, 1941, 51–73) provides further evidence—if any is needed—that he was capable of doing his full share. On the other hand, P's statement in his letter to Montagu of 4 Feb. 1707 (*B.M. Add. 7121*, 49–50), denying responsibility for the publication of *1707*—'part of the Mouse is likewise inserted, which I had little to say to otherwise than as I held the pen to what Mr. Montagu dictated'—is certainly flattering exaggeration. Speculation on the respective shares of P and Montagu (sum-marized by Macdonald, pp. 253–4) seems unprofitable; Sir James Montagu's account alone is evidence enough that the collaboration was a real one.

In the notes, we have given few specific references to *The Rehearsal* (1671), which is, as P states in his letter, the source of the dramatic framework and of many passages. Similarly, we have not attempted to give references to all the passages in *The Hind and the Panther* (abbreviated *H.P.*) that are burlesqued; but where *1687* calls attention to specific passages in *H.P.* by marginal references, we have noted the citation below, substituting line-numbers for the original page-numbers.

[Title.] *Transvers'd.* In *The Rehearsal*, I. i, Bayes says: 'Why, Sir, my first Rule is the Rule of Transversion, or *Regula Duplex*: changing Verse into Prose, or Prose into verse, *alternative* as you please. I take a Book in my hand . . ., if there be any Wit in't, as there is no Book but has some, I Trans-verse it; that is, if it be Prose, put it into Verse, (but that takes up some time) if it be Verse, Put it into Prose.'

[Motto.] Much . . . Wit. *H.P.*, l. 1295.

Nec . . . domari. A tag from Lily's *Grammar*, the section 'De Nominibus Heteroclitis', beginning, 'Quae genus aut flexum variant'.

[Preface.]

24. Rodriguez. See note to Preface, l. 50 below.

28–29. *H.P.*, ll. 877–8.

42–43. *H.P.*, l. 276; cf. l. 290 below.

46–47. *censure the* Turks. *H.P.*, ll. 376–9.

50. 'Difference betwixt a Protestant and *Socinian*, p. 62' (*1687*). At the end of his *Defence of the Paper Written by the Duchess of York, Against the Answer Made to it*, 1686 (*Works*, ed. Sir W. Scott and G. Saintsbury, Edinburgh, 1882–93, xvii. 253), Dryden remarked, 'among all the volumes of divinity written by the Protestants, there is not one original treatise, at least that I have seen or heard of, which has handled distinctly, and by itself, that Christian virtue of humility'. Stillingfleet, in his *Answer* (Dryden, *Works*, ed. Scott–Saintsbury, xvii. 280), replied that this was a deliberate falsehood, 'Since within a few years (besides what hath been printed formerly), such a book hath been pub-lished in London'. Thomas Tenison, in *The Difference Betwixt the Protestant and Socinian Methods: In Answer to a Book Written by a Romanist, and Intituled, The Protestants Plea for a Socinian*, 1687 (licensed 14 Dec. 1686), also replied (p. 62): 'I will tell him of one Book (as I could of many others) written singly upon that Subject. I mean a late Treatise by *Mr. Allen*, A Man who had considered many ways, but long before his Death, approv'd of that of the Church of *England*, as the most safe and Apostolical.' (A marginal note identifies the book: 'A Practical Discourse of Humility, by W. A. Lond. 1681.') In the Preface to *H.P.*, Dryden replied to Stillingfleet: '*the magnified Piece of* Dun-comb *on that Subject, which either he must mean or none, and with which another of his*

Fellows has upbraided me, was Translated from the Spanish of Rodriguez; *tho' with the Omission of the 17th, the 24th, the 25th, and the last Chapter, which will be found in comparing of the books.*' If Dryden was referring to a book other than Allen's, it has not yet been identified.

53–54. *makes the infallible Guide affirm.* H.P., ll. 1626–34.

60–61. *commanded him.* H.P., ll. 1576–84.

63. *inform us.* H.P., Preface: '*As for the Poem in general, . . . it was neither impos'd on me, nor so much as the Subject given me by any man.*'

70. The first line of Dryden's *Tyrannick Love, or The Royal Martyr* (1669), substituting 'his' for 'my'.

74. *Almanzor.* See note to *A Satyr on the modern Translators*, ll. 62–64.

83. *our Author's to the Dissenters.* In H.P., Dryden was, in accord with King James's early policy, conciliatory toward the Church of England and bitter toward the Dissenters. But James shifted his policy during the composition of the poem, and issued his first Declaration of Indulgence (4 April 1687) shortly before it was published. His new policy was conciliatory toward the Dissenters, attempting to make them allies of the Roman Catholics against the established Church. Dryden therefore explains in his Preface, with some embarrassment, that his satire is not intended to apply to those who have '*embrac'd this Gracious Indulgence of His Majesty in point of Toleration. . . . For those who are come over to the Royal Party are consequently suppos'd to be out of Gunshot.*'

[Text.]

4–5. H.P., Preface, first sentence.

16–17. The same sentence.

23. *Guide of Controversy. The Guide in Controversies: or a rational Account of the Doctrine of the Roman Catholics concerning the ecclesiastical Guides in Controversies of Religion; reflecting on the later Writings of Protestants, particularly of Archbishop Laud and Dr. Stillingfleet on this Subject*, 1666–7. (By A. Woodhead.)

24–25. *Considerations on the Council of Trent.* Another book (1671) by Abraham Woodhead (1609–78), who was the 'Romanist' answered by Dr. Tenison in the book cited in the note to Preface, l. 50 above.

25. *Good life.* H.P., l. 78.

38–39. H.P., l. 366.

44–45. H.P., l. 370.

48. H.P., l. 76.

49. *pamper'd Paunch.* H.P., l. 374.

51. *Fat Frier.* Dryden's *The Spanish Fryar*, 1680.

69. *Horace*'s design. *Satires*, II. vi. 79 ff.

90–93. H.P., ll. 1–4.

100–3. H.P., ll. 5–8.

118–19. H.P., ll. 9–10.

126. *Sanguis . . . Ecclesiæ.* Cf. Tertullian, *Apologeticus*, 50.

128–31. *H.P.*, ll. 13, 17–18, 25–26.

148–51. *H.P.*, ll. 27–34.

155. *H.P.*, l. 35.

163. *Armarillis*. In *The Rehearsal*, I. i, Bayes says, 'Why, I make 'em call her *Armaryllis*, because of her Armor: Ha, ha, ha.'

166–8. *H.P.*, ll. 37–38.

174–5. *H.P.*, ll. 39–42.

178. *H.P.*, l. 43.

182–4. *H.P.*, ll. 161, 164–5.

200. *H.P.*, ll. 180–1.

205. *H.P.*, ll. 686–92.

207–8. *H.P.*, ll. 184–9.

211. Catholick *Queen*. Milton mentions 'that old wives tale of a certaine Queene of *England* that sunk at *Charing-crosse*, and rose up at *Queene-hithe*' (*Animadversions*; *Complete Prose Works*, ed. Don Wolfe, New Haven, 1953, i. 708). There was a popular ballad, confusing the Queen Eleanor (wife of Edward I) whose memorial was at Charing Cross with the Queen Eleanor (his mother; wife of Henry III) who was associated with Queenhythe: *A Warning Piece to England against Pride and Wickedness: Being the Fall of Queen Eleanor, Wife to Edward the First, King of England, Who by Her Pride, by God's Judgment, Sunk into the Ground at Charing Cross and Rose at Queen Hithe* (as cited in the edition of Milton mentioned above). We are indebted to Professor J. A. Bryant for pointing out this reference.

213–14. *H.P.*, ll. 190–1.

219–20. *H.P.*, ll. 208–9.

244–6. *H.P.*, Preface, the penultimate paragraph.

256–7. *Cat with a Top-knot*. According to the Scott–Saintsbury edition of Dryden's *Works* (x. 257), there is an old caricature print of this description.

278–91. *H.P.*, ll. 253–60, 270–7.

301–6. *H.P.*, ll. 327–9, 399, 395, 1488.

315. *left Hand Marriage*. *H.P.*, ll. 351–6.

319–20. *H.P.*, ll. 408–9.

322–5. *H.P.*, ll. 382–7.

333–4. *H.P.*, ll. 1125–6.

337–45. See note to Preface, l. 83 above.

351. *Dear Joys Jests*. We have not identified this book. 'Dear-joy' was a familiar appellation for an Irishman (*O.E.D.*).

362–3. *H.P.*, ll. 511, 516.

370–2. *H.P.*, ll. 528–30.

378–9. *H.P.*, ll. 530–1.

384–5. *H.P.*, ll. 542–3.

393. *Viceroy*. *H.P.*, l. 549.

397–8. *Crown-General.* H.P., l. 982.

403. H.P., l. 570.

405–7. H.P., Preface, the penultimate paragraph.

425. H.P., l. 572.

429. *Tom. I——s.* Thomas Jenner (fl. 1631–56), author, engraver, and publisher. The last engraving in *Soules Solace*, 1631, shows a man sitting and smoking; under it are verses by Jenner with the burden, 'Thus thinke, then drinke Tobacco' (*D.N.B.*).

439–40. The Rhenish Wine Tavern in Channel Row was kept by P's uncle, Arthur Prior; the Rummer Tavern at Charing Cross was kept by another relative, Samuel Prior.

447. *Bishop Martin.* The Martin, in the third part of H.P., represents Father Petre, who had become James's chief adviser.

King Buz. The Buzzard, in H.P., iii, represents Gilbert Burnet.

451. H.P., ll. 1135–6.

462–3. H.P., ll. 1237–8.

468–70. H.P., ll. 632–7.

473. H.P., ll. 638–40.

480. *Poeta Loquitur.* H.P., l. 1230.

493. *Emission* or *Reception* of Light. H.P., ll. 647–8.

504. H.P., l. 970.

511. H.P., ll. 1793–5.

523. H.P., l. 1973.

527–31. H.P., ll. 501–4.

556–62. H.P., ll. 2366, 2253, 2318–19.

566. *person* of Honour. Dryden assisted Sir William Soames with his translation of Boileau's *Art of Poetry*, 1683, and Mulgrave (see note to *A Satyr on the modern Translators*, l. 25) and possibly Roscommon with several pieces.

575–6. H.P., ll. 790–3.

600. *French Author.* '*Varillas*' (*1687*). Dryden translated, or intended to translate Varillas's *History of Heresies* (Tonson entered it in the Stationers' Register, April 1686; Macdonald, p. 257); but the translation was never published. Gilbert Burnet assumed that his attack upon Varillas (*Reflections on Mr. Varillas's History* . . ., Amsterdam, 1686) caused Dryden to abandon the project, and that the incident explained Dryden's animus against him in H.P. In *A Defence of the Reflections on* . . . *Mr. Varillas's History* . . . *Being a Reply to his Answer* (Amsterdam, 1687), he said: 'I have been informed from *England*, that a Gentleman, who is famous both for *Poetry and several other things*, had spent three months in translating Mr. *Varillas's History*, but that as soon as my *Reflections* appeared, he discontinued his Labour, finding the credit of his Author was gone. . . . He has lately wreaked his Malice on me for spoiling his three moneths labour . . .' (pp. 138–9).

605–7. H.P., ll. 2435–52.

638–9. *H.P.*, ll. 31–32.

645. *H.P.*, ll. 252–6.

654. beating. See note to *A Satyr on the modern Translators*, l. 49.

686–7. *H.P.*, ll. 62–63.

691. *Pontack.* A sweet red wine of France.

695–6. *H.P.*, ll. 869–70.

713. *Beast of a Bird. H.P.*, l. 2307.

723–4. *H.P.*, ll. 2404–5.

726–8. *H.P.*, ll. 2053, 2571–2.

731–3. *H.P.*, ll. 1744–6.

    Bridewell. A house of correction for vagabonds and loose women.

    Compter. The Poultry Compter and the Bread Street Compter were debtors' prisons.

    737. *H.P.*, l. 2591.

(57)   *Epistle, to Lord* ——

MSS. *W*, 27 (P; ll. 44–51 only); *L 28*, 55 (D; emend. by Pope); *L 28*, 164 (D; ll. 44–51 only); *M*, 10 (A).

Pub. *1907*, p. 305.

Text. *L 28* (55) [D]. Collated: *W*, *L 28* (164), *M*.

Both in *L 28* and in the lost quarto miscellany which was the source of its text, the poem was preceded by the following letter:

If ever I had any Wit t'was when I had the honor to be with Your Lordship, and then too it was not mine by Nature but inspiration.

> So when the meanest Priest comes near the Cell
> Where the pleas'd Deity vouchsafes to dwell
> Farewell Humanity, a Nobler ray
> Descends and drives him from Himself away
> With mighty Joy his sacred Silence breaks
> And much the God inspires, and much the Prophet speaks.

Your writing to me I dare not thank You for: that were to undervalue it, It shal be the business of my life to acknowledge as it has been the honor of it to have received so great a favor. I deferr'd writing too well knowing my own inabilities to perform your Lordships Commands. Alas, my Lord, we have little Wit stirring at London (but what Harry Pain has brought up for the Dissenters) or if there were a Distribution made, so little would fall to my Share, that it would scarse be worth the sending.

                     (*L 28*, 54 (D); printed in *1907*, pp. 305, 399)

Both letter and poem were addressed to Lord Dorset, and both were written (as internal references indicate) in the summer of 1687. Probably they were sent to Dorset together, in response to his 'Commands' that Prior send him some poetry. The beginning of P's letter suggests that Dorset had complimented him upon his wit; the occasion may well have been *The Hind and the Panther Transvers'd.*

'Harry Pain' in P's letter is Henry Payne, author of *An Answer to a Scanda-lous Pamphlet, Entituled A Letter to a Dissenter concerning His Majesties late Declaration of Indulgence &c.* London, Printed for N. T. Anno Domini 1687. King James's efforts to win over the Dissenters, marked by the Declaration of Indulgence in April 1687, had caused a pamphlet warfare; this work defended James's policy.

4. United Honors. Charles Sackville inherited the titles of Lord Buck-hurst (1652) and sixth Earl of Dorset (1677) through the paternal line; through his mother, Lady Frances Cranfield, he became in 1675 Baron Cran-field and fourth Earl of Middlesex (Harris, *Dorset*, p. 62). Thus by 1677 the titles and estates—Knole and Copt Hall—of both families were united in him.

7. Strephon. John Wilmot, Earl of Rochester, frequently so called (as in Mrs. Behn's *On the Death of the late Earl of Rochester* and *Prologue to Valentinian*). Rochester, who had died in 1680, had been Dorset's close friend and, in the eyes of contemporaries, his poetic rival (Harris, *Dorset*, pp. 97–98). P, in *Dedication*, 1708, speaks of Dorset's 'Great Friend the Earl of ROCHESTER (that other Prodigy of the Age)'.

44–51. Much later, P recalled this passage in connexion with the line from Horace which is the source of l. 49: 'optat ephippia bos, piger optat arare ca-ballus' (*Epistles*, I. xiv. 43). The jottings he made at that time are preserved in *W*, 27, and Drift's transcript—presumably made while the original was more legible—in *L 28*, 164. After writing the first two words of the line from Horace and starting to illustrate it with some notes on examples from history, P put down from memory ll. 48–51, with the comment, 'I was very young when I wrote these 4 Verses in a Copy lost'. Afterwards, apparently trying to recollect the lines that introduced these four, he wrote a new couplet that expresses the same thought:

> Our Vice and Error chiefly spring from this
> Not that we want but use our Parts amiss.

Drift later inserted on this sheet a reference to p. 18 of *Pensées de Montaigne* (Paris, 1700), where Montaigne (in 'Un Traict de Quelques Ambassadeurs') quotes the same line from Horace and illustrates it.

66. Waller's *Instructions To a Painter*, 1665; see commentary on *Advice to the Painter* (1685).

69. Cf. P's *Dedication*, 1708: 'and King CHARLES did not agree with LELY, that my Lady CLEVELAND's Picture was Finished, 'till it had the Approba-tion of my Lord BUCKEHURST'.

77. *Pulton*. Andrew Pulton (1654–1710), joint master of the Jesuit college opened in the Strand at Whitsuntide, 1687. He held a conference with Dr. Thomas Tenison in Sept. 1687, which began a long controversy (*A True and Full Account of a Conference held about Religion, between Dr. Tenison and A. Pulton One of the Masters in the Savoy*, 1687).

Casuist *ABC*. Cf. Sir Edward Dering, *A discourse of proper sacrifice, in way of answer to A. B. C. Jesuite, another anonymus of Rome . . .*, 1644. Later Jesuits may have used the same pseudonym.

88. *Higden.* Henry Higden, lawyer, wit, and very minor poet, had just published a translation of Juvenal's tenth satire with complimentary verses by Dryden (see Macdonald, p. 43).

1688

(61) *To Mr Charles Montagu*

MSS. *B.M. Add. 7121*, 45 (P; the original sent to Montagu); *Bodl. Montagu d. 1*, 99 (P; ll. 21–26 only); *L 28*, 50 (D; emend. by Pope); *M*, 15 (A).
Pub. *1907*, p. 301; ll. 21–26 in *New Monthly Magazine*, ser. 2, i (1821), 253 (from *Bodl.*).
Text. *B.M.* Collated: *Bodl.*, *L 28*, *M*.

Charles Montagu (1661–1715), Prior's friend since their days at Westminster School and his collaborator in *The Hind and the Panther Transvers'd*, married Anne, widow of Robert Montagu, third Earl of Manchester, in Feb. 1688. The countess, who was much older than Montagu, brought with her a considerable fortune. Montagu's rapid rise to power began the next year; see note to *To Mr. Fleetwood Shepherd* (1689), ll. 64–66. Ten years later, on 9 Aug. 1698, P wrote to Montagu from Paris congratulating him on being made one of the Lords Regents: 'I remember I wrote six Verses to you 10 years since which had a spirit of prophecy in them, they had a litteral sence then and are verified to have had a typical meaning likewise'; he then quotes ll. 21–26 of the poem (*Bodl.*).

39. Cf. *To the E of D.* (1685), l. 78.

(63) *A Session of the Poets*

MSS. *L 28*, 46 (D).
Pub. *1907*, p. 299.
Text. *L 28*.

References in the poem fix the date of composition as after May 1688 (ll. 72–73), and well before the end of that year (ll. 1, 6); probably it was written in the summer. One passage, however, seems to have been written before Waller's death in Oct. 1687 (ll. 33–44), and another may date from 1689 or later (ll. 88–93); Prior never finished the poem, and he may have tinkered with it over a considerable period.

The genre to which the poem belongs was established in England by

Suckling's *Sessions of the Poets,* written about 1637. P's model was the most recent *Session,* that printed in Rochester's *Poems on Several Occasions* (Antwerp, 1680), p. 111; this was written about 1677 and, though its authorship has been much disputed, was probably by Rochester (see James Thorpe's edition of Rochester's *Poems,* Princeton, 1950, pp. 186–7). P is indebted to this poem for one line and several phrases; he writes in the same anapaestic couplet and satirizes many of the same poets (Dryden, Wycherley, Shadwell, Lee, Settle, Crowne, Behn, D'Urfey). These resemblances explain the note in *L 28:* 'Query if this has not been Finished, and Printed. Vide Miscellany Poems in 12:⁰ Page 96. Printed by Tonson 1716.' (The reference is to the second volume of the 1716 edition of *Miscellany Poems,* Case 172-2-e, p. 96, where Rochester's poem is reprinted.) P may have intended to supply an ironic ending to match the award of the laurel to an alderman in Suckling's poem and to Betterton in Rochester's poem.

1–8. Late in 1687 King James had begun a systematic purge of all who would not support his policies, replacing them by his own creatures. (Dorset was one of the lords lieutenants dismissed.) P compares this to a gambler at Loo (Lanterloo) taking the risky option of discarding his original hand in the hope that the dummy hand will be better. The poets complain that, in spite of all these changes, Dryden remains Laureate: Pam (l. 8), the knave of clubs, always ranked as the highest trump at Loo. Several phrases in the passage echo the first line of Rochester's *Session:* 'Since the *Sons* of the *Muses,* grew num'rous, and loud'.

9. Cf. Rochester, l. 9: 'In the *Head* of the *Gang* ℐ—— D——, appear'd.' P had used the same line in *A Satyr on the modern Translators* (1685), l. 23.

21. *The Sacrifice. A Tragedy. By the Honorable Sir Francis Fane, Knight of the Bath* was published in 1686 (2nd and 3rd editions, 1687). In the dedication to Dorset, Fane explains that he is publishing a play that has not been performed, 'Having long since devoted my self to a Country Life, and wanting Patience to attend the leisure of the Stage'. Fane, grandson of the first Earl of Westmorland, was a country gentleman; he was a friend and admirer of Rochester, to whom he dedicated *Love in the Dark* (1675), a comedy. Some of his poems are printed in Tate's *Poems by Several Hands,* 1685, pp. 11–17. He seems to have been a disinterested admirer of both Dorset and Rochester. Langbaine says, 'This Noble Person's Wit and Parts, are above my Capacity to describe' (*An Account of the English Dramatick Poets,* Oxford, 1691, p. 188).

22–26. Tamerlane the Great is the hero of Fane's *The Sacrifice;* he woos, unsuccessfully, Despina, wife of Bajazet, Emperor of the Turks (l. 26). L. 22 is made up of some of the more exotic names from the play, which is extremely heroic and melodramatic; the Mummy Priest shows the Crowned Mummies in the vault to Tamerlane and Axalla, and among them are '*Ochanti;* the Inventor of Printing', '*Huy Hannon.* He that found out the Philosophers Stone', and '*Tzinzummey.* The Inventor of Gun-powder'. *Rozarno* is one of a list of names read off by Axalla to Tamerlane in the first scene. L. 23 cites some of the more spectacular features; one stage direction reads: '*An Astrologer*, Axalla, Irene, *a Captain. Thunder, Lightning, Rainbows inverted, a bloody Arm, Comet, &c.*'

Lee in Bedlam. See note to *Satyr on the Poets*, l. 187.

32. W. R. Possibly Will Richards, an old servant of Dorset's. Harris (*Dorset*, pp. 75–76) cites a letter from him to Dorset written about 1688, which suggests that he was friend as well as servant.

41–44. See note to *A Satyr on the modern Translators*, l. 49.

45. Durfey. See notes to *A Satyr on the modern Translators*, l. 178; *Satyr on the Poets*, l. 18.

49. Mrs. Long. Possibly the Mrs. Long who was one of Davenant's four principal actresses when the theatre in Lincoln's Inn Fields opened in 1661 and was the mistress of Charles Stuart, third Duke of Richmond. We have not, however, been able to discover any song in which D'Urfey affronts her.

52. Maidwel. Langbaine writes in 1691: 'John Maidwel. An Ingenious Person, still living (as I suppose) in *London*; where some time ago he undertook the Care and Tuition of young Gentlemen, and kept a Private School' (p. 335). Maidwell (his name was Laurence, not John) wrote *The Loving Enemies: A Comedy* (1679; pub. 1680) and some translations.

60. Busby. Richard Busby (1606–95), headmaster of Westminster School from 1638 to his death.

62. Afra. For Aphra Behn (d. 16 April 1689), see notes to ll. 78–88 of *A Satyr on the modern Translators*. The reference here is to her latest production, *Lycidus: or the Lover in Fashion. Being an Account from Lycidus to Lysander, Of his Voyage from the Island of Love . . . By the same Author of the Voyage to the Isle of Love* (Feb. 1688; Case 184). P's *To the Bishop of Rochester* (1685) appeared in the Miscellany section of the volume.

64. Watches for Damon and Isis. In 1686 Mrs. Behn published *La Montre: or, The Lover's Watch* (translated from the French), in which Damon, a young nobleman, and Iris, a maid of quality, demonstrate the art of love in verse and prose.

66. Jack Hoyle. Mrs. Behn's lover, to whom she addressed many poems. He was a lawyer, a wit, and a highly disreputable person; V. Sackville-West (*Aphra Behn*, 1927, p. 52) quotes a contemporary comment: 'Mr Hoyle was an atheist, a sodomite professed, a corrupter of youth, and a blasphemer of Christ.'

71. Sir Courtly. See notes to *A Satyr on the modern Translators*, l. 177; *Satyr on the Poets*, l. 174. Of the performance of *Sir Courtly Nice* in May 1685, Downes says, 'This Comedy being justly *Acted*, and the Characters in't new, Crown'd it with a general Applause . . .' (*Roscius Anglicanus*, ed. M. Summers, 1928, pp. 40–41).

72–73. For Shadwell, see note to *Satyr on the Poets*, l. 10. His *The Squire of Alsatia* was produced in May 1688; Downes says that it had a run of thirteen days, and that '*The Poet receiv'd for his third Day in the House in* Drury-Lane *at single Prizes* 130£. *which was the greatest Receipt they ever had at that House at single Prizes*' (p. 41). Shadwell dedicated the play to Lord Dorset, stating that he had written the first act at Copt Hall.

78–82. See note to *Satyr on the Poets*, l. 12.

83. Sir Ch:. . . . . Sir Charles Sedley (1639–1701), one of the circle of court wits and an intimate of Dorset's, was famous as poet, playwright, and patron; his most recent play was *Bellamira*, 1687. See note to *Satyr on the Poets*, ll. 145–6. P may have in mind Apollo's rejection of Wycherley in Rochester's *Session*: 'No *Gentleman Writer*, that office shou'd bear | 'Twas a *Trader* in *Wit*, the *Lawrel* shou'd wear.'

87–88. Wycherley's last play, *The Plain Dealer* (1676), was performed at court in Dec. 1685, and the proceeds were used to free him from a debtors' prison. James II and Lord Mulgrave were his patrons.

91–92. This passage is puzzling. It appears to mean that the Test Acts would bar Wycherley, a Catholic, from the laureateship. However, even if Wycherley was re-converted to Catholicism in 1687 (and this is by no means certain, though there is some evidence that he died in that faith), this would be no bar to the laureateship held by the Catholic Dryden; and James's two Declarations of Indulgence had suspended the Test Acts in any case. The passage may have been written later than the rest of the poem, for after William's accession the Test applied again and no Catholic could hold the office.

(66)   *On Exodus iii. 14*

MSS. None.

Pub.   *Examen Poeticum*, 1693 (Case 172–3–a), p. 449; *Miscellanea Sacra*, ii, 1707 (Case 236–2), 17.
        Collected: *1707*, p. 84; *1709*, p. 1; *1718*, p. 1.

Text. *1718*. Collated: *1693, 1709*.

Prior is said to have been appointed to write this ode as part of the college's annual tribute to the Earl of Exeter (Johnson, *Lives*, ii. 181). We cannot find any definite evidence that the poem was written for this occasion, but the traditional story agrees with all the known facts. P was entered as a Keyton Fellow at St. John's on 3 April 1688, and the subtitle of the ode states that it was written there as an exercise in 1688. A member of St. John's preached a Burghley Sermon at Stamford each year on the Sunday after St. Luke's Day (18 Oct.), in memory of the benefactions of William Cecil, Lord Burghley, to the college in 1581. On this occasion Latin verses on scriptural texts were presented to the Earl of Exeter; the records do not mention the formal presentation of English poems, but this seems to have been customary. (We are indebted to Mr. F. P. White, the present librarian of St. John's, for some of the information summarized above; he kindly informs us that the college did not keep a register of these presentations.) Sir James Montagu, in his *Memorandums* (described in the commentary to *The Hind and the Panther Trans-vers'd*, 1687), f. 19, says, 'Dr Gower the Master of St Johns did cast his Eye upon him from the beginning and put him upon making particular exercises which produced that noble Ode on the 3d Chapter of Exodus.' By the end of 1688 P was in residence at Burleigh as tutor to Lord Exeter's sons.

This Cowleyan ode is the first poem in both of P's own collections of his verse (*1709* and *1718*). P may have begun the volumes with it simply because it was the earliest poem that he wished to acknowledge and preserve. The poems are not, however, arranged in these volumes strictly according to chronology; and it seems likely that P gave the ode this prominent position because of a special regard for it. It expresses a religious attitude that is a central theme throughout his verse and is developed at length in *Solomon* (1708).

21. Cf. Dryden, *Religio Laici*: 'The *Deist* thinks he stands on firmer ground;| Cries Εὕρεκα: the mighty Secret's found' (ll. 42–43).

25. Cf. Cowley, *The Tree of Knowledge. That there is no Knowledge. Against the Dogmatists*: 'The onely *Science* Man by this did get, | Was but to *know* he nothing *Knew*' (*Poems*, ed. A. R. Waller, Cambridge, 1905, p. 45).

58. new HYPOTHESIS. P may have in mind Newton's *Principia*, published in 1687.

67. Cf. Denham, *The Progress of Learning*: 'With their new Light our bold Inspectors press | Like *Cham*, to shew their Fathers Nakedness, | By whose Example, after-ages may | Discover, we more naked are than they' (*Poetical Works*, ed. T. H. Banks, New Haven, 1928, p. 120).

68–69. Cf. Cowley, *Christ's Passion*: 'Mountainous heap of wonders! which do'st rise | Till Earth thou joynest with the Skies! | Too large at bottom, and at top too high, | To be half seen by mortal eye' (*Poems*, p. 402).

88–92. Cf. Cowley, *Brutus*: 'Would have confounded *Humane Virtues* pride, | And shew'd thee a *God crucified*'; *Christ's Passion*: 'How Hell was by its Pris'ner Captive led, | And the great slayer Death slain by the Dead' (*Poems*, pp. 197, 402).

100–1. Cf. Dryden, *Religio Laici*: 'Not light us *here*; So *Reason*'s glimmering Ray' (l. 5); 'So pale grows *Reason* at *Religion*'s sight' (l. 10).

(70)   *The Orange*

MSS.   *L 28*, 62 (D); *B.M. Add. 29497*, 67 (X; a late collection).
Pub.   Broadside, without imprint [London, 1688]; *A Collection of . . . Poems . . . Against Popery*, 1689 (Case 189–1–a), p. 10; *A Supplement to the*

Collection . . . Against Popery & Slavery, 1689 (Case 191–2–a), p. 29;
The Muses Farewel to Popery & Slavery, 1690 (Case 191–1–b), p. 101;
P.O.A.S., 1697 (Case 191–d), p. 101; *P.O.A.S.* iii, 1704 (Case 211–3–a),
p. 288.
Collected: *1907*, p. 310.
Text. *1688*. Collated: *L 28*.

Each of the three copies of *1688* that we have examined (at Harvard, the
Bodleian, and the Wrenn Library at the University of Texas) represents a dis-
tinct issue; but there are no verbal or other significant differences among them.
We have taken the Wrenn copy as our text. All later printings reproduce *1688*.

References in the ballad indicate that it was written in Dec. 1688; it must
have appeared as a broadside in the same month, for *A Collection*, which
reprints it, is dated by Wood 'the latter end of December 1688' (Margoliouth's
ed. of Marvell, i. 209). All printings are anonymous; its inclusion in *L 28* is
the only evidence of Prior's authorship.

P's ballad is closely related to *A New Song of an Orange*, written in Nov.
1688, and published in several broadside versions, as well as in most of the
collections listed above (see H. E. Rollins, ed., *The Pepys Ballads*, Cambridge,
Mass., 1930–2, iii. 333). It begins:

> Good People, Come buy
> The fruit that I Cry,
> That now is in season, tho Winter is nigh,
> 'Twill do you all good,
> And sweeten your Blood,
> I'me sure it will please, when you've once understood,
>   'tis an Orange.

P's ballad is written to the same tune (called *A Pudding* and other titles;
W. Chappell, *Popular Music of the Olden Time*, 1859, i. 234) and expresses the
same general theme. But it is not a mere variant of *A New Song*, as is *The
Rare Virtue of an Orange* (*Pepys Ballads*, iii. 336), which brings it up to date
early in December. Nor is it an answer to *A New Song*, as the title in *L 28*
suggests; the advice to 'Throw the Orange away' is obviously ironic, and
the satire is directed at James and his followers. P's ballad is, rather, a new
poem on the same theme, without verbal resemblance to its predecessor.
We are obliged to Prof. Hyder E. Rollins for discussing this ballad with
us and for calling to our attention several rare broadsides in the Harvard
Library.

4. *Judith Wilk*. The queen's midwife. It was widely believed that Queen
Mary had worn cushions to counterfeit pregnancy, and that at the supposed
birth of the prince on 10 June 1688, the midwife had introduced the new-
born child of a tiler into the royal bed by means of a warming-pan.

8–10. On 28 Nov. King James had summoned Parliament for January and
had appointed commissioners to treat with William of Orange. William agreed

on 8 Dec. to abide by the decision of the Parliament and to keep his army at least 40 miles from London meanwhile, on condition that James should do the same. Probably the poem was written before this agreement was nullified by James's abortive flight of 11 Dec.; certainly it could not have been written after his final flight on 23 Dec.

13. *Calves-head.* The Calves' Head Club held dinners featuring this dish in disrespect to Charles I each year on 30 Jan., the date of his beheading.

15–17. At Salisbury late in November, James suffered a violent bleeding at the nose lasting three days.

26. *Da——.* Count Ferdinando D'Adda, the Papal Nuncio. He fled in disguise on 12 Dec.

29–30. In Nov. 1686 Louis XIV had undergone surgery for *fistula in ano*.

34. *open-arse.* The reference is probably to the suspicious ease with which Queen Mary gave birth to the prince. 'Open-arse' also meant 'medlar' (*O.E.D.*); cf. l. 31.

36–42. The Princess Anne, with Lady Sarah Churchill, escaped from the palace on 25 Nov., escorted by Bishop Compton and Lord Dorset. A week before, she had written to William expressing approval of his enterprise. Numerous fictions were invented to account for her voluntary flight: 'She had been grossly insulted: she had been threatened: nay, though she was in that situation in which woman is entitled to peculiar tenderness, she had been beaten by her cruel stepmother' (Macaulay, p. 1166).

43–45. Henry Mordaunt, second Earl of Peterborough (1624?–97), had been converted to Roman Catholicism in March 1687. A contemporary poem, *The Converts* (*The Muses Farewel*, 1689, p. 16), on those 'That chang'd their Faith to please their King', describes him thus: 'The first an Antiquated Lord, | A walking Mummy in a word, | Moves cloath'd in Plaisters Aromatick, | And Flannel, by the help of a Stick, | And like a grave and noble Peer, | Outlives his Sense by Sixty year. . . .' At the Revolution he attempted to escape from England, but was taken and put in the Tower on 24 Dec.

51–52. Lord Jeffreys, after almost being lynched by the mob that discovered him in disguise, was imprisoned at his own request on 12 Dec. and died in the Tower the next year. His son, John, had married a Catholic heiress; Luttrell writes on 21 July 1688: 'The lord chancellor's son hath married the late earl of Pembroke's daughter the lady Charlot, a papist; she is said to be worth 70,000£: they were married by a church of England man, and by a Romish Bishop . . .' (i. 451).

53. *D——s cause.* William Cavendish, first Duke of Devonshire (1640–1707), had in 1687 quarrelled with one Colepepper and been provoked into striking him at Whitehall. At the instigation of Jeffreys, he was fined £30,000 and imprisoned until he signed a bond for it. It was generally felt that he had been unfairly treated because of his opposition to James's policies. He signed the invitation to William, and led the rising in Derbyshire. After

the Revolution, the House of Lords reviewed his case, and decided that the Court had violated common justice.

55. *Herbert.* Sir Edward Herbert (1648?–98) as Chief Justice of the King's Bench had given judgement in the Hales case, 1686, for the dispensing power, and defended his action in a pamphlet. As a member of the ecclesiastical commission, he refused to support some of James's policies. However, he followed James in his flight to France and became his Lord Chancellor.

57. *Lobb, Penn.* Stephen Lobb (d. 1699), nonconformist divine, and William Penn (1644–1718), the Quaker, had attempted to win over the Dissenters to James's support in the spring of 1687.

(72)   *Journey to Copt-Hall*

MSS. *L 28*, 27 (D); *M*, 18 (A).
Pub. *1907*, p. 287.
Text. *L 28.* Collated: *M.*

This and the three following poems were written while Prior was at St. John's, 1683–8, but are not susceptible of more precise dating.

The present poem describes a journey from Cambridge to Copt Hall, Lord Dorset's seat in Essex, about 2 miles from Epping. Dorset lived in retirement there during most of James's reign; at the Revolution he re-entered public affairs, and was a strong supporter of William.

7. *Cordibeck.* Caudebeck, a kind of hat, from Caudebec in Normandy (*O.E.D.*).

11. *Hudibrass.* Referring to the end of the first canto.

18. *Machin.* Continuing the allusion to *Hudibras*:

> . . . They now begun
> To spur their living Engines on.
> For as whipp'd Tops, and bandy'd Balls,
> The Learned hold, are Animals:
> So Horses they affirm to be
> Mere Engines made by Geometry. (I. ii. 53–58)

23–24. Cf. *On the Coronation* (1685), l. 31: 'Whilst Zealous Crowds, like *Persians* run'; the verbal duplication suggests that P is mocking his own 'well-set Simile'.

25. *Lee.* Nathaniel Lee was patronized by Dorset before and after his confinement in Bedlam; see notes to *Satyr on the Poets*, ll. 187, 194–7.

26. *Durfey.* For Thomas D'Urfey, see notes to *A Satyr on the modern Translators*, l. 178; *Satyr on the Poets*, l. 18. Cf. also *A Session of the Poets*, ll. 45–51.

28. *Matron.* Probably a humorous allusion to the young countess, only 17 when Dorset married her in 1685 (see commentary on *To the E of D.*, 1685). If the poem was written before 20 April 1687, when Dorset's mother

died, she may be the 'Matron', though it appears that she lived at Knole and was not very close to her son and daughter-in-law.

(73)   *On Mr: F. S. Killing the French K . . .*

MSS. *L 28*, 29 (D); *B.M. Add. 27408*, 132 (X). (Index to *M.*)
Pub. *1907*, p. 288.
Text. *L 28*. Collated: *B.M.*

In *L 28*, the poem forms part of a letter to Lord Dorset:

My Lord
     After ten thousand thanks for the kindest entertainments I ever received, and as many Sighs for leaving C[opt] and Your Lordship, I presume to inform You that I have Obeyed Mr: Shep[herd's] commands, summond the Muses, told Them of his killing the F[rench] K[ing] and upon that subject presented him with such Poetry as Smal-beer and College Mutton cou'd Inspire.

     Then follows the poem, headed 'To F. S.'. Shepherd was a notorious liar; Prior wrote to George Stepney in 1694: 'The gravity of his follies is insufferable, and he wants a tutor more than my Lord Buckhurst. I thought you were not such a stranger in Israel as to fancy he expects to be believed . . .' (*H.M.C. Bath*, iii. 38). An example of Shepherd's prophecies is found in *Lpo 11*, 26 (X), headed, 'Sir Fleetwood Shepherd upon the Report of the Lord Capels death invented the Following Prophesy. . . .' It was printed, as *A Prophecy, by Sir F. S.*, in *P.O.A.S.* (*State-Poems; Continued*), 1697 (Case 211–1–c), p. 251. Another poem in *Lpo 11*, 27 (X), may possibly be the occasion of P's reply:

Epitaph on the French King
All Earthly glory's but a Farse—
Here Lyes a Monarch kill'd with his A——
The Papists pray for his sweet soul
That went out of a stinking hole
The Hugonites doe smile and simper
To see such an end of *Nec pluribus Impar*.
                              By Sir Fleetw: Shepherd.

For an account of Shepherd, see commentary on *To Mr. Fleetwood Shepherd* (1689).

     16. Raviliac. The assassin of Henry IV of France.
     20. The reference is probably to the Popish Plot of 1678. Thomas Pickering, a Jesuit, was executed (on Oates's evidence) for planning to shoot Charles II with a pistol loaded with silver bullets. *O.E.D.* quotes Oates's *Narrative*: 'by Tewxbury Mustard-balls, we are to understand Fire-balls.'

(74)   *There be Those*

MSS. *L 28*, 12 (D).
Pub. *1907*, p. 276.
Text. *L 28*.

For Lady Margaret, see commentary on the following poem. The form suggests that this poem may have been intended to be sung on some public occasion at St. John's.

(76)   *Many Daughters have done well*

MSS. *L 28*, 14 (D).
Pub. *1907*, p. 278.
Text. *L 28*.

Prior's Latin verses *Ad illustrissimam Dm: Margaritam* (1688) are very similar to this poem, some passages being so close that they seem to have been translated from Latin into English, or vice versa. Both poems show indebtedness to Cowley's *The Complaint* (*Poems*, ed. A. R. Waller, Cambridge, 1905, p. 436) in setting and structure: Cowley returns to Cambridge, sleeps, and has a dream-vision of the Muse of Pindar.

Lady Margaret Beaufort (1443–1509), Countess of Richmond and Derby, was the mother of Henry VII (l. 36), whose victory over Richard III at Bosworth Field in 1485 ended the Wars of the Roses. She planned Henry's marriage to Elizabeth of York in 1486, and in other ways influenced him towards reconciliation and peace. She was religious and charitable, a patron of learning, and a benefactor of the universities. Besides St. John's, she founded Christ's College, Cambridge (l. 46), and established divinity professorships at both universities.

4–6. Cf. Cowley, *The Complaint*: 'Where Reverend *Cham* cuts out his Famous way, | The Melancholy *Cowley* lay: | And Lo! a Muse appear'd to his closed sight.'

1689

(78)   *To My Lady Exeter*

MSS. *L 28*, 60 (D).
Pub. *1907*, p. 309.
Text. *L 28*.

The poem is dated '1689' in *L 28*. Lady Exeter was Anne Cavendish, daughter of the third Earl of Devonshire and widow of Charles, Lord Rich. She married John Cecil, fifth Earl of Exeter (1648?–1700), in 1670.

Sir James Montagu (*Memorandums*, fols. 19–23) thus describes Prior's stay at Burleigh:

Dr Gower Master of that Colledge hd recommended Mr Prior to the Patronage of John Earl of Exeter who had then two Sons at Home who wanted a tutor . . ., and by virtue of this recommendation Mr Prior came to be received into the Earl of Exeter's family. . . . And in that family Mr Prior continued sometime which gave him an insight into painting for the Earl of Exeter had many peices of the best hands in his House at Burleigh, and he being one that was thought to have skill in Pictures most of the Artists that way used to come to him, and from them Mr Prior learnt how to know and value good Pictures afterwards, and in that family he had likewise an opportunity of seeing much Company for no one at that time lived more splendidly than the Earl of Exeter; but upon the Prince of Orange's coming over and being declared King of England the said Earl not inclining to the Measures taken at the Revolution broke up his former way of Housekeeping and turn'd his thoughts to going into Italy to buy more Pictures for his fine House at Burleigh, and Mr Prior not liking to Continue a Tutor applyd again to the Earl of Dorset for his Patronage for at this time the said Earl was made Lord Chamberlain of the King and Queens Household, but waiting sometime longer than he expected Lord Dorset wou'd have permitted him to remain without something, He wrote that Epistle to Fleetwood Sheppard. . . .

The dates of P's residence at Burleigh are difficult to ascertain; he seems to have arrived before the end of 1688 (see *Epistola ad Magistrum*, Latin, 1688), and he stayed at least until 1 Aug. 1689 (see *The Crest of the Arms of the Earl of Exeter*, Latin, 1689) and possibly much longer. We know nothing definite of his movements until he went to Holland in Oct. 1690, as secretary to Lord Dursley. We can find no record of Lord Exeter's going abroad soon after the Revolution: he was at Burleigh in 1693 (*Gentleman's Journal*, Oct. 1693, p. 346) and in 1695 when William visited there (though, being a Nonjuror, he absented himself for the occasion); he seems not to have gone to Italy until 1699 (Luttrell, iv. 487, 563), and he died there the following year. P wrote a Latin epitaph for his monument (1704).

(79)   *To the Countess Dowager of Devonshire*

MSS.   None. (*L 28, 70*, contains the printed sheets from *1722*.)
Pub.   *A New Miscellany*, 1720 (Case 315), p. 12.
         Collected: *1722*, p. 1; *New Collection 1725*, p. 78.
Text.   *1720*.

'An Excellent POEM, *to the Countess Dowager of* DEVONSHIRE, upon a PIECE of WISSIN's, *whereon were all her* GRANDSONS *Painted*, (the last Performance of that Master, in his own Handwriting, without taking a COPY of it) He gave near Thirty Years ago to his friend ANTHONY HAMMOND, *Esq*; and to that Gentleman the Reader is now obliged for its first Publication' (Curll's *1722*

Memoirs). This history of the manuscript may be true, since the poem first appeared in *A New Miscellany*, edited by Hammond, more than thirty years after it was written.

The countess dowager was Elizabeth, daughter of William Cecil, second Earl of Salisbury; she had married William Cavendish, third Earl of Devonshire, in 1639. After his death in 1684 she lived at Burleigh with her daughter, Anne, Lady Exeter (to whom the preceding and following poems are addressed). Her seven grandsons (l. 5) were the four sons of Anne and Lord Exeter and the three sons of William, first Duke of Devonshire. Prior must have written the poem during his stay at Burleigh and before the death of the countess dowager on 19 Nov. 1689.

1. *WISSIN*. Willem Wissing (1656–87), a Dutch painter, came to England and studied under Lely. After Lely's death Wissing's work became fashionable; he was the favourite painter of King James. He died at Burleigh on 10 Sept. 1687, and Lord Exeter erected a tablet to his memory in St. Martin's Church, Stamford.

13. *Anna.* 'Eldest Daughter of the COUNTESS' (*1720*); Lady Exeter.

18. *Burleigh.* John, born 1674, Lord Burleigh until he succeeded to the title of Earl of Exeter in 1700.

(81) *To the Countess of Exeter*

MSS. None.
Pub. *Examen Poeticum*, 1693 (Case 172–3–a), p. 437; *Deliciae Poeticae*, 1706 (Case 240), p. 98.
   Collected: *1707*, p. 119; *1709*, p. 7; *1718*, p. 6.
Text. *1718*. Collated: *1693*, *1709*.

9–12. Cf. *Journey to Copt-Hall* (1688), ll. 23–24, and note.

14. See Cowley's *On Orinda's Poems* and *On the death of Mrs. Katherine Philips*.

19–20. Johnson, *Rambler*, in No. 143 (30 July 1751), noted that 'Prior was indebted for a pretty illustration to Alleyne's poetical history of Henry the Seventh'. The reference is to *The Historie of That wise and Fortunate Prince, Henrie of that Name the Seventh, King of England . . . In a Poem by Charles Aleyn . . .*, 1638: 'For onely *light* it selfe, it selfe can *show*, | And none but *Kings* can write, what *Kings* can *doe*' (p. 1).

36–37. According to medieval legend, St. Luke was helped by an angel in painting a portrait of the Virgin. There are several paintings representing this scene.

42. Perhaps suggested by the conclusion of Waller's *Of My Lady Isabella playing on the Lute*: 'So Nero once, with harp in hand, survey'd | His flaming Rome, and as it burn'd he play'd.'

(82)   *Picture of Seneca*

MSS. None.
Pub.   *1718*, p. 8.
Text. *1718*.

Lord Exeter was a great patron and collector of art; he spent much time abroad, '& in his Travels bought up an inestimable Treasure of Medals, Books, Pictures, Gems, & other Rarities of all sorts' (Francis Peck, *Desiderata Curiosa*, 1732, I. vi. 42). Peck, in his description of Burleigh, mentions this painting: 'In another Room are seven large Pieces, by *Lucas Jordano*, the Italian. Whereof the Principal is that of *Seneca* bleeding to Death. It is reckoned a most finished Picture, & one of the very best in the whole House' (I. vi. 43). Horace Walpole, writing to Dalrymple in 1790, remarks that Exeter knew Giordano in Rome and that this was why he acquired so many of his pictures; he thinks this one of Giordano's best, but not very good. The picture is still at Burleigh (Walpole, *Correspondence*, ed. W. S. Lewis, xv, New Haven, 1951, 204). The painter in question is Luca Giordano (1632–1705); misled by Prior's spelling, Evans (*1779*) and subsequent editors have confused him with the Dutch artist Jacob Jordaens (1593–1678).

(83)   *A Flower*

MSS. *Lpo 18*, 293 (X); *B.M. Lansd.*, *852*, 57 (X; misc. owned and annotated
       by Edward Lord Harley).
Pub.   *1718*, p. 290.
Text. *1718*. Collated: *Lpo, Lansd.*

Because of the close similarity in theme to *To the Countess Dowager of Devonshire*, ll. 1–8, and *To the Countess of Exeter*, ll. 36–41, and because there were flower-paintings by Verelst at Burleigh (F. Peck, *Desiderata Curiosa*, I. vi. 44), it seems probable that Prior wrote this poem during his residence there.

Simon Verelst (1637?–1710), a Dutch painter who settled in England during the reign of Charles II, was much admired for his flower-pieces. According to Horace Walpole (*Anecdotes*, 1876, ii. 114–16), he was excessively vain, called himself the God of Flowers, and went mad toward the end of his life. P owned a large 'Flower Piece' by him (H. B. Wright and H. C. Montgomery, 'The Art Collection of a Virtuoso in Eighteenth-Century England', *The Art Bulletin*, xxvii, 1945, 203).

(83)   *To Mr. Fleetwood Shepherd*

MSS. *Worcester Col.* (George Clarke's hand). (*L 28*, 96, contains the printed
       sheets from *1722*.) (Index to *M*.)
Pub.   *P.O.A.S.* (*State-Poems; Continued*), 1697 (Case 211–1–c), p. 193; *New*

Collection, 1705 (Case 237), p. 248; *Deliciae Poeticae*, 1706 (Case 240), p. 68.

Collected: *1707*, p. 27; *1716*, p. 39; *1722*, p. 39; *New Collection 1725*, p. 41. Text. *1697*. Collated: *1706*.

Col. C. H. Wilkinson kindly informs us that the variants in the Worcester College MS. are not significant; the text appears to be the same as *1706*.

Curll's *1722 Memoirs* states plausibly Prior's reason for not collecting 'his *First Epistle* to *Fleetwood Shephard, Esq:* which his great Modesty prevailed with him to withdraw, only upon there being in the Close of that Piece, an innocent Joke upon Mr. *Mountague*, late Earl of *Halifax*'. P's relations with Montagu after 1700 were not such as to permit much joking. Though the authenticity of the piece has never been doubted, the question of its date and occasion has produced a good deal of confusion; cf. Bickley, pp. 32–33; Eves, p. 44; *New Collection 1725*, pp. 29–30; Harris, *Dorset*, pp. 150–1; and the various dates given in collected editions.

The occasion of the poem was Dorset's appointment as Lord Chamberlain on 14 Feb. 1689, the day after William and Mary acceded to the throne. Since P sent his epistle as a substitute for a personal appearance among the crowd of petitioners (ll. 10–14), it was clearly written not long after the appointment was made. The date '1688' in the Worcester College MS. and in *L 28* must therefore mean 1688/9.

Fleetwood Shepherd (1634–98) had been Dorset's intimate friend since about 1674; at Copt Hall he acted as superintendent or steward, but was treated as friend rather than employee. He was a minor wit and poet, his most notable production being *The Countess of Dorset's Petition to the Late Queen Mary for Chocolate* (*P.O.A.S.* iii, 1698, 233–4). He was often flattered by writers seeking Dorset's favour: Rymer's *Tragedies of the Last Age*, 1678, is 'in a letter' to him, and Dennis dedicated *Poems in Burlesque*, 1692, to him, as Gildon did *Chorus Poetarum*, 1694. After Dorset became Lord Chamberlain, Shepherd 'sold offices in the Chamberlain's disposal' (Harris, *Dorset*, pp. 133, 216); in 1694 he was knighted and made Usher of the Black Rod. The poem makes it clear that Shepherd from the beginning had been involved in Dorset's patronage of P. P's two references leave it uncertain whether this dated from 1674 or 1676 (*H.M.C. Bath*, iii. 32, 38). The story of Dorset's discovery of P reading Horace in his uncle's tavern is told by Sir James Montagu in his *Memorandums* (quoted in *1889*, p. 210, and Eves, p. 14).

27. *S——d.* Robert Spencer, second Earl of Sunderland (1640–1702), had been Secretary of State for the Northern Department and one of King James's chief and worst advisers; he was dismissed in Oct. 1688 and fled to Holland.

Mun. St——n. John Mounsteven (1644–1706) had been Sunderland's secretary for some years, and held the post of undersecretary while Sunderland was Secretary of State. When Sunderland lost office he discarded him (*D.N.B.*).

38. Uncle. P's uncle, Arthur Prior, who kept the Rhenish Wine Tavern, had died in May 1687.

42. Prickt. Soured.

44–45. *Furney-Vall*'s-Inn. An Inn of Chancery belonging to Lincoln's Inn.

49. Whey-fast. Whey-faced.

64–66. Charles Montagu, P's collaborator in *The Hind and the Panther Transvers'd*, had married the wealthy Countess of Manchester in 1688 (see *To Mr Charles Montagu*), had been elected to Parliament in Jan. 1689 through Dorset's influence, and had purchased a clerkship to the Privy Council in February. The *Works and Life of . . . Halifax* (Curll, 1715) indicates that the clerkship is the preferment P refers to: 'As soon as Mr. Montagu . . . was in Possession of his first Place at Court, which was that of one of the Clerks of the Council, (an Introduction to more substantial Preferment, and which, upon his Marriage with the Countess of *Manchester*, at the very Time as he came up to be examin'd for Holy Orders, which he intended to take, for the Sake of a Benefice in the Church, he purchas'd for 1500£,) Mr. *Prior* took Occasion to put the Lord *Dorset* in Mind of himself by the following Letter address'd to Mr. (afterwards Sir) *Fleetwood Shepherd* . . .' (p. 65).

(85)   *An Epistle to Fleetwood Shephard*

MSS. None.

Pub. *Miscellany Poems*, 1692 (Case 197), p. 1; *Sylvae*, 1702 (Case 172–2–d), p. 196.
   Collected: *1707*, p. 102, *1709*, p. 13; *1718*, p. 11.

Text. *1718*. Collated: *1692*, *1709*.

25. each Year. Although the preceding epistle was written at most some three months before this one, the year had changed, according to the old style of reckoning, on 25 March. Prior may, of course, have written an earlier epistle which is not preserved, or he may conceivably have sent Shepherd the Latin declamation, *In Schola Westmr: May 14: 1688*, written exactly a year before.

41–50. Cf. *Hudibras*, I. i. 480–528.

51. The statue of Memnon at Thebes was said to emit musical sounds at daybreak; see Juvenal, *Satires*, xv. 5.

55–56. In *The Muses Farewel*, 1690 (Case 191–1–b), p. 170, there is a poem, attributed in the Index to Shepherd, called *A true and full Account of a late Conference between the wonderful Speaking-Head, and Father Pulton, as twas related by the Heads own Mouth to Dr. F——, 1686*. It begins:

> I that was once a humble Log,
> The pissing Post of ev'ry Rogue,
> And could hope for nothing high'r,
> Than to grace a Christmas Fire,

> From that Element did scape hard,
> By the favour of *Fleet Shephard*;
> Who being a Friend to th'Mathematicks,
> Does for Virtuoso's lay Tricks,
> And procur'd a Man of Art
> That gave me Voice articulate;
> Taught me Tongues the most difficile,
> To sing Sawney, laugh and whistle.
> Follow'd now by Court and City,
> I confound with my strange Ditty
> Both the Learned and the Witty:
> And make all the Talk at *Betty's*,
> By the help of my Friend *Pettis*.

It is an imitation of the fourth of Oldham's *Satyrs upon the Jesuits* (*S. Ignatius his Image brought in, discovering the Rogueries of the Jesuits, and ridiculous Superstition of the Church of Rome,* in *Works,* 1703, p. 68); for Pulton, see note to *Epistle, to Lord*—— (1687), l. 77.

63–64. Cf. Juvenal, *Satires,* xv. 1–10.

92. BUSBEY. See note to *A Session of the Poets* (1688), l. 60.

101. TONSON. Jacob Tonson (1656?–1736), the leading publisher of the time. From 1692 on he published most of P's work.

114. Granam. P's grandparents lived in Godmanstone, East Dorset, and apparently were Dissenters. See Wickham Legg, Appendix A.

115. LOBB. See note to *The Orange* (1688), l. 57.

128. Nuncio. See note to *The Orange,* l. 26.

134. England had declared war against France on 7 May.

161. Count LAUZUN. Antonin Nompar de Caumont, Marquis de Puyguilhem, Comte (later Duc) de Lauzun (1632–1723), soldier and courtier, attached himself to the court of James II; in 1688 he escorted the queen and the prince on their flight to France, and late in 1689 he led a French force to Ireland.

172. TOM TRAM. A popular jest-book: *The Mad Pranks of Tom Tram, Son-in-law to Mother Winter; whereunto is added his Merry Jests, Odd Conceits; and Pleasant Tales; very delightful to read.*

179. STAMFORD. Burleigh House is 1 mile south of Stamford, in Lincolnshire.

183. SHADWELL. Thomas Shadwell had been appointed Poet Laureate on 9 March 1689.

(91)   *On Fleet: Shepheards takeing*

MSS. *Worcester Col.* (George Clarke's hand).

Pub.   C. H. Wilkinson, 'The Library of Worcester College', *Oxford Bibliographical Society Proceedings and Papers,* i (1927), 289.
      Never collected.

Text. *1927.*

Col. Wilkinson, in the article cited above, attributes this poem to Prior because George Clarke, who was well acquainted with him, transcribed it between two others by P and inserted it in his copy of *1718* together with other pieces, manuscript and printed, not included in that collection. We have not found any other evidence to confirm the attribution, but neither have we found any reason to question it. The style and tone of this little mock-heroic strongly suggest P's authorship, and resemble those of the other poems to Shepherd, especially *On Mr: F. S. Killing the French K . . .* (1688). While there is no clue to the exact date of composition, it was probably written at about the same time as the other poems to Shepherd.

We are obliged to Col. Wilkinson for permitting us to reprint his transcript of the poem.

(92)   *To Mr: K——s Tune*

MSS.   *L 28*, 66 (D); *B.M. Harl. 7319*, 302 (X).
Pub.   *Comes Amoris*, 1689 (Day & Murrie, 102), p. 8 (ll. 1–18 only).
       Collected: *1907*, p. 313.
Text. *L 28*. Collated: *1689, Harl.*

James landed in Ireland on 12 March, and Prior's song may well have been written at about the time of the House of Commons' address advising William to declare war, 25 April 1689 (printed in Abel Boyer's *History of King William the Third*, 1702, ii. 77). The declaration of war came on 7 May. The composer was probably Robert King; see commentary on *Song* (1692).

(93)   *To Dr: F . . .*

MSS.   *L 28*, 53 (D); *M*, 24 (A).
Pub.   *1907*, 304.
Text. *L 28*. Collated: *M*.

We conjecture that this epistle was addressed to Samuel Fuller, D.D. (1635–1700), who, like Prior, was a Fellow of St. John's College. He was noted for his 'hospitality and wit', and he became such a good companion of his patron, the Earl of Exeter, that his portrait hung in the drinking-room at Burleigh House and he was pictured on the great staircase there as Bacchus astride a barrel. In 1695 King William hesitated to confirm Fuller's election as Dean of Lincoln because of his reputation for conviviality (*D.N.B.*).

It is probable that the 'my Lord' of l. 16 refers to Exeter, and that the poem was written during P's residence at Burleigh. In the lost Volume II (f. 6) of the quarto miscellany, from which Drift copied this poem into *L 28*, it immediately preceded *To Mr. Fleetwood Shepherd*. Both P and Fuller probably had acquaintances in Beverley, Yorkshire, because of the scholarships to St. John's College offered from the free-school there. A spa near the town was reputed to have healthful properties.

9. the Spaniard. Perhaps, among the 'stranger Matters' that P was reading at Burleigh (see *An Epistle to Fleetwood Shephard*, ll. 164–70) he had encountered *De Hominis Excrementis Libellus* (1613) by Rodericus Fonseca, a native of Portugal.

13–14. Apart from sermons, Fuller's only published work was *Canonica successio ministerii Ecclesiae Anglicanae reformatae tam contra Pontificios quam schismaticos vindicata* (Cantabrigiae, 1690). This may be the 'labour' to which P refers.

27. In the seal and motto of the University of Cambridge.

1690

(94)   *To Dr. Sherlock*

MSS. *Md* (D).
Pub. *Examen Poeticum*, 1693 (Case 172–3–a), p. 444.
      Collected: *1709*, p. 35; *1718*, p. 130.
Text. *1718*. Collated: *1693, 1709, Md*.

William Sherlock (1641?–1707), Master of the Temple, throughout the reign of James II had opposed Popery but upheld the doctrine of passive obedience. At the Revolution he refused to take the oaths, and stopped preaching on the day (1 Aug. 1689) fixed for suspension of Nonjurors. While excluded from his pulpit he wrote the *Practical Discourse*. He resumed preaching, however, on 2 Feb. 1690, and finally took the oaths in Aug. 1690, defending his action in a pamphlet, *The Case of Allegiance to Sovereign Powers Stated* (licensed 17 Oct. 1690). He was made Dean of St. Paul's on 15 June 1691.

A Practical Discourse Concerning Death was published early in Dec. 1689 (adv. *London Gazette*, 5–9 Dec.), and immediately became a devotional classic, going through twelve editions by 1703. Prior's poem was written probably before Sherlock resumed preaching in Feb. 1690, and certainly before he took the oaths in August. It was not printed with the book until the late eighteenth century. No connexion between P and Sherlock is known.

8. Cf. *Satyr on the Poets* (1687), l. 218: 'And Sing of wondrous Piety and You.'

27. Cf. Cowley, *To Dr. Scarborough* (*Poems*, p. 200): 'When all's done, *Life is an Incurable Disease*.'

49. Cf. *On the Coronation* (1685), l. 63: 'And for the Nations Bliss, defer his own'.

(96)   *A Pindarique on His Majesties Birth-Day*

MSS. None.
Pub.   [Title as in text.] By Mr. Prior. Printed for John Amery in Fleet street.
1690; Wise, *Catalogue*, iv. 68.
Never collected.
Text.   *1690.*

The original publication is extremely rare, but Wise's copy (now in the B.M.) is not, as he thought, unique; there is a copy in the Halliwell–Phillipps collection in Chetham's Library, Manchester (No. 1033 in *A Catalogue of Proclamations, Broadsides, Ballads, and Poems. Presented to the Chetham Library, Manchester, by James O. Halliwell . . .*, 1851). We are obliged to Miss H. Lofthouse of Chetham's Library for providing us with photostats of this and other rare works in that library. The two copies are identical except that *B.M.* has some manuscript alterations in a contemporary hand; we cite these, when significant, in the textual notes.

Although the title-page is the only evidence of Prior's authorship (except the similarities to his other poems pointed out in the notes below), we have not found any reason to doubt it. Presumably he did not collect the poem because he felt that it had been superseded by his later and better panegyrics on King William. 4 Nov. was not only William's birthday, but the anniversary of his marriage to Mary and of his landing in England (the latter date was actually 5 Nov., but it was moved forward a day to coincide with the others), as well as of the discovery of the Gunpowder Plot. This day of multiple significance was celebrated, according to *The London Gazette* (No. 2607, 3–6 Nov. 1690), with a 'very fine Consort of Musick, Vocal and Instrumental'; Luttrell (ii. 125) adds that a play was performed afterwards. These accounts do not mention P's ode, but presumably it was sung, as the title states. A few days before, P had arrived at the Hague, where he began his diplomatic career as secretary to Lord Dursley, the ambassador.

1–2. Cf. *An Ode in Imitation of Horace* (1692), ll. 49–50: 'See thy Arm'd Navies plow their glorious way | And with bold Prows assert their Masters Sea'; *Carmen Seculare* (1699), ll. 224–5: 'She thro' the raging Ocean now| Views Him advancing his auspicious Prow.'

32. *JERNE*. Ireland.

42. Henceforth the ode is prophetic: William did not go to the continent until Jan. 1691.

65–76. Cf. Virgil, *Eclogues*, iv. 4–10; Horace, *Carmen Saeculare*, ll. 57–60.

(98)   *To a Lady Sleeping*

MSS. *L 28*, 8 (D).
Pub.   *1907*, p. 274.
Text. *L 28*.

This poem and the eight which follow are placed here because they were originally included in Volume I of the lost quarto miscellany, from which Drift copied them into *L 28*. We know the contents of most of this lost volume from Drift's marginal references in *L 28*. It contained Prior's early verse, including most of his Latin poems, arranged generally (but somewhat erratically) in chronological order. The earliest date for which there is definite evidence is 1683; the latest, 1689. We therefore assume that these nine poems, which lack specific dates, were written not later than 1690. We have arranged them in the order in which they occurred in the lost volume.

2. Cf. *To My Lady Exeter* (1689), l. 23.

(99)   *Charity never faileth*

MSS. *L 28*, 9 (D).
Pub.   *1907*, p. 274.
Text. *L 28*.

This ode resembles, in style and theme, *There be Those* (1688) and *God is Love*, below. Prior's reason for not collecting it may have been that he felt that *Charity* (1703) superseded it. His statement in *Dedication*, 1708, ll. 257–61, suggests that he may have sent poems on this theme to Dorset.

29. Cf. Cowley, *To Mr. Hobs*: 'Long did the mighty *Stagirite* retain | The *universal Intellectual reign*' (*Poems*, p. 188).
44–49. Cf. *There be Those* (1688), ll. 17–20.
57–59. Cf. *There be Those*, ll. 29–32.

(101)   *Arria and Petus*

MSS. *L 28*, 19 (D).
Pub.   *1907*, p. 282.
Text. *L 28*.

The source is Martial, I. xiii. The full story may be found in Pliny (*Epistles*, III. xvi) and in Montaigne (Bk. II, ch. xxxv; ii. 825–7).

(101)   *God is Love*

MSS. *L 28*, 40 (D); *M*, 1 (A).
Pub. *1907*, p. 294.
Text. *L 28*. Collated: *M*.

Pope added a note to the Table of Contents in *L 28*: 'written very young'.

19–20, 23. Cf. *To the E of D.* (1685), ll. 22, 25, 28.
42–43. Cf. *On Exodus iii. 14* (1688), ll. 86–87.

(103)   *Letter to J . . .*

MSS. *L 28*, 52 (D; emend. by Pope); *M*, 23 (A).
Pub. *1907*, p. 303.
Text. *L 28* [D]. Collated: *M*.

Jane, or Jinny, may well be the same 'Flanders Jane' who was Prior's housekeeper and mistress and is celebrated in *Jinny the Just* (1708).

5. Nendick. The B.M. *Catalogue* lists *A Book of Directions and Cures Done
by . . . Nendick's Popular Pill* (1677?) and three other books in the 1670's
extolling the virtues of this pill.

(104)   *Caelia*

MSS. *L 28*, 67 (D).
Pub. *1907*, p. 314.
Text. *L 28*.

The opening couplet virtually duplicates the first couplet of *To Mr Charles
Montagu* (1688). There is no clue to the identity of the friend or of Caelia.
Both in *L 28* and in the lost miscellany, the poem was preceded by a longer
and presumably earlier version:

> Were Cælia Absent and remembrance brought
> Her and past Pleasures thick upon my thought,
> With Bacchus' Liquors I'd Loves flames defeat
> He'd soon leave flut'ring, if his Wings were wet.
> Else to my Books I'd dedicate my Days,
> Forget my Daphne whilst I saught the Bays.
> Or shou'd all other Cures successless prove
> To some kind Present She my Suit I'd move.
> Burns are expelld by fire and Love by Love
> But when I want my Friend, when my vext heart
> Beats short, and pants and seeks its nobler part,
> That absent one not Millions can attone
> Amidst a Multitude I'm Stil Alone.
> My mind like Telephus's hurt is found:
> The cause that gave can only Cure the wound.

(105)   *Song Set by Messrs: Pickering and Tudway*

MSS.   *L 28*, 65 (D).
Pub.   *1907*, p. 312.
Text. *L 28*.

Dr. Thomas Tudway (1646?–1726) was organist of King's College Chapel, Cambridge, from 1670, and later was Professor of Music at Cambridge. He was patronized by Lord Harley, who commissioned him to make a collection of English cathedral music (now in the B.M.), and was Master of the Music to Harley's chapel at Wimpole. Prior was acquainted with him, at this later period if not before; Tudway wrote on 7 April 1719, thanking P for sending him a copy of *1718* (*L 7*, 91), and he sent P academic gossip from Cambridge in Jan. 1721 (*H.M.C. Bath*, iii. 496).

We have not identified Mr. Pickering, and the setting does not seem to have survived.

(105)   *Song Set by Mr: K.*

MSS.   *L 28*, 64 (D; emend. by Pope). (Index to *M.*)
Pub.   *A Second Booke of Songs . . . Composed by R. King*, 1695? (Day & Murrie, 135), p. 29 (first stanza only); *1907*, p. 312.
Text. *L 28* [D]. Collated: *1695*.

King's book is undated. Day and Murrie conjecture 1695, the B.M. *Catalogue of Printed Music* (ed. W. B. Squire, 1912, i. 760) conjectures 1698, and W. C. Smith (*Bibliography of the Musical Works published by John Walsh during the years 1695–1720*, 1948, p. 6), 1696. See commentary on *Song* (1692).

(106)   *A Hymn to Venus*

MSS.   *L 28*, 68 (D).
Pub.   *1907*, p. 315.
Text. *L 28*.

The occasion of this poem may have been, as Eves (p. 11) assumes, the marriage of Prior's cousin Katharine to George Villiers on 4 Dec. 1690. There is, however, no evidence to substantiate this conjecture.

1–2, 5–6. Cf. *To the E of D.* (1685), ll. 19–20, 15–16.
25. Cf. *To the Countess of D . . . . t* (1685), ll. 26–28.
39–47. Cf. *To the E of D.*, ll. 76–84.

1692

(108)   *To the Honourable Charles Montague*

MSS. *B.M. Add. 23904*, 44ᵛ (X; a late collection).
Pub. *The Gentleman's Journal; or, the Monthly Miscellany*, Feb. 1692, p. 5;
     Examen Poeticum, 1693 (Case 172–3–a), p. 431; *A New Collection*, 1701
     (Case 223), p. 295.
     Collected: *1707*, p. 80; *1709*, p. 31; *1718*, p. 24.
Text. *1718*. Collated: *1692*, *1693*, *1709*.

Motteux, the editor of the *Gentleman's Journal*, thus introduced the poem:
'Whilst things like the following Stanza's made by Mr. *Prior*, shall be given
or sent me, you may believe I shall be prouder of making them publick than
my own.'

Charles Montagu (later Earl of Halifax) was by this time well launched on
his brilliant career in politics. See *To Mr Charles Montagu* (1688), and note to
To Mr. Fleetwood Shepherd (1689), ll. 64–66. On 21 March 1692 he was appointed a Lord of the Treasury.

The theme of this poem recurs frequently; it is most fully developed in the
second book of *Solomon* (1708) and the third canto of *Alma* (1718).

3–4. Cf. Montaigne, Bk. II, ch. xii; ii. 311–12.

13–20. Cf. Lucretius, iii. 944–9, 1080–4.

38. Cf. Dryden, *Aureng-Zebe*, Act IV: 'When I consider Life, 'tis all a
Cheat: | Yet, fool'd with hope, Men favour the Deceit. . . .'

(110)   *Song*

MSS. *M*, 78 (D). (*L 28*, 74, contains the printed sheet from *1722*.)
Pub. *Gentleman's Journal*, June 1692, p. 13, and Nov. 1692, p. 26 (with
     setting); *A Second Booke of Songs*, 1695? (Day & Murrie, 135), p. 8;
     Miscellany Poems, 1702 (Case 172–1–d), p. 258; *Oxford and Cambridge
     Miscellany*, 1708 (Case 248), p. 156 (on a cancel, L6, not present in all
     copies).
     Collected: *1716*, p. 17; *1722*, p. 17; *New Collection 1725*, p. 89.
Text. *1692* [June]. Collated: *M*, *1695*.

Motteux printed the words alone in the June 1692 *Gentleman's Journal*; in
the November issue he reprinted them with King's setting. Robert King (fl.
1684–1711) was a member of the private music of Charles II, James, William,
and Anne; he composed settings for a number of Prior's songs. See Ewing,
'Musical Settings'.

(110)   *An Ode* ('While blooming Youth')

MSS. None.
Pub. *Gentleman's Journal*, Aug. 1692, p. 1; *Examen Poeticum*, 1693 (Case 172–3–a), p. 433; *P.O.A.S.* iii, 1698 (Case 215), p. 127.
      Collected: *1707*, p. 114; *1709*, p. 10; *1718*, p. 9.
Text. *1718*. Collated: *1692, 1693, 1709*.

Motteux, introducing the poem in the *Gentleman's Journal* for Aug. 1692, says that it was written 'long before' *An Ode in Imitation of Horace*, which had recently been published by Tonson.

(112)   *An Ode in Imitation of Horace*

MSS. L 29, 17 (D & P). (*L 28, 75*, contains the printed sheets from *1722*.)
Pub. [Title as in text.] . . . By Mr. Prior. London, Printed for Jacob Tonson at the Judges-Head in Chancery-Lane near Fleetstreet. 1692; *Poems and Translations*, 1714 (Case 277), p. 225; *Odes and Satires of Horace*, 1715 (Case 287–d), p. 40.
      Collected: *1716*, p. 18; *1722*, p. 18; *New Collection 1725*, p. 45.
Text. *L 29*. Collated: *1692*.

The text in *L 29* appears to be the second stage of a thorough revision that Prior made probably with the intention of publishing the ode in either *1709* or *1718*. It consists of Drift's transcript of an extensive revision of *1692* and P's further alterations in his own hand.

The ode was written after the naval victory at La Hogue, 24 May 1692 (see ll. 51–56 and note) and published by August. Motteux, in the *Gentleman's Journal* for Aug. 1692 (p. 1), says that P 'wrote an Ode lately, published by Mr. *Tonson*, which, tho his extream Modesty makes him call it an Imitation of the 2d Ode of *Horace*'s 3d book, may justly be stiled an Original deserving the Admiration of the greatest Judges'. *L 29* and *1692* quote in footnotes the parallel passages from Horace that we cite below.

Curll, in his *1722 Memoirs*, said that P omitted the ode from his collections 'because he declared to have made some Use of that Piece in the Composing his *Carmen Saeculare*. Tho' it is rather to be presumed, this Omission was obtained by the persuasion of some Political-Friends, who thought the Revival of this ODE a Panegyrick too High for (a Prince above all Panegyrick) the late Immortal King WILLIAM of *Glorious Memory*.' Curll's insinuation is unwarranted: P collected other panegyrics on William at least as fulsome as this one. While there is no verbal duplication of this poem in *Carmen Seculare* (1699), P might justifiably have felt that the two poems were too similar for both to be preserved.

1. Horace, ll. 1–4.

9–11. William had gone to the continent on 6 March 1692, leaving Mary as vicegerent.

25. Horace, ll. 5–6.

35. Horace, ll. 25–26.

51–56. At the end of the naval battle of La Hogue, 19–24 May 1692, the English burned the French ships in their own harbour.

64. *Russel.* Edward Russell, Earl of Orford, commander of the English fleet in the victory of La Hogue.

68. Horace, ll. 6–12.

70–71. When William was slightly wounded by a cannon-ball at the Boyne, the report circulated in France that he had been killed; '. . . and, upon it, there were more public rejoicings than had been usual upon their greatest victories: which gave that court afterwards a vast confusion, when they knew that he was still alive; and saw that they had raised, in their own people, a high opinion of him, by this inhuman joy, when they believed him dead' (G. Burnet, *History of His Own Time*, 1818, iii. 55).

93. Horace, ll. 13–16.

123. *L 29* has the following note: 'Ils marchent droit au fleuve, où *Loüis* en Personne | Déja prest a passer, Instruit, Dispose, ordonne. &ca: Boileau Epis: 4th:'. These are lines 97–98 from Boileau's *Épître IV, Au Roi. Le Passage du Rhin* (1672).

130. Horace, ll. 17–20.

165. Cf. *On the Coronation* (1685), l. 57.

170. *L 29* has the note, 'Louis les animant du feu de Son Courage, | Se plaint de Sa Grandeur qui l'attache au rivage. Boileau 4 Ep:'. These are Boileau's ll. 113–14.

212. Horace, ll. 21–24.

241. Horace, ll. 29–32.

1693

(123)   *Considerations*

MSS. *L 27*, 63 (D); *M*, 3 (D).
Pub.   *Examen Poeticum*, 1693 (Case 172–3–a), p. 305 (on a cancel, X2, not present in all copies); *Miscellanea Sacra*, 1705 (Case 236–1–a), p. 5. Collected: *1740*, p. 15.
Text. *M*. Collated: *L 27*, *1693*, *1740*.

The text we print, from *M* (which agrees generally with *L 27* and *1740*), seems to be an authorial revision of that published in *1693*. The subtitle, 'A College Exercise, 1690', is found only in *1740*, and is without authority.

(Several titles in *1740* are erroneous: see commentaries on *On the Taking of Huy*, 1694, and *To a Child of Quality*, 1700.)

Examen Poeticum was published in July 1693 (*Gentleman's Journal*, July 1693, p. 239). P's poem was frequently reprinted in collections of religious verse; see *The Christian's Magazine*, vii (1766), 275, and citations in *N. & Q.*, 3rd ser., xii (1867), 347.

(124)   *Enigma*

MSS.   *L 28*, 174 (D). (Index to *M*.)
Pub.   *Gentleman's Journal*, Aug. 1693, p. 271; *Miscellany Poems*, 1702 (Case
           172–1–d), p. 259.
           Collected: *1740*, p. 112.
Text. *1693*. Collated: *L 28, 1740*.

Motteux gave the solution in the next issue of the *Gentleman's Journal* (Sept. 1693, p. 310): 'The *Enigma* by Mr. *Prior* in my last is the Knave of Clubs, or *Pam* at Lantrelu.' See note to *A Session of the Poets* (1688), ll. 1–8.

(124)   *An Epitaph on True*

MSS.   *Lpo 18*, 164 (X); *B.M. Harl. 7316*, 12ᵛ (X; misc. owned and anno-
           tated by Edward Lord Harley).
Pub.   *Gentleman's Journal*, Oct. 1693, p. 326.
           Collected: *Evans 1779*, ii. 226.
Text. *1693*. Collated: *Lpo 18, Harl.*

The Oct. 1693 issue of the *Gentleman's Journal* was called *The Lady's Journal* and was supposed to consist of 'Pieces written by Persons of the Fair Sex'. Motteux opened it with this poem, commenting: 'I cannot begin better than with the following Lines infinitely esteemable, for their Loyalty and their Wit.' The attribution, 'Written by a Young Lady of Quality', must represent a joke played either by or on Motteux, for there seems to be no doubt of Prior's authorship. Both manuscripts attribute the poem to him.

(125)   *Hymn to the Sun*

MSS.   None.
Pub.   *For the New Year: To the Sun. Intended To be Sung before Their Majesties
           on New-Years Day. 1693/4*. Written by Mr. Prior at the Hague. London,
           Printed for J. Tonson, at the Judges-Head near the Inner-Temple-Gate
           in Fleet-street. 1694; *The Annual Miscellany*, 1694 (Case 172–4–a),
           p. 287.
           Collected: *1707*, p. 123; *1709*, p. 39; *1718*, p. 26.
Text. *1718*. Collated: *1694* [Tonson], *1709*.

Only two copies of the original publication are known to exist: Wise's copy, now in the B.M., and one in the Bute collection, now in the Harvard University library. The latter has the date of publication written in: 19 Jan. 1693/4.

Since Prior changed the title from 'Intended To be Sung' in the first publication to 'Sung' in *1709* and *1718*, the ode must have been sung at court on 1 Jan. 1694, though we can find no mention of the performance. The setting is not preserved among the works of either Daniel or Henry Purcell.

We have not located the 'second edition', 1707 or 1708, mentioned by Waller (*1905*, p. 344), Wise (*Catalogue*, iv. 70), and G. A. Aitken ('Notes on the Bibliography of Matthew Prior', *Transactions of the Bibliographical Society*, xiv, 1915–17, 44), but not described by them; if it exists, it is probably the same as the version printed by Curll in *1707*, 'here Printed with Alterations; as it was Perform'd lately at a Consort of Musick, by the most Eminent Masters'. The alterations, for which it is extremely unlikely that P was responsible, consist chiefly in substituting regularly the names *Anna* and *Marlbro* for *Mary* and *William*. P made no such changes when he reprinted the poem in his own collections.

The idea of an address to the Sun probably derives from Horace's *Carmen Saeculare*.

1694

(128)   'Spare Dorsett's sacred life'

MSS. *St. John's Col. 409* (P; the original letter); *L 10*, 59 (X).
Pub. Peter Cunningham's edition of Johnson's *Lives* (1854), iii. 425 (from
      St. J); *H.M.C. Bath*, iii (1908), 20 (from *L 10*).
      Collected: *1892*, ii. 302.
Text. *St. J.* Collated: *L 10*.

These verses conclude a letter from Prior to Lord Dorset, dated 'Hague $\frac{14}{4}$ May, 94' (*L 10* gives the date, erroneously, as 30 April). After giving news of public affairs, P says, 'This letter may end like my last, with my prayers for Your Lordship's health and happiness'; the verses follow.

(129)   *To My Lady Dursley*

MSS. *Bodl. Add. B 105*, 82 (X; a late collection).
Pub. *The Annual Miscellany*, 1694 (Case 172–4–a), p. 110.
      Collected: *1709*, p. 24; *1718*, p. 19.
Text. *1718*. Collated: *1694*, *1709*.

Lady Dursley (1655?–1719) was Elizabeth, daughter of Baptist Noel, third

Viscount Campden; she married in 1677 Charles Berkeley (1649–1710), Viscount Dursley, later second Earl of Berkeley. Prior had been secretary to Lord Dursley since 1690. Probably he wrote the poem before Dursley left The Hague in Oct. 1693, but the date can be fixed only as before the *Annual Miscellany* was published in July 1694 (*Gentleman's Journal*, July 1694, p. 207).

In both *1709* and *1718*, P placed the following poem before his own:

To the Countess of Dorset. Written in her Milton. By Mr. Bradbury.

> See here how bright the first-born Virgin shone,
> And how the first fond Lover was undone.
> Such charming Words our beauteous Mother spoke,
> As MILTON wrote, and such as Yours Her Look.
> Yours, the best Copy of th'Original Face,
> Whose Beauty was to furnish all the Race:
> Such Chains no Author cou'd escape but He;
> There's no Way to be safe, but not to See.

This was first published in *A Collection of Poems*, 1701 (Case 151–e), p. 392, without attribution, and with the title, *To a Lady: With Milton's Paradise Lost*. It must have been written before the death of Mary, Countess of Dorset, on 6 Aug. 1691, for Dorset did not marry again until 1704. We have not been able to identify Mr. Bradbury; he may be the Francis Bradbury to whom William Winstanley dedicated his *Lives of the Poets* in 1687.

(129)   'That Heaven and Earth'

MSS.   *L 10*, 82 (X).
Pub.   *H.M.C. Bath*, iii (1908), 31.
       Never collected.
Text.   *L 10*.

The verses conclude a letter, dated at The Hague, 6 Aug./27 July 1694, from Prior to Charles Talbot (1660–1718), Duke of Shrewsbury, who had recently been made Secretary of State for the Northern Department. 'The Pensioner and Secretary of the Admiralty of Rotterdam complained of some abuses on this side from some of our officers. I desired them, if there was any ground for such a complaint, that it might be fairly drawn up, and that I would lay it before Your Lordship, and promised to have all abuses of that kind redressed on our side.' The verses follow.

(130)   *On the Taking of Huy*

MSS.   *M*, 67 (D); *L 29*, 16 (X).
Pub.   *Gentleman's Journal*, Aug.–Sept. 1694, p. 244.
       Collected: *1740*, p. 17.
Text.   *M*. Collated: *L 29, 1694, 1740*.

The text in *M* and *1740* seems to be an authorial revision of that in *1694* and *L 29*.

Huy was taken by the Allies early in Sept. 1694. Motteux introduced the poem in the *Gentleman's Journal* as one of 'two short Pieces, whose Insertion is not to be deferr'd; since they are on some new Events'. Although the victory was not impressive, Huy being a fortress of the third rank, it was the only important success of the year's campaign (Macaulay, p. 2455).

The title and date in *1740* (*On the Taking of Namur, 1692*), and the similar titles in both manuscripts, are erroneous. Namur was taken by the French in 1692, and was not recaptured by William until 1695. Probably the confusion arose because of the similarity of this poem to *An English Ballad* (1695), a similarity which also explains why Prior did not collect these verses.

1. Huy had opened its gates to the French in July 1693, without a battle. In the preceding month, Louis had retired from active direction of the campaign, and never afterwards made war in person (Macaulay, p. 2352).

1695

(130)   *An Ode. Presented to the King, 1695*

MSS. None.

Pub. *To the King, An Ode on His Majesty's Arrival in Holland, 1695.* By Mr. Prior. London, Printed for Jacob Tonson at the Judge's-Head near the Inner-Temple-Gate in Fleetstreet. 1695.

Collected: *1709*, p. 55; *1718*, p. 43.

Text. *1718.* Collated: *1695, 1709.*

Queen Mary died on 28 Dec. 1694, and the funeral was held on 5 March. In a letter to Lord and Lady Lexington (The Hague, 1 March 1695), Prior said: 'I am as yet so afflicted for the death of our dear mistress, that I cannot express it in bad verse, as all the world here does; all that I have done was to-day on Scheveling Sands, with the point of my sword:—

> Number the sands extended here;
> So many Mary's virtues were:
> Number the drops that yonder roll;
> So many griefs press William's soul.'

(*B.M. Add. 46539*, Lexington Papers, vol. xv, letter No. 10; published in *The Lexington Papers*, ed. H. Manners Sutton, 1851, p. 63). In a letter to Lord Dorset of 8/18 March, he wrote: 'We have had nothing new here for some months but volumes of bad poetry upon a blessed Queen. I have not put my mite into this treasury of nonsense, having been too truly afflicted by the subject to say anything upon it . . .' (*H.M.C. Bath*, iii. 49). P must have written his poem not long after this, however, for George Stepney had received a copy of it by 19/29 March (letter quoted in Eves, p. 95). He was expected to produce a poem, and could hardly refuse to do so; James Vernon, acknowledging receipt of the medal P designed for the occasion, said: 'if you think this will acquit you from the expectations people have of a poem from you, you will be mistaken, for they say you are not to come off with a posey and a shred of Horace; and they further desire, if you write anything in memory of the Queen, that you will take a little more notice of her than you do in your stamp . . .' (19/29 April; *H.M.C. Bath*, iii. 50). P wrote to Sir William Trumbull on 16/26 April: 'I have two summons from Tonson in your name commanding me upon receipt thereof to make my appearance at Parnassus, and answer for a sin of omission with which you are pleased to charge me. . . . Sir, I yield the question, and have a poem on the stocks to be given to his Majesty at his arrival here, which I will send to Mr. Tonson to be reprinted in England, and since that cur instigated the writing of it, I hope it may lie unsold, and contribute to the breaking of him' (*H.M.C. Downshire*, i. 465).

King William left for the Continent on 12 May; P, sending his poem to Lord Lexington on 17/27 May, remarked that he had 'given [it] to everybody but the King' (*Lexington Papers*, p. 88), implying apparently that he was not able actually to present the poem to the king on his arrival in Holland. Tonson published it by 27 May (adv. *London Gazette*, 23–27 May); if it was printed earlier in Holland, as P had intended, the Dutch edition has not survived. A Dutch translation, however, is extant: *Gezand aan den Koning, op zyn' Maj. aankomste in Holland, in den Jaare 1695*, Door Mr. PRIOR . . . Uyt het Engelsch in Nederl. Rym gebragt door W. Sewell. t'Amsterdam, ed. A. D. Oessaan, 1695.

P had severely criticized George Stepney's poem on this occasion, and Stepney, in a letter of 2/12 April 1695, retaliated by dissecting P's ode in great detail:

> For 1st you have chose Measures which are neither proper for Heroick nor Elegy. . . .
> 2ly. Throughout the whole Piece I see no design, allegory, or pretty Poeticall fiction or History to enliven the Composition: You have thrown away all yr Classick Learning, and have not imitated any Roman Poet. 3ly yr Stanza's are often as incohaerent as the Proverbs; and if you wou'd be at the pains to put them into Prose (which will not be very difficult) you must own they are inconsistent with one another, and without any drift or Method.

Stepney concludes: 'No, Mat, if I spoyld my Poem by writing too fast; you have spoild yours by dreaming too long. . . . Your Motto seems to me to be the best of the Piece: If I was in your Place, I'de print it alone, and leave out the Poem. . . .' The letter (*P.R.O., S.P. 105/55*) is printed in full by H. T. Swedenberg, Jr., 'George Stepney, My Lord Dorset's Boy', *Huntington Library Quarterly*, x (1946–7), 25–26.

[Motto.] Horace, *Odes*, I. xxiv. 1–3.

85. P wrote to Lord and Lady Lexington on 14/24 Jan.: '. . . 'tis impossible for me to tell you the sorrow that reigns universally in Holland: these people, who never had any passions before, are now touched, and marble weeps' (*Lexington Papers*, p. 47).

107. MAURICE and HENRY. Sons of William I of Orange: Maurice (1567–1625) and Frederick Henry (1584–1647).

110. Father. William II (1626–50) of Orange, son of Frederick Henry.

(139)   *An English Ballad*

MSS.   None.
Pub.   *An English Ballad: In Answer to Mr. Despreaux's Pindarique Ode on the Taking of Namure.* London, Printed for Jacob Tonson, at the Judge's Head near the Inner Temple Gate in Fleetstreet, MDCXCV.
       Collected: *1709*, p. 67; *1718*, p. 53.
Text. *1718*. Collated: *1695*, *1709*.

The *1740 History* gives the background of the poem:

The *French* King had taken *Namur* in the Campaign of 92, in Sight of the Army of the Allies, who were unable to raise the Siege. This was extolled by the Flatterers of that Prince, as a most inimitable Action; and the celebrated *Boileau* . . . had composed an Ode on this Occasion in Imitation of *Pindar*, wherein he pretended to assert the Character of that Antient against the Reflections of *Perrault*, at the same Time that he exalted his Hero above all the Heroes of *Greece*. Mr. PRIOR took this Occasion of turning the *Frenchman*'s darling Ridicule both on himself and his Master, by burlesquing his boasted Ode. . . . In a Word, he convinced all polite Readers . . . that the *English* HORACE was as much a more agreeable Writer than the *French* PINDAR, as he had made *Little Will, the Scourge of France,* a more amiable Hero than the divine LOUIS *le Grand.* (pp. 17–18)

William's recapture of Namur in Aug. 1695 marked the turning-point in the long struggle against France. On 13/23 Sept., Prior sent his poem to Tonson with a long letter in which he gave directions for printing Boileau's *Ode* on facing pages, suggested that Charles Montagu and Fleetwood Shepherd be consulted for possible improvements, and insisted on anonymity: 'A Secretary at thirty is hardly allowed the privilege of Burlesque' (the letter is printed in Eves, p. 97, and elsewhere; the original is now in the Yale library). Sir William Trumbull wrote on 17/27 Sept.: 'Care will be taken here of the poetry, and that it do not suffer in the printing, as it is pity it should. I see no reason why the author should be ashamed of battering B[oileau]'s poem, and reducing it, any more than we the Castle, since it is our honour that everything that concerns Namur be on our side. However, I have enjoyned T[onson] silence, as is desired, though it is not possible to keep it long a secret. I will add but one circumstance to that purpose, which is, that Fleet Shephard knows it'

(*H.M.C. Bath*, iii. 64). Tonson published the poem on 30 Sept. 1695 (adv. *London Gazette*, 26–30 Sept.).

[Motto.] Horace, *Odes*, IV. xii. 28.

4. Virgin of St. CYR. Mme de Maintenon established a school for young gentlewomen at St. Cyr, near Versailles, in 1687. She later made it into a convent.

22. MEGRIGNY and VAUBAN. The French engineers who were responsible for the fortifications.

29. Namur lies at the confluence of the Sambre and the Meuse.

54–56. Villeroy shelled Brussels in the hope of inducing the Allies to raise the siege of Namur; this caused much devastation in the defenceless city.

65–76. After the unsuccessful attempt on Brussels, Villeroy marched to Namur; he there confronted William's army for three days, and withdrew without fighting.

109. BOUFFLERS. Commander of the fortress or castle of Namur.

159–60. GUISCARD. Commander of the town of Namur, and second-in-command to Boufflers. After the surrender, Boufflers was detained until Louis promised to release the garrisons of Dixmuyde and Deynse, whom Villeroy had imprisoned in violation of the agreement for exchange of prisoners.

168. TOURVILLE. The French admiral defeated by Russell at La Hogue, 1692.

169. Upon his return to court, on 21 Sept., Boufflers was made a duke and awarded a grant of money.

(152)   *To My Lord Buckhurst*

MSS. None.
Pub.   *Poetical Miscellanies: The Fifth Part*, 1704 (Case 172-5-a), p. 218.
          Collected: *1709*, p. 25; *1718*, p. 20.
Text. *1718*. Collated: *1704*, *1709*.

The poem is said to have been inspired by a painting at Knole called 'Charles Sackville as a Youth', by an unknown artist. 'Charles is represented sitting down with the head of an enormous cat on his lap, the cat's hind feet being on the ground' (C. J. Phillips, *History of the Sackville Family*, 1930, i. 443). The 'Lord Buckhurst' addressed in the verses is, of course, not the one represented in the picture, but his son, Lionel, born in 1687 (see commentary on *To the E of D.*, 1687).

Although there is no way of dating the poem precisely, it is safe to assume that it must have been written some time before the following Prologue for young Buckhurst.

(153)   *A Prologue made for Lord Buckhurst*

MSS. *M*, 58 (D).
Pub. *1740*, p. 18.
Text. *M*. Collated: *1740*.

Dorset, as Lord Chamberlain, had prohibited Dryden's *Cleomenes* on 9 April 1692, because Queen Mary suspected it might contain Jacobite propaganda; the play was, however, quickly approved, and was acted a week later, on 16 April (Macdonald, p. 133). Harris (*Dorset*, p. 129) suggests that the 1695 performance may have been in honour of Dryden (who was, like Prior, an alumnus of Westminster) and comments that the audience 'must have found it amusing to hear the chamberlain's son blandly introducing a play which his father had suspended three years before because it impugned the government . . .'.

P used some passages from this prologue, which he never published, in his *Prologue to The Orphan*, 1720.

1696

(154)   *Presented to the King, 1696*

MSS. None.
Pub. *Verses Humbly presented to the King At His Arrival in Holland, After the Discovery Of the late horrid Conspiracy Against His most Sacred Person.* By Mr. Prior. London, Printed for Jacob Tonson, at the Judge's Head, near the Inner-Temple-Gate in Fleetstreet, 1696; Another issue: title as above, but without imprint.
        Collected: *1709*, p. 95; *1718*, p. 66.
Text. *1718*. Collated: *1696, N.D., 1709*.

The Assassination Plot to murder King William and effect a Jacobite restoration with the help of a French invasion was disclosed to the public on 23 Feb. 1696. Prior wrote to the Earl of Portland on 3/13 March expressing his joy at 'the great miracle God in His mercy has wrought amongst us in preserving His Majesty's person from a conspiracy that no history or age can equal' (*H.M.C. Bath*, iii. 73).

King William arrived in Holland on 7 May. P's poem was published in England by 21 May (adv. *London Gazette*, 18–21 May). The issue without imprint (B.M. shelf mark 11632.h.36) which we collate as *N.D.* may possibly have been printed in Holland for the actual presentation, or it may be a piracy of the Tonson issue. Sir Harold Williams kindly brought to our attention a bookseller's catalogue (Catalogue 92, 1943, of P. H. Muir [now Elkin Mathews Ltd.], Takeley, Bishop's Stortford, Herts.) in which an issue without imprint is described which 'appears to be a special edition printed in Holland for actual presentation to the King by Prior himself' (item 383). We have not been able to locate this copy, but it seems likely that it is identical with that in the B.M.

[Motto.] Horace, *Odes*, I. ii. 45–49.
1. Angels. P's use of this theme may have been inspired by Dryden's suggestion, in his *Discourse concerning the Original and Progress of Satire*, 1693, that guardian angels would make good machines for heroic poetry (*Essays*, ed. W. P. Ker, Oxford, 1900, ii. 34–37).
25–26. 1 Sam. xviii–xix.
28–30. See note to *An Ode in Imitation of Horace* (1692), ll. 70–71.

(157)   *In a Window*

MSS. *L 28*, 171 (D).
Pub. *1907*, p. 337.
Text. *L 28*.

Edward Villiers (1656–1711), Viscount Villiers from 1691 and first Earl of Jersey from 1697, was an alumnus of St. John's, and his cousin, Col. George Villiers, had married Prior's cousin Katharine. He arrived at The Hague as Plenipotentiary in Sept. 1695, and became very friendly with P.

2. Ratcliff. Dr. John Radcliffe (1650–1714), famous physician.

(158)   *Written in the Year 1696*

MSS. *W*, 22 (D & P); *L 28*, 137c (D; emend. by Pope). (Index to *M*.)
Pub. *1740*, p. 21.
Text. *W*. Collated: *L 28, 1740*.

The title, *The Secretary*, by which this poem has been commonly known, was first given to it in *1742* and is without authority.

13–14. When Peisistratus returned to Athens with Phya, a beautiful woman disguised as Athena, proclamations were made that the goddess herself was restoring the tyrant to power.

1697

(159)   *'Who would, says Dryden'*

MSS. *L 10*, 435 (X).
Pub.   *H.M.C. Bath*, iii (1908), 185.
      Never collected.
Text. *L 10*.

The verses occur in a letter to Charles, second Viscount Townshend (1674–1738), dated The Hague, 5 Nov. 1697. 'What a cursed thing, my Lord, is this! a secretary to be writing till midnight without having time to say one word to those whom he respects most or loves best. No matter; I shall see you within this fortnight, and in that thought adieu all the melancholy reflections that can be inspired by a huge bundle of papers without any method, or an ambassador without anything but method!' After the verses, he comments: 'I bronche, i'faith, and can no more rise in poetry than B. . . in prose. I hope the *Hoop* in Fish Street will give me some spirits, and cure an ill habit of mind contracted by a thick air of conversation. . . .'

Prior had been given the honour of bringing the official news of the Treaty of Ryswick to England, arriving at Whitehall on 24 Sept. and returning to Holland on the 28th. He returned to England again in William's train on 8 Nov., and remained there until the following January, when he left for Paris as secretary to Portland's embassy.

The allusion to Dryden seems to be to the last paragraph of the *Translation of the Latter Part of the Third Book of Lucretius* (*Sylvae*, 1685, p. 78), beginning:

> Why are we then so fond of mortal Life,
> Beset with dangers and maintain'd with strife?

(159)   *A New Answer*

MSS. *L 28*, 131 (D); *M*, 64 (D).
Pub.   [Title as in text.] London: Printed in the Year 1697; Another issue, without imprint; *P.O.A.S.* iii, 1704 (Case 211-3-a), p. 378; *New Collection*, 1705 (Case 237), p. 535.
      Collected: *1907*, p. 317.
Text. *1697*. Collated: *L 28*, *M*, *N.D.*, *1704*.

The broadsides are rare: the copy at Welbeck of the issue with imprint seems to be unique, and the issue without imprint (which may have been a piracy) is to be found only in Wise's collection, now in the B.M., and at

Harvard. We are obliged to Mr. F. R. D. Needham for providing us with a transcript of the Welbeck copy to use as our text.

As soon as the Peace of Ryswick was signed, there was a popular outcry for the immediate disbandment of the army. When Prior returned to England in November, the question of the disposition of the army was being urgently debated, in preparation for the meeting of Parliament on 3 Dec. The chief pamphlets were John Trenchard's *An Argument, Shewing, that a Standing Army Is inconsistent with A Free Government, and absolutely destructive to the Constitution of the English Monarchy*, and the reply by John, Lord Somers, commonly called the 'Balancing Letter' (both 1697). Trenchard and the malcontent Whigs argued from history that a standing army and a free constitution could not exist together, and that the fleet and the militia were sufficient protection, without a professional army. Somers and the ministerial Whigs replied that history showed that professional soldiers would always beat amateurs, and that it was necessary to balance one danger against another; Louis, being an absolute monarch, would give the English no time to form an army if he declared war. 'To trust to our fleet was to trust to the winds and the waves. The breeze which was favourable to the invader might prevent our men of war from standing out to sea. Only nine years ago this had actually happened' (Macaulay, p. 2739). Parliament voted on 10 Dec., however, to reduce the army from 87,000 to 10,000, its size in 1680.

P's ballad is an answer to Trenchard's pamphlet, along the same lines as the replies of Somers and the other ministerial Whigs. His correspondence (*H.M.C. Bath*, iii. 186–90) indicates that he had no confidence in Louis's pacific intentions. The poem was written in late November or early December, probably before the parliamentary decision on 10 Dec. The stanza-form and refrain had been used in earlier political ballads, for example, in *The Advice* (*The Muses Farewel*, 1689, Case 191–1–a, p. 13), urging King James to change his policies, and in *The Lord Chancellor's Speech to the Parliament* (*P.O.A.S.* iii, 1704, p. 116), written toward the end of Charles II's reign.

    11. A new parliament was to be elected in the summer of 1698.

(160)   *Upon this passage in Scaligerana*

MSS. *M*, 90 (D); *L 27*, 73 (D).
Pub.   *1740*, p. 60.
Text. *M*. Collated: *L 27, 1740*.

Presumably written during Prior's residence at The Hague. The passage quoted may be found on p. 14 of *Scaligerana ou Bons Mots, Rencontres Agreables, et Remarques Judicieuses & Sçavantes de J. Scaliger*. Avec des Notes de Mr. Le Fevre, & de Mr. de Colomies. Le tout disposé par ordre Alphabetique en cette Nouvelle Edition. A Cologne. Chez ***. M.DC.XCV.

1699

(161)   *Carmen Seculare*

MSS.   *Wm*, 12ᵛ–16, 88ᵛ–89 (P; the following lines only: 1–2, 190–3, 268–9,
       329–30, 338–43, 346–7, 458–9, 511, 542–7).
Pub.   [Title as in text.] London, Printed for Jacob Tonson, at Grays-Inn-
       Gate in Grays-Inn-Lane, 1700; *Carmen Sæculare To the King* . . . London:
       Printed for Jacob Tonson, within Grays-Inn-Gate in Grays-Inn-Lane,
       1701 [facing this is a Latin title-page: *Carmen Sæculare Serenissimo Prin-
       cipi Gulielmo III° Inscriptum* . . . Impensis Jacobi Tonson, 1701].
       Collected: *1709*, p. 138; *1718*, p. 133.
Text. *1718*. Collated: *Wm, 1700, 1701, 1709*.

   Published on New Year's Day, 1700 (adv. *Flying Post*, 2–4 Jan.). The
London Post for 3–5 Jan. says that the king 'designs to be to Morrow at St.
James, where is to be a great Ball upon account of her Royal Highness's
Birth-day, and the ode which was made for the new Year, will be there sung
before His Majesty'. The Latin translation by Thomas Dibben was much
admired, and was included by Prior in *1709* and *1718*. P made a few revisions
in the English text published with it in 1701, adopting one suggestion made
by J. Talbot in a letter (*H.M.C. Bath*, iii. 426–9). A piracy of *1700* was
published in Dublin by John Brocas, 1700.
   P takes from Horace's *Carmen Sæculare* little more than the title and general
theme.

   [Motto.] Virgil, *Eclogues*, iv. 52–54.
   32. Son of MARS. Romulus, founder of Rome. Cf. *Aeneid*, vi. 777–853.
   72. PHARAMOND. Legendary first King of France.
   88. DIDIER . . . ADOLPH. Sons of Walram II, founder of the elder line of
Nassau: Diether, Archbishop of Trèves (1300); Adolph, Emperor of Ger-
many (1292–8).
   93–94. CORNET. William, le Cornet, first Prince of Orange (eighth century). BEAU. Bertrand de Baux obtained the principality of Orange through
marriage in 1174, and was followed by nine princes of his line. CHALON.
John of Châlons became prince in 1393 through marriage. NASSAW. Phili-
bert, last of the Châlons line, was succeeded by René of Nassau-Châlons, and
he by William of Orange-Nassau in 1544.
   108. Name. 'MARY' (P's note).
   127–8. Cf. *Aeneid*, vi. 851–3.
   272. MUSCOVITE. Peter the Great. See P's Latin poem, *In adventum Cæsaris
Mosci in Angliam*, 1698.

280–3. P's version of the much-imitated lines from Denham's *Cooper's Hill*:

> O could I flow like thee, and make my stream
> My great example, as it is my theme!
> Though deep, yet clear, though gentle, yet not dull,
> Strong without rage, without ore-flowing full. (ll. 189–92)

For an account of the other imitations, see T. H. Banks's edition of Denham, pp. 342–50.

300. CHROMIUS. Victor in the chariot-race in the Nemean games, celebrated in Pindar's first Nemean Ode. THERON. Victor in the chariot-race in the Olympic games, celebrated in Pindar's second Olympic Ode. These are the only odes of Pindar translated by Cowley.

361. 'Whitehall, once belonging to the Archbishop of York. It was taken from Cardinal Wolsey by Henry the 8th, who made great improvements therein, and converted it into a royal palace. In 1698 the whole of it, except the Banqueting House, was destroyed by fire, and hath not since been re-built' (*Evans 1779*).

386. ORMOND. See commentary on *Seeing the Duke of Ormond's Picture* (1708).

397. DORSET. Dorset, P's first patron, was made K.G. in 1692 and held several posts of honour and responsibility during William's reign. See P's *Dedication* (1708).

406. CA'NDISH. See note to *The Orange* (1688), l. 53.

410. TALBOT. See commentaries on '*That Heaven and Earth*' (1694), *Written in Montaigne's Essays* (1713). SEYMOUR. Charles Seymour, sixth Duke of Somerset (1662–1748), like all the others mentioned, fought for William at the Revolution.

416. JERSEY. Edward Villiers, first Earl of Jersey, at this time Secretary of State for the Southern Department and one of the Lords Justices. See commentary on *In a Window*, 1696. There seems to be no record of Jersey's receiving the Garter (l. 421).

442–3. The Royal Society, to which P had been elected in 1698 (*H.M.C. Bath*, iii. 294).

444–5. The Society for the Reformation of Manners, founded in 696. In a manuscript fragment, P comments interestingly on Jeremy Collier's *Short View*, 1698:

Collier is not so much in the wrong: our plays are too licentious, and the poets affront the town when they Say that they write bawdy because nothing else takes: they may as well say that we like no musick but a Jigg, or that no pictures sell but Aretines postures: let them work up passion with grace and art and We shall be pleased with it: we liked the Mourning Bride thô Alphonso neither cursed like a swine or couched like a god thrô out the whole piece: and there will always be found so good Sence in the Nation that Some famous for having it will like what is truly good and the rest will not dare to contradict it at first, and form their gout Til afterwards: The French would not endure to hear a conquerour and a Princesse speak bawdy, and Yet that nation is as lewd as we can be for the hearts of Us, not from a dislike of the thing but from its being unnatural that such people talk so: our Imagination is so vitiated by such representations that in time it will be impossible for any thing fine to move them, we shall grow Moscovites putt pepper in our brandy; old lechers, be flogged in stead of being tickled.

But Collier makes too much work with his Character, for thô the thing be true that Divines should be abused he should only have touch't upon it lightly, and returned the ridicule where [it] is violently in earnest: and that the more because being a Clergy-man himself the Elogies he gives the Clergy are so many panegyricks upon himself, and one is not so much struck with the truths he evinces, that the Clergye have been always respected whilst one reflects that it is upon a principle of Interest that he proves they ought still to be so. . . . (*Wm*, 135ᵛ–7)

446–7. Roscommon and Dryden had desiderated an English academy, and Swift and others later revived the project. See Johnson's *Lives*, i. 232; ii. 185.

466. bright Effluence. Cf. *Paradise Lost*, iii. 6.

472–3. More than two-fifths of English exports consisted of cloth woven in England, and in 1700 £3,000,000 worth of woollen goods was exported. The wool industry was the most important source of wealth in England.

510–11. Cf. Dryden's *Alexander's Feast* (1697), ll. 33, 35.

1700

(181)   *A Fable*

MSS.   L *27*, 71 (D); L *28*, 130 (D; emend. by Pope); *M*, 63 (A); *B.M. Stowe 222*, 124 (X); *Lpo 11*, 23 (X); *U. Nott. Portland 1661*, iii. 384 (X).

Pub.   *P.O.A.S.* ii, 1703 (Case 211–2–a), p. 241; *New Collection*, 1705 (Case 237), p. 381; *Deliciae Poeticae*, 1706 (Case 240), p. 150.
        Collected: *1907*, p. 316.

Text.   *1703*. Collated: L *27*, L *28*, M, Stowe, Lpo.

First attributed to Prior by Malone, who noted that it is ascribed to Lord Jeffries in *1703*, but had been found in P's handwriting 'among his unpublished MSS., formerly in the library of the Duchess Dowager of Portland' (*Prose Works of Dryden*, 1800, I. i. 370). Sir Harold Williams (Swift, *Poems*, p. 1071) describes a manuscript of the poem transcribed into a copy of *Harward's Almanack* for 1666 in a hand attributed to Swift, and concludes that there is no basis for ascribing the poem to Swift. There is no doubt of P's authorship: the manuscript evidence is extensive, and the copy in *Stowe*, which belonged to Robethon, private secretary to King William, is endorsed on the back in Robethon's hand, 'Esops-tale, 1701, par le Sr. Prior' (*N. & Q.*, 8th ser., iv. 67; 22 July 1893). Furthermore, the theme of the *Fable* is closely paralleled in P's letters and other poems of the time. P frequently expressed his conviction that the king should be exalted above party, and should exercise his power to the full to diminish faction (*H.M.C. Bath*, iii. 318–26 and Introduction, p. xii; *1740 History*, pp. 143–85).

Although the poem cannot be dated precisely, it refers to the struggle over the Resumption Bill, which reached a climax in April 1700, and this date seems most likely.

The fable appears in Phaedrus (II. ii) and La Fontaine (I. xvii), as well as in Aesop.

(182) *Ballad*

MSS. *W*, 30 (P); *L 28*, 133 (D); *M*, 74 (A).
Pub. *1907*, p. 319.
Text. *W*. Collated: *L 28*, *M*.

The ballad is closely related in subject and theme to *A Fable*, and was written at about the same time, probably soon after the passage of the Resumption Bill by the Commons (2 April) and the Lords (11 April 1700).

3. Moses law. Lev. xvi.

6. Harlay and Mountagu. Robert Harley (later Earl of Oxford, and Prior's patron) was an anti-ministerial Whig; he had recently succeeded Charles Montagu as leader of the Commons. Both supported the Resumption Bill.

9–12. Gen. ix. 21–27.

14. Summers. John, Lord Somers (1651–1716), Lord Chancellor. See *On some Votes against the Lord S.*, Works of Doubtful Authenticity, 1700.

16. Ormond. See commentary on *Seeing the Duke of Ormond's Picture* (1708). The Resumption Bill contained a clause forgiving him all his debts to the Crown.

(183) *A Song*

MSS. None.
Pub. *Mercurius Musicus*, March–April 1700 (Day & Murrie, 186), p. 20; *Poetical Miscellanies: The Fifth Part*, 1704 (Case 172–5–a), p. 220; *The Virgin Muse*, 1717 (Case 304), p. 70.
Collected: *1709*, p. 28; *1718*, p. 22.
Text. *1718*. Collated: *1700*, *1709*.

The song was popular, and numerous later settings are preserved; see Ewing, 'Musical Settings'.

(184) *'This Man he took'*

MSS. *L 12*, 438 (D).
Pub. No publication known.
Text. *L 12*.

This epigram occurs in a letter from Prior to Jersey dated London, 17 Sept.

[1700], and is thus introduced: 'John is Still in the Country with his Lady, to his great Satisfaction he hopes her Father will Leave her All in Consideration of the many Children she may have. I must apply the Man in Chaucer to John and so conclude.' P had begun the story in a letter to Jersey on 30 Aug. 1700: 'John Swinford and his Monument are gone into Buckingham Shire to see her Father' (*L 12*, 419). Swinford (or Schweinfurt; the name is spelled variously) was a secretary in the diplomatic service who had been closely associated with P and Jersey since 1694 (*H.M.C. Bath*, iii. 21, 38).

It is not clear what passage in Chaucer P has in mind; perhaps the Wife of Bath's treatment of her rich and elderly husbands: 'I laughe whan I thynke | How pitously a-nyght I made hem swynke!' (*W.B. Prol.*, ll. 201–2).

(184)   *Hans Carvel*

MSS.   *B.M. Harl. 7315*, 298b (X); *U. Nott. Portland 1653*, 290 (X); *U. Nott. Portland 1661*, iii. 360 (X).

Pub.   *A Collection of Poems*, 1701 (Case 151–e), p. 445; *Poetical Miscellanies: The Fifth Part*, 1704 (Case 172–5–a), p. 221.

Collected: *1707*, p. 32; *1709*, p. 108; *1718*, p. 105.

Text.   *1718*. Collated: *Harl.*, *1701*, *1704*, *1709*.

Prior sent *Hans Carvel* to Lord Godolphin in Nov. 1700 (*L 12*, 465). Tooke entered the poem in the Stationers' Register on 17 Feb. 1701, as part of the contents of *A Collection of Poems*. Tonson entered it on 26 March, but evidently decided not to publish it separately.

As the title in *1709* and earlier printings indicated, P's tale is based on La Fontaine's *L'Anneau d'Hans Carvel* (*Contes*, II. xii); it is, however, a very free imitation, greatly expanded. La Fontaine took it from Rabelais (*Pantagruel*, III. xxviii), and Rabelais from Poggio (the 133rd of his facetiae, *Visio Francisci Philelphi*). It appears also as the 11th of *Cent Nouvelles Nouvelles*, at the end of Ariosto's fifth *Satire*, and the 89th of Malespini's *Ducento Novelle*, Part II. (This genealogy is first given in *Menagiana*, 3rd ed., 1715, i. 369.) There is, however, nothing to suggest that P had in mind any version other than La Fontaine's.

The title in *Harl.* adds 'Adapted to the E. of Ranelagh 1700'. Richard Jones, first Earl of Ranelagh (1636–1712), married a second wife (Margaret, daughter of James Cecil, third Earl of Salisbury) in 1696. The tale might well be applicable to him, as an old man who had recently married a young wife; but there is nothing to indicate that P had this or any specific couple in mind.

14–20. The tragedy described is Nathaniel Lee's *The Rival Queens, or the Death of Alexander the Great* (1677), which deals with the jealousy of Alexander's first wife, Roxana, for his second, Statira. Betterton, by this time an old man (b. 1635?), played Alexander. The tragedy remained popular well into the eighteenth century.

55. CLEOPATRA. A romance by La Calprenède (1614–63).

56. SCOT. John Scott (1639–95), author of *The Christian Life, from its Beginning to its Consummation in Glory . . . With Directions for Private Devotion and Forms of Prayer Fitted to the Several States of Christians*, 1681.

WAKE. William Wake (1657–1737), at this time Rector of St. James's, Westminster, and later Archbishop of Canterbury; author of numerous theological works.

127–8. An ironic allusion to the closing lines of Cowley's version of Catullus, XLV, portraying the happy lovers, Acme and Septimius. Cowley advises the gods to reward illustrious piety 'With such a Husband, such a Wife, | With *Acme*'s and *Septimius*' Life.'

139. The phrase, 'the devil looking over Lincoln', is used of a vitriolic critic or backbiter; it occurs in Heywood's *Proverbs*, 1562. Fuller, in his *Worthies*, says the phrase may allude either to the 'stone picture of the Devil which doth [1661] or lately did overlook Lincoln Colledge' or to a grotesque sculpture at Lincoln Cathedral (the Lincoln Imp). (*Brewer's Dictionary of Phrase and Fable*, revised ed., N.Y., N.D.)

(188) *Written at Paris, 1700*

MSS. None.
Pub. *1718*, p. 124.
Text. *1718*.

[Title.] *Méthode pour Apprendre Facilement la Géographie*, 1678, by Jacques Robbe (1643–1721).

(190) *To a Child of Quality*

MSS. *L 28*, 173 (D); *M*, 60 (A).
Pub. *Poetical Miscellanies: The Fifth Part*, 1704 (Case 172–5–a), p. 212.
       Collected: *1740*, p. 25.
Text. *1704*. Collated: *L 28*, *M*, *1740*.

1740, probably misled by the fact that Prior was 40 in 1704, dated the poem '1704'. Subsequent editions have continued this error.

In *L 28* a marginal note in Drift's hand identifies the Child of Quality as Lady Mary Villiers, daughter of Edward Villiers, first Earl of Jersey. Her date of birth is not known; in 1710 she married Henry Thynne of Longleat, was widowed, and the next year married George Granville, Lord Lansdowne; she died in 1735. P's close association with Jersey began in 1695 (see *In a Window*,

1696), and the poem must have been written after that date and before Oct. 1700, when P wrote to Jersey, 'Lady Mary, you see, writes very well, and is a very good child'; Jersey replied, 'I find you know my weakness, or else you would never have sent me Miss Mary's writing, though I must own it is very pretty for her age' (*H.M.C. Bath*, iii. 422, 425).

1701

(191) .   *Les Estreines*

MSS. None.
Pub.   *Lyric Poems 1741*, p. 16.
          Collected: *1742*, p. 136.
Text. *1741*.

Dated 'New Years day 1700/1'. Concerning *Lyric Poems 1741*, see commentary on '*Strephonetta Why*' (unknown date). The setting is by 'Mr. Smith', for whom see commentary on *Parting with Flavia* (unknown date).

[Title.] Les Étrennes, a New Year's gift.

(191)   *Song. Sett by Mr: Abell*

MSS. *L 28*, 172 (D); *L 27*, 67 (D); *M*, 75 (D).
Pub.   *A Collection of Songs . . . by Mr. John Abell*, 1701 (Day & Murrie, 192).
          Collected: *1740*, p. 59.
Text. *L 28*. Collated: *L 27*, *M*, *1701*, *1740*.

A Collection of Songs was published in May 1701 (adv. *Post Boy*, 22–24 May). John Abell (1650–1724), alto singer and lutanist, enjoyed the favour of Charles II and James II. After 1688 Abell, who was a Catholic, roamed the Continent; Prior mentions him in a letter to Charles Montagu, The Hague, 6 Jan. 1696: 'You will be pleased to let my Lord Godolphin know we do what we can to drive Abell over into England. He is perched at Amsterdam singing with great satisfaction in a city where he owes nothing: his debts at London make him afraid to venture at the kindness his patrons there offer him; and I have a fellow feeling for the poor minstrel . . . ' (*H.M.C. Bath*, iii. 67–68). By 1700 he had, however, returned to England. P's song may well have been written some time before 1701. It was later set to music again by John Travers in *Eighteen Canzonets 1745?*.

(192)   *Ballad*

MSS. *W*, 32 (P); *L 28*, 134 (D).
Pub. *1907*, p. 319.
Text. *W*. Collated: *L 28*.

The manuscript in *W* shows this ballad in process of composition, and is in Prior's hand. Otherwise, one would suspect the authenticity of the poem, for nowhere else does P express such a critical attitude toward King William. As in *A Fable* and *Ballad* (1700) P's criticism is directed mainly at the factions which have reduced William to impotence; the disrespect toward William himself is probably the result of a mood of cynical discouragement when the whole situation seemed hopeless (see the last stanza). In a letter to Jersey a few months before (14 Oct. 1700), P had expressed a hope which seemed ironic to him by the time he wrote the poem: 'But after all, for God's sake let somebody or other be ordained to rule us, for at present your Godolphins and Montagus equally deny that they have anything to do with us, and I think we are likely to fall between the two, though we might crush them both if we would act with vigour' (*H.M.C. Bath*, iii. 422).

The occasion of the ballad was probably William's address to Parliament on 10 Feb. 1701. (P was a member, representing East Grinstead, Dorset's pocket borough.) William urged Parliament to settle the question of succession to the Crown, in view of the death of the Duke of Gloucester, and to consider the dangerous situation on the Continent produced by the succession of Louis XIV's grandson, Philip, to the Spanish throne. He concluded: 'I Hope there will be such an Agreement and Vigour in your Resolutions, you shall take upon the import[ant] Matters now before you, as may make it appear we are firmly united among our Selves: And in my Opinion, nothing can contribute more to our Safety at Home, or to our being Considerable Abroad' (*A Collection of All the Speeches, Messages, &c. of His Late Majesty King William III . . .*, 1712, p. 42). The proceedings of Parliament were notoriously lacking in the unity and vigour William desiderated: although eventually the Act of Settlement was passed and William's preparations for the impending war were grudgingly supported, the violence and bitterness of party faction reached new heights. The Tories spent most of their energies in the effort to impeach the former Whig ministers, the Lords Somers, Portland, Halifax, and Orford; the Whigs accused the Tories of Jacobitism and irresponsibility.

5. Robert Harley (later Earl of Oxford) was Speaker, and Sir Edward Seymour, a high Tory, led the Commons, in this session.

16. without Troops or Pence. See *A New Answer* (1697); by this time Parliament had reduced the army to 7,000 men, all native-born.

20. Vernon. James Vernon (1646–1727) had been P's superior and friend

since 1694; he was Secretary of State from 1697 to 1702 (after May 1699, for the Northern Department alone). Vernon was not impeached with the other Whig leaders because it became clear that he had not known about the Partition Treaty and had not been in the king's confidence; 'By the king Vernon was treated rather as a clerk than as a minister' (*D.N.B.*).

22. Sunderland. See note to *To Mr. Fleetwood Shepherd* (1689), l. 27. Sunderland became powerful in William's counsels. He was regarded with so much fear and suspicion that he resigned his offices in 1697, but he manœuvred secretly thereafter to restore the Whigs to power.

25. Albemarle. Arnold Joost van Keppel (1669–1718) came over with William as page of honour, and was his constant companion and favourite. He was created Earl of Albemarle in 1696 and K.G. in May 1700, 'to the general Disgust of the Nobility' (*1740 History*, p. 177). William's foreign favourites, of whom Albemarle was chief after Portland had broken with the king, were extremely unpopular.

27. Cassie. Since P first wrote 'young Auverquerque', this is probably a nickname for Henry Nassau, Count of Auverquerque (1641–1708), another of the foreign favourites, captain of William's bodyguard and a general in his army. Like Albemarle, he was an able general and later distinguished himself in Marlborough's wars.

28. Miremont. The Marquis de Miremont was a French Protestant who emigrated to England on the Revocation of the Edict of Nantes, 1685. He commanded a regiment of dragoons in William's Irish campaign (Luttrell, iv. 418), and continued to serve under William and Marlborough.

31. Peregrine Bertie, a younger son of Robert, Earl of Lindsey, was Vice-Chamberlain from 1690 to his death in 1711; he was sworn of the Privy Council in May 1695 (Luttrell, iii. 470).

33. John Cutts, Baron Cutts of Gowran (1661–1707), called the 'Salamander' for his bravery under fire, was a close friend of William's and one of his most distinguished soldiers.

34. Jore. St. Jour, a French sea commander, 'deserted' to the English in 1690, was 'much caressed' by the king, and was not recognized as a spy until he escaped to France again in May 1691 (Luttrell, ii. 234).

Laloe. A 'Mons. Lalo' (or LaLoo), a French Huguenot, was reported in Oct. 1700 to have been made standard-bearer to the yeomen of the guard (Luttrell, iv. 694); Manchester had recommended another candidate and complained to P about the appointment (*H.M.C. Bath*, iii. 425). The Col. Lalo who was made a brigadier in 1709 and killed soon after (Luttrell, vi. 425, 485) may be the same man.

41. little Wales. James II's son. This stanza indicates clearly (as does l. 15) that the poem was written well before 14 May, when the Act of Settlement passed the Commons.

1702

(193)   *To a Young Gentleman in Love*

MSS.   None.

Pub.   [Title as in text.] London, Printed for J. Tonson, 1702; *Apollo's Feast*, 1703 (Case 230), p. 164; *Poetical Miscellanies: The Fifth Part*, 1704 (Case 172–5–a), p. 242.
Collected: *1707*, p. 92; *1709*, p. 100; *1718*, p. 99.

Text.   *1718*. Collated: *1702*, *1709*.

Prior sent this to Godolphin on 16 May 1702; it was printed (anonymously) by Tonson shortly thereafter, for P wrote to George Stepney on 16 June, 'This Paper of Verse is gotten into Print. You will guess the Author of it' (*L 13*, 7–8).

(195)   *Epitaph*

MSS.   L 27, 80 (D).

Pub.   *The Flying Post*, No. 4478, 19–21 Sept. 1721; *A Miscellaneous Collection*, Dublin, 1721 (Case 320–1), i. 58.
Collected: *New Collection 1725*, p. 27.

Text.   *L 27*. Collated: *1721fp*. [*Flying Post*].

The reference to NASSAU in the last line makes it probable that this was written before King William's death on 8 March 1702, though it was first published in the newspaper accounts of Prior's death. Many different versions were published in the next few years, and several answers; the best known was published with P's poem in *A Miscellaneous Collection*, 1721 (i. 58) and is attributed by Sir Harold Williams (*Swift, Poems*, p. 1151) to Concanen:

> Hold, Matthew Prior, by your leave
> Your epitaph is somewhat odd;
> Bourbon and you were sons of Eve,
> Nassau the offspring of a God.

S. W. Singer cited in *N. & Q.*, 1 ser., i (1850), 482, a Scottish prototype:

> Johnnie Carnegie lais heer,
> Descendit of Adam and Eve,
> Gif ony con gang hieher,
> I'se willing gie him leve.

1703

(196)   *A Song*

MSS. None.
Pub. *The Monthly Mask of Vocal Musick* (London Printed for & Sould by
I. Walsh), June 1703, p. 29.
  Collected: *1709*, p. 86; *1718*, p. 79.
Text. *1718*. Collated: *1703*, *1709*.

The setting in *1703* is by John Eccles (1650?–1735), one of the most
popular song-writers of the time. He had collaborated with Purcell on the
third act of *Don Quixote*, and in 1700 had become master of the King's Band
of Music. Prior's song was popular, and was published in numerous later
collections. It was sung, as set by Clayton, at a concert in 1711 organized by
Steele (Steele, *Correspondence*, ed. Rae Blanchard, 1941, p. 49 n).

(196)   *Adriani Morientis*

MSS. None.
Pub. *Poetical Miscellanies: The Fifth Part*, 1704 (Case 172–5–a), p. 211.
  Collected: *1709*, p. 35; *1718*, p. 128.
Text. *1718*. Collated: *1704*, *1709*.

The fifth part of *Tonson's Miscellanies*, in which this and the following ten
poems were first printed, was published on 21 Dec. 1703 (adv. *Daily Courant*).
   In both *1709* and *1718*, Prior's imitation was preceded by the Latin original
and by Fontenelle's French version (from the dialogue between Hadrian and
Margaret of Austria, in *Dialogues des Morts*, 1683):

> Animula, vagula, blandula,
> Hospes, Comesque Corporis,
> Quæ nunc abibis in loca,
> Pallidula, rigida, nudula ?
> Nec, ut soles, dabis joca.

> Ma petite Ame, ma Mignonne,
> Tu t'en vas donc, ma Fille, & Dieu sçaçhe où Tu vas:
> Tu pars seulette, nuë, & tremblotante, Helas!
> Que deviendra ton humeur foliçhonne ?
> Que deviendront tant de jolis ébats ?

   Pope discussed Hadrian's verses and translated them in a letter to Steele,
7 Nov. 1712, which was published in *Spectator*, No. 532. On 12 June 1713 he
sent to Caryll three poems on the subject, not identifying the authors—P's
imitation, his own translation, and *Christiani Morientis*, the first version of

his *Dying Christian to his Soul*—and invited comparison (Pope, *Correspondence,* ed. G. Sherburn, Oxford, 1956, i. 149–50, 176–9; *Minor Poems,* ed. N. Ault and J. Butt, 1954, pp. 91–95).

(197)   *The Despairing Shepherd*

MSS.   *B.M. Add. 14934,* 198 (X).
Pub.   *Poetical Miscellanies: The Fifth Part,* 1704 (Case 172–5–a), p. 231.
        Collected: *1709,* p. 29; *1718,* p. 23.
Text.   *1718.* Collated: *1704, 1709.*

The subtitle in *B.M. Add. 14934* (a late collection) is, 'Alexis's Minuet'. Prior may have had in mind the 23rd Idyll of Theocritus, translated by Dryden in *Sylvae,* 1685.

The piece was very popular. It was published in a pamphlet, with *Daphnis* and *The Despairing Lover,* London: Printed and Sold by H. Hills . . . 1709; the pamphlet was later included in *A Collection of the Best English Poetry,* 1717 (Case 294–1). In 1717 it also appeared in *The Virgin Muse* (Case 304), p. 10. The B.M. *Catalogue of Printed Music* (ed. W. B. Squire, 1912, i. 33) lists a setting by Gouge, 1720 (?), and an anonymous one, 1730 (?). Mr. W. N. H. Harding, of Chicago, has kindly permitted us to consult his first-line index to his remarkable collection of eighteenth-century songbooks, which lists the poem as appearing in fourteen songbooks between 1724 and 1749.

(198)   *The Lady's Looking-Glass*

MSS.   None.
Pub.   *Poetical Miscellanies: The Fifth Part,* 1704 (Case 172–5–a), p. 215.
        Collected: *1709,* p. 43; *1718,* p. 29.
Text.   *1718.* Collated: *1704, 1709.*

As the subtitle in *1704,* 'in Imitation of a Greek Idyllium', acknowledges, the first half of the poem is indebted to Moschus (Loeb Classical Library, *Greek Bucolic Poets,* p. 458). Frey (p. 135) cites also Horace, *Odes,* I. v.

3–4. *Evans 1779* cites the comparison of the Homer of the *Odyssey* to the setting sun, which retains its size but not its intensity, in the ninth chapter of Longinus.

44. Cf. Martial, *Epigrams,* XII. xlvii: 'nec tecum possum vivere nec sine te.'

(199)   *To the Author of Love and Friendship*

MSS.   None.
Pub.   *Poetical Miscellanies: The Fifth Part,* 1704 (Case 172–5–a), p. 604.
        Collected: *1709,* p. 49; *1718,* p. 34.
Text.   *1718.* Collated: *1704, 1709.*

In *1709* and *1718*, Prior's poem was preceded by Elizabeth Singer's *Love and Friendship: A Pastoral*, which begins:

AMARYLLIS.

> While from the Skies the ruddy Sun descends;
> And rising Night the Ev'ning Shade extends:
> While pearly Dews o'erspread the fruitful Field;
> And closing Flowers reviving Odours yield:
> Let Us, beneath these spreading Trees, recite
> What from our Hearts our Muses may indite.
> Nor need We, in this close Retirement, fear,
> Lest any Swain our am'rous Secrets hear.

SILVIA.

> To ev'ry Shepherd I would Mine proclaim;
> Since fair AMINTA is my softest Theme:
> A Stranger to the loose Delights of Love,
> My Thoughts the nobler Warmth of Friendship prove:
> And, while it's pure and sacred Fire I sing,
> Chast Goddess of the Groves, Thy Succour bring.

AMARYLLIS.

> Propitious God of Love, my Breast inspire
> With all Thy Charms, with all Thy pleasing Fire:
> Propitious God of Love, Thy Succour bring;
> Whilst I Thy Darling, Thy ALEXIS sing. . . .

Elizabeth Singer (1674–1737) had published *Poems on Several Occasions, written by Philomela* (1696) and other poems in miscellanies and periodicals. She was a protégée of Lord Weymouth, P's colleague at the Board of Trade and Plantations, and P met her while he was visiting Longleat in the autumn of 1703. Probably he wrote this poem shortly after the meeting. During the next year he carried on an epistolary flirtation with the lady; his letters, preserved in *L 13*, have been published, with commentary, by H. B. Wright, 'Matthew Prior and Elizabeth Singer', *Philological Quarterly*, xxiv (1945), 71–82. Miss Singer, who was an ardent Dissenter and writer of religious verse, seems to have tried to 'reform' P, taxing him with flippancy, idleness, excessive drinking, high churchmanship, and other defects; P's replies are in his best vein of teasing and facetious gallantry. In 1709 she married Thomas Rowe, a schoolmaster and Dissenting minister. When *1718* was published, she wrote a poem praising *Solomon* (*Miscellaneous Works*, 1739, i. 166).

(200) *To a Lady: She refusing*

MSS. None.
Pub. *Poetical Miscellanies: The Fifth Part*, 1704 (Case 172–5–a), p. 606.
      Collected: *1709*, p. 51; *1718*, p. 35.
Text. *1718*. Collated: *1704, 1709*.

The lady was Elizabeth Singer, according to the biography of Mrs. Rowe in her *Miscellaneous Works*, 1739, p. xviii (also in *Gentleman's Magazine*, ix, 1739, 282). The fact that in *1704*, *1709*, and *1718* this poem follows the one addressed to Miss Singer lends plausibility to this statement, as does the title given the poem in Lady Henrietta Harley's list (described in the commentary on *Out of the Greek*, Doubtful, 1684): 'Disputing wth Mrs Singer who left him in the Argument.'

(202)   *The Ladle*

MSS.   *B.M. Add.* 27407, 36 (X; a late collection).
Pub.   *Poetical Miscellanies: The Fifth Part*, 1704 (Case 172–5–a), p. 593.
          Collected: *1707*, p. 42; *1709*, p. 125; *1718*, p. 118.
Text.   *1718*. Collated: *1704*, *1709*.

Based on Ovid's story of Baucis and Philemon (*Metam.* viii. 626–724). The ending was apparently suggested (as an anonymous contributor to the *Gentleman's Magazine*, lvii, 1787, i. 399, pointed out) by a passage in *Pleasant Notes upon Don Quixot*, 1654, by Edmund Gayton (1608–66):

It cals to mind, a story of a poor, but simple woman, who for want of a graine or two of discretion, lost her husband the highest advantages of the World that ever was. For the good man had so spent his time in true and honest paines, contented and not murmuring, that Fortune seem'd to smile upon him, as oft as he came to worship at her Temple, whither he oft resorted; the gracious looks of the Goddesse encouraged him to aske something more then before he used, & yet considering with himselfe, that too bold a votary might be repuls'd, he modestly bounded his request with this sute, that her goodnesse would conferre three wishes upon 'um, which from the Oracle was answered; *Ratify'd; Wish, and be happy.* The joyfull man acquainted his wife strait, who having been the constant companion of his labours, was meet to share in his good fortunes; but shee was just such another Niddecook as *Ioan Gutierez*, and the first thing shee desired her husband, was, that one of these wishes, might be left to her disposall. The good old man, willing to gratifie her, said, yea Love, one I will spare thee: So to the Faire they came, whither they were bound, and the woman casting her eyes round about, to see what she should make the choyce of her wish, at last, (remembring what shee wanted at home) spied a handsome wooden ladle, which shee forthwith wish'd for, and as soon the thing was in her hand, which her husband seeing and impatient at the miscarriage of the first wish, wroth with his wife for her simplicity, wished the Ladle in her breech, which out of hand was instantly there. But the poor woman (like a fly with a straw in the same place) was so tormented, besides the shame, that she desired her husband, that as he ever hop'd to partake of the delights of the opposite place, he would remove this impediment, to which the uxorious man condiscended, and in charity to his wife, wish'd it out againe. So all the three wishes went in and out with a Ladle. (pp. 26–27)

We are much indebted to Miss Frances Mayhew for providing us with a transcript of this passage from Gayton. The subtitle in *1707*—'in Imitation of Fontaine'—is incorrect, and may have been intended for *Hans Carvel*, to which it would apply.

28. PAULO. Probably Paolo Cagliari, called Paul Veronese (1528–88).

CARACHE. Annibale Caracci (1560–1609), who, with his brother, Agostino, and his uncle, Lodovico, established a famous academy of painting in Bologna.

157. Plumb. 'The sum of £100,000' (*O.E.D.*).

(207) *Charity*

MSS. *Md* (D).
Pub. *Poetical Miscellanies: The Fifth Part*, 1704 (Case 172–5–a), p. 205.
    Collected: *1707*, p. 54; *1718*, p. 309.
Text. *1718*. Collated: *1704*, *Md*.

Cf. *Charity never faileth* and *God is Love* (both 1690).

(209) *Celia to Damon*

MSS. *B.M. Add. 40060*, 20ᵛ (X); *B.M. Add. 27987*, 79ᵛ (X).
Pub. *Poetical Miscellanies: The Fifth Part*, 1704 (Case 172–5–a), p. 234.
    Collected: *1709*, p. 87; *1718*, p. 38.
Text. *1718*. Collated: *1704*, *1709*.

The date, 'feb: 1702/3', in *B.M. 40060* is probably an error for 1703/4 (as the date of copying), since the text is copied from *1704*. Prior's epistle belongs to the tradition of Ovid's *Heroides*, but varies the theme: Celia is not deserted, but describes the torments of a happy love.

[Motto.] Lucretius, iv. 1141–2.
56. KNELLER. See commentary on *Seeing the Duke of Ormond's Picture* (1708).

(213) *The Wedding Night*

MSS. None.
Pub. *Poetical Miscellanies: The Fifth Part*, 1704 (Case 172–5–a), p. 247; *A Collection of Poems*, 1716 (Case 151–g), p. 16.
    Collected: *1740*, p. 75.
Text. *1704*. Collated: *1740*.

This poem and the two that follow were not reprinted by Prior in *1709* or *1718*, and the only evidence of his authorship is their inclusion in *1740*. All his poems in *1704* were printed anonymously; these three are contiguous to a group of ten poems, each of which was later acknowledged by P or is found in an authoritative manuscript. The present poem is attributed to Charles Tooke in *A Collection of Poems*, 1716 (Case 151–g), p. 16, but we can find nothing to support this ascription.

(213)   *The Third Ode of Anacreon*

MSS. *B.M. Add. 27407*, 100ᵛ (X).
Pub. *Poetical Miscellanies: The Fifth Part*, 1704 (Case 172–5–a), p. 199.
       Collected: *1740*, p. 116.
Text. *1704*. Collated: *1740*.

    Prior's version is rather a free imitation than a translation. *1740* prints on facing pages the translation by Thomas Stanley (1650). The ode is No. 33 in the Loeb Classical Library edition of the *Anacreontea*.

(214)   *To a Lady that design'd*

MSS. None.
Pub. *Poetical Miscellanies: The Fifth Part*, 1704 (Case 172–5–a), p. 202.
       Collected: *1740*, p. 76.
Text. *1704*. Collated: *1740*.

1704

(215)   *Prologue, Spoken at Court*

MSS. None.
Pub. [Untitled programme for the celebration.] London: Printed in the Year
       1703/4; [Title as in text.] London: Printed for Jacob Tonson. 1704;
       P.O.A.S. iii, 1704 (Case 211–3–a), p. 424.
       Collected: *1707*, p. 58; *1709*, p. 174; *1718*, p. 181.
Text. *1718*. Collated: *1704p* [the programme], *1704t* [Tonson], *1709*.

    Written for Queen Anne's birthday, 6 Feb. 1703/4. On 15 Feb. Prior wrote to Elizabeth Singer, 'The Ladys were very fine on the Queens Birth Day; My Prologue was not very well Spoken . . .' (*L 13*, 40). A copy of what seems to be the programme for the birthday celebration is preserved at Yale. There is no general title; the first heading is *Overture*, followed by *Prologue* (P's, printed complete but without attribution), then *Symphony*, then the five acts of a play (not identified), interspersed with music, songs, and various sorts of dances. The play was Dryden's *All for Love* (*Post Man*, 5–8 Feb. 1704).

    24. young AUSTRIAN. Prince Eugene of Savoy, recently placed in command of the Austrian forces.
    31. To Temples Zeal. Queen Anne's Bounty, announced in Feb. 1704, turned over the proceeds of the government tax on benefices ('first-fruits and

tenths') to be used to increase inadequate clerical stipends, and remitted all arrears in the tax.

Manners to the Stage. On 17 Jan. 1704 Queen Anne issued a proclamation stating that she had already given orders 'that Nothing be Acted in either of the Theatres contrary to Religion or Good Manners, upon Pain of our High Displeasure, and of being Silenc'd from further Acting; And being further desirous to Reform all other Indecencies, and Abuses of the Stage....; Our Will and Pleasure therefore is, and We do hereby strictly Command, That no Person of what Quality soever, Presume to go Behind the Scenes, or come upon the Stage, either before, or during the Acting of any Play. That no Woman be Allow'd or Presume to wear a Vizard Mask in either of the Theatres . . .' (quoted in J. Ashton, *Social Life in the Reign of Queen Anne*, New York, 1883, pp. 255–6).

(217)   *An Ode*

MSS. None.
Pub.   *1709*, p. 181; *The Odes and Satyrs of Horace*, 1715 (Case 287), p. 33; *1718*, p. 177.
Text. *1718*. Collated: *1709*.

Colonel George Villiers (son of George, fourth Viscount Grandison, and first cousin to Lord Jersey, Prior's friend and former superior) was the husband of P's cousin Katharine. In 1703 he was in command of a regiment of marines on board Sir Cloudesley Shovell's fleet. Returning home by way of Italy, he was drowned on 10 Nov. 1703, when his post calash capsized in the Piave river on the way back from a sight-seeing excursion. P had always been close to his cousin Katharine, and probably knew Villiers well. He helped the widow by writing to the English consul at Venice about Villiers' effects and the return of the body to England, if found (*L 13*, 30–33).

P sent this 'very moral Melancholly Poem' to Elizabeth Singer on 24 June 1704 (*L 13*, 46).

22. great HENRY's Tombs. The monuments in Henry VII's Chapel, Westminster Abbey.

HOLBEN's Dance. *The Dance of Death*, the famous series of woodcuts executed by Hans Holbein in 1524–6.

27. Young CHURCHILL. John, Lord Churchill, Marquis of Blandford, only surviving son of the Duke of Marlborough, died of smallpox in 1703 at the age of 17.

28. BRADFORD. Francis Newport, first Earl of Bradford (1619–1708).

32. SACKVILLE. See *Dedication*, 1708.

HYDE. Edward Hyde (1609–74), first Earl of Clarendon, statesman and historian, grandfather of Queen Anne.

39. As——L. John Asgill (1659–1738), lawyer and M.P., published in 1700 a treatise arguing that man may be translated into eternal life without passing through death.

(220)   *A Letter to M. Boileau*

MSS.   *W*, 26ᵛ (P; rough drafts of revisions of three passages for *1709*).
Pub.   [Title as in text.] London, Printed for Jacob Tonson, within Grays-Inn Gate next Grays-Inn Lane. 1704; *The Diverting Post*, 28 Oct.–4 Nov. 1704 (ll. 79–92 only).
       Collected: *1709*, p. 187; *1718*, p. 183.
Text.   *1718*. Collated: *W*, *1704* [Tonson], *1709*.

News of the victory at Blenheim reached England on 10/21 Aug. 1704; Prior's poem was published by Tonson on 29 Sept. (adv. *Post Man*, 28–30 Sept.). P wrote in his diary: 'upon the great victory of Hockstadt [i.e. Blenheim] I thought I had a fair occasion to shew the real respect I had for my Lord [i.e. Marlborough], and so vindicate myself for the scandal of having Lampooned him or his family, upon which I wrote my letter to Monsʳ Boileau, and as soon as it was printed sent 2 Copyes of it with a very civil letter to my Lady Dutchesse desiring her to do Me the honour to give one of those copyes to the Queen, I sent these by Ad. Churchill but was surprized some days after to find that the Dutchess sent Me back the pacquet by Mʳ Churchill unopen'd declaring that she would not receive anything of my writing' (Strong, *Catalogue*, p. 108). Cardonnel acknowledged cordially on 31 Oct. the copy P sent to the duke (*H.M.C. Bath*, iii. 433–4); but the duchess remained hostile. Apparently she was convinced that P had written *Faction Display'd* (1704), for which see the list of Works Wrongly Attributed.

P had carried on a poetic warfare with Boileau in *On the Taking of Huy* (1694) and *An English Ballad* (1695). Toward the end of P's first stay in Paris, during the interval of peace, they became acquainted; in the summer of 1699 he saw much of 'Boileau and the *beaux Esprits*', and wrote to Jersey, 'Boileau says I have more genius than all the Academy—good again' (quoted in Wickham Legg, pp. 84, 293). In the words of *1740 History* (p. 232), P's *Letter* comprises the 'various Beauties of a familiar Epistle, a genteel Satire, and an epic Poem' (the last phrase referring to the 'Plan of an Heroic Poem' in ll. 79–181). The *Diverting Post* states that ll. 79–92 'are now Setting to Musick'; but the setting apparently has not survived.

[Motto.] Horace, *Satires*, II. i. 12–14.

13. Max Emmanuel, Elector of Bavaria, was one of the three commanders on the French side. Disagreement between him and Marshals Tallard and Marsin was partly responsible for their defeat (G. M. Trevelyan, *England under Queen Anne: Blenheim*, 1946, pp. 374–5).

18. 'Epistre 4. du Sr. Boileau Dépreaux au Roy. *En vain, pour Te Loüer, &c'* (*1718*). Louis did not himself take part in the passage of the Rhine, and P taunted Boileau with this fact in *An Ode in Imitation of Horace* (1692), ll. 123–70.

20–21. *Épître IV*, ll. 15–16: 'Comment en vers heureux assiéger Doës-bourg, | Zutphen, Wageninghen, Harderwic, Knotzembourg?'

23. 'Wurts . . . Ah! quel nom, grand roi, quel Hector que ce Wurts! | Sans ce terrible nom, mal né pour les oreilles, | Que j'allais à tes yeux étaler de merveilles!' (ll. 144–6).

29. Marlborough's allies, Prince Eugene of Savoy and Prince Lewis of Baden.

34. HAMILTON. George Hamilton, first Earl of Orkney (1666–1737), Lieutenant-General, played a major part in the battle.

LUMLY. Lt.-Gen. Henry Lumley (1660–1722), cavalry commander; with Marlborough, he led the decisive charge that drove the French into the Danube.

35. INGOLDSBY. Lt.-Gen. Richard Ingoldsby; the most spectacular epi-sode in which he was involved was the capture of the two French brigades caught in the village of Blenheim.

PALMES. Col. Palmes led the famous cavalry charge that broke the Gendarmerie.

39–40. CUTTS . . . GOURAM. See note to *Ballad* (1701), l. 33.

42. WOOD. Another general; at Ramillies he captured two lieutenant-generals and almost captured the Elector of Bavaria and Marshal Villeroi (G. M. Trevelyan, *England under Queen Anne: Ramillies*, 1946, p. 116).

43. CHURCHILL. General Charles Churchill, Marlborough's brother, in-fantry commander at Blenheim.

46. DANE. A large body of Danish mercenaries took part in the battle, some as infantry under Churchill and some as cavalry. They fought bravely and suffered heavy losses (Trevelyan, *Blenheim*, p. 399).

76. LAMB. Patrick Lamb, author of *Royal Cookery: or, the Complete Court-Cook. Containing the choicest receipts . . . now in use in the Queen's Palaces* (1710).

121. bloody Cross. Insignia, with the emblem of St. George (l. 123), of the Order of the Garter, to which Marlborough was appointed in 1702.

143. The victory at Schellenberg on 2 July 1704 was the first great success of the Danube campaign.

(227)   *An English Padlock*

MSS. *B.M. Add. 40060, 59* (X).
Pub. *The Diverting Post*, 30 Dec.–6 Jan. 1704/5; [Title as in text.] London: Printed for Jacob Tonson, 1705; [Title as in text.] London: Printed for Jocab Tompson, 1705.
Collected: *1707*, p. 97; *1709*, p. 104; *1718*, p. 102.
Text. *1718*. Collated: *1705dp* [*Diverting Post*], *1705t* [Tonson], *1709*.

T. J. Wise has created some confusion among bibliographers by describing the 'Jocab Tompson' edition as the 'first edition' (*Catalogue*, iv. 72–73) and then 'correcting' this entry by describing it as Tonson's 'second edition' (x. 165); in both descriptions he has added to the confusion by altering the publisher's name to 'Tonson'. This is absurd: the edition is an incredibly careless piracy from the genuine Tonson edition (of which there was, as far as we can discover, no second edition or issue).

Prior's chief model is Ovid, *Amores*, III. iv; he may have had in mind also Wycherley's *The Country Wife* (1675).

2. HORACE. *Odes*, III. xvi. 1–11.
15–54. Cf. Ovid, *Ars Amatoria*, iii. 611–55; Juvenal, *Satires*, vi. 346–51.

1706

(229)   *Pallas and Venus*

MSS. None.
Pub. [Title as in text.] London: Printed for John Nutt near Stationers-Hall. 1706.
      Collected: *1709*, p. 93; *1718*, p. 98.
Text. *1718*. Collated: *1706*, *1709*.

Prior sent this to Lord Fitzharding on 2 March 1706: 'I venture to send you an Epigram which I made last Night, and will to morrow Morning ask You how you like it . . .' (*L 13*, 65). The first part is based on an anonymous epigram in the *Greek Anthology* (Bk. XVI, No. 174) or one of its numerous imitations; but there seems to be no precedent for Pallas' reply.

(230)   *An Ode, Humbly Inscrib'd*

MSS. None.
Pub. [Title as in text.] London: Printed for Jacob Tonson, within Grays-Inn-Gate next Grays-Inn Lane. 1706.
      Collected: *1709*, p. 273; *1718*, p. 245.
Text. *1718*. Collated: *1706*, *1709*.

The ode was published on 5 July 1706 (adv. *Daily Courant*, 6 July), and Prior sent a copy to Marlborough on that date (*L 13*, 72). Since Ramillies was won on 23 May, P had waited some time after the occasion. Late in June, an anonymous poet had exhorted him to write in *A Letter to Mr. Prior*,

Occasion'd by the Duke of Marlborough's Late Victory at Ramilly, and Glorious Successes in Brabant . . . Printed by W. D. for Edmund Curll:

> Shall MARLBRO' still new Victories obtain ?
> And shall the Muse be wanting to his Praise ?
> Exert, O PRIOR! thy melodious Voice,
> Convince the World, tho' tuneful *Dryden*'s gone
> A POET still remains, whose lofty Verse
> Can in just Numbers *Arms* and *Conquest* sing.

In his diary, P described the reception of the poem:

. . . upon the battle of Ramilies I made the ode in imitation of Spencer for which His Grace [Marlborough] returned me his particular thanks. I gave it to the Queen, who said she took it very kindly of me. The Whiggs tho' they did not openly censure this poem were no way satisfied that I had writt it; they say'd the Imitation was of a verse now grown obsolete, the Style a little hard, &c in the meantime none of them writt, at least none of note, except Dennis, and Walsh and Roe who came out about a year after; the Tories on the other side cryed up my poem too much.

(Strong, *Catalogue*, p. 109)

A poem that appeared in October is typical of the Whig attitude described by P: *A Modern Inscription to the Duke of Marlboroughs Fame. Occasion'd by an Antique, In Imitation of Spencer. With a Preface Unveiling some of the Beauties of the Ode, which has pass'd for Mr. Prior's.* London, Printed in the Year MDCCVI. In the Preface, the anonymous author insists ironically that this 'mean, cold, Performance' cannot possibly be P's; it is so poor that some have thought it 'a designed *Banter*, to turn the greatest of Actions into Ridicule. To address her *Majesty* in the Stile of Queen *Elizabeth*'s Reign, may be thought as much a Complement, as a *Jacobite Lady*'s coming to Court on an Inauguration Day, in a *Ruff* and a *Farthingal*.' He suggests that the author of the ode felt no enthusiasm for his subject, and accuses him of insulting the memory of King William and of not praising Marlborough sufficiently. The poem begins:

> As of his Faction's Downfal P——r sings,
> His Muse attempts to rise with broken Wings:
> When he shou'd praise an envy'd Fate, he cry'd,
> *A Good Man's grievous Loss, a faithful Servant dy'd.*

P's ode seems to have begun the vogue of imitating Spenser; he wrote to Lord Cholmondeley on 1 Aug. 1706 (*L 13*, 79): 'As to Spencer, my Lord, I think we have gained our point, every body acknowledges him to have been a fine Poet, thô three Months since not one in 50 had read him: Upon my Soul, tis true, the Wits have sent for the Book, the Fairy Queen is on their Toilette table, and some of our Ducal acquaintance will be deep in that Mythologico-Poetical way of thinking.'

[Motto.] Horace, *Odes*, IV. xiv, 49–52.
86. Max Emmanuel, Elector of Bavaria, had gained fame by his campagins against the Turks more than twenty years earlier.

102. AUVERQUERQUE. See note to *Ballad* (1701), l. 27. Auverquerque led the Dutch forces at Ramillies.

150–60. At the critical point of the battle, when the French cavalry broke through the Dutch, Marlborough was thrown from his horse and barely escaped death or capture. As he climbed on another horse, Col. Bringfield, who was holding the stirrup, had his head torn off by a cannon ball. 'The incident struck the imagination of England and Europe. Our newspapers seized on it as the symbol of Ramillies, as they had seized on "Tallard in the coach" for Blenheim' (G. M. Trevelyan, *England under Queen Anne: Ramillies*, 1946, p. 113).

175. SCHELLENBERG. See note to *A Letter to M. Boileau* (1704), l. 143.

223–8. TALBOT. See commentaries on '*That Heaven and Earth*' (1694), *Written in Montaigne's Essays* (1713).

SEYMOUR. Charles Seymour, sixth Duke of Somerset (1662–1748), was a supporter of William and favourite of Anne's; see also note to *Ballad* (1701), l. 5.

NEVIL. John Fane, seventh, otherwise thirteenth, Earl of Westmorland (1682?–1762), a descendant of the Nevilles, served under Marlborough.

CA'NDISH. See note to *The Orange* (1688), l. 53.

BUTLER's Sons. For James Butler, second Duke of Ormonde, see commentary on *Seeing the Duke of Ormond's Picture* (1708). His father was an admiral.

HERBERT. Thomas Herbert, eighth Earl of Pembroke (1656–1733), at this time Lord President of the Council; Arthur Herbert, Earl of Torrington (1647–1716); Henry, Baron Herbert of Cherbury (1654–1709).

CHURCHILL. See note to *A Letter to M. Boileau*, l. 43.

251. LUTETIA. Paris.

271. Column. 'There was an intention to erect some national monument to the glory of the Queen and her hero, the Duke of Marlborough; and Claud David of Burgundy published a large sheet-print, from the model of a fountain, with the statues of Queen Anne, the Duke of Marlborough on horseback, and several river gods, designed to be erected at the Conduit in Cheapside' (C. F. Secretan, *Memoirs of . . . Robert Nelson*, 1860, p. 238 n.).

282. young AUSTRIAN. Archduke Charles of Austria (aged 21), whom the Allies were trying to establish as Charles III of Spain. When the poem was written, the recent successes of Admiral Leake and Lord Peterborough in Spain made it seem likely that the Peninsular campaign could be won that summer.

292. VIGO. Won in 1702 by Sir George Rooke and the Duke of Ormonde.

GIBRALTAR. Taken in 1704 by Rooke, and successfully defended in 1704/5 by Admiral Leake and Prince George of Hesse-Darmstadt.

BARCELONE. Taken in Aug. 1705 by Peterborough, and successfully defended by him and Leake in May 1706.

295. Usurper BOURBON. Louis XIV's grandson, whom he had made Philip V of Spain.

311–20. After Ramillies, Brabant and Flanders welcomed the Allies and declared for Charles III.

335–6. The motto of the Order of the Thistle: 'Nemo me impune lacessit.'

350. The frontispiece to *1709* and *1718* illustrates this theme, with a motto from Horace, *Odes*, III. xxvi. 3–4.

1707

(244)   *A Simile*

MSS.   *Berks. Record Office Downshire Box 5*, bundle 3; *Christ Church Evelyn 18th cent. Lit. Misc. 1.*

Pub.   *1707*, p. 46; *P.O.A.S.* iv, 1707 (Case 211–4–a), p. 50; *Oxford and Cambridge Miscellany* [1708] (Case 248), p. 33.
       Collected: *1707*, p. 46; *1709*, p. 134; *1718*, p. 195.

Text. *1718*. Collated: *1707*, *1707p* [*P.O.A.S.*], *1709*.

Henry Danielson's catalogue No. 41 (1937), lists as part of item 248 (a collection made by Elijah Fenton of separately published pieces 1692–1707): '(Prior, Matthew) A Simile. First Edition. A single leaf, printed on both sides. "By Mr. Prior" in Fenton's autograph. Printed for Bernard Lintott, 1706. Of superlative rarity (? unknown to Bibliographers).' The publication is rare indeed, for we have been unable to trace this copy or to locate another one. On 19 Jan. 1706, Lintott advertised in the *Daily Courant* 'The SIMILY, a Poem. Price 2d.'; no author was named, but this may well be Prior's poem. Since *1707* probably reprints this separate publication—everything else in *1707* had been published earlier—we collate it in this instance. *1707* was published 31 Jan. 1707 (adv. *Daily Courant*).

Waller (*1907*, p. 408) notes that in his copy of the *Oxford and Cambridge Miscellany* the former owner, John Boyle, fifth Earl of Cork and Orrery, wrote opposite this poem, 'by M. Prior. Esq. To Tom Southerne'. Both manuscripts give the same identification of 'Dear THOMAS'. In 1719 P called Southerne 'my old acquaintance' (*H.M.C. Bath*, iii. 476).

(245)   *Epilogue to Phaedra*

MSS.   None.

Pub.   *Phaedra and Hippolitus. A Tragedy.* As it is Acted at the Queen's Theatre in the Hay-Market, By Her Majesty's Sworn Servants. By Mr. Edmund Smith. London, Printed for Bernard Lintott at the Cross-Keys between the two Temple-Gates in Fleetstreet. [1707].
       Collected: *1709*, p. 206; *1718*, p. 274.

Text. *1718*. Collated: *1707*, *1709*.

Edmund Smith's *Phaedra and Hippolitus. A Tragedy* was first performed on 21 April 1707 (adv. *Daily Courant*, 21 April), and was published in June. The play, modelled chiefly on Racine, was not successful; Addison commented: 'Would one think it was possible (at a Time when an Author lived that was able to write the *Phaedra* and *Hippolitus*) for a People to be so stupidly fond of the *Italian* Opera, as scarce to give a third Day's Hearing to that admirable Tragedy?' (*Spectator*, No. 18). Addison wrote the Prologue, and Johnson comments: 'No man was ever better introduced to the theatre than he who, in that violent conflict of parties, had a Prologue and Epilogue from the first wits on either side' (*Lives*, ii. 15). In a letter to Sir Thomas Hanmer of 24 June 1707, Prior says: 'Phaedra is a prostitute, and Smith's dedication [to Halifax] is nonsence—people do me a great deal of honour, they say when you and I had lookt over this piece for six months, the man could write verse; but when we had forsaken him, and he went over to St[eele] and Ad[dison] he could not write prose . . .' (Hanmer, *Correspondence*, ed. Sir Henry Bunbury, 1838, p. 111).

13–14. Smith's play has a happy ending, Hippolitus and Ismena being united.

1708

(247)   *Preface*

MSS. None.
Pub.   *1709*, p. xxiii; *1718*, Sig. c2.
Text. *1718*. Collated: *1709*.

Written for *1709*, which was published on 3 Dec. 1708 (adv. *Daily Courant*).

3. *a Collection of Poems*. *1707*, published by Edmund Curll on 31 Jan. 1707, was denounced in advance by Tonson (*Daily Courant*, 24 Jan.) and immediately repudiated by Prior (*Daily Courant*, 6 Feb.), who complained that 'some Pieces in the said Collection are not Genuine'. This disclaimer, repeated in the Preface now under consideration, was certainly false; it could be intended to apply to only three poems—*A Satyr on the modern Translators* (1685), *Satyr on the Poets* (1687), and *To Mr. Fleetwood Shepherd* (1689)—since all the others in *1707* were ultimately acknowledged by P; and there is conclusive evidence of the authenticity of these three pieces. P had lost his position on the Board of Trade in 1707, and was seeking another post or reinstatement in that one. He was therefore desperately anxious to avoid offending influential and important persons, especially Charles Montagu (now Lord Halifax). His letter of apology to Halifax, 4 Feb. 1707, makes it plain that he did not seriously deny the authorship of anything in *1707*, but that he found its publication highly embarrassing: 'Some rogue of a bookseller has

made a very Improper Collection of what He calls my writings, the whole is mutilated, Names printed at length and things written near Twenty years since, mingled with some written the other Day; in such a Manner as may do Me harm, part of the Mouse [*The Hind and the Panther Transvers'd*, 1687] is likewise inserted, which I had little to say to otherwise than as I held the pen to what Mr. Montague dictated; I mention this, my Lord, desiring your Lordship to believe this book was printed without my knowledge or consent . . .' (*B.M. Add. 7121*, 49–50). P's complaint that his writings had been 'mutilated' in *1707* was justified, one obvious example being the alteration of names in *Hymn to the Sun* (1693).

20. *Mr.* DIBBEN. Thomas Dibben's translation of *Carmen Seculare* was published by Tonson in 1701, with the English on facing pages. P reprinted it in *1709* and in *1718*; we omit it from the present edition. When Dibben was at work on the translation, P said that 'a little looking it over may make it the best thing in that kind that has been written since Buchanan' (*H.M.C. Bath*, iii. 423). Dibben was an alumnus of Westminster and of Trinity College, Cambridge; describing a convivial occasion in 1720, P calls him 'dirty Dibben, of Dorsetshire' (*H.M.C. Bath*, iii. 483).

24. *Mrs.* SINGER. See commentary on *To the Author of Love and Friendship* (1703).

(248)   *Dedication*

MSS. None.
Pub. *1709*, p. i; *1718*, Sig. A1.
Text. *1718*. Collated: *1709*.

As the reference in l. 2 indicates, this Dedication was written after *Preface*, above. The fact that it eschews conventional panegyric of the person addressed and presents instead a detailed analysis of the character of his father, Charles Sackville (1638–1706), sixth Earl of Dorset, who had been Prior's patron and friend for thirty years, has made it a primary source for biographers of that nobleman.

12. *Tu Marcellus eris.* Virgil, *Aeneid*, vi. 883.

52. Tacitus, *Dialogus de Oratoribus*, 2.

61. DRYDEN. In *Of Dramatick Poesie, An Essay* (1668), which was dedicated to Dorset. P's statement is the authority for the traditional identification of Eugenius as Dorset.

90. Rochester, *An Allusion to Horace* (*Poems*, ed. J. Thorpe, Princeton, 1950, p. 42).

93–94. Persius, *Satires*, i. 116–17.

119. a Song. '*To all you Ladies now at Land.*'

159. one great Man. Edward Villiers, first Earl of Jersey, P's friend since 1695, was Lord Chamberlain 1700–4.

219. Author. 'Sprat. *Hist. of the Royal Society*' (P's note), the end of Part II, sec. iv.

292–3. Adapted from *Aeneid*, v. 49–50.

300–5. As the *Postscript* added to this dedication in *1718* attests, the young earl did fulfil P's hopes; see also the Latin *Preamble* to his patent as duke that P wrote in 1720.

314. severer Studies. The major piece of this nature was *Solomon* (1708 below).

(256)   *An Ode* ('While from our Looks')

MSS. None.
Pub. *1709*, p. 27; *1718*, p. 21.
Text. *1718*. Collated: *1709*.

This and the eighteen following poems were first published in *1709* and may have been written at any time before that volume appeared on 3 Dec. 1708. Since there is no other evidence of their dates of composition, we present them in the order of *1709*.

An Ode was set to music by Charles Dieupart (*The Musical Miscellany*, 1731) and by at least three other eighteenth-century composers; see Ewing, 'Musical Settings'.

(257)   *Written in the Nouveaux Interests*

MSS. None.
Pub. *1709*, p. 33; *1718*, p. 127.
Text. *1718*. Collated: *1709*.

Gatien de Courtilz, Sieur de Sandras (1644–1712), *Nouveaux Interets des Princes de l'Europe, où l'on traite des maximes qu'ils doivent observer pour se maintenir dans leurs etats, & pour empêcher qu'il ne se forme une monarchie universelle*. Cologne, Chez P. Marteau, 1685. There were numerous later editions.

(257)   *Seeing the Duke of Ormond's Picture*

MSS. None.
Pub. *1709*, p. 53; *1718*, p. 37.
Text. *1718*. Collated: *1709*.

James Butler, second Duke of Ormonde (1665–1745), served under James against Monmouth and under William at the Boyne and on the Continent, and commanded the land forces at Cadiz and Vigo in 1702. From 1703 to 1707 he was Lord-Lieutenant of Ireland. He was the favourite of the High Tories, and early in Anne's reign was held up as rival to Marlborough, whom he succeeded as Captain-General in 1712. Prior had praised him in several earlier poems.

Sir Godfrey Kneller (1648–1723) was, after Lely's death in 1680, the leading portrait painter in England. P owned six portraits by him; see H. B. Wright and H. C. Montgomery, 'The Art Collection of a Virtuoso in Eighteenth-Century England', *The Art Bulletin*, xxvii (1945), 200–1.

The portrait of Ormonde by Kneller now in the National Gallery of Ireland is dated 1713, and therefore cannot be the one referred to in the poem. Mr. G. K. Adams, Director of the National Portrait Gallery (London), informs us that there are records of at least a dozen portraits of Ormonde by Kneller. There seems to be no way of identifying the one P saw. The fact that the battle of Landen (July 1693) is described suggests that the poem was written long before 1708. Dryden describes the same incident in his dedication of the *Fables* (1700) to Ormonde.

(258) *In Imitation of Anacreon*

MSS. None.
Pub. *1709*, p. 84; *1718*, p. 50.
Text. *1718*. Collated: *1709*.

The second stanza was probably suggested by the ode numbered 60A in the Loeb Library edition of the *Anacreontea*. Prior imitates the Anacreontic themes and attitudes, however, rather than any single poem.

15–16. Cf. the end of Waller's *Story of Phoebus and Daphne Apply'd*: 'Like *Phoebus* thus, acquiring unsought Praise, | He catch'd at Love, and fill'd his Arms with Bays.'

(259) *An Ode* ('The Merchant, to secure')

MSS. None.
Pub. *1709*, p. 85; *1718*, p. 51.
Text. *1718*. Collated: *1709*.

(259) *Paulo Purganti*

MSS. None.
Pub. *1709*, p. 116; *1718*, p. 111.
Text. *1718*. Collated: *1709*.

The motif of the husband who tries to conceal his impotence by inventing reasons for abstinence is common enough, as in La Fontaine ('Le Calendrier des Vieillards', *Contes,* II. viii) and Boccaccio (II. x), where a judge uses saints' days as a pretext, and his wife leaves him for a fresher lover. Prior's tale, however, seems to be his own invention; there is nothing to suggest that he was indebted to La Fontaine or Boccaccio.

[Motto.] Cicero, *De Officiis,* I. xxvii.

18. GUIDO. Guido Reni (1575–1642), Bolognese painter. P owned a *Madonna* by him.

21. JERSEY. See commentary on *In a Window* (1696).

22. BRADFORD. See note to *An Ode* (1704), l. 28.

28. KNAGS. Thomas Knaggs, a popular preacher, author of numerous sermons printed 1693–1720.

BURGESS. Daniel Burgess (1645–1713), presbyterian divine, famed for his 'merry' and histrionic preaching, was the most prominent nonconformist minister in London.

57–58. Cf. the Dryden–Soames translation of Boileau's *Art of Poetry,* i. 75–76; Pope, *Essay on Man,* iv. 379–80.

84. *Life of Lysander,* vii: 'Those who demanded that the descendants of Heracles should not wage war by deceit he held up to ridicule, saying that "where the lion's skin will not reach, it must be patched out with the fox's".' The saying does not seem to occur in the *Moralia.*

114. BLACKMORE. Sir Richard Blackmore (1654–1729), physician and poet.

HANS. Sir Hans Sloane (1660–1753), physician and scientist; Secretary and later President of the Royal Society.

129. COMINES. Philippe de Commines (1445–1509), French historian, called the father of modern history.

131–3. GROTIUS. Hugo Grotius (1583–1645), Dutch statesman, legal theorist, and theologian. His major work was *De jure Belli et Pacis,* 1625.

149. WARWICK-LANE. Site of the College of Physicians.

(264)   *Written in Mezeray's History*

MSS. *L 11,* 31 (D; ll. 7–12 only).
Pub. *1709,* p. 136; *1718,* p. 126.
Text. *1718.* Collated: *L 11, 1709.*

Prior wrote to Dr. William Aglionby from Paris on 24 March 1698:

Your application of the Passage in Horace [*Odes,* I. xxiv. 9–10] is so pretty that one would almost dye for it yet I am so dul but to think your occidit a Damn'd Verb, and am I think like to Live a good deal Longer notwithstanding all the fine things You can say of me in a winding Sheet; a Living dog is better than a Dead Lion, is, I think the Very wisest Saying of the wisest fellow that ever Lived; One

word as the Parsons Say and so conclude, it was, what I once writ in my Mezeray
when I was reading that book, and Splenetick and ill.

> Yet Let me Live, and I would Lye
> And growl, and whine, and scratch and cry
> On Dunghills Lowsy, and besh. . . .n
> Rather than decently to dye,
> To have been either Mezeray,
> Or any Monarch he has written.
>
> (*L 11*, 30–31; printed in *H.M.C. Bath*, iii. 202)

The book referred to is *Histoire de France depuis Faramond jusqu'à Louis le Juste*
(3 vols., 1643–51), by François Eudes de Mézeray (1610–83). P's copy, now
in the library of St. John's College, Cambridge, does not contain the verses.

8. *Invalides*. The Hôtel des Invalides in Paris, a hospital for disabled
soldiers founded by Louis XIV in 1670.

18. CAMBRAY. François de Salignac de La Mothe Fénelon (1651–1715),
Archbishop of Cambrai, renowned theologian and man of letters.

FONTAINE. P admired La Fontaine and had imitated him in *Hans Carvel*
(1700). He may have had in mind *La Mort et le Bûcheron* (*Fables*, I. xvi).

(265)   *The First Hymn of Callimachus*

MSS. None.
Pub.   *1709*, p. 167; *1718*, p. 298.
Text.   *1718*. Collated: *1709*.

Cf. *The Second Hymn of Callimachus* (1718).

(269)   *The Chameleon*

MSS. None.
Pub.   *1709*, p. 177; *1718*, p. 192.
Text.   *1718*. Collated: *1709*.

10. WILL's . . . TOM's. Two coffee-houses, both in Russell Street, Covent
Garden. Will's was the particular resort of poets and wits.

33. cheap *Port*. The Methuen Treaty with Portugal (1703) provided that
Portuguese wine be admitted at very low rates; port therefore became cheap
and popular.

34. The name seems to be fictional, but Addison mentions, in *Spectator*,
No. 9, the 'Hum-Drum club . . . made up of very honest Gentlemen, of
peaceable Dispositions, that used to sit together, smoak their Pipes, and say
nothing till Midnight'.

40–44. The description suggests the Kit-Cat Club, for which see note to
Jinny the Just (1708, below), l. 39. Tonson's *Miscellany Poems: The Fifth Part*,

1716 (Case 172–5–b), p. 60, contains a set of fifty-four *Verses Written for the Toasting-Glasses of the Kit-kat Club, in the Year 1703.*

(270)   *A Dutch Proverb*

MSS. None.
Pub.   *1709*, p. 179; *1718*, p. 110.
Text.   *1718*. Collated: *1709*.

The proverb is found in Erasmus, *Adagia*, II. ii. 48: 'Ignis, mare, mulier, tria mala.' The ultimate source is one of the monostichs of Menander (No. 231). We are indebted to Professor James Hutton for this information.

(270)   *To Cloe Weeping*

MSS. None.
Pub.   *1709*, p. 180; *1718*, p. 69.
Text.   *1718*. Collated: *1709*.

Set to music in 1710 (?) by John Reading, organist of St. John's, Hackney, in *A Book of New Songs (After the Italian Manner)* . . . with the title, 'Beauty in Tears'.

George Saintsbury, in *Minor Poets of the Caroline Period*, 1906, printed this as the first poem in his selection from Philip Ayres (ii. 354). S. J. Looker sent to I. A. Williams a letter pointing out that the poem is Prior's; Williams, supposing as did Saintsbury that the edition of Ayres in which it appeared was published in 1683, suggested possible explanations in the *London Mercury*, xi (1924–5), 525–6.

The fact is, however, that the first edition of Ayres's *Emblems of Love* (Bentley and Tidmarch, 1683) does not contain this poem. The poem, called *Cupid to Chloe Weeping*, appears only in three undated editions of Ayres's book: 'For John Wren'; 'Printed and sold by Hen. Overton'; 'For J. Osborn'. In the Wren edition, the first four leaves of the original edition are lacking (the rest of the book being from the same plates as the original), and two new leaves are substituted; the first contains a new title-page and the second, *Cupid to Chloe Weeping. A Sonnet.* This is clearly a bookseller's trick to dress up an old book. We have not been able to date the three editions precisely, but it is probable that they were all published after 1708.

(271)   *Love Disarm'd*

MSS. None.
Pub.   *1709*, p. 198; *1718*, p. 72.
Text.   *1718*. Collated: *1709*.

The French sources of *Love Disarm'd*, *Cupid and Ganymede*, and *Cupid Mistaken* were first pointed out in the 1720 reprint of *1718*. An unsigned letter 'sent to the Publisher' (pp. 454–5) cites the three French poems, calls attention to the superiority of Prior's versions, and states that the author of the French was Jean Bonnefons. We owe the identification of the true author to Mr. W. P. Barrett's unpublished doctoral dissertation, 'Matthew Prior and his Literary Relations with France', Cambridge University, 1931. The French poems are by Gilles Durant, Sieur de La Bergerie (1554–1615). In his *Imitations du Latin de Jean Bonnefons avec Autres Gayetez amoureuses de l'invention de l'Autheur* (Paris, 1610), they are not among the group of imitations of Bonnefons, but are in the section designated as Durant's original work. We quote from the beginning and ending of each only enough to indicate how it is related to P's poem.

Ode

> Amour tout las de voler
> L'autre jour au haut de l'air,
> S'élança d'une furie
> Dedans le sein de Marie.
>
> Trouvant l'endroit à propos
> Pour y prendre son repos,
> Il ageance ses deux aisles,
> Et s'endort sur ses mammelles.
>
> *   *   *   *
>
> Elle les prend, & soudain
> D'une diligente main,
> Elle de-serre & de-lie
> Amour, qui les autres lie.
>
> Depuis, ses traits redoutez
> Ne sont plus par luy portez:
> C'est Marie qui les garde,
> C'est Marie qui les darde.
>
> (Durant, p. 91 [F6ʳ])

(272)   *Cupid and Ganymede*

MSS. None.
Pub. *1709*, p. 201; *1718*, p. 75.
Text. *1718*. Collated: *1709*.

See commentary on the preceding poem.

Amour Jouant aux Echetz

> Contre Ganymede, un jour
> Le petit enfant Amour,
> Au jet d'Eschez, par gajeure
> Avoit perdu d'adventure,
> Son arc & ses traits aussi:
>
> *   *   *   *

> N'ayes peur qu'on ne m'honore:
> Charlotte a deux yeux encore:
> Tant que ces yeux dureront
> Les Dieux me redouteront.
> (Durant, p. 104 [G4ᵛ])

(275)   *For the Plan of a Fountain*

MSS. None.
Pub. *1709*, p. 205; *1718*, p. 191.
Text. *1718*. Collated: *1709*.

Cf. *An Ode, Humbly Inscrib'd* (1706), ll. 265–310 and note to l. 271.

(275)   *To Mr. Howard*

MSS. None.
Pub. *1709*, p. 209; *1718*, p. 70.
Text. *1718*. Collated: *1709*.

Prior had become acquainted with Hugh Howard (1675–1737), an Irish painter, at The Hague in 1697 (*H.M.C. Bath*, iii. 110–11), and Howard drew the frontispiece for *1709*. The portrait to which the ode refers hung in P's bedroom at the time of his death; the inventories made for his executors show that it was a picture of Flora posed by Anne Durham, to whom it was returned. Anne Durham, therefore, is the Cloe of this poem and of the two that follow: *Cupid Mistaken* and its companion piece, *Venus Mistaken*, which also refers to Howard's portrait. A group of later poems concerning her begins with *Her Right Name* (1718). She seems to have been P's mistress from 1708 or earlier (see commentary on *Jinny the Just*, 1708, below) until at least 1715. Before his death in 1721, P set her up in business, apparently as proprietress of a small shop, and in his will he bequeathed her £300. In 1722 she married William Hawkins of Maidstone, Kent.

5–20. Cf. Pliny, *Natural History*, xxxv. xxxvi. 86–87.

(276)   *Cupid Mistaken*

MSS. None.
Pub. *1709*, p. 212; *1718*, p. 78.
Text. *1718*. Collated: *1709*.

See commentary on *Love Disarm'd*, above.

Chanson

> Venus le long d'un̄ rivage
> S'alloit ébatant un jour,
> Quand le petit fils Amour
> De loin sa mere en-visage.

*   *   *   *

Amour etonné s'ecrie,
Helas! (dit-il) est-ce toy?
Ma mere pardonne moy,
Je pensoy blesser Marie.

(Durant, p. 90 [F5ᵛ])

A contributor to the *Gentleman's Magazine* (lvii, 1787, i. 138) cites a poem by Angerianus (Girolamo Angeriano, 1470–1512), *De Venere et Cupidine*, as source; but Prior's verses are much closer to Durant's. *Cupid Mistaken* was set to music, and numerous reprints indicate that it was very popular.

(277)   *Venus Mistaken*

MSS. None.
Pub.   *1709*, p. 213; *1718*, p. 78.
Text. *1718*. Collated: *1709*.

See commentary on *To Mr. Howard*, above. The first stanza derives ultimately from the epigrams in the *Greek Anthology* (xvi, Nos. 160, 162, 163, 168), which describe how Aphrodite saw the Cnidian Aphrodite of Praxiteles and asked where the sculptor saw her naked. The contributor to the *Gentleman's Magazine* (lvii, 1787, i. 138) cites Angerianus, *De Caeliae Pictura*; but this is no closer to Prior's version than the Greek epigrams. An unsigned Latin translation of P's poem appeared in *1740*, p. 380.

(278)   *Cloe Hunting*

MSS. None.
Pub.   *1709*, p. 211; *1718*, p. 74.
Text. *1718*. Collated: *1709*.

In *1709* this poem preceded *Cupid Mistaken*; we have changed the order to place it after the three poems which refer to the portrait of Anne Durham. The situation—Apollo mistaking Cloe for Cynthia—is parallel to that in *Venus Mistaken*. In *1718* Prior placed *Love Disarm'd* immediately before this poem to explain how Cloe gained possession of Cupid's weapons. It is possible that *Cloe Hunting*, like the three preceding poems, refers to a portrait, for in P's bedroom, with the pictures of Anne Durham and Elizabeth Cox, there was a painting by Kneller of 'Artemisa'. There is no way of identifying the woman who posed as Artemis; it is tempting to speculate that she may have been Jinny the Just, Anne Durham's predecessor.

The same contributor to the *Gentleman's Magazine* (lvii, 1787, i. 138) who suggested Angerianus as source for the two preceding poems cited, with much greater plausibility, the same writer's *De Caelia venante* as source for this one.

> Dum vaga venatur per nostros Caelia saltus,
> Hanc cernens subito Delius obstupuit.

*   *   *   *

> Venantes ambo, verum, sed dispare praeda
> Juno ait, haec homines conficit, illa feras.

(*Hieron. Angeriani Neapolitani* Ἐρωτοπαίγνιον. Florentiae. M.D.XII., Sig. C1ᵛ)

(278)   *Henry and Emma*

MSS. None.
Pub.   *1709*, p. 232; *1718*, p. 215.
Text.   *1718*. Collated: *1709*.

     John Oldmixon printed *The Nut-brown Maid. A Poem, near 300 Years Old* in the *Muses Mercury*, June 1707, pp. 134 ff. In his preliminary essay he states that his text is a copy of that in the Pepys collection of ballads, which was itself copied from an old book called *Customs of London*. 'This old Poem is a Compliment to the Fair Sex, who are often charg'd with Inconstancy: But the Author of those Verses gives you an Example of Female Truth, which no Trials cou'd shock. The Persons represented are a young Lord, the Earl of *Westmorland*'s Son; who, disguis'd like a Servant, had the good Fortune to be belov'd by a young Lady of equal Quality, tho she did not know his . . .' (p. 133). This publication of *The Nut-brown Maid* was the occasion of Prior's imitation. In both *1709* and *1718* he printed the text of *The Nut-brown Maid* before *Henry and Emma*, following Oldmixon in giving it the erroneous subtitle, '*Written Three Hundred Years Since*'. (Oldmixon thought *Customs of London* was printed *c.* 1472, and conjectured that the poem was written *c.* 1400.) Before 1718, however, P had obtained a copy of *Customs of London* (by Richard Arnold: Antwerp, 1503?; Southwark, 1521), in which *The Nut-brown Maid* was first printed, and had given it to Lord Harley; P wrote to Humphrey Wanley, who was helping him put *1718* through the press, suggesting that Wanley compare the text in that volume (*B.M. Harl. 3780*, 344, quoted by Wickham Legg, p. 260).

     Henry and Emma was extremely popular. It was translated into French prose by Mme Thiroux d'Arconville (*Mélanges de Poésie Angloise*, Paris, 1764), into German by F. J. Bertuch (Stralsund and Leipzig, 1753), and into Latin (with the English on facing pages; London: Lintott, Tonson, and Draper, 1748). Parts of it were set to music by Thomas Arne (*Songs in Henry and Emma . . . a New Musical Drama*, 1749) and by Sir Henry Bates Dudley in 1774. To Johnson's condemnation of it as 'a dull and tedious dialogue', Cowper replied: 'There are few readers of poetry of either sex in this country who cannot remember how that enchanting piece has bewitched them, who do not know that, instead of finding it tedious, they have been so delighted with the romantic turn of it as to have overlooked all its defects, and to have given it a consecrated place in their memories . . .' (Johnson, *Lives*, ii. 203 and notes).

The text of *The Nut-brown Maid* is readily accessible in modern editions (e.g. Percy's *Reliques*, ed. H. B. Wheatley, 1876–7; *Early English Lyrics*, ed. E. K. Chambers and F. Sidgwick, 1937).

5. Cloe may be Anne Durham (see commentary on *To Mr. Howard*, above). Elizabeth Cox, her successor as P's mistress, claimed that 'she was his Emma' (*Gentleman's Magazine*, lvii, 1787, 1039); but this is absurd, since he did not meet her until some years later.

39. In Spenser's *Faerie Queene* (IV. xi, st. 24), the Thame and his wife, the Isis, are represented as the parents of the Thames.

652. DEVA. The river Dee, which flows through Shropshire and Cheshire and forms part of the Welsh border. Cf. Milton, *Lycidas*, l. 55.

749. GAUL thrice Vanquish'd. Marlborough's three great victories: Blenheim (1704), Ramillies (1706), and Oudenarde (July 1708).

(300)   *Jinny the Just*

MSS. *L 29*, 65 (P); *L 29*, 69 (D).
Pub. *1907*, p. 360.
Text. *L 29* (P). Collated: *L 29* (D).

The poem indicates that Jinny was Prior's housekeeper and mistress during his residence at The Hague (1690–7) and at Paris (1698–9) and for some time after his return to England. *Letter to J* . . . (1690), if addressed to the same Jinny, shows that she was a widow and that P's intimacy with her had begun before he left England. P wrote to Charles Montagu from Paris, 9 Aug. 1698, that he was having his maid sent over from England because the French women were so unsatisfactory (*Bodl. Montagu d. 1*, 99–101), and it seems likely that Jinny was the maid referred to. On 8 Aug. 1699, P wrote to Jersey: 'Jane complains that his Excellence [Manchester] blows his nose in the napkins, spits in the middle of the room, and laughs so loud and like an ordinary body that she does not think him fit for an ambassador. She is of opinion that another Lord whom she knows is fitter to be a King than he to be a Lord' (Wickham Legg, p. 308). P's last reference to her occurs in a letter to William Fielding, 2 July 1706 (*L 13*, 71): 'I did not come home Drunk on Saturday Night as you maliciously insinuate in the Noble Epistle you left with Jane, but I was in tenebris till it was too late to write to you: By the by that Nymph is mighty Inquisitive, having read Your Letter about the Signification of the word Tenebræ, which She thinks is Latin for a baudy House.' Pope wrote on 12/13 July 1707, in a verse epistle to Henry Cromwell, ' 'Tis known, a Cook-maid roasted *Prior*' (*Minor Poems*, ed. N. Ault and

J. Butt, 1954, p. 26), which may well be a reference to Jinny. By 1708, P was celebrating a new mistress, Anne Durham (see commentary on *To Mr. Howard*, 1708, above). After P's death, Arbuthnot reported that Betty Cox (P's last mistress) 'owned, Flanders Jane was his Chloe' (*Gentleman's Magazine*, lvii, 1787, 1039); this gives us Jinny's nickname, though the statement that she was Cloe is untrue as applied to the poems of 1708 and after. Eves (p. 215) conjectures that the Jane Ansley who was P's housekeeper in 1721 and to whom P left a year's wages, mourning, and £50 was Flanders Jane.

The poem was written after 1700, but perhaps not long after (see notes to ll. 39 and 102). Four cancelled stanzas represent the beginning P originally wrote for the poem. The first of these is of interest as giving a specific situation and occasion. The second and third were incorporated, after revision, as ll. 100–2 and 97–99 respectively. The last line of the last stanza P used later in *For His own Epitaph* (1714). The whole passage makes it clear that Jinny was still alive, and still P's housekeeper, at the time of composition:

> With her Parrot and dogg on the sides of her bedd
> With the Key of the Celler close under her head
> Here J—— lyes extended as if She were Dead
>
> Then fancy Her turn'd to her primitive Clay
> For so I'm persuaded She must be one day
> What ever fantastic J—— Asgil may say
>
> And when that Day comes since no more can be don Her
> Then to take a due Care of her Corps and her honour
> Lest unsanctify'd Hands or Ill tongues light upon Her
>
> If a little before hand her praises I mention
> My hast You'l ascribe to my pious Intention,
> Go[o]d Doctors give Psysic by way of Prevention.
>
> (L 29, 66)

Jinny the Just is very similar in theme to *An Epitaph* (Doubtful, 1703) and employs the same metre and stanza, though there are no verbal resemblances. Certainly the two poems are closely related, though there seems to be no way of determining precisely what the relationship was. The most plausible hypothesis is that Dorset wrote *An Epitaph* and that *Jinny* was suggested by it.

Pope and Swift read the poem in manuscript, and liked it so much that they asked permission to print it in their *Miscellanies*; Pope wrote to Lord Oxford on 26 Dec. 1727: 'If you have no Material objection to suffering that Epitaph on Jenny of Mr. Priors to accompany some things of the same nature of the Dean of St Patricks & mine, it is what would be very agreable to him. He several times spoke of it to me to ask you . . .' (*Correspondence*, ed. G. Sherburn, Oxford, 1956, ii. 466). Oxford must have objected, for Pope wrote again two days later: 'If your objection to adding Jenny's Epit. to our Collection, be grounded on its being Own'd to be Mr Prior's, we need only set 2 initial Letters before it; But whatever you think right, I am sure I shall do the same.' Oxford evidently did not consent, for the poem was not printed.

39. J——. Probably Jacob Tonson, one of the founders and leading members of the Kit-Cat Club, which toasted reigning beauties. P belonged to this Whig club in 1700 (see commentary on *Prologue, By Sir John Falstaff*, Doubtful, 1700).

102. For John Asgill, see note to *An Ode* (1704), l. 39. The title of his book is self-explanatory: *An Argument Proving, That according to the Covenant of Eternal Life revealed in the Scriptures, Man may be translated from hence into that Eternal Life, without passing through Death, altho the Humane Nature of Christ himself could not be thus translated till he had passed through Death*, 1700. It was burned by order of the Irish House of Commons, 1703, and of the English Commons, 1707.

(304) *Florimel*

MSS. *W*, 26ᵛ (P); *L 28*, 156 (D).
Pub. *1907*, p. 330.
Text. *W*. Collated: *L 28*.

Prior's draft of this occurs on the same page in *W* as his drafts for revisions of some passages in *A Letter to M. Boileau* (1704), these revisions being incorporated in the version of that poem published in *1709*. Since *Florimel* precedes the revisions on the page, it seems reasonably certain that it was written by 1708.

(304) *Seneca, Troas*

MSS. *W*, 34 (D & P); *W*, 53 (D; ll. 12–19 only); *L 28*, 137 (D); *L 28*, 160 (D; ll. 12–19 only). (Index to *M*.)
Pub. *1907*, p. 321.
Text. *W* [34]. Collated: *L 28* [137]; for ll. 12–19: *W* (53), *L 28* (160).

Since almost half of this translation was incorporated in *Solomon* (1708), it must have been composed before that poem. Seneca's famous chorus had recently been translated by Rochester (*Poems*, 1680, ed. Thorpe, p. 50) and Glanville (*The Annual Miscellany*, 1694, Case 172–4–a, p. 306). Prior's version, however, shows no indebtedness to these.

3–8. Cf. *Solomon*, iii. 593–600.
20–33. Cf. *Solomon*, iii. 520–31.

(306) *Solomon*

MSS. *W*, 39ᵛ, 43, 44, 53ᵛ (P & D; the following passages only: i. 383–90, 682–98, 743–4, 754–9; ii. 477–8, 560–1; iii. 512–17, 787–8); *L 13*, 91 (D; ii. 576–7 only).

Pub. *1718*, p. 383.

Text. *1718*. Collated: *W, L 13*.

Prior's statement in the Preface (written in 1717 or 1718) that *Solomon* 'has *indeed been written and laid aside much longer*' than the nine years prescribed by Horace fixes the date of composition as not later than 1708, and probably some years before. On 2 Nov. 1706, P quoted a couplet from *Solomon* in a letter to Lord Cholmondeley (*L 13*, 91), and he mentioned 'my Solomon', as if completed, to Hanmer in June 1707 (*Correspondence of Sir Thomas Hanmer*, ed. Sir Henry Bunbury, 1838, p. 111). *Dedication*, 1708, refers to it by implication, as one of the 'Pieces of a very different Nature (the Product of my severer Studies)' that will be published later. *A letter from Sr: Wm: Windham to Mr. Prior April 18th 1714* (*B.M. Lansd. 852*, 56ᵛ; also in *Lpo 11*, 79ᵛ–80) praises *Solomon*, and describes a convivial evening when P entertained a group of 'Brothers' by reading from the poem. Erasmus Lewis, writing to Swift on 12 Jan. 1717, about the plan for publishing *1718*, says, 'we have a project of printing his Solomon and other poetical works, by subscription' (Swift, *Correspondence*, ed. F. Elrington Ball, 1910–14, ii. 360). The fact that the passages in *W* occur on the same pages as material intended for *Alma* and other poems of 1715–18 indicates that P did revise parts of *Solomon*; but *W* contains less than fifty lines out of a total of 2,652. P was disappointed in the reception of the poem, and annoyed at the general preference of *Alma*; see *The Conversation* (1720), ll. 61–64, and Johnson, *Lives*, ii. 206.

Whatever its worth as a poem, *Solomon* is an important document in literary and intellectual history. Pope made much use of it in the *Essay on Man*, as Maynard Mack's notes in his edition (1950) show. John Wesley (*Works*, 1831, xiii. 380–7) and William Cowper (*Works*, 1836–7, iv. 169) greatly admired the poem and were indebted to it. According to Ian Jack ('The "Choice of Life" in Johnson and Matthew Prior', *Journal of English and Germanic Philology*, xlix, 1950, 523–30), Johnson learned much from *Solomon* and shows its influence in *Rasselas* and *The Vanity of Human Wishes*.

For discussion of the background and meaning of *Solomon*, see three articles by M. K. Spears: 'Matthew Prior's Religion', *Philological Quarterly*, xxvii, 1948, 159–80; 'Some Ethical Aspects of Matthew Prior's Poetry', *Studies in Philology*, lxv, 1948, 606–29; 'Matthew Prior's Attitude Toward Natural Science', *P.M.L.A.* lxiii, 1948, 485–507.

Solomon was translated into Latin verse by William Dobson; the three books were separately published, Oxford, 1734–6, and the translation was reprinted in *1740*, pp. 227–379. Spence (*Anecdotes*, 1820, p. 179) says that Dobson 'got a great deal of reputation' by this translation. The second book was also translated into Latin by George Bally (Cambridge and London, 1743). A German translation by Simon Grynaeus was published in 1757 (Basel, J. J. Schorndorff).

To annotate *Solomon* fully would require disproportionate space, since the poem is intended to be a synthesis of traditional wisdom. Our citations of sources are to be regarded as representative rather than complete. Biblical sources and allusions are not identified, nor are Pope's numerous borrowings indicated.

[Motto 1.] From a lost play by Euripides. P might have found the quotation in Joshua Barnes, *Euripides* (Cambridge, 1694), p. 514. (We owe this reference to A. B. Conron.)

[Motto 2.] Cicero, *De Senectute*, xxiii. 83.

[Motto 3.] P takes this quotation not from the English *Advancement of Learning* (1605), but from an English translation of the enlarged Latin version, *De Augmenti Scientiarum*, of 1628: *Of the Advancement and Proficience of Learning or the Partitions of Sciences IX Bookes Written in Latin by the Most Eminent Illustrious & Famous Lord Francis Bacon . . .* Interpreted by Gilbert Wats (Oxford, 1640), p. 179.

Preface.

29. HORACE. *Ars Poetica*, l. 23.

70–71. *The Pleasures of Life . . . Miseries.* Cf. Montaigne, ii. 311–12, 319 (Bk. II, ch. xii).

71–72. *Death, as the only Cure of our Ills.* Cf. *To Dr. Sherlock* (1690), l. 27: 'And LIFE an Ill, whose only Cure is DEATH'; *Written in Mezeray's History* (1708 above), ll. 15–16.

83. Lucretius, iii. 1042–5.

91. Nec Deus . . . nodus. Horace, *Ars Poetica*, l. 191.

126. PHILIPPS. John Philips (1676–1709), whose *Splendid Shilling, Blenheim,* and *Cyder* are written in Miltonic blank verse.

132. *Friends now living.* E.g. Pope, whose translation of the *Iliad* had been appearing since 1715. (P was among the subscribers.)

134. *He that writes in Rhimes, dances in Fetters.* See George Saintsbury, *History of English Prosody* (1906–10), ii. 425.

142. Nonum prematur in Annum. *Ars Poetica*, l. 388.

166. *Lord* BATHURST. Allen, Earl Bathurst (1684–1775), and P were fellow members of the Brothers Club in 1711–12. He is said to have persuaded P to include *Alma* in *1718*; see commentary on that poem.

167. *whose Names do me great Honor . . . Book.* The list of subscribers prefixed to *1718*. 1,447 names are listed, including virtually all the notabilities of the time.

Book I

13. Cf. *To the Honourable Charles Montague* (1692), ll. 3–4 and note.

138–57. 'Who taught the Bee to sayle thorow such a vast sea of Aire, to the Flowers in the Fields; and to find the way so farre off to hir Hive againe? Who taught the Ant to bite every grain of Corne that she burieth in hir hill, lest it should take root and grow, and so delude hir hope?' (Gilbert Wats's translation of Bacon, *De Augmentis*, V. ii; p. 222).

185–8. 'Nos sens n'aperçoivent rien d'extrême . . . trop de distance et trop de proximité empêche la vue' (Pascal, i. 83; frag. 72).

189–90. Cf. Lucretius, iv. 353–5, 438–42.

231–6. Cf. Montaigne: 'Je dy donc . . . qu'il n'y a point d'apparence d'estimer que les bestes facent par inclination naturelle et forcée les mesmes choses que nous faisons par nostre choix et industrie. Nous devons conclurre de pareils effects pareilles facultez, et confesser par consequent que ce mesme discours, cette mesme voye, que nous tenons à ouvrer, c'est aussi celle des animaux' (ii. 254; Bk. II, ch. xii). See George Boas, *The Happy Beast in French Thought of the Seventeenth Century*, Baltimore, 1933.

339–40. The attempt to reconcile Genesis with the existence of savages in America and elsewhere led some writers to argue that the Flood was not universal and not all men were Noah's descendants; others argued that the Gentiles were created before Adam. See the citations of F. B. Kaye, ed., Mandeville's *The Fable of the Bees* (Oxford, 1924), ii. 196 n–198 n.

355–68. Cf. Lucretius, i. 782–8.

383–90. Cf. Montaigne: 'Les miracles sont selon l'ignorance en quoy nous sommes de la nature, non selon l'estre de la nature L'assuefaction endort la veuë de nostre jugement' (i. 207; Bk. I, ch. xxiii). The same idea is implied in *On Exodus iii. 14* (1688), st. vii. Clarke used this argument in his controversy with Leibniz: 'I affirmed that, with regard to *God*, no one Possible thing is more *miraculous* than another; and that therefore a *Miracle* does not consist in any *Difficulty in the Nature of the Thing to be Done*, but merely in the *Unusualness of God's doing it*.' Leibniz replied that this would make everything 'either equally *natural*, or equally *miraculous*. Will *Divines* like the former, or *Philosophers* the latter?' (*A Collection of Papers*, 1717, pp. 149, 265. The controversy is discussed in the note to *Alma* (1718), iii. 335.)

502–11. 'But *Velleius* the Epicurean needed not to have asked, why God should have adorned the heavens with starres and lights, as if he had bin an *AEdilis*; one that should have set forth some magnificent shewes or playes: for if that great Workman had conform'd himselfe to the imitation of an *AEdilis*, he would have cast the starres into some pleasant and beautifull workes, and orders, like the curious roofs of Palaces, whereas one can scarce find in such an infinite number of starres a Posture in square, or Triangle, or right-Line. *So different a harmony there is betweene the Spirit of man, and the Spirit of the world*' (Gilbert Wats's translation of Bacon, *De Augmentis*, V. iv; p. 251).

512–35. The astronomy of this passage is inconsistent with the geocentric description of ll. 254–5, above; but P has justified such anachronisms in the Preface. The concept of a plurality of inhabited worlds had been popularized by Fontenelle's *Entretiens sur la Pluralité des Mondes* (1686), of which P owned two copies.

536–9. Cf. Pascal: 'C'est une sphère infinie dont le centre est partout, la circonférence nulle part' (i. 73; frag. 72); also *Spectator*, No. 590.

549–62. Cf. Montaigne, ii. 398–9 (Bk. II, ch. xii).

635–6. Cf. Pascal: 'Juge de toutes choses, imbécile ver de terre; dépositaire du vrai, cloaque d'incertitude et d'erreur; gloire et rebut de l'univers' (ii. 346; frag. 434).

693–8. A prose draft of this passage, in P's hand, is found in *W*, 171: 'o flattery thou art the food of folly, the bane of virtue, the tares that choaks the corn and deformest the feild and Spoylst the harvest of our lives' (also in *L 28*, 324, as transcribed by Drift).

707–20. Cf. *On Exodus iii. 14* (1688), st. vi.

739–40. Cf. Denham, *The Progress of Learning* (1668), ll. 195–8:

> Through Seas of knowledg, we our course advance,
> Discovering still new worlds of Ignorance;
> And these Discoveries make us all confess
> That sublunary Science is but guess. . . .
>   (*Poetical Works*, ed. T. H. Banks, New Haven, 1928, p. 120)

744. The nature of Space and Time and their relation to God were muchcontroverted questions; see the note to *Alma* (1718), iii. 335.

760–7. Cf. Montaigne: 'Le soing de s'augmenter en sagesse et en science, ce fut la premiere ruine du genre humain; c'est la voye par où il s'est precipité à la damnation eternelle' (ii. 330; Bk. II, ch. xii).

Book II

52. Cf. *To the Honourable Charles Montague* (1692), st. vii.

128. elanc'd. A Gallicism apparently peculiar to P.

360. ABRA. P considered *Zilpha* and *Zilla* before deciding on the name *Abra*, as his jottings in *W*, 52ᵛ show.

539. The image of the passions as winds was a commonplace in discussions of the 'use of passions'; see Mack's notes to *Essay on Man*, ii. 105–8. P's version reverses the usual optimistic connotation.

617–22. Cf. *Aeneid*, iv. 133–9.

730–4. Cf. *Aeneid*, iv. 86–89.

812. Cf. Ovid, *Metam.* ii. 846–7.

851–8. Cf. *Aeneid*, ii. 305–8.

916. Cf. Milton, *On the Morning of Christ's Nativity*, ll. 211–12.

922. See *An Epistle to Fleetwood Shephard* (1689), ll. 63–64 and note.

959–62. Cf. Dryden, *Conquest of Granada, Pt. I*, III. i: 'Ah, Why did Heav'n leave Man so weak Defence, | To trust frail Reason with the Rule of Sense! | . . . like a Captive-King, 'tis born away; | And forc'd to count'nance its own Rebel's sway'; Boileau, *Satire IV*: 'En vain certains rêveurs nous l'habillent en reine, | Veulent sur tous nos sens la [la raison] rendre souveraine.' See also Mack's note to Pope's *Essay on Man*, ii. 149–50.

Book III

86–94. Cf. Montaigne, i. 458–61 (Bk. I, ch. xxxix); Lucretius, iii. 1053–75.
95–101. See note to l. 223 below.
    102. A correspondent in *N. & Q.* (vi, 1852, 158) points out that Diogenes Laertius (v. 18) attributes this thought to Aristotle; a later correspondent notes that Stobaeus attributes it to Pindar. P may also have found it in Bouhours, *Pensées Ingenieuses* (1692), which was in his library: 'L'Esperance a esté appellée par un ancien Sage . . . le songe d'un homme éveillé' (p. 159).
    103–5. Based on Motto 2, from Cicero.
    136–97. Cf. Juvenal, *Satires*, x. 188–245.
    163. dim Suffusion. Cf. *Paradise Lost*, iii. 25–26.
    167. Grateful Vicissitude. Cf. *Paradise Lost*, vi. 8.
    223. Cf. *To the Honourable Charles Montague* (1692), l. 9: 'Against Experience He believes'; Pascal (ii. 322–3; frag. 425): 'Une épreuve si longue, si continuelle et si uniforme, devrait bien nous convaincre de notre impuissance d'arriver au bien par nos efforts. Mais l'exemple nous instruit peu: . . . nous attendons que notre attente ne sera pas déçue en cette occasion comme en l'autre. Et ainsi, le présent ne nous satisfaisant jamais, l'expérience nous pipe, et de malheur en malheur, nous mène jusqu'à la mort, qui en est un comble éternel.'
    225–41. Based on Theognis, 425–8.
    253. Cf. Cowley's translation of Horace, *Odes*, III. i. 1: 'Hence ye profane, I hate ye all | Both the great vulgar and the small.'
    323–30. Cf. Juvenal, *Satires*, x. 56–77.
    424. Cf. *On Exodus iii. 14* (1688), and Dryden's *Hind and the Panther*, i. 65: 'Thy Throne is darkness in th'abyss of light.'
    470. Tube. Telescope.
    520–31. Here, as at ll. 593–600, the translation of *Seneca, Troas* (1708, above) is incorporated.
    588. A traditional argument for immortality; see Mack's note to Pope's *Essay on Man*, iv. 347–8.
    613–18. Cf. Cowley, *Life and Fame*, ll. 10–11: 'Vain, weak-built *Isthmus*, which dost proudly rise | Up betwixt two *Eternities*'; Pascal (ii. 88–90; frag. 172): 'Nous ne nous tenons jamais au temps présent. . . . Le présent n'est jamais notre fin: . . . le seul avenir est notre fin. Ainsi nous ne vivons jamais, mais nous espérons de vivre; et, nous disposant toujours à être heureux, il est inévitable que nous ne le soyons jamais.' Cf. also *Spectator*, No. 590: '. . . many

witty Authors compare the present Time to an Isthmus or narrow Neck of Land, that rises in the midst of an Ocean. . . .'

645–6. Pascal describes man as 'entre ces deux abîmes de l'infini et du néant'; 'un milieu entre rien et tout' (i. 78; frag. 72).

696–9. Cf. *Paradise Lost*, i. 25–26; Pope, *Essay on Man*, i. 16.

735–809. Cf. the vision of the future that Michael shows to Adam in the last two books of *Paradise Lost*.

822–3. Cf. Montaigne, ii. 320 (Bk. II, ch. xii).

836–7. Cf. *On Exodus iii. 14* (1688); also *Paradise Lost*, viii. 119–22.

1709

(385)   *To Isaac Bickerstaff*

MSS.   *M*, 194 (D & A); *L* 27, 69 (D; verses only).
Pub.   *1740*, p. 127 (verses only). No publication of the prose letter is known.
Text.   *M*. Collated: *L* 27, *1740*.

This is listed first among the prose works in the Index to *M*. Since it is not mentioned in the *Tatler*'s occasional acknowledgements of communications received and is not in Charles Lillie's *Original and genuine Letters sent to the Tatler and Spectator . . . None of which have been before printed*, 1725, it may never have been submitted. Walter Wou'd have Wit's statement (l. 27) about his birthday, 'which you see I place about the middle of May', seems to indicate the approximate date of composition. The latest *Tatler* to which specific allusion is made is No. 13, 7 to 10 May 1709. The letter could not have been written after the publication of No. 75, 29 Sept. to 1 Oct. 1709, for in that issue Isaac Bickerstaff announced that he had disposed of Jenny, and in No. 79 he dated her marriage to Tranquillus as having occurred on 8 Oct.

Prior had some part in another letter to the *Tatler*, published in No. 258, 30 Nov. to 2 Dec. 1710, a short note in which he collaborated with Swift and Rowe (Swift, *Journal to Stella*, 2 Dec. 1700).

1–2. Steele introduced Isaac's half-sister, Jenny Distaff, in *Tatler*, No. 10, 30 April to 3 May 1709, which purports to have been written by her.

7–8. *Tatler*, No. 11, contains a genealogy of the Staff family in a letter from Isaac's kinsman, D. Distaff, a genealogist at the Heralds' Office.

17–18. Jenny took Isaac's place as 'author' of Nos. 10, 33, 36, 37, 38, and was consulted by him in regard to the Chamber of Fame in No. 68.

33–34. Steele in *Tatler*, No. 1, 12 April 1709, maintained the fiction that the writer of the *Tatlers* was the same Isaac Bickerstaff who in the pamphlets written by Swift had predicted the death of John Partridge, maker of astrological almanacs, and had insisted that it occurred on 29 March 1708, in spite of the victim's protests that he was still alive.

44–47. In *Tatler*, No. 4, Steele had discussed the charms of Chloe and Clarissa and described the pastoral picture of them by Charles Jervas, in which Chloe wore a straw hat. Jervas had been a friend of P's since at least 1699, when he drew the poet's portrait in crayons. See G. A. Aitken, ed., *The Tatler*, 1899, i. 38 n.

48. *Honthurst* and *Houseman*. Gerard van Honthorst (1590–1656) and Jacob Huysmans (1636?–96) were mediocre Dutch and Flemish portrait painters who achieved a fashionable success in England.

52. bite. In *Tatler*, No. 12, Steele had ridiculed this new word for a new form of wit. See further comment in Swift, *Correspondence*, ed. F. Elrington Ball (1910–14), i. 40, and in *Spectator*, Nos. 47 and 504.

57. *Dictinna, Pastorella*. The names of two young women whose characters are sketched in *Tatler*, Nos. 9 and 13.

61–64. J. J. Heidegger's English adaptation of the opera *Clotilda* was first performed at the Haymarket on 13 March 1709 (A. Loewenberg, *Annals of Opera*, 1943, p. 59). Steele had attacked Italian opera in *Tatler*, No. 4, and in No. 12 had called Heidegger 'a surgeon, who cuts any foreign fellow into an eunuch, and passes him upon us for a singer of Italy'.

68. Gilles Ménage, *Dictionnaire Etymologique*, 1650; Antoine Furetière, *Dictionnaire Universel*, 1690.

1710

(388)   *A Fable*

MSS. None.
Pub.   *The Examiner: or, Remarks upon Papers and Occurrences*. Numb. 3. From Thursday, August 10. to Thursday, August 17. 1710.
       Collected: *1740*, p. 39.
Text. *1710*. Collated: *1740*.

The Examiner, the Tory ministry's answer to Whig propaganda, commenced publication on 3 Aug. 1710. The first issue began by 'examining' a Whig pamphlet, *A Letter from Monsieur Pett[icu]m to Monsieur B[u]ys. Faithfully Translated from the French Original*. London, Printed in the Year 1710. This *Letter*, purporting to be written by the agent of Holstein to the Dutch Deputy, concerned English affairs, especially the dangers involved in a dissolution of Parliament at that time. *Examiner*, No. 3, which continues the attack begun in No. 1, says: 'I know to what Hand common Fame ascribes it; but I will not, I cannot believe her, because I think I can make it pretty plain, that 'tis writ without Art or Wisdom; and that the Writer, whoever he was, could neither be a good *English-man*, nor a faithful *Subject* to the *Queen*, nor even a true *Friend* of the present *Ministers*.' In addition to condemning the author for his untruths and his political views, the *Examiner* criticizes his lack of skill in maintaining the fiction: 'This Gentleman, whoever he be, that has writ a Letter in the Name of Mr. *Pett——m*, has but an ill Hand at personating; and has err'd in two material Points, which a good Counterfeit should always take Care of, first to choose a proper Subject for him he represents, and then to make him speak consistently with his Character, and the Characters of those he has to deal with' (No. 1). *A Fable* is introduced at the end of No. 3: 'In the mean time, having Examin'd the Pretences of this *Personated* Writer, I shall dismiss him, by applying to this terrible Performance of his, what is said of the Player's *Mask* in the Fable. . . . Which I take the Liberty to translate for the Use of some of Mr. *Pett——m*'s Friends, who don't understand the Original.' The note in *1740*, p. 39, identifying the subject of *A Fable* as the 'Author of the Medley. 1710' may be intended as an ascription of the *Letter* to Arthur Mainwaring or to John Oldmixon, although their *Medley* did not begin publication until almost two months after the third *Examiner*.

The prose part of *Examiner*, No. 3, has never been specifically attributed to P. (For discussion of his part in the early *Examiners*, see the list of Works Wrongly Attributed.) The ascription of *A Fable* to him rests upon the authority of *1740* alone.

[Motto.] Phaedrus, *Fabulae*, I. vii.

(389)   *The Examiner. Numb. 6*

MSS. None.
Pub.   *The Examiner*. Numb. 6. From Thursday, August 31. to Thursday,
          September 7. 1710.
          Collected: *1740*, p. 37 (verse only); *1740 History*, p. 318.
Text. *1710*. Collated: *1740*.

Addison, in *The Whig-Examiner*, No. 1, recognized the author of this number of *The Examiner* as the man who wrote *Hans Carvel* and *The Ladle*; and according to *1740 History*, p. 318, it 'is universally allowed' to be by Prior. Its occasion was the publication of *A Poem to the Earl of Godolphin. By Dr. G[art]h*, a Whig eulogy of Godolphin upon his being forced to resign as Lord Treasurer on 8 Aug. 1710. Addison defended Garth's poem against P's criticisms in *The Whig-Examiner*, No. 1, 14 Sept. 1710, and attacked this paper again in *Tatler*, No. 239, 19 Oct. 1710.

[Motto.] Horace, *Epistles*, II. i. 266–7.

2. *Kit cat.* See note to *Jinny the Just* (1708), l. 39 and commentary on *Prologue, By Sir John Falstaff* (Doubtful, 1700).

4. Sir *Harry F——e.* We cannot identify this man.

6. *H——y.* Harley; see commentary on the next poem.

7–8. R. J. Allen (*The Clubs of Augustan London*, Cambridge, Mass., 1933, p. 50) believes this refers to Lady Harcourt, whose husband had defended Sacheverell against the Whig impeachment.

10. 'This *Club* can have but *Thirty-Nine* Members' (J. Macky, *A Journey Through England*, 1714, p. 188).

13. *Squire Trelooby*, an adaptation of Molière's *Monsieur de Pourceaugnac* by Congreve, Vanbrugh, and Walsh, was first performed on 30 March 1704, with a prologue written by Dr. Garth (A. Nicoll, *A History of Early Eighteenth Century Drama*, Cambridge, 1925, pp. 152, 363).

14–15. See commentary on *Epilogue to Phaedra* (1707).

20. Richard Bentley (1662–1742), great textual critic, Whig, cleric, and enemy of Swift's.

60–62. Garth's poem *The Dispensary* had, since its first appearance in 1699, gone through a series of editions 'corrected by the author' and had in 1706 reached a sixth edition 'with several descriptions and episodes never before printed'. P quotes from Canto I, p. 12, of this revision.

63–64. Beginning with the second edition (1699), *The Dispensary* included Christopher Codrington's verses 'To my Friend the Author, Desiring my Opinion of his Poem', which judge the work according to this criterion:

> Criticks, and aged Beaux of Fancy chast,
> Who ne'er had Fire, or else whose Fire is past,
> Must judge by Rules what they want Force to Taste.
> I wou'd a Poet, like a Mistress, try,
> Not by her Hair, her Hand, her Nose, her Eye;
> But by some Nameless Pow'r, to give me Joy.

112. *Five Stars.* Two days after Godolphin's dismissal, the Treasury was put in the hands of a commission of five.

132. *Busby.* See note to *A Session of the Poets* (1688), l. 60.

137–9. The official medal distributed at Queen Anne's coronation pictured her as Pallas Athena hurling thunderbolts against a double-headed monster; the legend was 'VICEM GERIT . ILLA . TONANTIS' with reference to Anne's determination to follow the policy of King William in opposition to France (E. Hawkins, *Medallic Illustrations*, 1885, ii. 228).

144. Dryden, *Don Sebastian*, III. i.

191–4. The answer to Oedipus' riddle is given in *1740*, p. 38 n., as 'A Prime-Minister'. Specifically, the lines refer to Godolphin, who gained the Lord Treasurer's staff of office, lost it, and then crawled off the scene.

(394)   *Horace Lib. I. Epist. IX*

MSS.   *W*, 4 (D & P); *Lpo 11*, 74ᵛ (D); *B.M. Lansd. 852*, 51ᵛ (X).
Pub.   [Title as in text.] To the Right Honourable R . . . . . H . . . . ., Esq.
       Printed for Bernard Lintott, at the Cross-Keys, between the two
       Temple-Gates in Fleet-street. [1711]; *Miscellaneous Poems and Transla-
       tions*, 1712 (Case 260–1–a), p. 72.
       Collected: *1716*, p. 14; *1718*, p. 283.
Text. *1718*. Collated: *W*, *Lpo*, *Lansd.*, *1711*.

In *Lansd.*, which was collected for and annotated chiefly by Edward Lord
Harley, there is the following note: 'These Verses were sent to Mr. Read,
Mr. Harleys Porter, That if he liked them to shew them to his Master. 1710.'
Robert Harley (1661–1724), leader of the moderate Tories, became Chan-
cellor of the Exchequer in Aug. 1710.

    1. DICK. Richard Shelton; see note to *Alma* (1718), l. 1. Prior's plea was
not immediately successful, for he wrote to Harley again in 1712 and in 1713
seeking preferment for Shelton (Strong, *Catalogue*, pp. 280, 288) and to
Bolingbroke in Sept. 1713: 'Poor Dick Shelton dines sometimes, I think, in
York-Buildings; he has done so these three years; but cholic, spleen, and
disappointment, hinder peoples digestion. Pray persist in your good opinion
of him, my Lord, for he really deserves it from you. I have likewise engaged
the Duke of Shrewsbury to put in a kind word in his behalf; for what, in
God's name, do we translate our odes, and write our little stuff, but to be
able to do our friends some good? and why is a man, who may be useful to
the public, and whose heart is with us, to lie fallow till either we have not
the power to do him service, or till he wants health to enjoy our friendly
offices?' (Bolingbroke, *Correspondence*, ed. G. Parke, 1798, iv. 266–7). Shelton
finally got his preferment early in 1714, and P wrote to Halifax in Oct. 1714
asking 'that our old Fellow Collegiate and my *fidus Achates* Mr Richard
Shelton, whom my Lord of Oxford after 4 years importunity on my part,
made a Commissioner of the Stamp office some months since, may by your
favour be retained still in his employment . . .' (Wickham Legg, p. 223, from
B.M. Add. 15947, 1).

(395)   *To the Lady Elizabeth Harley*

MSS.   *L 29*, 15 (P); *W*, 43ᵛ (P; title only); *Lpo 11*, 80 (D); *B.M. Lansd. 852*,
       53ᵛ (X).
Pub.   *1718*, p. 291.
Text. *1718*. Collated: *L 29*, *W*, *Lpo 11*, *Lansd.*

    In *Lansd.* there is this note: 'The following Lines by Mr Prior: On a
Pillar drawn by Mrs. Elizabeth Harley 1710.' Lady Elizabeth Harley married

Peregrine Hyde Osborne, Marquis of Carmarthen (who later became third Duke of Leeds) on 15 Dec. 1712. She died in Nov. 1713.

In *W*, 54ᵛ, there is in Prior's hand a discarded attempt at a similar quatrain:

> future time shal say
> How Harley's daughter studious past the day
> While four fold to her father she restor'd
> Blessings, which from him She at Morn implor'd.

In Drift's transcript (*L 28*, 159) the quatrain is entitled: 'On the Marchioness of Caermarthen'.

(396) *Gualterus Danistonus*

MSS. *B.M. Lansd. 852*, 52 (X).

Pub. *Walter Danniston, Ad Amicos. Imitated by Mr. Prior* [N.D.]; *Archibaldi Pitcarnii Scoti. Carmen. Anno Aetatis suae LX. Imitated by Mr. Prior* [1712]; *Miscellaneous Poems and Translations*, 1712 (Case 260–1–a), p. 67. Collected: *1716*, p. 9; *1718*, p. 297.

Text. *1718*. Collated: *Lansd.*, *N.D.*, *1712*, *1712m* [*Miscellaneous Poems*].

The title of the second publication listed above dates the Latin poem 1712, when Pitcairne was 60; this publication appeared early in 1712 (G. A. Aitken, 'Notes on the Bibliography of Matthew Prior', *Transactions of the Bibliographical Society*, xiv, 1915–17, p. 54). In *Lansd.*, however, Prior's imitation is dated 1710; and since the dates in *Lansd.* are usually reliable and often confirmed by other evidence, we accept this date.

The Latin poem, as P printed it in *1718* before his imitation, is as follows:

> Dum Studeo fungi fallentis munere vitæ,
>   Adfectoque viam sedibus Elysiis,
> ARCTOA florens Sophiâ, SAMIISQUE superbus
>   Discipulis, Animas morte carere cano.
> Has ego corporibus profugas ad sidera mitto;
>   Sideraque ingressis otia blanda dico;
> Qualia conveniunt Divis, queis fata volebant
>   Vitäi faciles mollitèr ire vias:
> Vinaque Cœlicolis media inter gaudia libo;
>   Et me quid majus suspicor esse viro.
> Sed fuerint nulli forsan, quos spondeo, cœli;
>   Nullaque sint DITIS Numina, nulla JOVIS:
> Fabula sit terris agitur quæ vita relictis;
>   Quique superstes, Homo; qui nihil, esto Deus.
> Attamen esse hilares, & inanes mittere curas
>   Proderit, ac vitæ commoditate frui,
> Et festos agitâsse dies, ævique fugacis
>   Tempora perpetuis detinuisse jocis.
> His me parentem præceptis occupet Orcus,
>   Et Mors; seu Divum, seu nihil esse velit:
> Nam Sophia Ars illa est, quæ fallere suavitèr horas
>   Admonet, atque Orci non timuisse minas.

We have not found any publication of this Latin poem dated before its appearance with P's imitation; however, the National Library of Scotland and the Bodleian Library have copies of a single-leaf quarto without imprint that may be earlier. This text has a variant first line, 'Dum prudens utor redituræ munere vitæ', and two additional lines between ll. 18 and 19. Even the texts published with P's verses vary strangely from one another. The one published as *Archibaldi Pitcarnii Scoti. Carmen* [1712] has twenty-four lines, the first of which reads, 'Dum moriens laetor redeuntis munere vitae'. The version in *Selecta Poemata Archibaldi Pitcarnii* (Edinburgh, 1727), p. 1, has the title *Johannis Sylvii de seipso carmen*; and the first of its twenty-two lines reads, 'Dum brevis adnitor momentum fallere vitæ'. In *L 28*, 394 there is a copy by Drift of a twenty-line version with the same title and first line as this last, but with several lines that differ in part from any of the published texts. At the bottom of *Archibaldi Pitcarnii Scoti. Carmen*, I Cor. xv. 19 is quoted in both Latin and English.

Archibald Pitcairne (1652–1713) was an eminent Scottish physician. He was Professor of Medicine at Leyden in the 1690's when P was in Holland, and P may have met him there; he made a complimentary allusion to P in an ode written in 1708 (L. Bradner, *Musae Anglicanae*, 1940, p. 249). George Sewell, in the Preface to his translation of Pitcairne's *Whole Works*, remarks: 'And it was not long before he died, that he gave us that excellent Picture of himself in a Copy of Verses, which are at least equal, both in their Easiness, Simplicity, and Elegance of Thought and Stile, to any of CATULLUS, and far superior to any modern Composition of that kind. They have been printed by MR. PRIOR, who honoured them with an Imitation . . .' (2nd ed., 1727; the Preface is dated 1715). Pitcairne engaged in Latin poetical competitions with his friend Walter Daniston, a country schoolmaster, and sometimes circulated his Latin verses among his friends under Daniston's name. See *Biographia Britannica* (1760 ed.), s.v. *Pitcairne*; W. Anderson, *The Scottish Nation* (1877), pp. 290–1.

(397)   *To a Person who wrote Ill*

MSS. None.
Pub.   *1718*, p. 198.
Text. *1718*.

This and the following poem may be dated 1703–10 on the basis of the reference to BRAG in l. 8. PHILO cannot be identified with certainty, but Daniel Defoe seems to fit the description reasonably well. (We are indebted to Mr. Spiro Peterson for help in the discussion of Defoe.)

Benjamin Bragg, or Bragge, was active as a bookseller from 1703 to 1710, when his name appeared on a title-page apparently for the last time (see No. 49 in W. J. Cameron, *A Bibliography of English Poetical Miscellanies*, Turnbull

Library Bulletin, No. xi, Wellington, N.Z., 1953). During this period Prior was under attack for turning Tory and for supposedly writing satires on his former friends and superiors. The most important satires on P were: *The Blasted Laurel* (1702), a long poem devoted entirely to abuse of P; *Faction Display'd. A Poem. Answered Paragraph by Paragraph* (1704), which denounced P as the supposed author of the libel it answered; and a vicious passage of twenty-four lines in *Reformation of Manners* (1702), pp. 30–31.

All three of these publications were anonymous, and Bragg's name did not appear on any of them. The authors of the first two are still unknown, and we cannot tell what guesses P may have made about their identity and their connexion with Bragg. The authorship of *Reformation of Manners* was, however, not long a secret; for in 1703 it was reprinted, not only in *P.O.A.S.*, vol. ii, but also in two collections of Defoe's works. In 1704 Bragg was one of the publishers of the *London Post*, edited by Defoe; in 1705 Bragg advertised Defoe's *Double Welcome* in the *Term Catalogues* (iii. 465–6) and put his imprint on three of Defoe's other works. In one of these, *The Consolidator*, Defoe impugned the competence of all the Commissioners of Trade and, on p. 27, again attacked P personally. By 1705, then, Defoe could easily have been recognized as an enemy and Bragg identified as his publisher. By that time, also, Defoe was in close enough contact with political leaders so that his '*vivâ voce* Reflection' (l. 10) could be dangerous (J. Sutherland, *Defoe*, 1938, pp. 49, 148–53). And in his *Review*, with its witty 'Advice from the Scandal. Club', he was boasting of his ability as a linguist (vol. ii, No. 38, 31 May 1705).

(397)   *On the Same Person*

MSS. None.
Pub.   *1718*, p. 199.
Text. *1718*.

3. TEAGUE. In Sir Robert Howard's *The Committee* (v. i), honest Teague, the prototype of many other stage Irishmen, explains that the Devil would not let him go where he wanted but made his legs carry him 'to this little long place, and t'other little long place'.

1711

(398)   *To Mr. Harley*

MSS. *Lpo 11*, 75ᵛ (D); *Lpo 17*, 126ᵛ (X); *B.M. Lansd. 852*, 52ᵛ (X).
Pub.   *To the Right Honourable Mr. Harley, Wounded by Guiscard*. London: Printed for Jacob Tonson at Shakespear's-head, over-against Catherine-street in the Strand. MDCCXI; Abel Boyer, *The Political State of Great*

Britain, Vol. I. London: Printed, and Sold by J. Baker . . . 1711, p. 333.
Collected: *1718*, p. 285.
Text. *1718*. Collated: *1711* [Tonson], *Lpo 11*, *Lpo 17*, *Lansd.*

Antoine de Guiscard, a French adventurer who called himself the Marquis
de Guiscard and had once been an abbot, had been employed by the Godolphin ministry. Harley did not like him and reduced his pay; Guiscard then
sold himself back to France and began a trade in English military secrets.
When his spying was discovered, he was arrested and brought before the
Committee of the Privy Council on 8 March 1711. During the examination
he stabbed Harley with a penknife, which broke at the first blow. Harley
recovered from the wound after about six weeks, and before this time Guiscard had died in Newgate. Swift wrote *To Mr Harlyes Surgeon* (*Poems*, p. 140)
on this occasion, and he also began, and assisted Mrs. Manley to finish,
A True Narrative Of what pass'd at the Examination of the Marquis De Guiscard . . .
(J. Morphew, 1711), in which Guiscard is said to have intended to assassi-
nate the queen and to have stabbed Harley as a substitute.

Prior's poem was written by 30 March, when Swift wrote in the *Journal
to Stella*: 'Prior shewed me a handsome paper of verses he has writ on Mr.
Harley's accident: they are not out; I will send them to you. . . .' It was
advertised in *Spectator*, No. 35, 10 April 1711. Wise (*Catalogue*, iv. 75) mentions an unauthorized edition published by J. Morphew, but we have been
unable to discover any record of such a publication. Possibly Wise confused
the poem with the *True Narrative*, which Morphew did publish.

In the *Thynne Papers* at Longleat, vol. lxxvi, f. 249, on a separate, smaller
sheet inserted in the manuscript volume, there are three short poems in an
unknown hand. One of them is a quatrain headed, 'by Mr. PRIOR':

> Weltring in blood, when Harley calls to mind
> That those dire stabs were for his Queen design'd;
> Proud of the Pain, the Patriot form'd this prayer,
> May all such wounds light rather here, than there.

These verses also occur in *Lpo 11*, 57 (X); *Lpo 11*, 77 (D); *B.M. Lansd. 852*,
53 (X); *B.M. Harl. 7316*, 36ᵛ (X); and the Halliwell-Phillipps MSS. at
Chetham's Library in Manchester. In all these manuscripts, the verses are
without ascription. The copy by Drift in *Lpo 11*, 77 is part of a collection of
poems written on or addressed to Harley that Drift transcribed for presentation to Edward Lord Harley; after the title of these verses (*On Mr. Harley's
being Stab'd*), he has, 'By ——'. If P had written the quatrain, it is inconceivable that Drift would not have known it. It is clear, therefore, that
the attribution in the *Thynne Papers* is simply an error on the part of the
copyist.

[Motto.] Horace, *Odes*, IV. iv. 59–60.
13–16. Trevelyan comments, '. . . Harley's narrow escape turned public

and royal sympathy so strongly in his direction that no intrigue and insinuation could for a while divert it. . . . Even the Whigs . . . sent him private messages of support, exhorting him to take firm charge of the government of the country, which tottered while he lay sick' (*England under Queen Anne: The Peace*, 1946, p. 121). As soon as he recovered, he was made Lord Treasurer and raised to the peerage as Earl of Oxford and Mortimer.

1712

(399) *An Extempore Invitation*

MSS. *Lpo 11*, 79 (D); *B.M. Lansd. 852*, 56ᵛ (X).
Pub.   *1718*, p. 286.
Text. *1718*. Collated: *Lpo 11, Lansd.*

Lansd. gives the specific date, Wednesday, 16 April 1712. The invitation is to a meeting of the Brothers' Club, in which the leading Tory statesmen and wits assembled each Thursday evening (see R. J. Allen, *The Clubs of Augustan London*, Cambridge, Mass., 1933, pp. 77–82). Oxford was not a member, but the patron and frequently invited guest of the club. A little later (1713–14) he stood in the same relation to the Scriblerus Club, and numerous verse invitations to their gatherings are preserved (Swift, *Poems*, pp. 184–8; *Memoirs of Scriblerus*, ed. C. Kerby-Miller, New Haven, 1950, pp. 351–8).

2. Prior had occupied a house in Duke Street, Westminster, since some time before June 1701 when he leased the land between his house and the wall of St. James's Park to use as a garden (Wickham Legg, p. 118).
14. DORSET. See *Dedication* (1708).

(400) *An Imitation of Chaucer*

MSS. *B.M. Add. 11258*, 12 (X; a late collection).
Pub.   *Miscellaneous Poems and Translations*, 1712 (Case 260–1–a), p. 74; *The Carpenter of Oxford, or, the Miller's Tale, from Chaucer. Attempted in Modern English, by Samuel Cobb* . . . *To which are added, Two Imitations of Chaucer,* I. *Susannah and the Two Elders.* II. *Earl Robert's Mice. By Matthew Prior, Esq;* London: Printed for E. Curll, at the Dial and Bible, R. Gosling, at the Mitre, and J. Pemberton, at the Buck and Sun in Fleet-street. 1712 [Prior's two imitations have a separate title-page and new pagination]; *Poems and Translations*, 1714 (Case 277), p. 244; *Poems on Several Occasions*, 1714 (Case 278), p. 143; *A Collection of Original Poems, Translations, and Imitations, by Mr. Prior* . . . *and other Eminent Hands* . . .

E. Curll . . . *1714* [a made-up miscellany, incorporating Curll's *1712* publication, listed above].
  Collected: *1716*, p. 6; *1718*, p. 290.
Text. *1718*. Collated: *1712m* [*Miscellaneous Poems*].

Miscellaneous Poems and Translations, in which the poem first appeared, was published on 21 May 1712 (adv. *Daily Courant*). Prior's imitation is of Chaucer's style and manner, not of any specific passage. For the contemporary attitude toward Chaucer, see G. Tillotson's introductions to Pope's translations and imitations of Chaucer in *The Rape of the Lock and Other Poems*, 1940.

In Curll's publication, *The Carpenter of Oxford*, P's imitation is followed by *Susannah and the Two Elders, Attempted in a Modern Stile*, beginning: 'When Fair SUSANNAH in a cool retreat . . .'. This 'modern' paraphrase is attributed to Samuel Cobb in *Poems on Several Occasions, By the Earls of Roscommon, and Dorset*, 1721 (Case 323–2–a), p. 117.

(400)   *Erle Robert's Mice*

MSS.   *B.M. Lansd. 852*, 54 (X). (The printed sheets of the Morphew edition
       are in *L 29*, 11).
Pub.   [Title as in text.] *A Poem in Imitation of Chaucer, &c* . . . London: Printed
       for A. Baldwin, near the Oxford-Arms in Warwick-Lane. MDCCXII;
       [Title as in text.] *A Tale, in Imitation of Chaucer, &c* . . . Corrected from
       the Errors of a Spurious Edition. London: Printed for John Morphew
       near Stationers-Hall. MDCCXII; *The Carpenter of Oxford . . . To which
       are added, Two Imitations of Chaucer . . . By Matthew Prior, Esq;* London:
       . . . E. Curll . . . *1712; Poems on Several Occasions*, 1714 (Case 278), p. 139;
       A Collection of Original Poems, Translations, and Imitations . . . E. Curll . . .
       1714.
       Collected: *1716*, p. 1; *1718*, p. 287.
Text. *1718*. Collated: *Lansd.*, *1712m* [Morphew].

The Baldwin edition, which was unauthorized and very corrupt, was advertised in the *Post Boy*, 4–7 Oct. 1712; the Morphew (authorized) edition appeared on 16 Oct. (adv. *Daily Courant*). The poem was probably written before 6 Aug. 1712, when Prior left with Bolingbroke for France.

  2. Erle ROBERT. Robert Harley had been created Earl of Oxford and Mortimer on 23 May, and made Lord Treasurer on 29 May 1711.
  9. Henry St. John had been created Viscount Bolingbroke on 7 July 1712.
  17. CHARLES. Charles Montagu, Baron Halifax since 1701; see *To Mr. Fleetwood Shepherd* (1689), ll. 64–66 and note.
  18. Sir TOPAZ. See commentary on *In Chaucer's Stile* (1718).

'Squire QUARLES. Francis Quarles (1592–1644), author of *Emblems, Divine and Moral*, 1635.

46. St. STEPHEN's Court. 'Exchequer' (*1718*).

54. Montagu had taken for himself in 1699 the sinecure of Auditor of the Exchequer, held for life and paying at least £4,000 a year, as insurance against political misfortune (Johnson, *Lives*, ii. 44 n). P suggests a similar post, as Teller, for himself.

1713

(402)   *Written in Montaigne's Essays*

MSS. None.
Pub.   *1718*, p. 313; *Letters and Correspondence . . . of . . . Bolingbroke*, ed. G.
        Parke, 1798, iv. 74.
Text.   *1718*. Collated: *Ltr*.

Prior enclosed this poem in a letter to Bolingbroke, dated Paris, 8 April 1713. The Peace of Utrecht had been signed on 31 March. Charles Talbot (1660–1718), twelfth Earl and first Duke of Shrewsbury, had arrived in Paris in Jan. 1713, as Ambassador. He was a cultured and witty valetudinarian of great ability and charm, the 'King of Hearts'. P had corresponded with him since 1694 (see '*That Heaven and Earth*', 1694), when Shrewsbury was Secretary of State, and found him highly congenial. Shrewsbury had resigned his offices in 1698 and gone to Italy, where he remained during the first half of Anne's reign; he was a great connoisseur and collector of art objects. P compliments his Italian wife in *Frederic* (1714).

(403)   *Doctors Differ*

MSS. *Lpo 11*, 39 (X); *Worcester Col.* (George Clarke's hand). (Index to *M*.)
Pub. *1740*, p. 106.
Text. *1740*. Collated:, *Lpo 11*, Clarke.

George Clarke's title probably gives an accurate description of the epigram: 'Dialogue between Dr Bentley & Dr Willis when Dr Sprat Bp of Rochester was preaching before the Queen at St James.' Sprat was High Church and Tory; Willis and Bentley were Low Church and Whig. Prior had praised Sprat in *To the Bishop of Rochester* (1685) and had made a complimentary reference to his *History of the Royal Society* in *Dedication* (1708). Richard Willis (1664–1734), a famous Whig preacher, is called 'of Ephraim' because of the controversial sermon on Isa. xi. 13–14 he preached in 1705, in which he seems to have called for the Dissenters (Ephraim) and the Church of England (Judah) to unite against the common enemy, the Roman Catholics. For Bentley, see note to *The Examiner. Numb. 6* (1710), l. 20.

The epigram must have been written before Sprat's death in May 1713; the occasion may have been the sermon he preached before the queen at St. James's in 1712 (which was published). The note in *1740* identifying 'Rochester' as Francis Atterbury (Sprat's successor) carries less authority than Clarke's earlier identification. Furthermore, Willis probably would have been referred to by his title after he became Bishop of Gloucester in 1714.

(403)   *Beauty*

MSS. *W*, 54ᵛ (P); *L 28*, 159 (D; emend. by Pope).
Pub.   *1907*, p. 333 (from *L 28*).
Text. *W*. Collated: *L 28*.

On *W*, 54ᵛ–55 (one continuous sheet) occur also Prior's drafts of a variant of *To the Lady Elizabeth Harley*, written probably in 1710, and certainly before Nov. 1713, when Lady Elizabeth died. These verses were probably written at about the same time.

Drift, in *L 28*, copied all P's drafts from *W*, including preliminary versions that P clearly meant to reject. We have attempted to reconstruct P's intentions from *W*. P may have intended to put the last couplet first or to expand it into a quatrain; otherwise, the poem seems to be substantially complete.

1714

(404)   *Frederic*

MSS. *W*, 63–68, 71ᵛ–76ᵛ (P); *W*, 68ᵛ–71 (D & P); *W*, 77–80 (D); *L 28*,
        175 (D; emend. by Pope); *M*, 124 (A & D).
Pub.   *1907*, p. 339.
Text. *W* (D). Collated: *W* (D & P), *L 28*, *M*.

The manuscripts in *W* consist of Prior's rough drafts and revisions of scattered passages; a transcript of ll. 1–134 by Drift, revised and supplemented by P; and finally, a fair copy by Drift of these same lines, as further revised and supplemented, and possibly dictated by P from the preceding transcript. We present only this finished portion in our text. Interspersed throughout the manuscripts are numerous drafts for later parts of the narrative; since these represent an early stage of composition, we print them as a note to l. 134.

Frederic was written after the marriage of the Duke of Grafton on 30 April 1713 (see l. 71), and before the death of Queen Anne on 1 Aug. 1714 (see ll. 91–94). Since it is addressed to the Duchess of Shrewsbury, it was probably composed before she left Paris with the duke on 31 Aug. 1713. On the Duke of Shrewsbury, see commentary on *Written in Montaigne's Essays* (1713). During his Italian sojourn he had married, in 1705, a young widow, Adelaide, daughter of Andrea, Marquis Paleotti, of an ancient family of Bologna, and descended on her mother's side from Sir Robert Dudley. The duchess (naturalized in 1706) was beautiful, accomplished, and eccentric; she died in 1726.

The title is misleading, for P's source was definitely La Fontaine's *Le Faucon* (*Contes et Nouvelles*, III. v) rather than Boccaccio; in fact, P merely borrowed La Fontaine's subtitle: *Nouvelle Tirée de Boccace*. There is nothing to show that P knew Boccaccio's story, which differs in several respects from that of La Fontaine (for instance, the lady in Boccacio is named Monna Giovanna; P follows La Fontaine in calling her Clitia). It is apparent, however, that P intended to do more than merely translate La Fontaine; he follows the main outlines of the story, but does not hesitate to adapt it. He makes Clitia a widow to begin with, instead of having Frederic woo her while her husband is still alive; and he invents the character of Thestylis, the old nurse (perhaps suggested by the 'vieille édentée' mentioned by La Fontaine at l. 90). These changes tend to make the tale more simply moral and pathetic, as does P's omission of La Fontaine's witty and satirical touches; since the whole is couched in Miltonic blank verse, the total effect produced is quite different from that of La Fontaine's story. The prelude (ll. 1–96), of course, owes nothing to La Fontaine. P wrote in blank verse partly in order to please Shrewsbury (see l. 15 and note); but he had used that metre previously in his translation of *The First Hymn of Callimachus* (1708).

15. Eves, p. 290, quotes a letter from Shrewsbury to George Stepney in 1705:

I wish we did more generally take up the use of those blank verses, more noble and unconfined than the Gothick monkish fashion of gingling rhime, which serves as a crutch to support lame verses and weak thoughts.

For P's opinion of rhyme, see the Preface to *Solomon* (1708), and *Protogenes and Apelles* (1718), ll. 5–6.

43. Scuderys learned Sister. Madeleine de Scudéry (1607–1701), sister of Georges de Scudéry; author of *Artamène ou le Grand Cyrus*, *Clélie*, and other romances and poems.

44. Fabers Daughter. Mme Anne Dacier (1654–1720), scholar and translator; daughter of Tanneguy Lefebvre (Tanaquillus Faber), 1615–72, classical scholar.

65. Finch. Daniel Finch (1647–1730), Earl of Nottingham, leader of the High Church Tories, satirized by Swift as 'Dismal'.

Harcourt. Simon Harcourt (1661?–1727), Viscount Harcourt, Lord Chancellor 1713–14, the 'best speaker of his day' (*D.N.B.*).

71. Buckingham. John Sheffield (1648–1721), whom, as Earl of Mulgrave, P had ridiculed in *A Satyr on the modern Translators* (1685) and *Satyr on the Poets*

(1687), was created first Duke of Buckingham and Normanby in 1703. He was Lord President of the Council 1710-14. In 1705 he married, as his third wife, Lady Catherine Darnley, natural daughter of James II; she survived him.

Grafton. Charles Fitzroy, second Duke of Grafton, married on 30 April 1713 Lady Henrietta Somerset. She died in 1726.

92. Hester. Esther.

Deborah. See Judges v.

99-104. In *W*, 72 and 80, there is a preliminary version of these lines:

> Liv'd Frederic, noble his Discent, his person
> In comely Strength erect and flow'r of Manhood
> Noble his race, his breeding and behavour
> Liberal, tho large his Lands, his mind yet larger
> Repleat with all those open Virtues bright.

134. The rest of the story in La Fontaine is as follows: Frederic spends all his wealth wooing Clitia, but she remains obdurate. Now a poor man, he retires to a small farm, with nothing left but one old servant and his beloved falcon. Clitia's husband dies; her son falls sick and insists that he must have Frederic's falcon. Clitia therefore visits Frederic to ask of him the only thing he has left; having no other food, he kills the falcon and serves it to her. When she learns of this final sacrifice, she is moved at last, and returns his love. Her son dies, and in spite of the objections of her brothers, she marries Frederic and brings him great wealth.

We present here P's drafts for the rest of the narrative, taking the text from *W* but some readings, where *W* is illegible, from Drift's copy in *L 28*. We omit rough and disconnected fragments, and add suspension periods.

[On Clitia's willingness to let Frederic ruin himself in wooing her:]

> . . . Strange Sex, that would be woed
> Refusing to be won.   (*W*, 72)
> . . . A Seeming Complaisance
> Child by a cold disdain . . .
> . . . Cruel conflict
> Where those who persevere shall be undone
> And those who wearied leave the fight, are Securest
> To be recall'd to conquest . . . .   (*W*, 76)
> . . . and all that chain of mad expence
> Whose extreme link is ruine. Lands are Sold
> And Mortgages contracted, false Trustees . . .
> And faithless Stewards joyn to wrong the Master
> . . . and profit by those negligences
> Which 'twas their only Service to retrieve. . . .   (*W*, 75)
> Till now too late two points he saw delude
> His love unprosperous and his ruine certain.   (*W*, 72)

[Frederic retires to his farm:]

> Thus spending more then his abilities could mentain . . .
> A farm, and what had he reserv'd there, but a poor hawk

But the change of his condition did not change his love.
He complains to himself of his ill fortune . . .
Poverty not abasing his spiritt, hid his poverty
Fortuna animum mutare non potest.   (*W*, 63ᵛ)

[Thestylis, his old nurse, accompanies him:]

                . . . for not the noble Matron
Whose womb bore pensive Frederic lov'd him better
Then did old Thestylis whose breast had fed him.
           . . . as he now has fed
His darling hawk, and in his garden water'd
The Rose and Jess'mine or with carefull hand
Propt the figg tree luxuriant from the danger
Of its own weight, or view'd the cluster'd Grape
Half purple round the verdant Elm encircled
His little hopes of Vintage. . . .   (*W*, 75)

[Clitia arrives:]

Runs Thestylis, she bids her master come:
Horsemen were in the court, the Coach was stop't
And Clitia just allighted: what surprise
What Joy what fear divided Frederics heart:
He came he saw he welcom'd her, he sigh'd.   (*W*, 76ᵛ)

[Frederic prepares the meal:]

               . . . Of fig tree or the Vine
Torn from their branches are the largest Clusters
And heap't the basket with abundant fruits
That She may chuse the ripest: Frederic fears
Least none be ripe enough . . .
Thus speaking, on the perch he spyes his hawk
Seizes the bird, and Sudden wrings her Neck
Then flinging it to Thestylis enjoyns her
So in the dressing to disguise the Meat
That Clitia while She eats may not descern it.   (*W*, 76ᵛ)
. . . He laid the bread and Salt and Napkins . . . .   (*W*, 63ᵛ)

[Clitia requests the hawk for her son:]

But what we ask, good Manners in your Sex
Is bound to grant: we rather think how much we wish a thing then how
     reasonable it is to be granted . . . .   (*W*, 64)

[Frederic reveals his sacrifice of the hawk:]

Poor Frederick trembling heard her speech; his eye
Downcast endeavour'd to conceal yet told
His Inward woe: (*W*, 64)
Now alass nor bird have I nor Clitia
Nor shall have: short he stopt, compos'd his look
And charg'd his Manhood to conceal his greif . . .
He said, and from his Tongue persuasive Verses
Great harbinger and friend of Love Shott forth
Propitious; but then the God, the God himself
Oer the Youths thoughtfull modest flaming Eye
Elated, from out his fiery Quiver lanc't
The Chosen beam Transfixing Clitia's heart.   (*W*, 66–66ᵛ)

[Clitia returns his love at last:]

Not Snow melts faster on the craggy Mount
The Alp, or Appenine, when Sol in Spring
Arising cheers the world, not Waves and Winds
Subside more sudden, when great Neptune rears
His awfull trident, and commands a Calm
Then in one Moment fell from Clitia's breast
The coldness of disdain, the Widdows pride
And Prudery of the Sex.   (*W*, 67)
For better then my Self thee Thee I love
My Self how can I name having prefer'd
My Ease to Thine, having in Lux' and wealth
Securely slept, while thou perchance hast Wakt
With fear of debts alarm'd and shame of want.   (*W*, 76)
O to thy Arms receive that penitent
That never shall again repent of aught
But of too late Conversion. Oh, my Frederic
Mine wilt thou be, receive thy Clitia thine
And be our next endeavor joyn'd to save
The lingring life of him, whom Natures will
And Thou will grant I next to thee shou'd love
My Son.   (*W*, 75ᵛ)
She said and kneeling he embraced her Knees
And taking with respectfull awe her hand
Kist it, unable to express his Joy
And Impotent of Speech.   (*W*, 63ᵛ)

[Clitia's son dies:]

She sigh'd She wept and gave the Year to mourning
As decency requir'd, but mighty Love
Had erst possess't her heart, that Monarch god
Admitts no rival power, his ardent flames
Dispell the little damps which Sorrow casts
Upon the Soul, nor suffers other tears
To fall adown the Cheek, but those alone
Which his attendant Cares and fears create.
But when Necessity obliges, Patience
Lessens the Ill, and grief is born away
Upon the Wings of time.   (*W*, 65)

[Conclusion:]

Succeeding Years beheld the happy pair
Blest in their lives, distributive of good . . .   (*W*, 67ᵛ)
Here since Great Maro does not doubt to Sing
Cayeta Nurse to his eternal Hero,
Let poor Good Thestylis my Muse be mention'd
Not without praise: fresh flowers upon her grave
Were strew'd by Clitia's hand,
And on her tombstone stand engrav'd her virtue
Gracious acknowledgments of faithfull Service.   (*W*, 68)
. . . The Mem'ory of Kind Frederic and good Clitia
They drink, and tell the Story of the Hawk.   (*W*, 73)

(408) *An Epistle*

MSS. None.
Pub. *1718*, p. 314.
Text. *1718*.

Queen Anne died on 1 Aug. 1714. Prior made the formal announcement to Louis XIV on 9/20 Aug. (*1740 History*, p. 411). Since Shrewsbury's departure in Aug. 1713, P had been 'acting ambassador'. The opening lines of the poem reflect the disappointment of his hopes of receiving a suitable reward for his contribution to the Peace of Utrecht.

33-34. Cf. Horace, *Odes*, I. v. 13-16.

(409) *For His own Epitaph*

MSS. L 27, 77 (D).
Pub. *1740*, p. 129.
Text. L 27. Collated: *1740*.

The date of composition is fixed by the reference to Prior's age in l. 9; the occasion was evidently (l. 5) the completion of the bust by Charles Antoine Coysevox (1640-1720), which was placed on P's monument in Westminster Abbey. (The frontispiece of *1740* is an engraving of this monument.) The bust is described as 'done at Paris 1714' in the reports of P's executors at Welbeck Abbey (i. 17). Hearne states that the bust was made 'at the Expence of the late King of France', and remarks that Coysevox was 'one of the finest Artists in Europe' (*Remarks and Collections*, vol. vii; Oxford Historical Society Publications, xlviii, 1906, 282-3).

1. Cf. the last of the cancelled stanzas in the commentary on *Jinny the Just* (1708).
12. Cf. *Jinny the Just*, l. 8.

(410) *The Remedy, Worse than the Disease*

MSS. None.
Pub. *1727*, p. 45.
Text. *1727*.

The epigram must have been written before Dr. John Radcliffe's death on 1 Nov. 1714. *In a Window* (1696) contains a favourable reference to Radcliffe and indicates that he was then Prior's physician. From 1711 on P was intimate with Dr. Arbuthnot (a fellow member of the Brothers' Club); Radcliffe 'was laughed at in the Swift-Arbuthnot circle; and about town whimsical stories concerning him were the order of the day, more often jocular than contemptuous' (L. M. Beatty, *Dr. John Arbuthnot, Mathematician and Satirist*, Cambridge, Mass., 1935, p. 122). Radcliffe was M.P. in 1690 and again in 1713. In spite of his sometimes brutal frankness, he had the largest practice of the day.

(411)   *True Statesmen*

MSS. *W*, 49 (D); *L 28*, 156 (D; emend. by Pope); *M*, 117 (A).
Pub.   *1907*, p. 331.
Text. *W*. Collated: *L 28*, *M*.

The references to the queen (l. 31) and to Dr. Charles Davenant (ll. 21–26), as well as the conjectural references in l. 18, indicate that the verses were composed between 1710 and 1714, and probably nearer to the former date. The theme is similar to those of Prior's earlier poems against faction, *A Fable* and *Ballad* (both 1700).

18. Pope, who also supplied the title, filled in the second of these blanks in *L 28*: 'H——y.' The names intended are, almost certainly, 'St. John' and 'Harley'; the occasion may have been any of the numerous conflicts between them 1710–14.
21. Doctor. Dr. Charles Davenant (1656–1714), Tory pamphleteer and political economist.
26. T. D. 'Tom Double', a regular character in Davenant's pamphlets. P owned two of these: *The True Picture of a Modern Whig, set forth in a Dialogue between Mr. Whiglove and Mr. Double* . . . 1705; *Sir Thomas Double at Court* . . . *In Two Dialogues, between Sir Thomas Double and Sir Richard Conover, alias Mr. Whiglove* . . . 1710.
35. Grey Coat Boys. Charity students at Westminster.

(412)   *Thos: Britton, Small-Coal-Man*

MSS. None.
Pub.   A print by T. Johnson from a painting by J. Woolaston, *c.* 1714; Sir
       John Hawkins, *A General History of the Science and Practice of Music*,
       1776, v. 75.
       Collected: *Evans 1779*, ii. 224.
Text. *1714.*

First attributed to Prior by Sir John Hawkins, who quotes the poem from the print and comments:

The above verses were scribbled by Prior with a view to recommend Vertue, then a young man, and patronized by Edward earl of Oxford, though they are little less than a sarcasm on Woolaston and Johnson. It is suspected that the insignificant adverb *artfully* was inserted by a mistake of the transcriber, and that it originally stood *probably*.

Hawkins states that his information about the Woolaston portraits of Tom Britton was 'related by Mr. Woolaston himself to the author of this work', thus implying that Woolaston told him P wrote the verses (which are unsigned in the print). Since Woolaston is an authoritative source, and Hawkins is generally careful and scrupulous in his treatment of such matters, we accept the poem as genuine.

The painting by J. Woolaston from which this print was made seems to have disappeared, and little is known of the engraver, Thomas Johnson. Mr. William Parrish, curator of prints at the Henry E. Huntington Library and Art Gallery, kindly informs us that the print was probably made very soon after Britton's death in 1714, since this was the time when Vertue first became established as collaborator with Kneller. Vertue himself, in his *Note Books* (published by the Walpole Society), v, 95, described in 1730 a copy of the print and quoted the verses; but he made no comment other than that the print was made after Britton's death. P's verses were obviously composed for the print. It is hardly necessary to point out that Hawkins's proposed emendation is absurd.

In the print Britton is represented tuning a harpsichord, with a violin hanging on the wall of the room and shelves of books before him. There is another painting of Britton, also done by J. Woolaston, which shows him in his smock with his small-coal measure in his hand. It is dated 1703, and is now in the National Portrait Gallery, London. From this painting also a print was made, with verses by John Hughes, beginning, 'Tho' mean thy Rank, yet in thy humble Cell . . .' (*Works of the English Poets*, ed. A. Chalmers, 1810, x. 33).

Thomas Britton (1644–1714) is important in the history of music as the organizer of the second series of public musical concerts in London, and perhaps in the world. Handel and Pepusch were among the performers, as were John Hughes and Woolaston; men of fashion and ladies of rank climbed up the ladder to the low room above Britton's shop in which the concerts were held. Britton was a collector of books, prints, and manuscripts, as well as of music and musical instruments. He was sometimes employed by Lord Oxford, and is said to have collected the Somers Tracts for Lord Somers. See *D.N.B.*, Grove's *Dictionary of Music*, and Walpole's *Anecdotes of Painting* (1876), ii. 236–7.

1. *Small Coal.* Charcoal.

8. *Kneller.* See commentary on *Seeing the Duke of Ormond's Picture* (1708).

Vertue. George Vertue (1684–1756), engraver and antiquary. Lord Harley had him make an engraving of the Richardson portrait of P that is better known than the painting itself, which is our Plate I. See *H.M.C. Bath*, iii. 476.

1715

(412) ## To a Lady

MSS. *L 29*, 13 (P); *B.M. Lansd. 852*, 86 (X).
Pub. *1907*, p. 355.
Text. *L 29*. Collated: *Lansd.*

This French poem, like the following one, was probably written at some time during Prior's residence in France, 1698–9 and 1712–15, and before he left France for the last time on 25 March 1715.

(413) ## To the Horse of Henry the Fourth

MSS. *L 29*, 13 (P); *B.M. Lansd. 852*, 86 (X); *Harvard Eng. 629F*, 74 (X).
Pub. *1907*, p. 355.
Text. *L 29*. Collated: *Lansd., Harv.*

See the preceding commentary. In *Harv.* the epigram has the following title: 'On Seeing ye. King of France on a very Little horse, the following Lines were made Extempore by Monsieur Malherbe.' The attribution to Malherbe seems to be without basis; *Harv.* is a late collection (after 1729). There is no clue to the occasion of the epigram; perhaps it was suggested by an equestrian statue of Henry IV.

(413) ## Fragment

MSS. *W*, 53ᵛ (D & P); *L 28*, 158 (D; emend. by Pope).
Pub. *1907*, p. 333.
Text. *W*. Collated: *L 28*.

Written before Burnet's death in March 1715, and probably after Sacheverell's trial in 1710. In *B.M. Lansd. 852*, 27ᵛ, there is what seems to be a completed version of this epigram. It is unsigned, undated, and written in the same unidentified secretarial hand as most of *Lansd. 852*. There is no way of telling whether or not Prior was responsible for this version; it may represent someone else's completion of his fragmentary epigram. Since it may well be P's, however, we give it in full:

Dr: Sacheverel and Ben: Hoadley

Among the high Churchmen I find there are several
That stick to the Doctrine of Henry Sacheverell.
Among the Low Church too I find that as odly
Some pin all their Faith on Benjamen Hoadley.

> But wee moderate Men do our judgment suspend
> For God only knows where those Matters will end
> For Salisbury-Burnet, and Kennett-White show
> That as the time vary so Principles go.
> But twenty years hence for ought I or you know
> Twil be Hoadley the High and Sacheverel the Lowe.

1. K . . . . . t call'd White. White Kennett (1660–1728), Dean and later (1718) Bishop of Peterborough. A strong Whig and Low Churchman, he wrote a reply to Sacheverell's famous sermon of 5 Nov. 1709, and the next year refused to congratulate the new Tory ministry.

Burnet Gil—. Gilbert Burnet (1643–1715), Bishop of Salisbury, a leading Whig, latitudinarian, and opponent of Sacheverell.

4. Hoadly. Benjamin Hoadly (1676–1761), chief of the Low Church party. Later, as Bishop of Bangor (1715–21), he was the centre of the Bangorian controversy.

Sachevril. Henry Sacheverell (1674–1724), leader of the High Church faction. His sermon of 5 Nov. 1709, asserting the doctrines of passive obedience and non-resistance and attacking the Whigs and Dissenters, resulted in his impeachment by the Whig ministry. His trial (Feb.–March 1710), making him a martyr in the eyes of the Tories and the populace generally, brought about the fall of the Whigs.

6. Followed, in both manuscripts, by a fragmentary line: 'Grace —— & Sweet Burnet.'

(413)   *Daphne and Apollo*

MSS. *W*, 18 (D & P); *W*, 95ᵛ (P; rough draft); *L 28*, 138 (D; emend. by Pope); *M*, 82 (A).
Pub.   *1740*, p. 4.
Text. *W* (D & P). Collated: *W* (P), *L 28*, *M*, *1740*.

The reference in l. 16 fixes the date of composition as before the death of John Partridge on 24 June 1715. The subtitle, 'Faithfully Translated . . .', is ironic: Apollo's speeches are based on *Metam.* i. 504–24, but Daphne's replies are entirely Prior's invention. *1740* prints Dryden's translation of Ovid on facing pages.

When Pope described P's unpublished manuscripts to Spence, he remarked: 'I remember there was a dialogue of about two hundred verses, between Apollo and Daphne, which pleased me as much as any thing of his I ever read' (Spence, *Anecdotes*, ed. Singer, 1820, p. 48).

1. Cf. Dryden's translation, l. 688: 'Abate thy speed, and I will bate of mine.'

16. John Partridge (1644–1715), astrologer and almanac-maker. See note to *To Isaac Bickerstaff* (1709), ll. 33–34.

22. Syphacio. Giovanni F. G. Siface (1653–97), famous *castrato*. John Evelyn noted in his *Diary* for 30 Jan. 1687, that he had heard 'the famous eunuch, Cifaccio . . . esteemed one of the best voices in Italy'.

45. Father. Peneus, the river-god.

47. Courant. *The Daily Courant* (1702–35), the first successful daily newspaper in England.

93. Bavius. A poetaster ridiculed by Virgil (*Eclogues*, iii. 90).

(417)   *Observations on Homer*

MSS.   *W*, 112 (D & P); *L 28*, 235 (D).
Pub.   No publication known.
Text.   *W*. Collated: *L 28*.

There is no clue to the identity of the person to whom Prior addressed this epistle, nor any indication that it was actually sent; it is likely that P meant to revise it further before sending it. Although it is, as P says, a 'Diary' of his study of the *Iliad* rather than a finished essay, it is his most extended piece of criticism, and we print it entire.

Observations was written by 1715, for after that time it is inconceivable that P should not take notice of Pope's *Iliad* (1715–20), to which he subscribed and which he mentioned twice in *Alma*, 1718 (ii. 91–120; iii. 5–8). Furthermore, the manuscript in *W* contains indications that P was revising *Observations* at the time he was making preliminary drafts for *Alma*, which was begun in 1715.

The French translation that P says he used (l. 2) was probably one of the two in his library: Antoine Houdar de La Motte's (1714) and a 1711 edition of Anne Dacier's; the Latin one was almost certainly Joshua Barnes's edition of *Ilias et Odyssea* in Greek and Latin (Cambridge, 1711). When, after P's death, Drift listed Barnes's edition among the books sent to Harley, he described it as containing 'remarks MS by Mr Prior' (Welbeck MSS., *Accounts of Prior's Executors*, i. 69). This kind of notation is unusual in the catalogue and must indicate a substantial amount of manuscript—probably the original from which Drift transcribed the text in *W*, which was then revised by P. If these are the books P used, he cannot have begun *Observations* before 1711.

9. *Ars Poetica*, l. 359.

38–39. An echo of *The Rehearsal*; see note to *Learning* (1721), ll. 226–7.

43–45. *Aeneid*, i. 50–74.

46–47. 2 Chron. xviii. 22. Cited in margin of *W* and *L 28*.

49–51. Julius Caesar Scaliger, *Poetices libri septem* (1561), Bk. V, ch. ii; P owned a copy of the fifth edition (Heidelberg, 1617). Scaliger in this chapter ridicules some of Homer's absurdities much as P does, and in the next argues the superiority of Virgil.

56. Sir Richard Blackmore, author of three epics: *Prince Arthur* (1695), *King Arthur* (1697), *Eliza* (1705). See *Paulo Purganti* (1708), l. 114 and note.

105. Horace, *Epistles*, I. ii. 3–4.

133. *Aeneid*, viii. 626–728.

(423)   *The Viceroy*

MSS. None.
Pub.   *1740*, p. 40.
Text. *1740*.

On 16 June 1715, Prior was examined by the Secret Committee, of which Coningsby was the most violent and insulting member. *1740 History* notes at the end of P's account of the examination (pp. 417–35): 'Lord *Coningsby*'s Behaviour during this Examination, seems to have been the Ground of that Resentment express'd against him by Mr. PRIOR in his Ballads of *Down-Hall*, and the *Viceroy*. . . .' On 18 June Coningsby was made Baron Coningsby in the English peerage (he had been Baron Coningsby of Clanbrassil in the Irish peerage since 1692); probably this is the elevation referred to in st. xlviii. The ballad was probably written soon after these events rather than in 1714, as the table of Contents to *1740* states.

Thomas Coningsby (1656?–1729) was one of the Lords Justices of Ireland 1690–2, and for some months in 1693 was at the head of the administration. His cruelty, together with his shameless extortion and embezzlement, made him much hated, and in Dec. 1693 the Earl of Bellamont moved his impeachment in the English House of Commons. 'But the Earl laying his Charge too high [i.e. high treason], the Commons resolved That there were not sufficient Grounds to support it, and so the Measures complained of, as arbitrary and violent, passed without Examination' (*1740, History*, p. viii). Coningsby continued to enjoy King William's favour, and in 1698 was made paymaster of the forces in Ireland. Under Queen Anne he was a strong Whig; he was one of the managers of Sacheverell's trial, and lost his seat in the Tory reaction. After the accession of George he was in high favour; his family had an hereditary feud with the Harleys, and he moved the impeachment of Lord Oxford and prosecuted the Tory leaders with great bitterness.

Of all P's ballads, this one is closest to the street-ballads in style.

[Title.] *The Lady Isabella's Tragedy: or: The Step-Mother's Cruelty* may be found in *Roxburghe Ballads*, ed. J. W. Ebsworth, 1869–79, vi. 650–2.

17. patriot. The Earl of Bellamont, who moved Coningsby's impeachment.

25. articles. '*Sabbati* 16. *die Decembris* 5 *Gulielmi & Mariae* 1693' (*1740*),

i.e. in the *Journal of the House of Commons.* From l. 33 to l. 120, P follows the Articles of Impeachment. As summarized in *The History and Proceedings of the House of Commons,* 1742, ii. 427, these were:

1. That the said Lord Coningsby hath traitorously abus'd the Power and Authority of his Government . . . by discouraging and terrifying the Militia, and framing and imposing on them a new, arbitrary, and illegal Oath . . . [cf. ll. 33–40]
2. That [he] . . . did traitorously, &c. exact and force free Quarters for the Army; and did also by Force of Arms levy Money on the Protestant subjects, &c. [cf. ll. 41–44]
3. [That he] . . . caus'd a great Scarcity of Provision in the Army before Limerick, by obliging the Sutlers to take out Licenses . . . [cf. ll. 45–60]
4. That the said Lord, assuming to himself a tyrannical and arbitrary Power over the Lives as well as the Properties of the People, did, in Council by Word of Mouth, order one Gafney to be hang'd without Trial . . . [cf. ll. 61–88]
5. That [he] . . . did traitorously carry on a Trade with the Subjects of the French King [cf. ll. 89–96]
6. That [he] . . . did embezzle vast Quantities of their Majesties Stores . . . [cf. ll. 97–108]
7. And that [he] . . . did favour and support the Papists in their Robberies and other Outrages &c. [cf. ll. 109–20]

77–84. Gafney was 'an evidence against one *Sweetman,* for the murder of some of Colonel Foulkes' Souldiers: But the said *Sweetman* giving all his real Estate . . . to Mr. *Culliford,* besides the sum of 500 l. to Mr. *Fielding,* Lord *Coningsby*'s secretary, for being his Bail, was never prosecuted for the said murder: And the said *Gafney* was immediately executed, according to the said verbal Order' (from the full text of Article 4, as given in A. Grey, ed., *Debates of the House of Commons,* 1769, x. 365 n.). Gafney had confessed to complicity in the same murder, but retracted his confession; Coningsby furiously ordered him to be hanged, without a trial or even a written order for the execution.

182. Queen Anne's birthday was 6 Feb.

190. Coningsby was made Lord Lieutenant of Herefordshire in Nov. 1714, and Baron Coningsby in the English peerage on 18 June 1715. Later, in April 1719, he was created Earl Coningsby.

220. DE-WITTED. John and Cornelius de Witt, Dutch statesmen, were lynched by a mob in 1672.

1716

(431)   *Cantata*

MSS. None.

Pub.   *Six English Cantatas After the Italian Manner Compos'd by Mr: Galliard.* London Printed for J: Walsh Servant in Ordinary to his Britanick Majesty . . . & J: Hare . . . [1716], p. 15 (*Cantata IV. The Words by*

Mr. Prior); *Horace and Venus. A Song. By Mr. Prior. Never before publish'd*
[E. Curll, 1719]; *The Court Miscellany*, 1719 (Case 308–1), p. 22.
Collected: *1718*, p. 266.
Text. *1718*. Collated: *1716*.

Six English Cantatas was published in Nov. 1716 (adv. *Post Man*, 27–29
Nov.). Curll's broadside was published in Feb. 1719 (adv. *Post Boy*, 26–28 Feb.).
Johann Ernst Galliard (1687?–1749) was oboeist and organist as well as com-
poser, and taught music in the royal family after coming to England in 1706.
The other cantatas in the 1716 volume have words by John Hughes and
William Congreve. Hughes seems to have begun the writing of cantatas in
English; see the Preface to his *Six Cantatas*, set by Pepusch, in *Works of the
English Poets*, ed. A. Chalmers, 1810, x. 30. P's cantata is based on Horace,
Odes, IV. i.

(432)   *Epigram*

MSS. *L 14*, 316 (D).
Pub. *1740*, p. 91.
Text. *L 14*. Collated: *1740*.

Prior sent this epigram to Lord Chesterfield on 27 April 1721, stating that
he wrote it 'while under confinement' (*L 14*, 316), i.e. 1715–16 (see commentary on *Song in Prison*, Works of Doubtful Authenticity, 1716). It was set
to music in *Eighteen Canzonets 1745?*.

1717

(432)   *The Dove*

MSS. *Worcester Col.* (George Clarke's hand).
Pub. *The Dove. A Poem* . . . London: Printed for J. Roberts, near the Oxford-
      Arms in Warwick-Lane. MDCCXVII.
      Collected: *1718*, p. 80.
Text. *1718*. Collated: *1717*.

Published on 15 Jan. 1717 (adv. *Daily Courant*). Col. C. H. Wilkinson
describes the Worcester College MS. (in George Clarke's commonplace book)
in *Oxford Bibliographical Society Proceedings and Papers*, i, 1927, 288. We are
obliged to Col. Wilkinson for informing us that this manuscript contains no
significant variants.
   In *B.M. Add. 29497*, 113, there is an anonymous poem, *Love Disarm'd or
Blindman's Buff* (beginning, 'As Truant Cupid on ye Rake'), written in the
same metre and stanza as Prior's *Dove* and telling a similar story: Cupid

searches Cloe, in bed, for his lost arrows, and says, 'Mama I'm sure I feel their Feathers'.

[Motto.] *Aeneid*, i. 11.
20. Cf. *Democritus and Heraclitus* (1718).
29–33. As in numerous other poems 1708–18, Cloe is probably P's mistress, Anne Durham, who lived in the parish of St. Dunstan's in the West, at least in 1722 (H. B. Wright, 'Matthew Prior's Cloe and Lisetta', *M.P.* xxxvi, 1938, 15).

(437)   *Epistles*

MSS.   *B.M. Harl. 7316*, 130 (X).
Pub.   *Evans 1779*, ii. 226.
Text.   *Harl.*

Lord Harley's annotations in *Harl.* date these epistles '1716–17' and identify Prior as the author. The signing of Elkanah Settle's name is obviously a joke: Settle was by this time a completely ridiculous and abject figure, and about 1718 he entered the Charterhouse (see note to *Satyr on the Poets*, 1687, l. 12). Since P had recently emerged from confinement and of course was without employment under the new régime, he probably intends the wry suggestion that his position is as bad as Settle's. The epistles seem to involve other, more private jokes. Apparently they were delivered together by P's servant, Jonathan (for whom see note to *Alma*, 1718, iii. 613).

These two trifles are of interest as the first indication of P's intimacy with Lord Harley and his family; his earliest letter to Harley is dated 14 Sept. 1717 (*H.M.C. Bath*, iii. 448). Edward Lord Harley (1689–1741), the only son of Robert Harley, first Earl of Oxford, was P's close friend and patron for the rest of his life. On 31 Oct. 1713 he had married Lady Henrietta Cavendish Holles (see Swift's poem on the marriage, *Poems*, p. 176).

We are indebted to Mr. James William Johnson for kindly re-checking the manuscript of these poems for us.

(437)   *Epilogue to Lucius*

MSS.   None.
Pub.   *Lucius, The First Christian King of Britain. A Tragedy*. As it is Acted
        at the Theatre-Royal in Drury-Lane . . . By Mrs. Manley. London:
        Printed for John Barber . . . and sold by Benj. Tooke . . ., 1717.
        Collected: *1718*, p. 276.
Text.   *1718*. Collated: *1717*.

Lucius was performed on 11 May 1717, and published in June (adv. *Daily Courant*, 24 June). Steele wrote a prologue for it, and the play is dedicated to him. Mrs. Mary de la Rivière Manley (1663–1724) had succeeded Swift as editor of *The Examiner* in 1711 and had written numerous books and pamphlets on the Tory side. Her dedication and Steele's prologue mark the end of their political feud.

On 19 March 1720, Mrs. Manley wrote to Prior that *Lucius* was being revived for her benefit, 'and gracious Mrs. Oldfield has agreed to speak that admirable epilogue you honoured me with'; Mrs. Oldfield wished P to instruct her in speaking it (*H.M.C. Bath*, iii. 480).

(439) *To my Lord*

MSS. *L 29*, 37 (Lady Henrietta Harley's hand); *L 28*, 143 (D); *L 27*, 65 (D); *Lpo 18*, 238 (X); *B.M. Harl. 7316*, 130 (X); *Welbeck* (Lady Henrietta Harley's hand; printed in Strong, *Catalogue*, p. 99).
Pub. *1740*, p. 132.
Text. *L 29*. Collated: *L 28*, *L 27*, *Lpo 18*, *Harl.*, *Wel.*, *1740*.

Lord Harley added the following note in *Lpo 18*: 'September 1717. Mr. Prior and I sitting in the library at Wimpole a message came to me from my Wife for paper, pen, & ink &c the following lines were made by Mr. Prior extempore.' Harley added similar but less detailed notes in *L 29* and *Harl.* Since the copy at Welbeck is not at present accessible to us, we collate it from the text given by Strong.

(439) *Engraven on a Column*

MSS. *L 29*, 89 (P).
Pub. Verses: *1718*, p. 312. Prose inscription: *Evans 1779*, i. 344 n.
Text. Verses: *1718*. Collated: *L 29*, *Memorial plate* in St. Andrew's Church, Halstead, Essex.
     Prose inscription: *L 29*. Collated: *Memorial plate*, the text of which was kindly furnished by the Reverend A. W. Swallow, Rector of Halstead.

Prior wrote this memorial in 1717, probably not long before the end of November, when John Morley was making arrangements for it to be engraved on a copper plate 'as big as has been formed since the days of Alexander the Coppersmith' (*H.M.C. Bath*, iii. 450). At the time of composition, Fiske was still alive, and a deleted line in the rough draft asserted he was 'much to be lamented when he dyes'. In its final form, however, the memorial displayed the additional legend '*obiit* April 21, 1718 *aet* 64', and a separate plate reading, 'John Morley to the Memory of his Good friend and neighbour Dedicates this plate'. (For Morley, see commentary on *Down-Hall*, 1721.)
Among the antiquarian collections of William Holman of Halstead there is

a satire on Fiske's spire, which begins, 'In times like these with wonders so adorned' and concludes:

> 'Tis clumsy tot'ring empty and indeed,
> The perfect model of the doctor's head.

Alfred Hills ('Matthew Prior in Essex', *Essex Review*, xliv, 1935, 236–42) suggests that it was written by P after he had been drinking too much with his friend Morley. Fortunately, there is no reason whatever to suppose that P wrote the doggerel, drunk or sober.

1718

(440)   *Postscript*

MSS. None.
Pub.   *1718*, Sig. d1.
Text. *1718*.

In *1718*, Prior reprinted *Dedication* and *Preface* from *1709* and added this *Postscript*. The volume was in print (except for the list of subscribers) by the end of Sept. 1718, though it was not issued until March 1719.

13. Horace, *Odes*, III. xxx. 1.
35–37. Molière, *Le Bourgeois Gentilhomme*, IV. v.
38–40. In a fragment (*W*, 44^v) written at about this time, P noted: 'Cloe may help to make Solomon sell.'

(441)   *A Lover's Anger*

MSS. None.
Pub.   *1718*, p. 85.
Text. *1718*.

Set to music by Thomas Arne (*Vocal Melody*, Part I, 1746; *Clio and Euterpe*, 1762, iii. 89), by 'Mr. Larken' (*Gentleman's Magazine*, xviii, 1748, 181), and others.

(442)   *Mercury and Cupid*

MSS. None.
Pub.   *1718*, p. 86.
Text. *1718*.

(443)   *Her Right Name*

MSS. None.
Pub.   *1718*, p. 267.
Text. *1718*.

We have changed the order of *1718* in this one instance in order to place this poem before a group of poems about a Cloe whose 'right name' seems to be 'Nancy', i.e. Anne Durham.

28. See the beginning of *Henry and Emma* (1708).

(444)   *On Beauty*

MSS. None.
Pub.   *1718*, p. 88.
Text. *1718*.

This poem and the seven that follow it constitute a distinct and inter-related sequence, in which Cloe fears that she will be supplanted by a new mistress, Lisetta, and is reassured. In *Cloe Jealous*, Cloe refers specifically to the preceding five poems as the basis of her jealousy, and the last two poems answer her complaint. As the commentary to the next poem will show, it is probable that the sequence reflected a real situation.

19–20. In horror at the rape of Lucretia by Sextus Tarquinius, the people overthrew his father, the last king of Rome, and prepared the way for the republic.

21. LAIS. Thais, not Lais, was the courtesan who incited Alexander to burn the palace at Persepolis. Dryden, in *Alexander's Feast* (1697), originally made the same mistake; his letter reminding Tonson to correct it is quoted by Malone (*Prose Works*, 1800, I. ii. 60).

(445)   *The Question*

MSS. None.
Pub.   *1718*, p. 90.
Text. *1718*.

Lisetta in this and the next poem probably represents Elizabeth Cox, who, with her husband, John Cox, kept a tavern in Long Acre. *Song in Prison* (Works of Doubtful Authenticity, 1716) describes Prior's flirtation with her in 1715–16, when he was under confinement at the messenger's house in Brownlow Street, nearby. Cloe probably represents Anne Durham, as in the other poems of this group, and she is clearly still the poet's mistress. (See commentary on *To Mr. Howard*, 1708.)

The date when Elizabeth Cox did supplant Anne Durham is not known, but P's will and the records of his executors indicate that it was a considerable time before his death in Sept. 1721. The will, dated 9 Aug. 1721, shows that P had provided for Mrs. Durham some time before, and therefore left her only a small legacy. Mrs. Cox, however, was one of the two principal beneficiaries. The records of P's executors give us most of the information we have concerning Elizabeth Cox's character and her relations with P. The letters P had sent her were of such a nature that the executors took great pains to get them out of her hands in order to prevent her from proudly showing them to the company at the ale-house, which she still maintained. Her impatient, grasping behaviour in relation to her legacy caused Drift to call her a 'most Ungenerous and most Ungrateful Female Fury', 'more Fell than a Tigress'. According to Dr. Arbuthnot, she was 'a brimstone bitch'. By May 1723, Mrs. Cox had married Henry Kirby, a peruke maker; and a document that Mr. Needham has recently found at Welbeck Abbey shows that later she became the wife of a Richard Waddington. (See H. B. Wright, 'Matthew Prior's Cloe and Lisetta', *M.P.* xxxvi, 1938, 13–16, 19–23.)

(446)   *Lisetta's Reply*

MSS. None.
Pub.   *1718*, p. 90.
Text. *1718*.

  See the preceding commentary.

(446)   *The Garland*

MSS. None.
Pub.   *1718*, p. 91.
Text. *1718*.

  See commentary on *The Question*, above. *The Garland* was set to music several times, and reprinted both separately and in such songbooks as *A Complete Collection of . . . Songs*, 1736 (Case 400–5), *The Vocal Miscellany*, 1738 (Case 388–2–b), *The Merry Companion*, 1739 (Case 424), *Philomel*, 1744 (Case 444).

(448) *The Lady who offers her Looking-Glass to Venus*

MSS. None.
Pub.   *1718*, p. 93.
Text. *1718*.

  As Dr. Johnson pointed out in *Rambler*, No. 143 (30 July 1751), Prior's

source was an epigram attributed to Plato in the *Greek Anthology* (vi. 1).
P may also have had in mind Ausonius, *Epigrams*, LXV, or some other of the
very numerous imitations.

(448)   *Cloe Jealous*

MSS. None.
Pub. *1718*, p. 93.
Text. *1718*.

(450)   *Answer to Cloe Jealous*

MSS. None.
Pub. *1718*, p. 95.
Text. *1718*.

The 'same Stile' refers particularly to the concluding stanza of the preceding poem, in which Cloe's pathos becomes sentimental.

(450)   *A Better Answer*

MSS. None.
Pub. *1718*, p. 96.
Text. *1718*.

During his flirtation with Elizabeth Singer in 1703-4 (see *To the Author
of Love and Friendship*, 1703), Prior wrote a letter to the sentimental young
poetess that constitutes an interesting parallel:

You have contrefaited the Spleen so long Dear Philomela [Miss Singer], that
I begin to fancy you have it in Earnest, your melancholly Gloom & unfrequented
Shades, Dying Strains & complaining Lyres are sure Symptoms of a Person very
far gone in that Distemper; Sweet Bardolph says Sir John Falstaffe, talk to a Body
like a man of this world, & let one hear a little how your Tea Table is furnished,
how much butter a good huswife Country Lady makes in a Season, how much
higher the Coquets head Knot is then that upon the fore Horse of her Team; What
Phanatick Parson got his maid with Kidd, & what Orthodox Dean fell drunk
from his horse. . . . The sum of all this is that I would have you merry, and think
nothing in the World worth much Anxiety. . . . Hark ye, take my Advice get into
Company & dont play with edge Tools. Loves Dart may cut your finger, & his
flames burn 'em . . . (*L 13*, 36).

This poem concludes the Cloe–Lisetta sequence that began with *Her Right
Name*.

3-4. *2 Henry IV*, v. iii. 99-101.
23-24. Cf. *A Midsummer-Night's Dream*, III. ii. 171-3 (first cited in *Evans
1779*).
26. *Odes*, III. ix.

(451)   *A Passage in the Moriae Encomium*

MSS. None.
Pub.   *1718*, p. 129.
Text. *1718*.

Prior owned a Latin edition (Amsterdam, 1685) of the *Moriae Encomium*
and a French translation (Leyden, 1713). The passage imitated seems to be
the first paragraph of the book: but the imitation is a very free one. The
theme occurs frequently in P's verse; see especially *Solomon* (1708), ii. 774–91.

(452)   *Merry Andrew*

MSS. None.
Pub.   *1718*, p. 194.
Text. *1718*.

The poem may have been based on a real incident, as an anecdote in the
Gentleman's Magazine, xlvii (1777), 77, suggests:

Hold your tongue, and eat your pudding, said a Mountebank to his Merry-Andrew,
who while he was stuffing of pudding with one hand, in the other held a stag's
tongue. Sir Jonathan Trelawney, Bishop of Winchester, passing by in his coach,
and being caught with the appearance of this *living rebus*, stopped to see what it
was, and then, passing on, said to Mat. Prior, who was in the coach with him,
'This fellow is no fool.'

The anecdote may, of course, be based on nothing more than the poem; but
the identification of the bishop as Trelawney, at least, is plausible. Bishop
Trelawney was a friend of Prior's, and in 1707 offered him a post as his secretary, which P accepted and then, upon reflection, declined (*Correspondence of
Sir Thomas Hanmer*, ed. Sir Henry Bunbury, 1838, pp. 109–10). Later in the
same year the bishop joked with P about the rumour of his taking orders
(*H.M.C. Bath*, iii. 436).

1–3. Southwark Fair (Our Lady Fair) was the City fair, held 7–9 Sept. In
1697 the Lord Mayor published an ordinance regulating vicious practices and
banning plays at Bartholomew Fair; plays and interludes were also banned
in 1700, 1702, and 1708 (Henry Morley, *Memoirs of Bartholomew Fair*, 1859,
pp. 336, 343).

(453)   *The Flies*

MSS. None.
Pub.   *1718*, p. 196.
Text. *1718*.

Possibly suggested by the beginning of Bacon's essay, 'Of Vain Glory'.

(454)   *From the Greek*

MSS. None.
Pub. *1718*, p. 197.
Text. *1718*.

An imitation of Meleager's epigram in the *Greek Anthology*, ix. 331. We are indebted to Professor James Hutton, of Cornell University, for pointing out this source to us.

(454)   *Epigram*

MSS. None.
Pub. *1718*, p. 197.
Text. *1718*.

(454)   *Another* ('To John I ow'd')

MSS. None.
Pub. *1718*, p. 197.
Text. *1718*.

An imitation of the epigram *Bienfait Publie* by Jean Ogier de Gombauld (1570–1666), in *Les Epigrammes de Gombauld* . . . A Paris, chez Augustin Courbé . . . M.DC.LVII., p. 48:

> Si Charles, par son credit,
> M'a fait un plaisir extréme,
> J'en suis quitte; il l'a tant dit,
> Qu'il s'en est payé luy-mesme.

Lord Hailes in 1779 sent a note to Johnson through Boswell pointing out Prior's indebtedness to Gombauld in this and two other epigrams: *An Epigram. Written to the Duke de Noailles* and *An Epitaph*, both 1718, below. (See Boswell's *Life of Johnson*, ed. G. B. Hill and L. F. Powell, Oxford, 1934, iii. 396, 533.) Johnson did not use this information in his Life of P, but remarked: 'I have traced him among the French epigrammatists, and have been informed that he poached for prey among obscure authors' (*Lives*, ii. 207).

Lord Hailes referred to Gombauld's epigrams as printed in *Recueil des plus belles pièces des Poètes François* . . ., Paris, 1692. P owned this anthology, and about a dozen of the French poems that he imitated are to be found in it. We have not been able to use a copy of the 1692 edition; the 1752 edition, however, contains the same poems, though the texts are sometimes modernized and the pagination is slightly different. We therefore cite the 1752 edition as evidence that the poem was in the 1692 one, but take our text from early editions of the individual poets. *Bienfait Publie* is in the 1752 edition, iii. 81; according to the reference of Lord Hailes, it is in the 1692 edition at iii. 25.

Gombauld's epigram may have been suggested by Martial, v. lii, which Frey (p. 178) cites as P's source.

(454)　　　　　　　*Another* ('Yes, every Poet')

MSS. None.
Pub. *1718*, p. 198.
Text. *1718*.

As C. A. Ward pointed out in *N. & Q.*, 5th ser., vi (1876), 67, Prior's source was an epigram by Scévole de Sainte-Marthe (1536–1623):

> Je confesse bien comme vous,
> Que tous les poëtes sont fous:
> Mais puisque poëte vous n'êtes,
> Tous les fous ne sont pas poëtes.
> (*Les Poètes François, depuis le XIIe Siècle jusqu'à Malherbe . . .*,
> Paris, 1824, v. 88)

An *Epigram from the French*, based on the same source, was published in the third volume of the Swift–Pope *Miscellanies*, 1732 (Case 344-4-a), p. 66:

> Sir, I admit your gen'ral Rule
> That every Poet is a Fool:
> But you yourself may serve to show it,
> That every Fool is not a Poet.

Norman Ault, in his introduction to *Pope's Own Miscellany* (1935), argues that Pope is the author.

(454)　　　　　　　*Another* ('Thy Naggs')

MSS. None.
Pub. *1718*, p. 198.
Text. *1718*.

Suggested by *Sur un homme qui avoit de mauvais chevaux qu'il nourrissoit fort mal*, an epigram by Antoine Le Brun, in *Epigrammes, Madrigaux, et Chansons Par Monsieur Le Brun* (Paris, 1714), p. 5:

> Albin nourrit à peu de frais
> Deux Rosses; celui qui les mene,
> Ne les fait marcher qu'avec peine;
> Il dépense plus en foüets,
> Qu'Albin ne dépense en aveine.

Le Brun's book was in Prior's library.

(455)   *Quid sit futurum*

MSS. None.
Pub.   *1718*, p. 199.
Text. *1718*.

     The title is from Horace, *Odes*, I. ix. 13.

(455)   *Written in an Ovid*

MSS. *W*, 1 (P).
Pub.   *1718*, p. 268.
Text. *1718*. Collated: *W*.

     Prior's source was *Sur l'art d'aymer d'Ovide, A Philis. Madrigal*, by Gabriel Gilbert (*c.* 1610–*c.* 1680), in *Les Poësies Diverses de Monsieur Gilbert, Secretaire des Commandemens de la Reyne de Suede, & son Resident en France* (Paris, 1661), p. 146:

> Cette lecture est sans égale
> Ce livre est un petit Dedale,
> Où l'esprit prend plaisir d'errer;
> Philis suivez les pas d'Ovide,
> C'est le plus agreable Guide,
> Qu'on peut choisir pour s'égarer.

Gilbert's poem was reprinted in various miscellanies; P may have found it in *Recueil des plus belles pièces des Poètes François*, 1692 (1752 ed., iv. 256). It was first identified as P's source in *Evans 1779*, i. 289–90.

(455)   *A True Maid*

MSS. *W*, 1 (P).
Pub.   *1718*, p. 269.
Text. *1718*. Collated: *W*.

     Based on *De Sylvie* by De Cailly, in *Diverses Petites Poésies du Chevallier D'Aceilly* (Paris, 1667), p. 57:

> Je veux mourir, disoit Sylvie,
> Avecque ma virginité;
> C'est grand dommage, en verité;
> Que cette charmante beauté
> Veuille si-tost perdre la vie.

Prior may have found this in *Recueil des plus belles pièces*, 1692 (1752 ed., v. 8).

     2. ROSE. P's drafts in *W* show that he tried the names 'Jane' and 'Mol' before arriving at 'Rose'.

(455)   *Another* ('Ten Months after Florimel')

MSS. None.
Pub.   *1718*, p. 269.
Text. *1718*.

Probably suggested by *Contre Iris* by De Cailly (see preceding commentary), in *Diverses Petites Poésies*, p. 196:

> Iris se plaignoit du tourment
> Qu'elle avoit enduré dans son accouchement,
>   Et contre l'hymen disoit rage.
>   L'hymen n'avoit pas tort pourtant;
> Cette belle savoit qu'avant son mariage
> Elle avoit bien souffert autant.

De Cailly's verses are in *Recueil des plus belles pièces*, 1692 (1752 ed., v. 30).

(456)   *A Reasonable Affliction*

MSS. *B.M. Add. 5832*, 167 (X; a late collection).
Pub.   *1718*, p. 269.
Text. *1718*.

Based on *Le Mari Malade* in Le Brun's *Epigrammes*, 1714, p. 20 (see commentary on *Another*, 'Thy Naggs', above):

> Malgré les soins des Suppôts d'Esculape,
> Dave gémit & sent des maux affreux:
> Sa femme en souffre; ils craignent tous les deux,
> Lui qu'il n'en meure, elle qu'il n'en rechappe.

(456)   *Another Reasonable Affliction*

MSS. None.
Pub.   *1718*, p. 270.
Text. *1718*.

From *Sur le mesme sujet* [i.e. Contre une femme qui se fardoit] by Georges
de Brebeuf (1618–1661), in *Poësies Diverses de Mr de Brebeuf*. Imprimées à
Rouen, Et se vendent A Paris, Chez Antoine de Sommeville . . .M.DC.LXII.,
p. 51:

> Avant-hier Alizon partit si follement
>   Pour un long & fascheux voyage,
> Que sortant de chez elle avec empressement,
>   Elle oublia ses gans, ses dens, & son visage.

Prior may have found this in *Recueil des plus belles pièces*, 1692 (1752 ed., iii. 268).

(456)   *Another* ('Her Eye-brow-Box')

MSS. None.
Pub. *1718*, p. 270.
Text. *1718*.

(456)   *On the same Subject*

MSS. None.
Pub. *1718*, p. 271.
Text. *1718*.

(457)   *On the Same*

MSS. None.
Pub. *1718*, p. 271.
Text. *1718*.

(457)   *Phyllis's Age*

MSS. None.
Pub. *1718*, p. 272.
Text. *1718*.

Based on an epigram in De Brebeuf's *Poësies Diverses*, 1662, p. 49 (see commentary on *Another Reasonable Affliction*, above):

> Quel age a cette Iris dont on fait tant de bruit,
> Me demandoit Cliton n'aguere,
> Il faut dis-je vous satisfaire,
> Elle a vingt-ans le jour & cinquante ans la nuit.

De Brebeuf's epigram is part of a series 'contre des femmes fardées'. It is in *Recueil des plus belles pièces*, 1692 (1752 ed., iii. 268).

(458)   *Forma Bonum Fragile*

MSS. None.
Pub. *1718*, p. 272.
Text. *1718*.

The title is taken from Ovid, *Ars Amatoria*, ii. 113. The baron's name may have been suggested by a comedy by Raymond Poisson (1630–90), *Le Baron de la Crasse*.

(458)   *A Critical Moment*

MSS. None.
Pub. *1718*, p. 273.
Text. *1718*.

(458)   *An Epigram*

MSS. None.
Pub. *1718*, p. 273.
Text. *1718*.

As Lord Hailes pointed out to Dr. Johnson in 1779 (see commentary to *Another*, 'To John I ow'd', above), Prior was probably indebted to *Le Moyen de se deffaire de quelqu'un*, by Gombauld, in *Recueil des plus belles pièces*, 1692, iii. 30 (1752 ed., iii. 86). We take the text from Gombauld's *Epigrammes*, 1657, p. 108:

> Tu veux te deffaire d'un homme,
> Et jusq'icy tes vœux ont esté superflus.
> Hazarde une petite somme;
> Preste luy trois Loüys; tu ne le verras plus.

Adrien-Maurice, Duc de Noailles (1678–1766), succeeded to the title in 1708 and was a distinguished soldier and courtier. P wrote to the duke in 1715 and 1716 (*L 14, 167, 169*), and in 1717 sent the duchess a gold watch made by Quare (*L 7, 64*); in 1720 the duke reproached P for his long silence (*L 7, 126*).

(459)   *The Thief and the Cordelier*

MSS. *W*, 2 (P).
Pub. *1718*, p. 278.
Text. *1718*. Collated: *W*.

As Dr. Johnson observed (*Lives*, ii. 207–8), Prior's ballad was probably suggested by *De Sacerdote Furem consolante*, by Georgius Sabinus, 'a poet now little known or read, though once the friend of Luther and Melancthon':

> Quidam sacrificus, furem comitatus euntem
>   Huc ubi dat sontes carnificina neci,
> Ne sis mœstus, ait; summi conviva Tonantis
>   Jam cum cœlitibus (si modo credis) eris.
> Ille gemens, si vera mihi solatia præbes,
>   Hospes apud superos sis meus oro, refert.
> Sacrificus contra; mihi non convivia fas est
>   Ducere, jejunans hac edo luce nihil.
>   (As quoted by Johnson from Sabinus, *Poemata*, 1558)

A correspondent in the *Gentleman's Magazine*, lxxxi (1811), 513, cites Alexander Brome's *On a Priest and a Thief* as P's source; but Brome's epigram is merely a translation of Sabinus, and bears no verbal resemblance to P's ballad. The story occurs in Montaigne (i. 87–88; Bk. I, ch. xiv) and is used in an epigram by John Owen (*De Bardella, latrone Mantuano*); but in both Montaigne and Owen it is the thief who says he is fasting.

A photograph of the manuscript of the ballad may be found in D. Flower and A. N. L. Munby, *English Poetical Autographs*, 1938, pp. 13–14. For the tune—the same to which *Down-Hall* (1721) is written—see *Pills to Purge Melancholy*, 1706 (Day & Murrie, 210A), iv. 28. The B.M. *Catalogue of Printed Music* (ed. W. B. Squire, 1912), ii. 683, lists a folio reprint of the ballad with the music in 1725(?).

1. *Greve.* La Place de la Grève, or Place de l'Hôtel-de-Ville.

8. 'Squire of the Pad. A highwayman (pad = road).

Knight of the Post. '[i.e. (?) of the whipping-post or pillory.] A notorious perjurer; one who got his living by giving false evidence' (*O.E.D.*). Cf. *Hudibras*, I. i. 583.

(461)   *An Epitaph*

MSS. None.
Pub. *1718*, p. 281.
Text. *1718*.

This is the third and last of the poems for which Lord Hailes noted a source in Gombauld (see commentary to *Another*, 'To John I ow'd', above). Cf. *La Vie de Guillaume* in Gombauld's *Epigrammes*, 1657, p. 34:

> Guillaume ne fut bon à rien.
> Nul n'en scent le mal ny le bien.
> Il ne fit la paix ny la guerre.
> Tantost assis, tantost debout,
> Il fut soixante ans sur la terre,
> Comme s'il n'estoit point du tout.

[Motto.] Seneca, *Thyestes*, the famous chorus at the end of Act II, translated by Marvell (ed. Margoliouth, i. 54), Cowley (*Of Obscurity*, 1668), and Sir Matthew Hale (*Contemplations, Moral and Divine*, 1676).

29. Cf. note to *The Chameleon* (1708), l. 33.

48. Bottom. 'A clew or nucleus on which to wind thread; also a skein or ball of thread' (*O.E.D.*).

(462)   *In Chaucer's Stile*

MSS. None.
Pub.   *1718*, p. 289.
Text. *1718*.

Prior evidently wrote this to accompany his two Chaucerian imitations of
1712; he printed it between them in *1718*. 'Topaz' is mentioned in l. 18 of
Erle Robert's Mice; the name, of course, comes from Chaucer's 'Sir Thopas'.
A note in *1793*, p. 450, identifies him as Sir Richard Blackmore, a notoriously
dull and long-winded poet; see note to *Observations on Homer* (1715), l. 56.
    The epigram may have been suggested by Martial, III. xlv.

(463)   *Protogenes and Apelles*

MSS. None.
Pub.   *1718*, p. 291.
Text. *1718*.

The tale comes from Pliny (*Historia Naturalis*, XXXV. xxxvi. 81–83), as Prior
notes in l. 13. Austin Dobson (*1889*, pp. 227–8) cites Horace Walpole's
Introduction to *Aedes Walpolianae* (1752) on the superiority of P's version to
Pliny's:

> I cannot conclude this topic of the ancient painters without taking notice of an
> extreme pretty instance of Prior's taste, and which may make an example on that
> frequent subject the resemblance between poetry and painting, and prove that taste
> in the one will influence the other. Everybody has read his tale of Protogenes and
> Apelles. If they have read the story in Pliny they will recollect, that by the latter's
> account it seemed to have been a trial between two Dutch performers. The Roman
> author tells you, that when Apelles was to write his name on a board, to let Proto-
> genes know who had been to inquire for him, he drew an exactly straight and
> slender line. Protogenes returned, and with his pencil, and another colour, divided
> his competitor's. Apelles, on seeing the ingenious minuteness of the Rhodian master,
> took a third colour, and laid on a still finer and indivisible line. But the English
> poet, who could distinguish the emulation of genius from nice experiments about
> splitting hairs, took the story into his own hands, and in a less number of trials,
> and with bolder execution, comprehended the whole force of painting, and flung
> drawing, colouring, and the doctrine of light and shade into the noble contention
> of those two absolute masters.

5–6. Cf. the Preface to *Solomon* (1708) and note to l. 15 of *Frederic* (1714).
The Duke of Shrewsbury and Bishop Atterbury, among P's friends, were
opponents of rhyme and may have influenced him; but Milton, Sir William
Temple, and others furnished ample precedent for this view.

(465)   *Democritus and Heraclitus*

MSS.   *W*, 170 (P; first line only).
Pub.   *1718*, p. 295.
Text.   *1718*. Collated: *W*.

An imitation of an epigram in the *Greek Anthology*, ix. 148. (We are obliged to Professor James Hutton of Cornell University for pointing out this source.)

(466)   *For my own Tomb-stone*

MSS.   None.
Pub.   *1718*, p. 295.
Text.   *1718*.

After Prior's death, Atterbury wrote to Pope (27 Sept. 1721): 'He is buried, as he desired, at the Feet of Spencer; and I will take care to make good in every respect what I said to him when living; particularly as to the Triplet, he wrote for his own Epitaph; which while we were in good Terms, I promised him, should never appear on his Tomb, while I was Dean of Westminster' (Pope, *Correspondence*, ed. G. Sherburn, Oxford, 1956, ii. 85).

(466)   *The Second Hymn of Callimachus*

MSS.   None.
Pub.   *1718*, p. 303.
Text.   *1718*.

Cf. *The First Hymn of Callimachus* (1708).

(470)   *Alma*

MSS.   *W*, 39, 39^v, 43, 53, 126, 128, 128^v, 135 (P & D; the following passages only: i. 130–3, 270–1, 369–83, 421–34; ii. 63–86, 125–8, 133–4, 214–21; iii. 192–3, 320–3, 366–7, 373, 526–31); *L 30* (X; fair copy on vellum).
Pub.   *1718*, p. 317.
Text.   *1718*. Collated: *W*, *L 30*.

According to Ruffhead, Prior told Pope that he wrote *Alma* 'to relieve the tedious hours of my imprisonment, while in the messenger's hand' (Owen Ruffhead, *Life of Pope*, 1769, p. 482). If this report is authentic, it means that the poem was composed between June 1715 and June 1716. The manuscripts show, however, that P revised and altered the poem extensively, deleting numerous passages and adding others. References in two passages (ii. 91–120, 287–306) fix their date as after June 1717, and it is likely that most of the revision was done after this date. P quoted the poem in a letter to Harley on 30 Nov. 1717 (*H.M.C. Bath*, iii. 450), and must have sent it to Atterbury at about this time, for Atterbury's letter returning it is dated 1 Jan. 1717/18 (*H.M.C. Bath*, iii. 458).

According to J. H. Burton (*Life and Correspondence of David Hume*, 1846, ii. 501), Lord Bathurst told Hume that he was with P reading the pieces to be published in *1718*, and 'asked him if he had no more poems. He said, No more that he thought good enough. "What is that?" said Bathurst, pointing to a roll of paper. "A trifle," said Prior, "that I wrote in three weeks, not worthy of your attention." It was *Alma*.' The story gains plausibility from the fact that P states in the Preface to *Solomon* that Bathurst and Harley induced him to print that poem. The incident must have taken place, however, early in 1717, when *1718* was first being planned and before *Alma* had been revised. P certainly thought *Alma*, in its final state, worthy of Bathurst's attention, for Bathurst returned it with a complimentary letter in Sept. 1718 [?] (*H.M.C. Bath*, iii. 458). Possibly P decided to revise it after Bathurst encouraged him to print it.

For discussion of the background and meaning of the poem, see W. P. Barrett, 'Matthew Prior's *Alma*', *Modern Language Review*, xxvii, 1932, 454–8; M. K. Spears, 'The Meaning of Matthew Prior's *Alma*', *E.L.H.*, xiii. 1946, 266–90; id., 'Matthew Prior's Attitude Toward Natural Science', *P.M.L.A.*, lxiii, 1948, 485–507.

There are numerous passages in *W*, *L 28*, and *L 29* that are either labelled or immediately recognizable as rejected drafts for *Alma*. (Those from *L 28* were printed in *1907*, pp. 325–30.) Most of them seem to be parts of the poem as originally composed, deleted in the later revision; others are clearly trial drafts. We print in the notes those that seem worth preserving.

Alma was translated into Latin verse by Thomas Martin in 1763 (Typis E. Easton: Sarum, 1763).

[Title.] As W. P. Barrett noted (in the article cited above), the name 'Alma' for the soul was probably derived from Spenser's House of Alma (*Faerie Queene*, II. ix). The subtitle may have been suggested by Donne's *Of the Progresse of the Soule* (*The Second Anniversarie*).

[Motto.] From Hugo Grotius's additions to *Dicta Poetarum Quae apud Jo. Stobaeum Exstant* (Parisiis, apud Nicolaum Buon, 1623), xcvii (pp. 412–13), labelled 'Incertus'. In the *Greek Anthology* (x. 124) it is attributed to Glycon.

Canto I

1. RICHARD. Richard Shelton had been P's schoolfellow at Westminster; writing to Halifax in Oct. 1714, P calls Shelton 'our old Fellow Collegiate

and my *fidus Achates* (*B.M. Add. 15947*, 1, quoted in Wickham Legg, p. 223). In 1710 P wrote *Horace Lib. I. Epist. IX* asking a place for Shelton, whom he describes as 'the Partner of my inmost Soul' (l. 22); after repeated solicitations by P, Shelton finally got his preferment, as Commissioner of the Stamp Office, early in 1714. The letter to Halifax quoted above is a plea that he be allowed to keep this place; we do not know how successful the plea was. At any rate, Shelton was obliged to borrow so much money from P that P thought it sufficient legacy to cancel all his 'Bonds, Notes, or Obligations'. His wife may have been the Mrs. Dorothy Shelton who received one of the mourning rings at P's death, and whose name follows Shelton's in the list of subscribers to *1718*. His son, George (cf. iii. 464–5, below) was remembered in P's will: he was left £300 to be paid in six annual instalments after the boy had entered the university or undertaken some employment.

Shelton seems to have been with P constantly from 1717 on, and is frequently mentioned in P's letters. Writing to Harley in 1720, P calls him 'Surly Dick' (*H.M.C. Bath*, iii. 489), and in another letter of the same year he illustrates the description:

> Dick Shelton accosted me this morning; when I asked him why [he] had not writ oftener to us, he replied that writing was nonsense, and before a good deal of company he told me that I looked very well, and that my boil had done me good. I did but touch upon South Sea, and he asked me what I could expect better from a conjunction of scoundrels at Court with sharpers in the City; so, you see, whatever may change, Dick is *semper idem*. (*H.M.C. Bath*, iii. 493)

Shelton's translations from Tibullus and Ovid are printed in *1740*, pp. lxvii–lxxxvii.

5–6. Cf. *Daphne and Apollo* (1715), ll. 91–92.

10. JACOB. Jacob Tonson, publisher of *1718* and of most of P's verse since 1692.

15–21. Cf. Aristotle, *De Anima* (ed. and trans. R. D. Hicks, Cambridge, 1907): 'If, then, we have to make a general statement touching soul in all its forms, the soul will be the first actuality of a natural body furnished with organs. Hence there is no need to enquire whether soul and body are one, any more than whether the wax and the imprint are one . . .' (p. 51). 'Now it needs no proof that the soul—or if it is divisible into parts, certain of its parts —cannot be separated from the body . . .' (p. 53). The interpretation that P burlesques is that of the scholastics; St. Thomas Aquinas said, 'The soul is wholly in the whole body and at the same time wholly in each part of the body' (*Summa Theologica*, i. 76. 8; for background on this point, and on the history of speculation about the seat of the soul, see F. I. Mackinnon, *Philosophical Writings of Henry More*, New York, 1925).

23. Men of OXFORD. The conservative Aristotelianism of Oxford at this time is well attested; see Sir Charles Mallett, *History of the University of Oxford* (New York, 1924–8), ii. 401. Christ Church, as the Battle of the Books indicates, was a centre of hostility to the New Science.

24. CAMBRIDGE Wits. The scientists generally, and specifically Sir Isaac Newton and his followers. Aristotle had been out of fashion at Cambridge since at least the mid-seventeenth century, and Descartes had a powerful influence there; see J. B. Mullinger, *The University of Cambridge from the Earliest Times to the Accession of Charles I* (Cambridge, 1883), iii. 135-6, 606-7. P owned three copies of Rohault's compendium of Cartesian physics, and probably used it as a textbook at St. John's. (See S. L. Lamprecht, 'The Rôle of Descartes in Seventeenth-Century England', *Studies in the History of Ideas*, edited by the Department of Philosophy of Columbia University, iii, 1935, 181-243.)

29. A proverbial expression. E. Partridge (*Dictionary of Slang and Unconventional English*, 2nd ed., 1938) lists it and says: 'Origin obscure: even Nares failed to discover it.' A poem in *Wits Recreations*, 1641 (Case 95-b), p. 442, called *A proper comparison*, begins: 'As there are three blue beanes in a blue bladder; | As there are thrice three rounds in a long ladder, | . . . There are three Universities.'

30-79. Descartes conceives of the mind as communicating with the body only through the brain, and not the whole brain, but 'une certaine glande forte petite, située dans le milieu de sa substance'—the pineal gland, or conarion (*Œuvres*, ed. C. Adam and P. Tannery, Paris, 1904, xi. 352). The animal spirits surround and permeate the conarion, and are the medium of communication between soul and body: a sort of vapour refined from the blood in the brain, they are barely material, like 'vent tres subtil, ou plutost une flame tres vive et tres pure' (xi. 129). The conarion, delicately balanced among the animal spirits, can be inclined by the soul, and so change the direction of the surrounding spirits which, flowing through the nerves into the muscles, control the body.

Newton accepted, in general, the Cartesian account of perception and volition, though he substituted for the 'animal spirits' the equally ambiguous medium of the 'ether' (see note to iii. 60 below). E. A. Burtt, in *The Metaphysical Foundations of Modern Physical Science*, 1932, gives an account of the position of Newton and the other scientists on these philosophical questions.

90-101. The argument that the mind, if in the brain at all, must be extended, goes back as far as Gassendi's objections printed with the first edition of Descartes' *Meditations*. Gassendi pointed out that logically the mind cannot be in even the smallest part of the brain if the mind is unextended, 'since, however small the part be, it is nevertheless extended, and you are coextensive with it, and consequently are extended' (*Philosophical Works of Descartes*, tr. E. Haldane and G. R. Ross, Cambridge, 1912, ii. 198-9). Subsequent criticism of the Cartesian distinction between *res cogitans* and *res extensa* was widespread.

102-5. A rejected draft in *W*, 129, illustrates this theme:

> Now if you happen to fall Ill
> Let your Desease be what it will

The doctor asks you how you do
Only for complement and show.
He feels your pulse, and as that beats
Judges your bodyes colds or heats.
Your head he thinks don't understand
These things so Clearly as your hand.

134–5. The following much-revised and partly illegible draft in *W*, 129, shows that P originally intended to illustrate the point, but gave it up:

If we for Instance should suppose
You draw your hand cross Surly's Nose
That touch will put his honour to't
As Much as Kicks from head to foot.
Clap but your hand in Celia's breast
You make her understand the rest:
The touch does as much Love discover
As if you fumbled her all over.
The stroaks you see tho' much the Same
Provoke the Squire, and please the Dame.

136–43. Cf. Lucretius, iv. 823–57. For Creech, see notes to *A Satyr on the modern Translators* (1685), ll. 111–27.

170. *Monmouth*-Street. This street (now called Dudley Street) in St. Giles was inhabited by cheap tailors and sellers of second-hand clothing.

190. MEMMIUS. To whom Lucretius dedicated *De Rerum Natura*.

198. FAUBERT's. 'Monsieur, or Major, Faubert's riding academy. Faubert's Place in Regent Street marks its site' (Dobson, *1889*).

213. The sound of Bow bells called Dick Whittington back to London to be three times Lord Mayor.

218. THEODORET. Theodoretus (*c.* 390–*c.* 457), Bishop of Cyrrhus, wrote no commentary on Aristotle, and we cannot locate any argument in his works for the natural immortality of the soul.

ORIGEN. Origen (*c.* 185–*c.* 254) represented the soul as incorporeal and imperishable; souls are imprisoned in mortal bodies as punishment for sin, and at the Resurrection will put on heavenly bodies. Origen did not write a commentary on Aristotle.

224. SIMPLICIUS. Simplicius of Cilicia, one of the last Neoplatonists, lived in the first half of the sixth century. He wrote a commentary on Aristotle's *De Anima*, in which he maintained the immortality of the soul; P has him on the wrong side of the controversy.

THEOPHRAST. Theophrastus (*c.* 372–287 B.C.) was Aristotle's favourite pupil and successor as leader of the Peripatetic School. He wrote a commentary on *De Anima*, and seems to have considered the soul mortal.

DURAND. Guillaume Durand (d. 1334), or Durandus of Saint-Pourcain, wrote a treatise on the condition of souls after separation from the body. He seems to have argued that unaided human reason cannot prove the immortality of the soul; but his name is hardly appropriate in this context.

245. GASSENDUS. Pierre Gassendi (1592–1655), who attacked Aristotelian philosophy and maintained the Epicurean doctrines against Descartes; friend of Galileo and Kepler. See G. S. Brett, *The Philosophy of Gassendi*, 1908.

252–65. As William Jackson (*The Four Ages*, 1798, pp. 254–5) first pointed out (see also W. P. Barrett's article, cited above), P's 'system' was probably suggested by the following passage in Montaigne's 'De l'Yvrognerie' (ii. 31; Bk. II, ch. ii):

> La chaleur naturelle, disent les bons compaignons, se prent premierement aux pieds: celle là touche l'enfance. De là elle monte à la moyenne region, où elle se plante long temps et y produit, selon moy, les seuls vrais plaisirs de la vie corporelle: les autres voluptez dorment au pris. Sur la fin, à la mode d'une vapeur qui va montant et s'exhalant, ell'arrive au gosier, où elle faict sa derniere pose.

304. FRIEND. Dr. Robert Freind (1667–1751), headmaster of Westminster School, 1711–33, a lifelong friend of P's and author of his Latin epitaph.

SNAPE. Andrew Snape (1675–1742), headmaster of Eton 1711–19.

339–42. Cf. *Memoirs of Scriblerus*, ed. C. Kerby-Miller (New Haven, 1950; discussed in note to ii. 251–80 below), p. 158:

> . . . he hath been verily persuaded, that the Organ of Generation is the true and only *Seat of the Soul*. That this part is seated in the middle, and near the Centre of the whole body, is obvious. . . . From thence, like the sun in the Centre of the world, the Soul dispenses her warmth and vital influence. . . .

357. Lucretius, iv. 1059–60.

359. OVID. e.g. *Tristia*, IV. x. 65–66.

361. HORACE. *Odes*, IV. i. 12: 'torrere iecur'.

362. Based on the phrase, 'curiosa felicitas', which Petronius uses of Horace's verse. P quotes it in the Preface to *An Ode, Humbly Inscrib'd* (1706).

363. We can find no reference by Virgil to the liver as the seat of love.

399. HORACE owns. *Epistles*, I. i. 10–12.

405–15. Referring to Lucretius' invocation of 'alma Venus' (i. 1–43)—in which, however, there is no mention of Cupid—and his description of the indifference of the gods, which followed immediately in editions of P's time but is printed as ii. 646–51 in modern editions.

418. SCAPIN's Cheats. In Molière's farce, *Les Fourberies de Scapin* (1671), adapted by Otway as *The Cheats of Scapin* (1677).

484. TALL-BOY. The awkward young lover in Richard Brome's *The Jovial Crew* (1641), which was still performed regularly in the early eighteenth century.

491. EDWARD our Fourth. Edward IV (1442–83) married in 1464 Elizabeth, daughter of Richard Woodville, Lord Rivers, and widow of Sir John Grey, though Warwick had planned for him to marry a French princess. Warwick therefore turned against him, and several battles resulted.

497. FRANCE's fourth HENRY. Henry IV of France (1553–1610) defeated

the Duc de Joyeuse at Coutras in 1587. In 1590 he fell in love with Gabrielle d'Estrées (1573–99); her father married her to another man, but in 1592 she became Henry's mistress and later bore him several children.

519–20. A reference to the quarrel concerning the ancients and the moderns, for which see Swift's *Battle of the Books* (1704) and the commentaries thereon. *Alma* is obviously related to this conflict—Aristotle *v.* Descartes—and P's position in it is much like his friend Swift's.

Canto II

4. The argument of the first canto of *Hudibras* ends:

> Th' *Adventure of the Bear and Fiddle*
> *Is sung, but breaks off in the middle.*

9–16. Cf. Pliny, *Letters*, IX. xxvi: 'Nam ut quasdam artes ita eloquentiam nihil magis quam ancipitia commendant. Vides, qui per funem in summa nituntur, quantos soleant excitare clamores, cum iam iamque casuri videntur. Sunt enim maxime mirabilia, quae maxime insperata, maxime periculosa ...' (first cited in *Evans 1779*). As Mrs. Piozzi (*Thraliana*, ed. K. C. Balderston, Oxford, 1942, i. 443–4) pointed out, P may also owe something to Dryden: '. . . like a skilful dancer on the ropes . . . who slips willingly, and makes a seeming stumble, that you may think him in great hazard of breaking his neck, while at the same time he is only giving you a proof of his dexterity' (*Essays*, ed. W. P. Ker, Oxford, 1900, ii. 149).

25. *Clare-obscure.* Or *clair-obscur*, French translation of Italian *chiaroscuro*. This is the first use of the term cited by *O.E.D.*

32. *Birth-Day.* It was customary to wear magnificent clothing for the royal birthday celebrations; cf. Pope, *Rape of the Lock*, i. 23.

91–120. In the third volume of Pope's *Iliad*, published in June, 1717, occurs the following note to ix. 450:

> But it seems *Poltis* King of *Thrace* was of another opinion, who would have parted with two wives, out of pure good-nature to two mere strangers; as I have met with the story somewhere in *Plutarch*. When the *Greeks* were raising forces against *Troy*, they sent embassadors to this *Poltis* to desire his assistance. He enquir'd the cause of the war, and was told it was the injury *Paris* had done *Menelaus* in taking his wife from him. "If that be all, said the good King, let me accomodate the difference: Indeed it is not just the *Greek* Prince should lose a wife, and on the other side it is pity the *Trojan* should want one. Now I have two wives, and to prevent all this mischief, I'll send one of them to *Menelaus*, and the other to *Paris*.["] It is a shame this story is so little known, and that poor *Poltis* yet remains uncelebrated: I cannot but recommend him to the modern Poets.

Poltis was later celebrated by Joseph Mitchell, who quotes Pope's note and the passage from *Alma*, in *Poltis, King of Thrace: or, The Peace-Keeper* (*A Tale and Two Fables in Verse*, 1727).

131. TEAGUE. See note to *On the Same Person* (1710), l. 3.

151. P's rough drafts for the foregoing passage are preserved in *W*, 135:

> You still may gape about
> Thô either of your Eyes be out
> And thô you chance to lose your Ear
> Erect the other, you shall hear:
> The Demi loss no Creature knows
> Provided still your Hatt sett close . . .
> But if you cleft his heart in twain:
> Or kindly scoopt out half his brain
> The Mutilated man no doubt
> Would neither be discreet nor stout.

A rejected draft for an additional passage is found in *W*, 133ᵛ (it is transcribed by Drift in *L 28*, 152, and *M*, 115; it was printed from *L 28* in *1907*, p. 328):

> Odd is the Justice of that land
> Which only lopps the theifs right hand.
> The left before inurd to robb
> Is each new Sessions in your fobb:
> In Britain we with wiser care
> Chastise a limb that has no pair;
> And when You hang him by the neck
> E'en trust him for a second trick.
> But that of which he was bereft
> Alass, had ne'r a fellow left.

194–8. The Leibniz–Clarke correspondence (discussed in the note to iii. 335 below) may have suggested this image: 'Man's Soul may be compared to a Balance, wherein Reasons and Inclinations are in the place of Weights . . . the Will of Man is like a balance, which stands always unmoved when the Weights in both Scales are equal' (*A Collection of Papers . . .*, 1717, p. 383).

199. MAH'MET's Tomb. Cf. *Hudibras*, II. iii. 441–2: 'But in the *Airy Region* yet, | Hangs like the Body of *Mahomet*.'

200–13. Based ultimately on the medieval sophism known as 'Buridan's Ass' (the ass died of hunger midway between two hayricks of equal size and quality). Cf. Montaigne, ii. 557 (Bk. II, ch. xiv) and the Leibniz–Clarke correspondence: 'There is never any such thing as an *Indifference in aequilibrio*. . . . 'Tis *true*, if the Case (of the Ass standing between *Two Green Fields*, and equally liking *Both of them*) was possible, we *must say* he would suffer himself to be *starved to Death*' (p. 385).

228. HENAULT. Charles Jean François Hénault (1685–1770), jurist and writer, President 1710–31 of the Chambre des Enquêtes of the Parlement de Paris; a very wealthy man.

245. Attraction. The common term for Newton's law of gravitation. Thomas Baker says that Newton 'seems to resolve all into Attraction; which tho it may be true and pious withal, perhaps will not be thought so philosophical' (*Reflections upon Learning*, 4th ed., 1708, p. 103); Swift has the ghost of Aristotle conclude that '*Gassendi* . . . and the *Vortices* of *Descartes* were equally

exploded. He predicted the same fate to *Attraction,* whereof the present
Learned are such zealous Asserters' (*Gulliver's Travels,* ed. H. Davis, 1941,
pp. 181–2).

251–80. Chapter XII of the *Memoirs of . . . Martinus Scriblerus* (ed. C. Kerby-
Miller, New Haven, 1950, p. 137) deals with Martinus's attempts to discover
the seat of the soul:

> Sometimes he was of opinion that it lodg'd in the Brain, sometimes in the
> Stomach, and sometimes in the Heart. Afterwards he thought it absurd to confine
> that sovereign Lady to one apartment, which made him infer that she shifted it
> according to the several functions of life: The Brain was her Study, the Heart her
> State-room, and the Stomach her Kitchen. But as he saw several offices of life went
> on at the same time, he was forced to give up this Hypothesis also. He now con-
> jectured it was more for the dignity of the Soul to perform several operations by her
> little Ministers, the *Animal Spirits,* from whence it was natural to conclude, that she
> resides in different parts according to different Inclinations, Sexes, Ages, and
> Professions. Thus in Epicures he seated her in the mouth of the Stomach, Philo-
> sophers have her in the Brain, Soldiers in their Hearts, Women in their Tongues,
> Fidlers in their fingers, and Rope-dancers in their Toes. At length he grew fond
> of the *Glandula Pinealis,* dissecting many Subjects to find out the different Figure
> of this Gland, from whence he might discover the cause of the different Tempers
> in mankind.

The rest of the chapter consists of a letter from the Society of Free-Thinkers
to Martin, informing him that his failure to find the soul proves that it does
not exist, and giving him 'an easy *mechanical Explication* of *Perception* or
Thinking'. In Chapter XV, after the episode of the Double Mistress, the
lawyers debate as to whether or not the 'Organ of Generation is the true and
only *Seat of the Soul*'.

The *Memoirs* were not published until 1741, and the date of composition
of the passage quoted is not known. Possibly Arbuthnot was the author,
and he may have written it in 1714, when the latter part of Chapter XII
apparently was composed, though Kerby-Miller (pp. 57, 285) thinks this
passage was probably written later. It is therefore conceivable that P, who
was on intimate terms with Swift and Arbuthnot, was influenced by the
passage. It is much more likely, however, that the influence was the other
way, and that the specific parallels to *Alma* in this passage—as in others
from the *Memoirs* cited in these notes—are the result of Pope's extensive
revision of the *Memoirs* shortly before their publication.

255. NICHOLINI. Nicolini Grimaldi (1673?–1726?), famous Italian *castrato,*
in England 1708–17. He frequently sang in *Pyrrhus and Demetrius* (a translation by Owen Swiney or MacSwiney of Morselli's *Pirro e Demetrio*).

257. PEDRO. Probably Pietro Castrucci (1697–1752), famous violinist who
came to England in 1715 and became leader of Handel's opera-band.

287–304. *Eloisa to Abelard* first appeared in the volume of Pope's *Works*
which was published on 3 June 1717.

305–6. John Sheffield, Duke of Buckingham, prefixed complimentary verses to Pope's 1717 volume. P had satirized him (as Earl of Mulgrave) in *A Satyr on the modern Translators* (1685) and *Satyr on the Poets* (1687), but later became friendly with him; P sent *Solomon* to him before publication, and mentions dining with him in 1720 'at a sort of *convivium poeticum*, for Pope and Gay are the other two guests' (*H.M.C. Bath*, iii. 458, 482).

A fragment in P's hand in *L 29*, 60 (transcribed by Drift in *L 29*, 49, and printed in *1907*, p. 358) seems worth preserving. Because the original is partly illegible, we take some readings from Drift's copy:

> Broghil did Cowley's thankfull Muse commend
> And is not Broghil's Grandson Priors friend?
> Roscommons verse indulg'd Poor Dryden's pride
> While to the Patrons voice the Bard reply'd:
> Roscommon writes to that unerring hand
> Muse slay the bull that spurns the Yellow Sand.
> Sheffeild great Buckingham illustrious Name
> Old in Poetic's and in civil fame
> Transfer'd his Lawrell to his pupil Pope
> The Patron's goodness pass'd the Poet's hope.

'Broghil' was Roger Boyle (1621–79), Baron Broghill and first Earl of Orrery; his grandson was Charles Boyle (1676–1731), fourth Earl of Orrery. The reference in line 3 is to Roscommon's commendatory poem for the 1683 edition of *Religio Laici*. In lines 5–6, Prior adapts what must be the most absurd couplet Dryden ever wrote, from *To the Earl of Roscommon, on his Excellent Essay on Translated Verse*, 1684, ll. 66–67:

> *Roscomon* writes, to that auspicious hand,
> Muse feed the Bull that spurns the yellow sand.

401. HEYLYN. Probably Peter Heylyn (1600–62), author of *Microcosmus, A Little Description of the Great World*, 1629, which P owned.

415–22. Many of the following examples of exotic customs are drawn from *A New Voyage round the World*, by Captain William Dampier (1652–1715). Dampier writes of the Hottentot women:

. . . their legs are wrapt round with Sheep-guts two or three Inches thick, some up as high as to their Calves, others even from their Feet to their Knees, which at a small distance seems to be a sort of Boots. These are put on when they are green; and so they grow hard and stiff on their Legs, for they never pull them off again, till they have occasion to eat them; which is when they journey from home, and have no other Food; then these Guts which have been worn, it may be, six, eight, ten or twelve Months, make them a good Banquet. (4th ed., 1699, p. 538)

427–30. Dampier says that at Tonquin 'Their teeth are as black as they can make them; for this being accounted a great ornament, they dye them of that colour . . . they say they should else be like Brutes; and that would be a great shame to them to be like Elephants or Dogs; which they compare those to that have white teeth' (*Voyages and Descriptions*, 2nd ed., 1700, ii. 41). There is no 'King CHIHU' in Dampier, but the name may have been suggested by the title, 'Choua', of one of the two kings of Tonquin.

441–8. 'Prince GIOLO' is presumably Dampier's 'Jeoly, the Painted Prince',
who was tattooed 'by pricking the Skin, and rubbing in a Pigment' (*A New
Voyage*, p. 514). Dampier bought him in Mindanao, where he had been en-
slaved, and brought him to England, where he died. He told Dampier that
most people on his native island, Meangis, in Malaya, were so painted.

463–8. Cf. *Memoirs of Scriblerus*, ed. Kerby-Miller, p. 108: 'But what most
conduced to his easy attainment of this Language, was his love of Ginger-
bread; which his Father observing, caused it to be stampt with the Letters
of the Greek Alphabet; and the child the very first day eat as far as Iota.'

481–92. Dampier, *A New Voyage*, p. 328:

A *Comrade* is a familiar Male-friend; a *Pagally* is an innocent Platonick Friend
of the other Sex. All Strangers are in a manner oblig'd to accept of this Acquaintance and Familiarity, which must be first purchased with a small Present . . .
and as often as the Stranger goes ashore, he is welcome to his *Comrade* or *Pigally's*
House, where he may be entertained for his Money, to eat, drink, or sleep. . . .

Dampier is describing, however, not China but Mindanao in the Philippines.
P seems to confuse this custom with prostitution, which, Dampier says, is
also customary in China and the East Indies: '. . . the chief Factors and
Captains of Ships have the great Mens Daughters offered them, the *Man-
darins* or Noblemens at *Tunquin*, and even the King's Wives in *Guinea*; and
by this sort of Alliance the Country people are ingaged to a greater friendship'
(pp. 395–6).

497. POMONQUE. P seems to be referring to the Pamaunkee (Paumonkey)
tribe of American Indians encountered by the first settlers in Virginia. We
have not, however, found a report of any such ceremony as that described.

505–28. Cf. Montaigne: 'Quelle bonté est-ce que je voyois hyer en credit,
et demain plus, et que le trajet d'une riviere faict crime? Quelle verité que
ces montaignes bornent, qui est mensonge au monde qui se tient au delà?'
(ii. 493; Bk. II, ch. xii). Cf. also Pascal: 'Trois degrés d'élévation du pôle
renversent toute la jurisprudence. . . . Plaisante justice qu'une rivière borne!
Vérité au deçà des Pyrénées, erreur au delà' (ii. 216; frag. 294).

Canto III

4. twofold Hedge of Teeth. A literal translation of a phrase in *Iliad*, iv.
350 and ix. 409. Pope does not so translate it and does not comment on the
phrase.

9. The following passage in *W*, 40–41 (transcribed in *L 28*, 147, and *M*,
111, and printed from *L 28* in *1907*, pp. 325–6), is an earlier version of Dick's
objection and Matthew's reply. The last lines clearly led P into the verses
on conscience that he placed in *Vicar of Bray and More* (1721):

> All this says Richard is but nonsence
> For what's the Will without the Conscience
> That mighty power by whom the thought
> Is from Kings Bench to Chanc'ry brought.

What seat for Her have You assign'd
Where She may view and sway the mind?
   Dear Dick at Surgeons Hall they tell You
There are two Regions in the Belly
The Diaphragma (You love Greek)
The Midriff as the vulgar speak
Lyes between both that thou mayst know
How far the bounds of either go
As in the Tennis Court the nett
Determines either parties bett
Or Berwick whilome did Distinguish
The Limits between Scotts and English.
   For hark You, Richard, shou'd we putt
The conscience lower towards the Gutt
It wou'd remain inept and quiet
And stil go downward with our Diet
Hence the desires She wou'd produce
Wou'd all be sordid base and Loose.
   Now place her in a higher part
Amidst the Region of the heart:
From thence so many conduits lead
Directly upward to the head
That mounting by too swift advances
And bursting in ten thousand fancies
She wou'd from Neighbourhood of place
Be always flying in Your face
And fire your brain with so much heat
That You cou'd neither Sleep nor eat.
   For Dick Your Conscience like your Horse
Shou'd never &ca—

43–52. For Pythagoras' rule of silence and of abstention from beans, see
Diogenes Laertius, vii. 10, 33–34. P's line of attack is like Montaigne's:

Il est bien aisé, sur des fondemens avouez, de bastir ce qu'on veut: car, selon la
loy et ordonnance de ce commencement, le reste des pieces du bastiment se conduit
ayséement, sans se démentir. . . . Quiconque est creu de ses presuppositions, il est
nostre maistre et nostre Dieu: il prendra le plant de ses fondemens si ample et si aisé
que, par iceux, il nous pourra monter, s'il veut, jusques aux nües.

(ii. 413–14; Bk. II, ch. xii)

53–60. Lucretius had posited (i. 329–97) a void or vacuum in which the
atoms move, and which explains the penetrability and differing densities of
bodies. Descartes, however, conceived of the world of extended bodies as
a *plenum*, with motion communicated only by immediate impact; he denied
all possibility of action at a distance (i.e. without material media). Hence it
was necessary to suppose bodies to swim in an infinite ether ('subtle matter'
or 'first matter') which forms whirlpools or vortices in which bodies are
carried about. While Newton refuted, in the *Principia*, the vortex theory of
planetary motion, and rejected the concept of ether as a dense fluid, he
formulated an elaborate hypothesis concerning a similar medium:

And now we might add something concerning a certain most subtle spirit which pervades and lies hid in all gross bodies; by the force and action of which spirit the particles of bodies attract one another at near distances, and cohere, if contiguous; and electric bodies operate to greater distances . . . and light is emitted, reflected, inflected, and heats bodies; and all sensation is excited, and the members of animal bodies move at the command of the will, namely, by the vibrations of this spirit. . . . (*Mathematical Principles of Natural Philosophy*, ed. F. Cajori, Berkeley, 1934, p. 547)

'And is not this Medium exceedingly more rare and subtile than the Air, and exceedingly more elastick and active? . . . And is it not, (by its *elastick force*) expanded through all the Heavens?' (*Opticks*, ed. E. Whittaker, New York, 1931, p. 349).

P's criticism of this doctrine was probably indebted to the Leibniz–Clarke correspondence (see note to iii. 335, below). Leibniz argued that Newtonian physics involved a perpetual miracle, else it is impossible that 'bodies should *attract* one another at a distance, without any intermediate Means' (p. 115). Clarke replied that the attraction does not take place without intermediate means, 'But the *Means* by which Two Bodies attract each other, may be *invisible* and *intangible*', non-mechanical, yet regular (p. 151). The ether gives bodies an elastic force, so that, when two bodies strike, they rebound not only with the original force, but 'with a *new Force* impressed by the others Elasticity' (p. 327); the quantity of motion is not constant, else there would be an absolute mechanism, and the ether is the source of new motion. Leibniz denied such 'natural' miracles, and contended that God created the universe perfect, and does not need to intervene.

61–62. Alchemy was not yet discredited; even Robert Boyle and Newton pursued alchemical experiments.

68. The dispute over *plenum* or *vacuum*, discussed in the note to ll. 53–60, above.

81. Cunning-Man. Astrologer. Cf. *Hudibras*, II. iii. 106.

103. *Ideas*—Plato and the Neoplatonists; *Forms*—Aristotle and the schoolmen. What sect P means to suggest by *Intellects* is not clear: perhaps the Thomists, since Aquinas defined the various intellects at length.

105. The controversy over transubstantiation.

113–16. The image is reminiscent of Horace, *Odes*, I. xxiii (first noted by Dobson in *1889*).

125–6. See note to *Frederic* (1714), l. 65. Nottingham in 1711 made a bargain with the Whigs: in exchange for their support for the Occasional Conformity Bill he joined them in opposition to the peace that P was secretly negotiating. Swift attacked him (as 'Dismal') in two poems (*Poems*, pp. 141, 161). His followers were called the Whimsical Tories.

128. 'Quoth *Hudibras*, I smell a *Rat*; | *Ralpho*, thou dost prevaricate' (*Hudibras*, I. i. 821–2).

129. Your Sect. Presumably the Pyrrhonists or philosophical sceptics.

152–81. Cf. Swift's *Mechanical Operation of the Spirit* (1704), and the latter

part of Chapter XII of the *Memoirs of Scriblerus*, with Kerby-Miller's notes
(see note to ii. 251–80, above).

205. Belly-Timber. Cf. *Hudibras*, I. i. 331.

215. Cf. *Hudibras*, I. i. 314.

225. BURNET. Probably the work P has in mind is his *Exposition of the
XXXIX Articles*, 1699. See note to *Fragment* (1715), l. 1.

HEYLYN. See note to ii. 401, above. Author of such works as: *Ecclesia
Restaurata, or History of the Reformation*, 1661; *Cyprianus Anglicus*, 1668; *Aerius
Redivivus, or History of Presbyterianism*, 1670.

231. *Mohack*. The Mohocks were a gang of rakes who terrorized London
in 1712; see R. J. Allen, *The Clubs of Augustan London* (Cambridge, Mass.,
1933), pp. 105–18.

235. nicking Sashes. The Nickers broke windows with halfpennies; cf.
Gay's *Trivia*, iii. 323–4 (first cited by Dobson in *1889*).

240–1. Cf. the *Memoirs of Scriblerus* (ed. Kerby-Miller, p. 106): 'Consider,
Woman, the different Temperaments of different Nations: What makes the
English Phlegmatick and melancholy but Beef? What renders the Welch so
hot and cholerick, but cheese and leeks? The French derive their levity from
their Soups, Frogs, and Mushrooms. . . .'

248. CONGREVE. See *Concerning Humour in Comedy*, 1695, in *Comedies*, ed.
B. Dobrée, 1939, p. 11.

265. QUARE. Daniel Quare (1648–1724), a Quaker and famous clock-
maker; he invented repeating watches.

291. RUSSEL. An undertaker.

335. See *A Collection of Papers, Which passed between the late Learned Mr. Leib-
nitz and Dr. Clarke, in the Years 1715 and 1716. Relating to the Principles of Natural
Philosophy and Religion*, 1717. This controversy, which has already been cited
as probably influencing several passages in the poem, seems to have made
a deep impression upon P. The central question at issue was the nature of
Space and Time, and their relation to God. Leibniz criticized Newton's
concept of Space as the *sensorium* of God, and objected to the notions of
absolute Space and Time chiefly because they were inconsistent with his
principle of Sufficient Reason: if Space and Time are uniform, there is no
reason why an event should occur at one time or in one place rather than
another. Clarke, in turn, attacked the concept of Sufficient Reason, which
would subject God to a kind of necessity, and argued that Space and Time
are constituted by God's omnipresence and eternity. As Ernst Cassirer remarks ('Newton and Leibniz', *Philosophical Review*, lii, 1943, 366–91), the
controversy shows a fundamental conflict of two philosophical methods,
based on different standards of truth and different frames of reference; the
presuppositions of Leibniz and Clarke are so at variance that neither can
comprehend the other's point of view.

342. Philosopher. Zeno of Elea, who denied the possibility of motion

in the famous paradoxes of Achilles and the Tortoise and the Flying Arrow.

346–9. Perhaps Galen, who denied that the heart was muscular or had propulsive force because he believed that muscle was incapable of such incessant motion.

350. CHRYSIPPUS. P has reversed the positions of Epicurus and Chrysippus (Stoic philosopher, *c.* 281–207 B.C.). Cicero, in *De Fato*, x and xvi–xix, says that Epicurus, in order to avoid fatalism, had maintained that some propositions are neither true nor false; Chrysippus, however, argued that every proposition is either true or false, and hence that all events are caused by fate.

354. MALBRANCH. Nicolas de Malebranche (1638–1715) held that we can know nothing but God directly and immediately. We know matter only through its ideas, i.e. in God; we are more certain of the existence of our minds (through *conscience* or *sentiment intérieur*) than of our bodies, but we know even less of the nature of our minds than of our bodies. Other minds are known only through conjecture. (*Recherche de la Vérité*, 1674–5, Bk. III, Pt. II, ch. vii.)

369. WH——N. William Whiston (1667–1752), eccentric divine, scholar, and mathematician, proposed in 1714, with Humphrey Ditton, a means of working out the longitude by means of bomb-vessels. The scheme was unsuccessful, and frequently ridiculed; cf. the *Memoirs of Scriblerus*, ed. Kerby-Miller, pp. 167, 334.

383. *Darii . . . Bocardo.* Forms of the syllogism.

402–11. Probably a reminiscence of Swift's Preface to *A Tale of a Tub* (ed. A. C. Guthkelch and D. Nichol Smith, Oxford, 1920, p. 46).

423. BAYS's Dance. See *The Rehearsal*, Acts II and V.

424. L'AVARE. Cf. Molière's comedy, *L'Avare*, 1668, and Horace, *Satires*, II. iii. 111–23.

436. PEDRO. See note to ii. 257, above.

465. GEORGY. Shelton's son; see note to i. 1, above.

471. Two fragments in the manuscripts probably were a part originally of the preceding passage (ll. 418–71). They are more sombre in tone than the rest of the poem, and may have been deleted for that reason. The first (*L 28*, 149; printed in *1907*, p. 326) is labelled, 'The following Lines were in Alma but left out—':

> Yet happy Human race my Friend
> Did here the sickly madness end.
> But Mitis troubl'd half the Nation
> About his Offsprings Education;
> And urg'd by some unhappy fate
> Gave him Two Thirds of his Estate
> To settle the sad Wretch in Mariage
> (This of his life the Sole Miscariage).

> Yet Hopeful counts his Fathers Years,
> And blames the Sloth of Clotho's Sheers;
> That thus protracts the long wish'd death;
> Of whom? the Man who gave him breath.
> Say this, and the ill jesting Calf
> Replyes ye with an impious laugh:
> His Mother help'd, and he cou'd spare
> Her too, from all this Worldly care:
> Were She, good Soul, but once in Heav'n
> Her Jointure wou'd set matters even.
> Wou'd Fate this double Blessing give
> A happy Orphan he shou'd Live.

The second occurs in P's hand in *W*, 42, and *L 29*, 64 (transcribed in *L 28*, 150, and *M*, 112; printed in *1907*, p. 327); in *W* it is labelled 'Original Brouillon', and in *L 29*, 'Fragment for Alma. (not finished) therefore Omitted'. The lines satirize Lord Coningsby, whom P had attacked in *The Viceroy* (1715). We print them from *W*:

> Hence frantic Att All's endless rage
> Hates the recess requir'd by age.
>
> Most people live by drink and Diet,
> He feeds on other Mens disquiet.
> Eternal Watch the Mad man keeps
> When e'er he knows his neighbour sleeps.
> Scar'd with His own injurious Deed
> He thinks it safest to proceed
> Hears jingling Chains and clinking Fetters
> And wou'd impose 'em on his betters.
> Which does the Bedlam fear the most
> Harly alive or Gaphneys Ghost?
> Leave him as God and Man has done
> And let the Muse go gently on.

480–91. 'L'âme est jetée dans le corps pour y faire un séjour de peu de durée. . . . Il ne lui en reste que très peu [de temps] dont elle puisse disposer. Mais ce peu qui lui reste l'incommode si fort et l'embarrasse si étrangement, qu'elle ne songe qu'à le perdre. Ce lui est une peine insupportable d'être obligée de vivre avec soi et de penser à soi. Ainsi tout son soin est de s'oublier soi-même. . . . C'est l'origine de toutes les occupations tumultuaires des hommes, et de tout ce qu'on appelle divertissement ou passe-temps. . . . Sa joie consiste dans cet oubli; et il suffit, pour la rendre misérable, de l'obliger de se voir et d'être avec soi' (Pascal, ii. 53 n.; a passage added by the Port-Royal editors). For discussion of this concept of *divertissement*, see M. K. Spears, 'Some Ethical Aspects of Matthew Prior's Poetry', *Studies in Philology*, lxv (1948), 606–29.

515. TOM O' STILES . . . JOHN O' NOKES. Fictitious names used by young lawyers in stating cases; cf. *Hudibras*, III. i. 616, and *Spectator*, No. 577 (6 Aug. 1714).

516–19. In *The Rehearsal*, IV. i, the two kings of Brentford lament and quarrel over Lardella's coffin, then discover that it is empty and she is alive.

531. In *W*, 128, there is a rejected passage that probably came here:

> Now as we both my dearest friend
> Into the Vale of Years descend
> And your grey hairs and my dry Cough
> Show that sad prospect not far off. . . .

547. P owned more than 130 paintings; prints and drawings appraised at over £250; a library of more than 2,500 volumes; and a sizable collection of coins, medals, antique bronzes, jewels, and trinkets. See H. B. Wright and H. C. Montgomery, 'The Art Collection of a Virtuoso in Eighteenth-Century England', *The Art Bulletin*, xxvii (1945), 195–204.

578. Cf. Shakespeare, Sonnet LXVI: 'Tir'd with all these, for restful death I cry. . . .'

602. Addison's *Cato*, 1713.

609. WANLEY. Humfrey Wanley (1672–1726), scholar and antiquary, librarian to Robert Harley, Earl of Oxford, and to his son. He helped P correct proof for *1718*; P was evidently on cordial terms with him from 1717 on, and mentions him frequently in his letters.

610. DRIFT. Adrian Drift (1676–1737) was P's secretary at least by 1699, and in 1700, when P became a Commissioner of Trade and Plantations, Drift was made clerk to the board. P succeeded in having him released from his duties to serve as his secretary on his last mission to France; but after the death of the queen, Drift lost his post at the Board of Trade. By 1717 P had taken him to live with him, more as friend and companion than as secretary. Of his affection and admiration for P there is ample evidence; see, for example, his poems in *1740*, pp. lvii, lviii, lxii.

612. Two rejected passages in *W*, 43–44 (transcribed in *L 28*, 151 and in *M*, 114; printed in *1907*, pp. 327–8) cast interesting sidelights on P's view of the basic conflict represented in the poem:

> Besides a Man must never put
> His Oar into anothers Boat.
> Are there not Bells in ev'ry Steeple
> To Summon in the Docile People
> And Deans and Prebends whose great Care
> Some two and fifty times a Year
> Shou'd to their Parish gravely read?
> But if they send them in their Stead
> Some Curate who can hardly Spell
> This some conceive does e'en as well.

> Besides, Dear Dick, thô you and I
> With ipse dixet shou'd comply,
> He never will obtain his Ends
> On many of our Gresham Friends;

Who with Authority Dispense
And in its place have setled Sense.

The World was 2000 Year in the Dark following Aristotle . . .
Till great Descart and his Sectators
Light up their Philosophic Papers
Which say the Aristotelians again
Were but Jackalents, by which Men
thinking [they] saw mistook their way more than before.

613. JONATHAN. P's servant, mentioned in letters of 1717–18 (*H.M.C. Bath*, iii. 451–2, 455).

(516)   *Song*

MSS. *W*, 1ᵛ (P); *L 28*, 161 (D); *M*, 79 (A).
Pub. *1740*, p. 125.
Text. *W*. Collated: *L 28*, *M*, *1740*.

In *1740*, there are footnotes identifying 'Dick' (l. 2), as 'Mr PRIOR's intimate Friend RICHARD SHELTON, Esq' and 'N[anny]' (l. 4) as 'Mrs. ANNE DURHAM'. These identifications are probably correct; the description fits Shelton (see note to *Alma*, i. 1), and the situation resembles that in *The Question* and the other poems of the Cloe–Lisetta sequence (1718, above). Presumably this poem was written at about the same time.

8. B—— fair. Bartholomew Fair began on 24 Aug.

(517)   *Answer to the Female Phaeton*

MSS. *W*, 57 (D & P); *L 28*, 165 (D; emend. by Pope).
Pub. *1907*, p. 335.
Text. *W*. Collated: *L 28*.

See the commentary on *Upon Lady Katherine H—de's first appearing* (Works of Doubtful Authenticity, 1718). Curll's edition of that poem, in which it is called *The Female Phaeton* and attributed to Prior, was published in April 1718, immediately after the first edition. This *Answer* was probably written soon thereafter. If it was sent to Curll, it had no effect, for he continued to attribute *The Female Phaeton* to P.

5. Thou. Edmund Curll (1675–1747) published two unauthorized collections of P's verse (*1707* and *1716*) in addition to many separate pieces, always unauthorized or spurious; he was the publisher of many of the works listed under Works Wrongly Attributed. See Pope's *Dunciad*, ii. 116, 130, and notes (ed. J. Sutherland, 1943), and R. Straus, *The Unspeakable Curll*, 1927.

14. Mother. Jane Hyde (d. 1725), Countess of Clarendon and Rochester,

a famous beauty. Her eldest daughter was Jane (l. 25), her second Kitty (l. 26), the 'Female Phaeton'.

61. In 1716 Curll was tossed in a blanket by the boys of Westminster School and was given an emetic by Pope; see George Sherburn, *The Early Career of Alexander Pope* (Oxford, 1934), pp. 161–72.

1719

(520)   *A Prologue*

MSS.   *L 28*, 169 (D); *M*, 86 (A [ll. 1–42] & D [ll. 43–49]).

Pub.   *Chit-Chat. A Comedy. As it is Acted at the Theatre-Royal in Drury-Lane . . .* Written by Mr. Killigrew. London: Printed for Bernard Lintot, between the Temple Gates. [1719]; *A Miscellaneous Collection*, 1721 (Case 320–1), ii. 162.

     Collected: *1907*, p. 338.

Text.   *L 28*. Collated: *M*. (Full text of 1719 pub. is given below.)

Chit-Chat, the only play by Thomas Killigrew the younger (1657–1719), was performed on 14 Feb. 1719; through the influence of the Earl of Argyle it ran for eleven nights and made a profit of £1,000 (A. Nicoll, *A History of Early Eighteenth Century Drama 1700–1750*, Cambridge, 1925, p. 188). Among the actors were Booth, Wilks, Cibber, and Mrs. Oldfield.

Chit-Chat was published by Lintot on 28 Feb. 1719 (adv. *Daily Courant*). The unsigned prologue published with the play (and reprinted in *A Miscellaneous Collection*, 1721) looks very much like a revision of the version in *L 28* (which is dated 'Feb: 1719'); it uses most of the manuscript version, except for the last nine lines, but alters it extensively. It is possible that Prior did the revision himself, unknown to Drift; but in this case it is odd that his name was not used with the published version. Perhaps he gave his rough draft to someone else to revise and complete. Nothing is known of any relation between P and Killigrew. The printed version is as follows (from the first edition of the play):

The Prologue

> The ugly Beau by frequent Use of Glass, ⎫
> Instead of hating, comes to like his Face, ⎬
> And grows the Plague of every publick Place. ⎭
> Just so it fares with Fops of Phæbus Strain, ⎫
> They read their Nonsense or'e and o're again, ⎬
> And find strange Charms in what gives others Pain ⎭
> This from our Author I am bid to say,
> As some Excuse for his first Coup d'Essay.
> At once he boldly soars to highest Life,
> And paints a very, very modish Wife:

> *In whose Example this sad Truth appears,*
> *The Husband's hated for his Worth, not Years.*
> *They crave for Fops, as Girls green Fruit devour,*
> *Not that 'tis young, but that they love what's sowre.*
> *But one Word more for these loose following Scenes;*
> *Ye all will ask what 'tis the Scribbler means?*
> *Where is the Order, Method, the Design,*
> *And all that makes a well-wroght Drama shine?*
> *Why, if his Conduct merits not Applause,*
> *Consider, Sirs, they are your Lives he draws.*
> *As for his Wit, if that be under-grown,* ⎫
> *Make it not less, by making it your own.* ⎬
> *And then for Moral: Faith, like you, he has none.* ⎭
> *His Plot he's sure will plead for every Fault,*
> *Such deep Designs no* Spanish *Priest e're thought,* ⎫
> *Nor darker* Machiavel *to Borgia taught.*   ⎭
> *Observe him well, ye learn'd in State Intrigues,*
> *Who deal in Politicks, and powder'd Wigs:*
> *Your Schemes, as soon as form'd, are all reveal'd;*
> *But here the Action's done, and yet the Plot's conceal'd.*

'Corinna', in *Critical Remarks on the Four Taking Plays of this Season* . . . (1719), speaks as if she thinks Killigrew himself wrote the prologue: '. . . the Author frankly owns all that can be said in his Prologue, which is, that there is no *Order*, no *Design*, no *Plot*, nor any thing that *Comedy* requires . . .' (p. 55).

35. Alberoni. Giulio Alberoni (1664–1752), Spanish-Italian cardinal and statesman, was at this time immensely powerful in Spain.

40. Cf. Epilogue to *The Rehearsal*, l. 1: 'The play is at an end, but where's the plot?'

(521)   *Verses*

MSS. L 29, 33 (D); L 27, 5 (D). (The printed sheets from *1720* are included in L 28, 184.) (Index to M.)

Pub.   [Title as in text.] Cambridge, Printed for Cornelius Crownfield; And are to be Sold by Jacob Tonson, Bookseller in London. [1719]; [The same, without imprint]; [Title as in text.] London: Printed for Jacob Tonson, at Shakespear's-Head over-against Katharine-Street in the Strand. MDCCXX.
       Collected: *New Collection 1725*, p. 62.

Text. *1719*. Collated: L 29, L 27, *1720*.

First published on 25 Nov. 1719 (adv. *Daily Courant*). The broadside without imprint listed above was printed from the same setting of type as the Cambridge edition, and probably preceded it; perhaps it was distributed to those present on the occasion. Prior wrote to Swift on 8 Dec. 1719:

Having spent part of my summer very agreeably in Cambridgeshire with dear

Lord Harley, I am returned without him to my own palace in Duke Street, whence I endeavour to exclude all the tumult and noise of the neighbouring Court of Requests, and to live *aut nihil agendo aut aliud agendo*, till he comes to town. But there is worse than this yet: I have treated Lady Harriot at Cambridge—good God! a fellow of a college treat—and spoke verses to her in a gown and cap. What! the plenipotentiary so far concerned in the damned peace at Utrecht; the man, that makes up half the volume of terse prose, that makes up the report of the Committee, speaking verses! *Sic est, homo sum*; and am not ashamed to send those very verses to one, who can make much better. . . . (Swift, *Correspondence*, ed. F. Elrington Ball, 1910–14, iii. 38–39)

A verse introduction to P's poem by Charles Caesar is discussed in the section of Works Wrongly Attributed. Thomas Baker wrote to Hearne on 13 Dec. 1719: 'My Lord and my Lady were here, and dined with Mr. Prior, who spoke a copy of verses (in the Library) in compliment to my Lady with some Intimation of a charitable design' (*Remarks and Collections*, Oxford Historical Society Publications, xlviii, 1906, 80). It appears that the 'charitable design' was the building of a new chapel for the college; see the letter of John Newcome of St. John's to P, 27 Nov. 1719 (*H.M.C. Bath*, iii. 472–3).

4. Neighbour. Lord Harley's seat, Wimpole, was in Cambridgeshire.
25–28. For Lady Margaret, foundress of St. John's, see commentary on *Many Daughters have done well* (1688).

(522)   *Engraved on Three Sides*

MSS.   *L 29*, 44 (D & P); *M*, 128 (D); *Worcester Col.* (George Clarke's hand; apparently copied from the engraved plates).
Pub.   With engravings of the lamp [1720?].
       Collected: *1740*, p. 223.
Text.   *L 29*. Collated: *M*, *1720*, *1740*, *Pedestal* at Welbeck.

The date of composition is set by Prior's letter to Lord Harley, 15 Dec. 1719, which also tells us that the Latin inscription and the translation of P's quatrain into Latin Sapphics are by Dr. Robert Freind: 'Bob has writ the prose inscription for the lamp, and we had a friendly squabble last night about the verse. He says my last of the four is harsh, *i.e.*, he can't stuff so much excellent sense—as I told him—into two stanzas of sapphic; well, the last verse is made softer, the four are turned otherwise; Gibbs shall have the whole *debito tempore* . . . (*H.M.C. Bath*, iii. 475). P had bought the lamp from the Colbert collection when he was in Paris in 1698 (P to Père Montfaucon, 12 May 1721; *L 29*, 7ᵛ). Before presenting it to Lord Harley, he had made for it a three-sided wood pedestal about 9 inches high with these inscriptions written in gilt on the side panels. This pedestal is now at Welbeck Abbey, although the lamp itself has been lost. Harley was so pleased with the gift that he ordered engraved plates of the 'profiles of it' for distribution to his friends (P to the Earl of Chesterfield, 27 April 1721; *L 14*, 315–17). The Society of Antiquaries of London has a copy of these plates as well as the original drawings, ascribed to Grisoni. Miss Pamela Wynn Reeves, Curator of Artistic Possessions, tells us that in these the lamp appears to resemble an ornate sixteenth-century Italian centre-piece for a dining table. P collected antique lamps, as *Alma* (iii. 458–9) indicates.

1720

(523)   *The Conversation*

MSS.   *W*, 16 (P; ll. 1–14, 17–20, 35–36 only); *L 27*, 18 (D); *L 29*, 34 (D). (The printed sheets from *1720* are included in *L 28*, 186.) (Index to *M*.)

Pub.   [Title as in text.] London: Printed for Jacob Tonson, at Shakespear's-Head, over-against Katharine-Street in the Strand. MDCCXX. Collected: *New Collection 1725*, p. 66.

Text.   *1720*. Collated: *W*, *L 27*, *L 29*.

Published on 18 Feb. 1720 (adv. *Post Boy*, 16–18 Feb.). Prior sent a copy to Pope before publication, with a request for criticism; Pope replied: 'I can find nothing to be objected or amended in what you favor'd me with, Unless you shou'd think the first Speech you put into your own mouth a little too long. It is certainly no Fault, & I don't know whether I should speak of it; but as a proof that I would . . . find something like a fault, to show my zeal, & to have the vanity of pretending, like Damon himself, to have Advis'd you' (*Correspondence*, ed. G. Sherburn, Oxford, 1956, ii. 30). 'Damon' obviously represents a type rather than a specific person; but a letter from Robert Ingram to P, 8 March 1718, reveals one 'friend' who exemplified the type perfectly: 'I have often alter'd the Countenance of Strangers to me; by hinting, that yourselfe had read many Parts of your Solomon to me. . . . In the decent Liberty I have always allow'd Myselfe, & from the sole Principle of Humanity & Benevolence to Mankind, in frankly speaking my Thoughts with relation to the four last years of the Queen; I never once utter'd a disrespectful Word of you, & have ever endeavour'd to divert others from it, by timely professing my long Acquaintance with & great Esteem for you' (*L 7*, 70).

The following fragments in the manuscripts seem to indicate that P began a poem relating more directly to his own experiences. The first may represent his resolution before his examination by the Secret Committee in 1715:

Anaxarcus; being upon the Torture in hopes of some Discovery bit out his Tongue and Spit it into the Tyrants Face—The Tongue thus separated from the dear Root

> Thus wounded and thus spit
> Express'd more Wisdom Sence and Wit
> Then Homer Sung or Plato writ.
>
> Tho bad I sing thô worse I speak
> Nor Latin understand nor Greek
> To save Your Life
> For what You value more Your fame
> For all that Man with the hard Name
> This foolish Tongue wou'd do the same.
>
> Virtue and Love instruct me well
> What to Conceal and what to tell.
>
>   (*W*, 60ᵛ [D]; also in *L 28*, 152 [D].
>   Printed, in part, in *1907*, p. 329.)

The second may describe his examination and confinement:

> Who er [a] Serious view will take
> Of that learned book the Almanack
> Will find a figured Man pierct thrô
> With Sundry Darts from head to toe.
> Just so a Year at least stood I
> Smote breast and back and hip and thighe.
> Full twenty Foes around Me came
> And Each took several aim
> Against Some part Each took
> One at my head with malice strook
> T'other ram'd Perjury at my throat
> This with Sophisticated reason
> Shot at my head for writing treason.
> Against them all I stood.
>
> (*W*, 46 [very rough draft in P's hand], with some readings
>   from *L 28*, 154 [D]. Printed in *1907*, pp. 329–30.)

The third seems to represent a speech by a friend of P's who remained loyal in spite of an estrangement, and helped obtain subscriptions for *1718*:

> Yet distancd and undone by those
> Whom sure thou did'st Excell in Prose
> When thou thy long mistake did'st see
> And los'd from Prison came to Me
> Say, did I not receive Thee, Say
> As thou had'st never gone astray?
>
> To make thy fortune fair amends
> In raising Thee twelve hundred friends
> By which succeeding age may See
> Who lov'd the Muse and pardon'd Thee.
>
> I Saw a thousand Illook't foes
> Their dagger to thy Breast oppose.
>
>   (*W*, 45 [P], with some readings from *L 28*,
>   152 [D]. Printed in *1907*, p. 329.)

36. Dr. Samuel Clarke's *Scripture Doctrine of the Trinity*, 1712, was attacked as Arian in tendency by Dr. Daniel Waterland and others.

50. Dunstable. 'Used proverbially as a type of directness and plainness' (*O.E.D.*), the road from London to Dunstable being remarkably straight and even.

88. DORSET. See *Postscript* (1718), and *Preamble to the Duke of Dorsets Patent* (Latin, 1720).

(526)   *Prologue to The Orphan*

MSS.   *L 27*, 8 (D). (The printed sheets from *1720* are included in *L 28*, 185.) (Index to *M*.)

Pub.   [Title as in text.] London: Printed for Jacob Tonson, at Shakespear's-Head over-against Katharine-Street in the Strand. MDCCXX. Collected: *New Collection 1725*, p. 64.

Text.   *1720*. Collated: *L 27*.

Published on 10 March 1720 (adv. *Daily Courant*). The play was Otway's *The Orphan* (1680). 'Lord Duplin' was Thomas Hay (1710–87), Viscount Dupplin since 1719, when his father became seventh Earl of Kinnoull. His mother (Abigail, Countess of Kinnoull) was the daughter of Robert Harley, Earl of Oxford, to whom she wrote on 18 Feb. 1720: 'About a fortnight ago some of the Westminster scholars acted a play called "The Orphan", Lord Erskine's part was Monimia, and Tommy acted Cordelio the page; they both did their parts mighty well. Mr. Prior made a prologue which Tommy spoke as well as I could wish. He told me he would send you a copy of it, which I hope he has done' (*H.M.C. Portland*, v. 593). *B.M. Add. 27408*, 124, contains a *Prologue ye Orphan by Mr. W. Herbert. Spoken by Toby Dore*, which is based on Prior's prologue and quotes it extensively.

In *L 29*, 58, there are drafts in P's hand (transcribed by Drift in *L 29*, 48, and printed in *1907*, pp. 357, 403, as separate fragments) for what seems to be another prologue to be spoken by Lord Dupplin at a similar performance in the next year, 1721. The first line appears to refer to Dupplin's performance in *The Orphan*, the second stanza jokes about the youth of the actors, and the third deals with Westminster School. Perhaps because the reading of the proper names in ll. 3–4 is uncertain, we have not been able to identify the play. We base our text on P's drafts, taking some readings from Drift where the original is illegible:

> . . . and I was last year a ladys page
> Thus serve her better in a riper age.
> When I in fact shall act Tiphax part
> Lett every fair Lessandra guard her heart.
>
> What amrous Cares did Psyche's mind employ
> And yet the God of Love was but a Boy.

Diana too forsook her other cares
To teach Endimion to observe the Stars.
Stopt in the Montains where her Lover lay
And rose but very little before day.

Early in life we learn the Mighty rule
Taught by old Bess the foundress of our School
Neither to flatterers nor to frowns to bend
To scorn our foe but dye to serve our friend.

1–6. These lines are taken almost verbatim from P's *Prologue made for Lord Buckhurst* (1695; not published until 1740), ll. 2–4, 9, and 15–16.

20. See notes to *A Session of the Poets* (1688), l. 60; *Alma* (1718), i. 304.

(527)   *A Letter*

MSS. *L 1*, 64 (P); *L 27*, 66 (D); *B.M. Harl. 7316*, 129 (X). (Index to *M*.)
Pub. *1740*, p. 133.
Text. *L 1*. Collated: *L 27*, *Harl.*, *1740*.

The holograph from which we print is written on a single leaf bound into a section of *L 1* that consists chiefly of Prior's letters to Lord Harley. Plate II is a photograph of this manuscript.

Lady Margaret Cavendish Holles-Harley, only surviving child of Edward Lord Harley and Lady Henrietta, was born on 11 Feb. 1715 (Swift, *Correspondence*, ed. F. Elrington Ball, 1910–14, ii. 269 n.). P mentions her constantly and affectionately in his letters to Harley from 1717 on, and she remarked, much later, that he 'made himself beloved by every living thing in the house, —master, child, and servant, human creature or animal' (Pope's *Works*, ed. W. Elwin and W. J. Courthope, 1871–89, viii. 193 n.). She married William Bentinck, second Duke of Portland (1709–62) in 1734, and died in 1785.

(527)   *'Fame counting Thy books'*

MSS. *Welbeck Harley Papers*, xxxiv, 176 (P). (Index to *M*.)
Pub. *N. & Q.*, 3rd ser., iii (1863), 109.
        Collected: *1892*, ii. 301.
Text. *Wb* [*Welbeck Harley Papers*]. Collated: *1863*.

Prior sent this couplet to Lord Oxford from Wimpole on 23 Dec. 1720, remarking: 'Being a very laborious poet, I made these two verses in a morning in the library, and was never in my life better pleased with my own work than to hear little Mlle. Harley repeat them the next morning with the prettiest tone and manner imaginable' (*H.M.C. Portland*, v. 611; the original letter at Welbeck is our text). Francis Trench, in *N. & Q.* (cited above), says that the couplet is 'preserved in the library at Wimpole . . . and was copied by the writer there'. His version adds, after the couplet, '*Written in the Library*, Dec. 2, 1720. | M. P.' Viscount Clifden has kindly informed us that these verses were not at Wimpole during the period he was in possession of the house.

Like his father, Edward Lord Harley was a great collector. After his death, his printed books (estimated at 50,000 volumes, with 350,000 pamphlets) were sold to Osborne the bookseller for £13,000; the Harleian MSS. were sold to Parliament in 1753 for £10,000 as one of the foundation collections for the British Museum.

(528)   *Epitaph for Sir Thomas Powys*

MSS. *Bodl. MS. Hearne*, vol. cxxxviii, Thomas Hearne's Diary for 25 Jan. 1733 (transcript from the monument). (Index to *M.*)

Pub. *Desiderata Curiosa. Volume the First*, ed. Francis Peck, 1732, lib. vi, p. 28. Collected: *Evans 1779*, ii. 280 (omitting ll. 1, 4–17, 28–30).

Text. *Monument* in the church of St. John the Baptist, Achurch, Northamptonshire, where it has been transferred from St. Peter's Church, Lilford. From this all other extant texts have been derived. The transcript here reproduced was kindly supplied by Mr. Vincent H. Sykes of Thrapston.

The authenticity of this epitaph is proved by a letter from Ambrose Powys, third son of Sir Thomas, to Prior, sending him a gratuity and thanking him 'for the very great obligation you have conferr'd upon our Family by transmitting the character of my Father in the most elegant manner to his Posterity, from which I hope we shall learn to be wise and be instructed' (*L 7*, 110). This letter is dated merely 'Lincolns-Inn, July the 27th', but the will of Thomas Powys, eldest son of Sir Thomas, makes it almost certain that it was in 1720 that P composed the memorial. In Thomas's will, signed on 27 Feb. 1719[–20], he made his brother Ambrose, as one of his executors, responsible for carrying out the plans on which they had already agreed for setting up their father's monument (Somerset House, Probate, 14 March 1719/20).

(529)   *Virgils Georgic 4*

MSS. *L 7*, 110^v (D); *L 28*, 163 (D); *Lpo 18*, 260^v (X).
Pub. *1907*, p. 334.
Text. *L 28*. Collated: *L 7*, *Lpo 18*.

The copy in *L 7* is written in Drift's hurried hand (as if from dictation) upon the back of the letter from Ambrose Powys quoted in the preceding commentary. Presumably the verses were composed soon after the date of the letter, 27 July [1720]. We follow the text of *L 28* because part of *L 7* is lost in the binding. In *Lpo 18*, 260–1, Prior's is the third translation of this passage in a series containing six others by Miss Verney, Dryden, Mr. Ogilby, the Earl of Mulgrave, the Earl of Lauderdale, and Thomas May.

(529)   *Ronsard's Franciade*

MSS.   *L 29*, 42 (D).
Pub.   *1907*, p. 356.
Text.   *L 29*.

The manuscript is dated 'W.[impole?] Dec. 1720'. The reference in the title locates the passage in the edition of Ronsard that Prior owned (*Œuvres*, Paris, 1584); P did not, however, write out the translation in his own copy, now in the library of St. John's College, Cambridge. In *L 29*, Drift transcribed the passage from Ronsard before the translation. It consists of the six lines beginning, 'Mille ans apres, les Tourangelles plaines', near the end of the *Franciade* (Ronsard, *Œuvres complètes*, ed. G. Cohen, Paris, 1950, i. 779). In the Preface to *Solomon* (1708), P calls the *Franciade* '*incomparably good as far as it goes*'.

P discovered later that the passage is an imitation of Virgil (*Georgics*, i. 493–7); he noted in *L 29*, 109^v: 'Virg: Geor: 1 towards the End: Scilicet et tempus veniet is just the verses of Ronsard that I have translated.'

6–7. A separate couplet, the first transcribed by Drift under the heading 'Fragments Written at Down-Hall', in *L 28*, 147, seems to be an alternate version of these lines: 'The Plowshares now deform the martial plain | Raking the Sculls of the once glorious Slain.' The existence of this fragment suggests that P may have tried the translation in couplets before deciding on blank verse.

(529)   *The Turtle and the Sparrow*

MSS.   *W*, 7 (D & P; ll. 1–441 only); *B.M. Harl.* 6947, 202 (X; ll. 1–441 only); *L 27*, 37 (D); *L 29*, 30 (D; ll. 442–53 only); *W*, 163^v (P; ll. 232–9 only); *L 28*, 160 (D; ll. 442–53 only); *Lpo 18*, 96 (X; ll. 442–53 only). (The printed sheets from *1723* are included in *L 28*, 218.) (Index to *M*.)

Pub.   *The Turtle and the Sparrow. A Poem.* By the late Matthew Prior, Esq; London: Printed for J. Roberts, near the Oxford-Arms, in Warwick-Lane. MDCCXXIII [ll. 1–441 only]; [Two 'second editions', 1723, one by J. Roberts, the other by Thomas Osborn; 'third edition', London Printed, and Dublin Re-Printed, 1723]; *1740*, p. 67 [ll. 442–53 only].

Collected: *New Collection 1725*, p. 1 [ll. 1–441 only].

Text. *W* [D & P], for ll. 1–441; *L 29* for ll. 442–53. Collated: *L 27, 1723*, for ll. 1–441; *W* (P) for ll. 232–9; *L 27, L 28, Lpo 18, 1740* for ll. 442–53.

On Harley's orders, Drift inserted advertisements in the newspapers protesting against the unauthorized publication of this poem and *Down-Hall* by Roberts in 1723 (see commentary on *Down-Hall*, 1721). We therefore take *W* (which was revised by Prior and is partly in his hand) rather than *1723* as our text for ll. 1–441; for ll. 442–53 we take *L 29*, which seems to be Drift's transcript from P's original: it contains a note from Drift to Harley, 'Your Lordship has the Original in Mr Priors own hand'.

In *L 27*, the poem is dated 'MDCCXX', and other evidence confirms this date. P's *The Dove* (1717) is mentioned at l. 143, and Southerne's *Spartan Dame* (1719) at ll. 221–3. On 22 June 1720, P wrote to the Duke of Buckingham, 'Upon Your Graces Opinion I shal know if I ought to Correct or to burn this enclosed Dialogue . . .' (*L 14*, 288); on 14 Jan. 1721 he wrote to the Earl of Chesterfield, 'I presume to send You a little Fable, to which in truth, you are justly entituled; For I own, I took the hint from those uncommon and Fine thoughts relating to the happy State of Matrimony which you were so good as to communicate to me . . .' (*L 14*, 299). Both these letters appear to refer to *The Turtle and the Sparrow*.

The Index to *1727* describes the poem as 'Wrote in Compliment to Queen Anne, on the Death of Prince George' (i.e. 1708), and this description is repeated in many later editions. It is not only erroneous, but absurd. The note added to the conclusion (ll. 442–53) in many of these editions, 'Written long after the tale', has no basis except the editor's inference that, if the tale was written in 1708, the conclusion, addressed to Lady Margaret Harley, who was born in 1715, must have been written 'long after'.

Two short poems in *Recueil de Pieces Galantes en prose et en vers, de Madame La Comtesse De La Suze, et de Monsieur Pelisson, Augmenté de plusieurs Pieces nouvelles de divers Autheurs* (Lyon, 1695), iii. 12–13 (*Avanture d'un Moineau & d'une Tourterelle* and *Avis à la Tourterelle*) may possibly have suggested the theme and situation to P.

13–70. As the Sparrow suggests in l. 182, the Turtle's lament is modelled on Bion's *Lament for Adonis*.

109. FATES lean Tipstaff. The figure suggests Holbein's Dance of Death (cf. *An Ode*, 1703, l. 22).

135. STRADA's Nightengale. Faminiano Strada (1572–1649), Jesuit historian and poet; he was 'the *Cleveland* of his Age, and had a Multitude of

Admirers' (*Spectator*, No. 617). Several translations of his *Nightingale* were
published in the miscellanies, e.g. *New Collection 1725*, p. 109.

221. TOM SOUTHERN. Probably referring to the following passage in
The Spartan Dame (1719), I. i:

> Tender, and Chaste, and Fair! nay, she was once
> The boasted Pride, and Judgment of my Choice:
> So she was thought, and so I valu'd her:
> But she's my Wife—and nothing but a Wife,
> With all her Charms, cou'd have been stale so soon.
> O Curse of Marriage! . . .

The Spartan Dame, though written much earlier, was first acted in Dec. 1719,
and published the same year. P helped Southerne (whom he called 'my old
acquaintance') sell tickets for the play, and wrote to Harley on 2 Jan. 1720:
'The *Spartan*, or, as they call it here, the *Smarting*, *Dame* has just done Tom
S[outherne']s business, and both he and the town are satisfied it has been
acted, and are not troubled that it is laid aside' (*H.M.C. Bath*, iii. 477).

231. DUNMOW Bacon. At Dunmow, in Essex, a flitch of bacon was given
to any couple who would swear at the end of the first year of marriage that
they had never quarrelled and had never wished to untie the knot. The
award is still made.

309–14. Cf. La Fontaine, *La Coupe Enchantée* (*Contes*, III. iv), ll. 34–35.

327–30. *Joconde* (*Contes*, I. i), ll. 99–103. Cf. also *La Coupe Enchantée*,
ll. 163–4.

399. bandore. A widow's head-dress.

442–53. In *L 27*, 61, these lines are preceded by a headnote: 'The follow
ing Verses to Mrs: Margaret Harley were intended for the Conclusion of the
foregoing Poem, but left unfinished.' *L 28*, 160, has the note, 'Intended to be
added at the End of the Dove and Sparrow', and the Index calls the verses,
'Inscription of the Turtle and the Sparrow to Lady Margaret Harley'. *1740*
gives them a separate title, 'Application of the Turtle and Sparrow'. For Lady
Margaret Harley, see commentary to *A Letter*, 1720 above; the lines were
apparently written for her birthday in 1721. Drift's reason for describing
them as unfinished is not apparent from the verses themselves.

(542)   *Epigram*

MSS. *W*, 163ᵛ (P); *L 27*, 76 (D); *L 28*, 164 (D).
Pub. *1740*, p. 65.
Text. *W*. Collated: *L 27*, *L 28*, *1740*.

In *W*, this epigram occurs on the same sheet with Prior's working drafts of ll. 232–9 of *The Turtle and the Sparrow*. Presumably it was composed at about the same time as that poem.

(543)   *The Lame and the Blind*

MSS. *L 28*, 153ᵛ (D); *M*, 116 (D).
Pub.   Broadside engraving, N.D.
          Collected: *1740*, p. 124.
Text. *L 28*. Collated: *M*, *N.D.*, *1740*.

   The broadside engraving shows the lawyer eating the oyster and giving the shells to the lame defendant and blind plaintiff; on the B.M. copy, 'M.P.' is written in ink after the verses, showing that someone recognized their authorship. According to the signatures, the print was engraved from a painting by William Dobson (1610–46) by John Simon (1675?–1751), a Huguenot engraver who came to England early in the reign of Anne; it was published by E. Cooper. The print is not dated, but Mr. P. H. Hulton, Assistant Keeper of the Department of Prints and Drawings in the British Museum, kindly informs us that it is probably not earlier than 1714, before which Simon published his own plates, nor later than 1720, when he seems to have finished working for Cooper, the printseller. W. T. Morgan, in his *Bibliography of British History, 1700–1715* (Indiana University Studies, 1934–42), Sec. C, No. 253, describes a similar engraving containing these verses, signed 'Sutton Nichols, Exc., Aldergate Street', and dates it conjecturally 1700. We have not, however, been able to locate a copy of the print he describes.

   In *L 28*, the verses are followed by the title, 'Written under a Picture Painted by Mr: Howard'. It is clear from the markings in the manuscript that Drift meant the title to apply to these verses, though he names the wrong painter. Waller, in *1907*, p. 330, erroneously applied the title to the next verses on the page, *Invocation to Fortune* (unknown date).

   Prior found the story in La Fontaine, *L'Huître et les Plaideurs* (*Fables*, IX. ix) or Boileau (conclusion of *Épître II*), though his verses are rather an epigram or emblem than a re-telling of the story.

   In *1740*, another couplet is printed as a conclusion to this poem. The evidence of the manuscripts, however, makes it very doubtful that it was so intended: in both *L 28*, 154, and *M*, 116, it is set off by a separate title, 'Law', and the page in *L 28* on which it occurs is one containing numerous fragments. We give the text from *L 28* (in *1740* the tense is changed to the present):

Law

So Judges word decreed the Peoples right
And Magna Charta was a Paper Kite.

(543)   *Truth and Falshood*

MSS.   None.
Pub.   *The Country Journal: Or, The Craftsman.* No. 133, 18 Jan. 1729.
       Collected: *1740*, p. 139.
Text.   *1740.* Collated: *1729.*

    The reference to 'rising-stock' in l. 38, which *1740* annotates, 'South-Sea',
fixes the date. South Sea stock, tremendously inflated in the summer of 1720,
began to fall in August; the bubble burst in September, and the parliamentary investigation began in December (see Prior's letters in *H.M.C. Bath*,
iii. 488–9, 493).

    The version printed in *The Craftsman*, 1729, agrees with *1740* through l. 34.
From this point on it is altered extensively:

> At *Court*, appears extreamly wise,   35
> And rolls, at *Church*, her Saint-like Eyes.
> Talks, in the *City*, much of *Trade*,
> And Seizures on the *Spaniards* made;
> Sometimes in pompous, fustian Rhimes,
> Extolls our blest Saturnian Times,   40
> Our *Wealth* and *Power* o'er *Europe*'s Fate,
> And *Wisdom* in Affairs of State;
> Or when the Nation quite on Fire is,
> Writes *London Journals* and *Enquiries:*
> But most affects, in ———   45
> To State *Accounts* and *Represent*,
> To prove that *Two and Two make Seven*,
> That *White is Black*, and *Odds are Even;*
> Pleads, as Time serves, for *Peace* or *War*,
> And makes a Jest of *Gibraltar*,   50
> Speaks *pro* and *con*, like honest *Y*———
> And always sticks to what is wrong.
>   Mean while poor *Truth*, in this Distress,
> Robb'd of her old, engaging Dress,
> Became, unhappy Maid! the Sport   55
> Of Country, City, Camp and Court,
> And, scorning from her Cause to wince,
> Hath gone *stark naked* ever since.

This version cannot have been written before about 1728; it follows the line
of the *Craftsman* in attacking the Whig Sir William Yonge (l. 51) and the
pro-Walpole *London Journal* (l. 44) and in protesting that the question of
Gibraltar had not been settled by the Treaty of Seville, 1728 (l. 50). It was
reprinted in *A Collection of Poems on Several Occasions; Publish'd in the Craftsman.
By Caleb D'Anvers* . . . London: Printed for R. Francklin . . . 1731, pp. 60–
63, and *The Dublin Magazine*, 1733 (Case 382), pp. 44–46. There is a transcript in *B.M. Add. 28253*, 16, dated 1729. None of these texts is signed, and
the poem is nowhere attributed to any one of the three authors of the

Craftsman: Bolingbroke, William Pulteney, and Nicholas Amhurst. (W. Sichel, *Bolingbroke and his Times*, 1902, ii. 250, states that Bolingbroke wrote *Craftsman*, No. 133, but does not mention the verse specifically.)

It appears that one of these men (perhaps Bolingbroke) took P's poem, revised the ending to include topical attacks on the Walpole ministry, and thus converted it into a political satire. P may have given Bolingbroke a copy of the original poem, or Pope may have made a copy when he read P's manuscripts in 1723 and passed it on to Bolingbroke or Pulteney. The alternative conjecture is that the version published in *1740* is not by P; but we can discover nothing to support this conjecture. The situation is like that in *A Prologue* (1719), where someone else appears to have revised P's manuscript. In this case, however, we can at least be sure that P had nothing to do with the revision.

1721

(545)   *Colin's Mistakes*

MSS. L 29, 38 (D); L 27, 11 (D). (The printed sheets from *1721* are included in L 28, 192.) (Index to *M*.)
Pub. [Title as in text.] London: Printed for Jacob Tonson, at Shakespear's-Head over-against Katharine-Street in the Strand. MDCCXXI. Collected: *New Collection 1725*, p. 72.
Text. *1721*. Collated: L 29, L 27.

On 14 Feb. 1721, Prior sent this to Chesterfield, describing it as 'a thing of another kind than the last [presumably *The Turtle and the Sparrow*], the produce of reading Spenser last Season at Wimpole, and a mark of my respect to the Lady of that place. I gave it to her on her Birth-day Saturday last' (L 14, 300). On the same day he sent a copy to Lady Morpeth, a friend of Lady Henrietta Harley's, with a similar description (L 14, 303). Probably these were printed copies; Tonson advertised the poem in the *Daily Courant* on 15 Feb. Lady Henrietta's birthday was the same as her daughter's, 11 Feb.

The poem is written in the modified Spenserian stanza of P's *An Ode, Humbly Inscrib'd* (1706). There is a blank verse fragment in *W*, 62—perhaps written when P was working on *Frederic* (1714)—that is of interest as showing P's attitude toward Spenser:

> Bid me Climb the highest Hill and fetch the Eagles Nest.
> Bid me Dive into the Sea and bring the Coral.
> The Mountain shou'd not seem high nor the Sea deep . . .
> But when Thou bidest me Imitate Spencer I drop my Pen.
> As well I might go out with Arthurs Sheild or Edwards Sword.

[Motto.] Horace, *Odes*, III. iv. 5–6.

(549)   *Epitaph* ('Meek Franco')

MSS. *L* 29, 36 (D); *B.M. Add. 31152*, 34 (X).
Pub. *The Works of Alexander Pope*, ed. W. Warburton, 1751, viii. 103 n.
   Collected: *Evans 1779*, ii. 213.
Text. *L* 29. Collated: *1751, B.M.*

 As late as Aug. 1718, Prior was on excellent terms with Francis Atterbury, Bishop of Rochester and Dean of Westminster (see *H.M.C. Bath*, iii. 456–7). By the end of the following year, however, Atterbury had taken up a position which was to alienate him from P, Lord Harley, and other friends. Atterbury insisted that the new dormitory at Westminster School be placed in the college garden, in spite of the strong opposition of the headmaster, Dr. Robert Freind. Starting as a dispute within the chapter, the quarrel was taken to Chancery, which referred it to the King's Bench in June 1720. Early in the next year Atterbury appealed to the House of Lords, which finally (May 1721) decided in Atterbury's favour. (See F. Williams, *Memoirs and Correspondence of Francis Atterbury*, 1869, i. 272–5; H. C. Beeching, *Francis Atterbury*, 1909, pp. 207–11.) The Harley group, supporting Dr. Freind, were shocked by the tactics of the bishop, and when he began to solicit Whig support in the House of Lords they denounced him as a traitor to his party (see *H.M.C. Portland*, v. 618–19; vii. 259, 277, 287–98). P wrote to Swift on 25 April 1721: 'Roffen. is more than suspected to have given up his party as Sancho did his subjects for so much a head. . . . His Cause therefore which is something originally like that of the Lutrin is opposed or neglected by his ancient friends, and openly sustained by the Ministry. He cannot be lower in the opinion of most men than he is . . .' (Wickham Legg, pp. 271–2). P's 'share in the public service of humbling Ruffe' (Stratford to Harley, 5 April 1721, *H.M.C. Portland*, vii. 294) consisted of the present poem and the three that follow it. Although their authorship was supposed to be kept a secret, Atterbury knew that P had written verses against him (see Atterbury's letter to Pope, quoted in commentary on *For my own Tomb-stone*, 1718).

 Epitaph was written after June 1720, when the Lord Chancellor referred the case to the King's Bench (see l. 5), and before 3 Jan. 1721, when P wrote to Harley, 'Francis [Bishop] of Chester is well, and likes the epitaph of *his grave was his ground*' (*H.M.C. Bath*, iii. 493). P's other verses against Atterbury were written soon thereafter; on 2 March Stratford wrote to Harley that an epitaph and an epigram suspected to be by P had just reached Oxford (*H.M.C. Portland*, vii. 292).

(549)   *The Epitaph upon Gilbert Glanvill*

MSS.   *W*, 81ᵛ (P & D); *L 29*, 41 (D).
Pub.   *1907*, p. 356.
Text.   *W*. Collated: *L 29*.

In both manuscripts the translation is accompanied by this text of the original 'epitaph':

> Glanville Gilbertus nullâ bonitate refertus
> Hic jacet Immitis, & Amator Maximè Litis;
> Et quia dum vixit sic Lites solet amare,
> Nunc ubi pax nulla est, est aptior Inhabitare.

The Latin version, at least, was being circulated in Jan. 1721 by Robert Freind's supporters, who delighted in citing the parallel between the character of the earlier Bishop of Rochester and that of Bishop Atterbury (William Stratford to Lord Harley, 17 Jan. 1721, *H.M.C. Portland*, vii. 287).

In spite of the title, the Latin verses were not in Rochester Cathedral, which, in fact, contains no monument for Gilbert de Glanville, the bishop who died in 1214. They are to be found, however, in John Weever's *Ancient Funerall Monuments*, 1631, p. 313, where they are introduced by this explanation: 'Betweene this man and his Monkes of Rochester was long and continuall debate. . . .' The monks so hated him that 'they would afford him no manner of Obsequies, but buried him most obscurely, or rather basely, without either ringing, singing, or any other solemnities; and furthermore abused him with such like rime-doggerell'.

(550)   *Epigram* ('My Lord there's a Christ'ning')

MSS.   *L 29*, 36 (D); *L 29*, 40 (D); *L 29*, 42 (D); *B.M. Add. 31152*, 34 (X); *Ketton MS.* (X).
Pub.   *H.M.C. 12th Rep.*, App. IX, 1891, p. 189 (from MSS. of R. W. Ketton). Collected: *1907*, p. 355.
Text.   *L 29* (36). Collated: *L 29* (40); *L 29* (42); *B.M.*

In *B.M.*, the title is, 'Liberty to D: F: to christian his children in the abbye'. If, as seems likely, 'D: F:' is Dr. Freind, the epigram is related directly to the Freind–Atterbury dispute, and may possibly reflect a real incident. In any case, its position in *L 29* indicates that it was a part of the campaign against Atterbury early in 1721: one copy is on the same page as *Epitaph*, one on the page preceding *The Epitaph upon Gilbert Glanvill*, and one on the page following it.

Bishop Atterbury had in 1719 started a serious effort to discourage private baptism in his diocese and had begun to insert in every minister's licence a clause prohibiting it (F. Williams, *Memoirs and Correspondence of Francis Atterbury*, 1869, i. 265–7).

550)   *On Bishop Atterbury's Burying the Duke of Buckingham*

MSS. None.
Pub. *1727*, p. 46.
Text. *1727*.

The death of John Sheffield, Duke of Buckingham, on 24 Feb. 1721, offered Prior another opportunity for continuing the attack on Atterbury, of which the three preceding poems are a part. As Dean of Westminster as well as Bishop of Rochester, Atterbury read the funeral service in the abbey, although the duke had, in his will, prescribed for his tomb an epitaph that was considered agnostic:

> Dubius, sed non improbus vixi,
> Incertus morior, sed inturbatus;
> Humanum est nescire & errare:
> Christum adveneror, Deo confido
> Omnipotenti, benevolentissimo:
> Ens entium, miserere mei.
>   (*Character of John Sheffield*, 1729, p. 44)

On the day of the funeral, the newspapers printed an incorrect text of the epitaph, which was even more offensive because it gave the last clause of the fourth line as 'Deo *soli* confido'. A 'correct' copy which P received from Pope, he sent to Lord Harley on 16 March adding that 'various copies run about, and everybody comments on it *pro libitu*; Franco objects against its being put up' (*H.M.C. Bath*, iii. 498). On 19 March Edward Harley, junior, sent his aunt a satirical 'translation' of the epitaph 'by an unknown hand' (*H.M.C. Portland*, v. 619), perhaps the same as that now in Harvard MS. *Eng. 629F*, f. 47. Atterbury was undoubtedly embarrassed, and it is said to have been at his insistence that in the text of the inscription actually placed on the duke's monument the words *Christum adveneror* were omitted and the last phrase of the second line was altered to *non perturbatus* (F. Williams, *Memoirs and Correspondence of Francis Atterbury*, 1869, i. 289–90).

(550)   *Down-Hall*

MSS. L 27, 24 (D). (The printed sheets from *1723* are included in L 28, 200.) (Index to *M*.)
Pub.   *Down-Hall: A Poem*. By the Late Mr. Prior . . . London, Printed for J. Roberts, in Warwick-Lane, MDCCXXIII.
      Collected: *New Collection 1725*, p. 27.
Text. L 27. Collated: *1723*.

On Lord Harley's orders, Drift inserted five advertisements in the news-papers in July 1723, protesting against the 'unwarrantable Publication of the Poems'—i.e. the publication by Roberts of *Down-Hall* and *The Turtle and the Sparrow* (Welbeck MSS., *Executors' Reports*, ii. 10ᵛ). Since 1723 was thus un-authorized, we take *L* 27 as our text. Roberts's Preface to 1723 is of interest, however, as an indication of Prior's contemporary reputation:

> *The uncommon Success that always attended the Works of Mr. PRIOR, is sufficient Encouragement to any one, to publish any Performance of that Gentleman's. But stronger were the Motives that induced me to it; I thought it an Injury done to the Memory of the Dead, and a Wrong to the World, to screen from Light any Thing of that immortal Man's; especially when it was in my Power to oblige the World there-with.*
>
> *I thought it proper, on this Occasion, to inform the Reader, that the posthumous Works of Mr. PRIOR, publish'd some Time ago by Mr. C——l, are thought to be spurious. That this is genuine, will surely be doubted by none, unless of a very depraved Taste. Look on the* Thief *and* Cordelier, *and* Down-Hall, *then think if they could be wrote by separate Hands. See the Easiness of Thought, and Nature so artificially drawn, and judge if they can be any one's but a* PRIOR's.
>
> *Such are the Sentiments of some judicious Correspondence; by whose Advice I no longer conceal'd the following Poem, (the Copy of which has been above a Year in my Hands) but took this Opportunity to favour the Ingenious with it.*

John Morley's letter (1740, p. lxxxviii; original in *L* 7, 84) discussing the early negotiations for the purchase of Down-Hall is dated 'New-Year's-Day, 1719' (meaning, as the rest of the correspondence shows, 1 Jan. 1720), and it appears that P had not then seen the property. His journey there with Morley must have occurred after this time and before 2 July 1720, when he wrote to Harley: 'I have been at Down, surveyed the estate, and done everything—as to taking a rent-roll, discoursing my tenant, &c.—that Morley calls wisdom. It is impossible to tell you how beautiful a situation Down is, and how fine the wood may be made; but for the house, as all the cross unmathematical devils upon earth first put it together, all the thought and contrivance of man cannot make a window to be looked out of, or a door to be shut' (*H.M.C. Bath*, iii. 483). Probably the ballad was written in the summer or autumn of 1720; we can say with certainty only that it was written some time before P's reference to it in a letter to Harley on 14 June 1721 (see note to l. 176).

Down-Hall is in Essex, 3½ miles from Harlow and 3 miles south-west of the church of Hatfield Broad Oak. When P bought it, Lord Harley paid half the purchase price; at P's death, the estate reverted to Harley, who lived there occasionally. From the summer of 1720 until his death, P spent a great deal of time making and projecting improvements at Down. The architect James Gibbs designed a new house, and P consulted other 'virtuosi' about landscaping, gardening, and the like (*H.M.C. Bath*, iii. 488–90).

The tune to which the ballad is written is the same as that for *The Thief and the Cordelier* (1718). In *New Collection 1725* there is an engraving by

G. van der Gucht to illustrate the ballad; it was included in many of the earlier editions.

15. JOHN. John Morley of Halstead, the greatest land-jobber in England, Lord Harley's agent, and P's friend since 1717 (see commentary on *Engraven on a Column*, 1717).

23. P left England on his first diplomatic assignment in Nov. 1690.

35. OLIVER MARTIN. Oliver Martin, of the Middle Temple, Lord Harley's lawyer; see *1740*, p. lxxxix.

41. SOUTH-SEA. See commentary on *Truth and Falshood* (1720).

45. For Coningsby, see commentary on *The Viceroy* (1715).

57. RALPHO. P's horse, named after Hudibras's squire.

NEWMAN. The 'John Oeman or Newman' named as a servant in P's will. He was at Down Hall with P when Lord Harley visited there in June 1721 (*L 1*, 103; this letter is misdated in *H.M.C. Bath*, iii. 482).

59. HODSDON. 'Hoddesdon, on the River Lea, is a hamlet in Hertfordshire, which straggles along the highway between Broxbourne and Ware. Sir Marmaduke Rawdon, who had a house there, having supplied it with water from a spring about half a mile off, proceeded to erect in the middle of the town . . . an aqueduct or conduit for the benefit of the inhabitants, which aqueduct or conduit he further embellished by "the effigies of the Samaritan woman" ' (*1889*, p. 232).

106. Secret Committee. The committee which had examined P and the Tory leaders in 1715.

158. JEMMY GIBBS. James Gibbs (1682–1754), architect of the Radcliffe Camera at Oxford, King's College Library at Cambridge, and numerous churches and mansions. The plans he made for P's house at Down-Hall may be found in his *Book of Architecture*, 1728, Mr. F. R. D. Needham kindly informs us that there is at Welbeck Abbey a detailed set of plans, dated 1720, probably the original ones. Gibbs is mentioned frequently in P's letters of 1720–1, and he designed P's monument in Westminster Abbey.

162. JOHN BALLOTT. Former owner of Down-Hall (*1889*, p. 231).

173. touch Thumbs. Alluding to 'the licking and joining of thumbs by the parties concerned in token of the completion of a bargain' (*O.E.D.*).

176. First Part. P may have intended to write a second part, as this line suggests. At any rate, he was urged to do so by Morley; P wrote to Harley on 14 June 1721: 'Morley himself was never so unreasonable as to ask for another Volumn of Solomon, however He may expect the Second part of the Ballad of Down' (*L 1*, 107–107ᵛ; printed, inaccurately, in *H.M.C. Bath*, iii. 505). John Bancks, in editing *1740*, wrote to Morley's son to ask if he knew of the existence of a second part; the son's negative reply is printed in *1740*, p. xci. There is nothing in the manuscripts or elsewhere to suggest that P ever wrote a second part.

(558)   *Translated from the Original French*

MSS. *L 29*, 102ᵛ (D & P); *L 29*, 43 (D); *L 28*, 144 (D).
Pub. *1907*, p. 322.
Text. *L 29* (D & P). Collated: *L 29* (D); *L 28*.

In *L 29*, 102ᵛ, the translation is thus introduced:

Theobald the IVth: Comte of Champaign, called le faiseur de Chansons made
these Verses to Blanche the Wife of Louis the 8th: King of France in 1200, by which
we may see what the French Language was 500 Years ago, comparing it with the
Traduction. Vide the Chansons du Roy de Navarre.

The original and a modern French version are then given, with a reference
to the *Journal des Sçavans*, 26 May 1721, xx. 308–9. The passage translated
is the fourth stanza of a poem beginning, 'Je n'os chanter trop tart ne trop
souvent'; see *Les Chansons de Thibaut de Champagne, roi de Navarre*, ed. A.
Wallensköld (Société des Anciens Textes Français), Paris, 1925, pp. 229–32.
We give the French texts from the *Journal des Sçavans*:

> *Moult me sçeut bien esprendre & allumer,*
> *En biau parler, & accointement rire.*
> *Nus ne l'orroit si doucement parler,*
> *Qui ne cuidast de s'amour être Sire.*
> *Par Dieu amour ce vous ose bien dire,*
> *On vous doit bien servir & honorer,*
> *Mais on s'y peut bien d'ung pou trop fier.*

> Traduction.

> Elle sçut bien m'embraser & me prendre
> Par ses discours, ses ris pleins de douceur,
> Et l'on croiroit seulement à l'entendre,
> Etre déja le Maître de son cœur.
> O Dieu d'Amour, on vous dit d'un air tendre
> Qu'on vous doit bien servir & reverer,
> Mais on pourroit un peu trop s'y fier.

(558)   *The Old Gentry*

MSS. *W*, 23, 25 (P); *L 28*, 162 (D; emend. by Pope). (Index to *M*.)
Pub. *1740*, p. 102.
Text. *W*. Collated: *L 28*, *1740*.

These verses are an expansion of a shorter poem written by either Prior
or Pope and published in 1717 (see commentary on *The Old Gentry* in Works
of Doubtful Authenticity, 1717). In *L 28*, 162, Pope has inserted the title and
first stanza of the earlier poem, and the text published in *1740* incorporates
these additions. Although we reject the other changes introduced by Pope
and Drift, we print the title and first stanza as supplied by Pope because

they are necessary to an understanding of the poem; otherwise, we follow P's text in *W*. Since this text shows the poem in process of composition (see F. R. D. Needham's transcript in *M.P.*, xxxv, 1937, 185–6), there can be no doubt of its authenticity. The second stanza is indebted to the 1717 version; the other stanzas are related to it only in theme. As our text makes clear, P did not complete the poem; it may be that he intended to make it independent of the earlier version.

References in the poem fix the time of composition as 1719–21, and memoranda on the versos of the sheets in *W* fit this date.

9. Kenoul. George Hay, whose wife was Abigail, daughter of Robert Harley, Earl of Oxford, became seventh Earl of Kinnoull in 1719. P wrote *Prologue to The Orphan* for their son (Thomas Hay, Lord Dupplin) to speak in 1720, and from 1718 on was on intimate terms with the family—he sometimes calls the parents 'Dup and Duplinia' (*H.M.C. Bath*, iii. 453–5, 457, 459, 477). The Hays traced their lineage back to William de Haya, King's Butler to William the Lion (1143–1214), King of Scotland.

12. P's family were originally farm labourers in Godmanstone, Dorset, and some of them remained there (Wickham Legg, pp. 3–4 and Appendix A).

20. Anstis. John Anstis (1669–1744), Garter King-of-Arms. He obtained the reversion of this office in 1714, but did not actually fill it until 1718.

(559)   *Epigram* ('Stil craving yet')

MSS. *L 28*, 147 (D).
Pub. *1907*, p. 325.
Text. *L 28*.

According to Drift's notation in *L 28*, this is a fragment 'Written at Down-Hall'. The date of composition would therefore be between July 1720, when Prior first stayed at Down, and 10 Aug. 1721, when he left it for the last time.

(559)   *Predestination*

MSS. *L 28*, 279 (D; emend. by Pope). (Index to *M*.)
Pub. *1907*, p. 345.
Text. *L 28* [D].

Drift's title-page in *L 28*, 279, reads: 'Brouillon of a Poem Begun at Wimpole in August 1721. Transcribed From the Authors Papers since his Death.' *Predestination* was thus, almost certainly, Prior's last work: he arrived at Wimpole for his last visit on 10 Aug., and was stricken by his fatal illness on 11 Sept. Drift's transcript consists of ten separate 'brouillons' in varying stages of completion, from prose notes and jottings to finished verse. They are carefully lettered and numbered from 'A. No: 1.' through 'A. No: 10.'; but, since No. 10 contains what is obviously the final version of the first part of the poem, it is evident that the numbers do not represent any attempt on Drift's part to arrange the fragments in order. As we have seen in considering works for which both P's original drafts and Drift's transcripts are preserved, Drift, though a meticulous copyist, was not a particularly intelligent one: he sometimes misread P's hand and often misinterpreted his directions as to the order of lines and the superseding of one version by another. We have not hesitated, therefore, to change the order of these brouillons or to substitute one passage for another when such changes seem clearly to be required. We print first the beginning of the poem (ll. 1–161) from Brouillon 10, and then Brouillons 6–9, with some deletions and substitutions (indicated in the notes). Brouillons 1–5 consist mostly of rough fragments and preliminary versions; we have placed two finished passages from them in the text (ll. 192–9, 264–76), but the rest of this material we have either relegated to the notes or omitted. Most of the punctuation in the manuscript seems to have been inserted later, presumably by Pope; since it is impossible to distinguish with certainty between the original and later punctuation, we have retained it all. For comment on the theology of the poem, see M. K. Spears, 'Matthew Prior's Religion', *Philological Quarterly*, xxvii (1948), 159–80.

1–161. From Brouillon 10 (*L 28*, 292–6). Brouillon 1 (*L 28*, 280) is clearly P's outline for this part of the poem:

I was made by God, and am preserved by him, else I shal be annihilated. [Cf. ll. 1–28.]
  Whence ill? [Cf. ll. 29–52.]
  Calvin says we were all Predestinated. [Cf. ll. 53–80.]
  The consequences are that we are Machines, that our good Endeavors signify nothing. [Cf. ll. 81–88.]
  Yet the Apostle says we are Clay in the hands of the Potter. [Cf. ll. 89–92.]
  That Argument Answered, Man and Inanimate being compared. [Cf. ll. 93–119.]
  The Solution of this Doubt that God foresaw and permitted, which is just the same as if he Predestinated. [Cf. ll. 120–61.]

23. A preliminary version of this imperfect line is cancelled in Brouillon 5 (*L 28*, 282): 'Where did this Guide my wandring steps forsake.'
  25–34. A preliminary version, cancelled in Brouillon 5, is of interest:

> Yet conscious to my self I sadly find
> A thousand Errors vex my wav'ring Mind
> The Crooked Biass of my violent will
> I find averse to God and prone to ill.
> Whence rises this depravity of Thought
> Is it for mine or my forefathers fault?

> Shal I allow and say that Death and Sin
> Did from our Parents pristin fault begin
> Or placing their Original too high
> Give good and Evil coeternity?

89. Apostle. Rom. ix. 21.

162–91. From Brouillon 6 (*L 28*, 284–5). After l. 165, we omit four lines that seem not to belong here:

> If God does Universal Vows reject
> Or only justifys his own Elect
> Or those in Climes remote who never heard
> His Word reveal'd are from his Anger Spar'd.

A prose fragment in Brouillon 5 (*L 28*, 282) outlines the same problem, which P apparently decided not to consider in the poem: 'Could the Heathen by the dictates of Nature obtain Salvation, where was the necessity of Christs coming, and if they could not, how happens it that they were not called to pertake the benefit of his passion.'

177. After this line, Brouillon 6 repeats ll. 162–5.

192–9. From Brouillon 2 (*L 28*, 280). We substitute this passage for the following lines in Brouillon 6, which develop the same theme but do not fit the context:

> As running Streams their parted Waters spread
> Adown the hill or thrô the flow'ry Mead
> Here rising bold and Turbulent in waves
> There sunk in Sand or sunk in Rocky Caves
> The human Eye may stil collect and bring
> To their first Murmer and Original Spring:
> So from the various action of our mind
> To pleasure better or to grief enclin'd
> Glitt'ring in Courts and shining bright in Arms
> Fond of Mans praises and of Womans charms
> Or flying Crowds desiring more to dwel
> In the thick Woods or Melancholy Cell.

199. The following passage from Brouillon 2 (*L 28*, 280) seems to belong to this part of the argument, though it does not fit into the text:

> Against Gods Spirit here we fight
> Had leave to chose but wou'd not use it right
> Our ill produc'd and we must suffer Woe
> But had we merit or Perfection, No.
> In vain You cite this Liberty of Will
> Free to do good, but more inclin'd to ill.

200–30. From Brouillon 7 (*L 28*, 287). We omit a couplet at the end of this passage that seems to be a preliminary version of ll. 196–7 above:

> Before we Grant or Answer let us bring
> Our pow'r of Thought to its primaeval Spring.

231–51. From Brouillon 8 (*L 28*, 289). The following passages from Brouillon 5 (*L 28*, 282–3) appear to be early drafts for ll. 247–51: 'Nor do I ask whence Sin came, but it was such that to Save the World from it the Son of God must Dye.'

> Whence else a Dying Saviors grief and Fame
> And dire Convulsion of this general frame
> That shook the Earth made frighted Nature groan
> And the great Fathers will that must be done?

252–63. From Brouillon 9 (*L 28*, 291).
264–76. From Brouillon 3 (*L 28*, 281).

(567) *Ladislaus*

MSS. *W*, 136 ('Argument' in D's hand, drafts for scenes in P's); *L 28*, 297 (D).
Pub. No publication known.
Text. *W*. Collated: *L 28*.

Our dating of both *Ladislaus* and *Britanicus* depends upon the fact that in *L 28* Drift placed his transcription of them at the end of the English works, after poems completed in 1721 and together with pieces that Prior was composing at the time of his death.

In addition to the 'Argument', the manuscripts of *Ladislaus* contain drafts for four disconnected scenes. The 'Argument' seems to be in a reasonably finished state. The dramatic scenes, on the other hand, are in a very rough condition, and are therefore printed here only in the notes. Since P's drafts of these scenes in *W* are unfinished and the sheets on which they were written have suffered some damage, we have, in a few matters, been obliged to follow the transcript in *L 28*; we accept Drift's reading of obliterated letters and words, give the names of speakers, and spell out all proper nouns.

P's argument is based on *Venceslas* (1647), the best-known play of Jean de Rotrou (1609–50), and follows the main lines of Rotrou's plot. It is clear, however, that P meant to do more than merely translate Rotrou. In the argument, he changes the name of Rotrou's 'Féderic, duc de Curlande' to Conon, Duke of Courland, because he uses the name Frederic (Earl of Coningsberg) for Cassandra's father, who is not named in Rotrou. He adds several spectacular stage effects, such as the ring given to Frederic and the scene in the chapel when Alexander's murder is discovered and his body brought in upon a bier. The first speech is almost a translation of Rotrou, I. ii: 'Vous, téméraire, | Vous la main sur l'épée, et contre votre frère!' Nothing else is so close, although the speech we print in the notes to ll. 111–14 is based on Rotrou, IV. iv. The longest and most finished of P's drafts (see note to ll. 116–19) has no prototype in Rotrou, and is not described in the 'Argument'.

20–29. P's rough draft for these scenes (*W*, 137ᵛ, 141ᵛ; *L 28*, 304–5):

The King chides Alexander: Insolent, your hand upon your Sword, against your brother, your elder brother whom the rights of Nature and Customs of Establisht Law have made your Master.

Alexander.   Soverein father hear Me. Thô I would not extenuate my Error, I will wait on him till he shall say he is satisfied.

Vinceslaus.   Ha young assassin too well I understand that feign'd Submission, You would privately See him and then provoke him to do something worse to thee, and have in Murder some small appearance of Glory. No, the Submission shall be Equal to the affront, not a Man that was at the Chase but shall see thee bend thy Knee to him.

Alexander.   It is a father's Command and shall be obey'd.

                                                          Exit.

Vinceslaus.   O cruell Nature whither wouldst thou drive Me
              Why do I love these two Young Men so well
              And why do they so little love Each other?
              Why do I chide him who had no fault
              And dare not chide him that was to blame?
              But Theodora my daughter has all goodness.

                    Enter Theodora.

The King desires her to prepare her brother Ladislaus.

                                                Exit Vinceslaus.

                 Enter Ladislaus to his Sister.

Theodora.   Brother when did You see the King?

Ladislaus.   Sister when did you See Cassandra. Kind Mediatress, good Sister, to thee I'l kneel that art the only good of our family. Exert thy good offices to Cassandra, and I'l be tame, I'l ask my brother's pardon.

Theodora.   Brother is the Course you take the means to make her love you? But See she Comes.

                    Enter Cassandra.

Cassandra the Musick will be in the grove at Eight, till then I leave you.

Cassandra.   I'l vow I'l go.

Ladislaus.   Stay Sister stay.

                 The Hectoring Scene ends.

Learn to please: call her back, no, I'l murther any body else that dare attempt her, I'l dye for love.

92–96. P's notes for dramatizing this section (*W*, 145; *L 28*, 306):

King.   In the appartement joyning to the Chappell be he confin'd.

The King promises Cassandra she shall have justice.

In my wars against thy father I slew two Sons, thou revengest their deaths.

                                                          Exeunt.

                 Manent Frederic and Theodora.
                        Love Scene

                        2 Act:

                    King and Frederic.

King resolves Ladislaus shall dye.

> Ah, Sir, thô all my arguments are vain
> Theodora's life
> I'l leave you.

111–14. A speech (by the King?) intended for this point (*W*, 146; *L 28*, 307):

Before the weeping People are assembled keep this a Secrett from all Men but from the Confessor, but ah take care that he may timely be advised,

> Stern Justice
> Demands no further then the Murtherers life
> Then blood for blood, She leaves to gentle Mercy
> The Man's immortal part, and while the Judge
> Forct by strict law transmitts the Malefactor
> An Exil from this world, and human race
> Whom he by Crimes has injured, Kind clergy
> With fervent tongues and hands lift up are suffered
> To send their wishes up that Heaven would pardon
> The dying Penitent, and guarding Angells
> Convey his parting Spirit to endless Joy.

116–19. The following scene (*W*, 151–2, 148; *L 28*, 308–9), though not described in the Argument, was probably written to fit in about here:

King.   Ha is the Infection then grown universal
        Have I for fifty row[ling] years beheld
        As many thousand Scimiter'd right hand[s]
        Prompt to distribute Deaths as I directed
        And is there not One Pole one Lithuanian
        That will do Justice to his Countryes Cause
        And execute a Trayter and a parricide
        Thô the law dictates and the King commands it?

Octavius. Not one, the City magistrates in vain
          Offer large farms and gold Immense to Men
          Steep't to lipps in poverty, and freedom
          To Captives mourning under pondrous Chains,
          Not one will strike the blow.

King.   Am I abandond then am I betray'd?
          Mark Me . . . ere to morrow dawns
          This young Usurper, more obey'd then I
          Will find a hand to execute his orders
          And sheath the dagger in his fathers heart.

Therefore Octavius on thy allegiance aid thy King distrest. Find me out sudden some Illustrious Wretch to strike his head off, or I at least will find one to strike off Thine.

Octavius. Sir that Grim Tartar whom last Night the Captain
          Seiz'd near the Arsinal, his horridness
          And gastly looks and estate bespeak him
          Fit for your Cruel purpose, the sad Custom
          Of his fierce Country. No regards
          Oblige, no kindness binds his savage heart
          To Ladislaus.

King.   O rightly hast thou judged,
        My Loyal Subject and my faithfull friend
        Immediate bring the Man.

                Soliloque.

           Enter Octavius with . . . .

King.   Speak'st thou the Polish language ?

Tartar.   Language I have little.

King.   I hope at least thou understandst Me while I tell thee that thou
must do a deed
        Which will oblige a King to thee for Ever.
        Give me thy hand in token of thy friendship
        Give me thy horrid hand which thus I honour,
        Receive this Scymeter, and with it freedom
        Wealth and Command all that a Soul like Thine
        Immers't in flesh can wish, and in return
        Bring Me that Head divided from its body
        Which while united I esteem'd the dearest.
        Octavius double the guards.

Octavius. The Rascians, Sir, as fiercest and armd with battle axes——

[King.]   That again was justly thought, lett them draw out around the Scaffold,
once more forestall the hour.
        Stay not till Noon, at ten be sure Octavius
        The blow be strook.

An additional passage (*W*, 150; *L 28*, 303), which was intended to be inserted in the Argument, may be related somehow to this scene:

Gustavus, comes from the Army which has beaten the Muscovite, brings Ernest with him whom the Prince when he commanded the Army had stroke and he therefore had gon over to the Muscovite Service, Gustavus had taken him his prisoner; and had brought him privately to Warsaw hoping to entreat his pardon, he tells Frederic so, the Duke Frederic tells him by no Means, that he cannot move the King in it, for fear of disobliging the Prince, assures him of his good offices.

(571)   *Britanicus*

MSS.   *W*, 153–62ᵛ, 165–9 (P); *L 28*, 311 (D).
Pub.   No publication known.
Text.   *W*. Collated: *L 28*.

As in the case of *Ladislaus*, we date this work on the basis of its position in *L 28*, and suppose that the composition of it was interrupted by Prior's death. The original drafts in *W* are in a very confused state. They consist of a mixture of rough notes, synopses, and dramatized scenes, written on sheets, half-sheets, and small scraps of paper that have been put together in accidental order. From these brouillons we have selected those passages of dialogue that are most finished, and have given them the arrangement that best accords with the clues in the manuscripts and with the chronology of the plot. We have numbered the scenes thus reconstructed, headed each with the names of the characters present, and spelled out all proper names.

As the notes below indicate, P based his play on Racine's *Britannicus*, from which the characters and plot are taken and a few passages freely translated. As in *Ladislaus*, however, he meant to do more than merely translate: he introduces one character, Pallas, who is mentioned but does not appear in Racine, and many of the speeches and outlines of the action have no counterpart in the French tragedy. He may have intended simply to adapt Racine to English taste, or he may have planned an independent play using the same material and adapting some of Racine's best scenes.

1–25. *W*, 159–60; *L 28*, 316–17. This scene was probably intended to come early in Act I. It has no counterpart in Racine, though it is somewhat like his first scene, in which Agrippine similarly unburdens herself to Albine. P seems to have intended to substitute Pallas for Albine, who, as the traditional *confidante* of the French stage, would be out of place on the English. He made two outlines for the first act; but, since they are very rough and entirely inconsistent, we do not print them. It is worth noting, though, that neither follows Racine.

26–41. *W*, 158; *L 28*, 318. Possibly suggested by Racine, II. i, though it does not correspond to this scene in detail.

42–86. *W*, 161–2ᵛ; *L 28*, 320–1. These scenes do not correspond to any in Racine. They show (especially l. 86) P's intention to enliven the French play by adding the pageantry and movement demanded by the English stage.

87–102. *W*, 155ᵛ; *L 28*, 321ᵛ. A free translation, much abbreviated, of Racine, I. iii–iv.

103–6. *W*, 168ᵛ; *L 28*, 323ᵛ. These lines are found as a separate fragment in *L 29*, 105, as well as with the other fragments from the play in *W* and *L 28*. Waller printed them in *1907*, p. 355, with the title, '[Fragment from *Britanicus*]'.

107–48. *W*, 156ᵛ, 165, 159ᵛ; *L 28*, 322ᵛ, 319, 316ᵛ. Based on Racine, II. ii. Ll. 120–36 are partly translated from Racine, but expanded and developed.

149–64. *W*, 156; *L 28*, 322. Has no counterpart in Racine.

165–220. *W*, 167ᵛ–8, 156ᵛ, 154, 157; *L 28*, 324, 322ᵛ, 312, 314. Based on Racine, IV. iv. P outlined the preceding scene (Racine, IV. iii) but did not write it. In this scene he takes from Racine only the situation and dramatic action, in which Narcissus brings Nero to his final decision to murder Britannicus; the sketch for one speech (ll. 188–91) is freely translated, but the rest does not correspond to the French.

193. Mustroms. The poison with which Agrippina murdered Claudius was said to have been sprinkled on a mushroom (Tacitus, *Annals*, xii. 67).

220. P wrote nothing for the fifth act except a brief plan corresponding to Racine's Act V.

(578)   *Learning*

MSS. *L 25*, 1 (A); *L 26*, 1 (D). (Index to *M*.)
Pub.   *1907*, p. 180. (Two passages—ll. 168–98, 208–16—were published by
        E. Malone in his edition of Dryden's *Prose Works*, 1800, i. 545–6; iii. 73.)
Text. *L 25*. Collated: *L 26*.

It appears that Prior intended to develop these loosely organized 'heads'
into a longer treatise, in the form of a letter (l. 14). There are among his
manuscripts—especially in the commonplace book for 1720–1 in *L 29*—many
unpublished prose fragments relating to this subject, and we have given in
the notes several of the more finished passages that P may have intended
to incorporate.

P evidently worked on this material over a considerable period. The
reference to 'the late Earl of Ranelagh' (l. 210) would be possible only after
1712, and Dr. Smalridge, mentioned as living (l. 135), died in 1719. It seems
likely that most of the essay was written toward the end of P's life, when he
was concerned with the other prose pieces.

The extant manuscripts are independent transcripts made after P's death
from a copy now lost. Since we know that the anonymous copyist elsewhere
reproduced the details of his copy-text more exactly than Drift did in tran-
scribing other works into *L 26*, we base our text upon *L 25*, but substitute
the reading of *L 26* when it corrects an error.

29–33. In his commonplace book for 1720–1 (*L 29*, 113), P expands this
point with more specific detail:

> A too intense application to any study to which a Man is born by his natural
> Genius becomes tyresome and ridiculous in Conversation, a Mathematician is
> dividing your Chamber into Cubes and Triangles, and a Naturalist stops at an odd
> blade of grass in your Garden, Catches a strange butterfly, and wonders at a black
> peble: but I have known Some poets worse Company than all these, they have often
> with great absence of Mind asked Me what News just after I had read aloud the
> Gazette or Dayly post and in melancholy Silence withdrawn their mind to the com-
> posing a Stanza or searching a Rhime while every man else has been communicating
> his thought to the Company, and the Subject of the conversation has been mirth
> and friendship.

69–70. William I, Prince of Orange (1533–84), wrote a famous 'Apology
or defence . . . against the proclamation . . . by the King of Spain . . . by
which he proscribeth the said Lorde prince', 1581.

81–84. The commonplace book for 1720–1 (*L 29*, 103ᵛ–105, 112ᵛ) shows
P working on a fuller discussion of the limitations of classical studies:

> I believe no Man now alive is so absolutely Master of the Greek or Latin tongue
> as to be able to read one Sentence without stopping a little to consider the Gram-
> matical construction of it: add to this that the Customs of these Nations, their
> Cloathing, their Utensils, their Houses, husbandry, Encampments, their laws, the

manner of their pleadings, and the placing their words, their proverbs in common discourse are so different from Ours, that whole Volumes of Critics & Commentators must not only be read but remembered before a Man is master of One oration of Demosthenes or Cicero of One Comedy of Aristophanes or a Satyr of Horace or Juvenal. . . . And as We generally read these books when we are Young So that in truth we know more of these matters when we come from the College then we do all our life time after and when we come into the world We are obliged to Study the laws of our own Country, to turn our thoughts to the transactions of our own times, to make our selves masters of the modern languages as they are usefull to us all in our travel abroad, and to many in their Several professions at home. Now the Ancient Authors and their readers for Several Generations took all this into their ordinary way of life, their Orations were carrying on their own or their Clients law suits while they speak in those terms that confound Us or writing to those Friends who at first view apprehended the force of words written in their own Native language, and the Circumstances upon which the Sence of their letter depended. The finest allusions of their Poets regarded times actions and persons then present or at least so near as to be generally known and easily understood so that a Modern of the greatest natural parts, most unwearied Industry and most happy Memory upon 40 years study could not, generally speaking, understand Greek or Latin so well as Cobler in the —— at Athens or a private Souldier in the Army of Augustus. Turn the tables and suppose a Greek or Roman boy bred up to their own language instructed in the civil and religious rights of their Country, and Learning Those of England only from some few British books and philosophers that happened to travel that way, in this case could this Man come to any competent degree of knowledge ? . . . I do not say this to discourage the Study of ancient learning but to mortify the pride of those that think there is no knowledge besides it, and neglect all the rest as if this were the Universal[?] necessarie. This considered I do not doubt but that prevention laid aside and unbiassed Judgment exercised, any English reader will find that King Charles the 1st writes better then Julius Caesar whom I just now named, and my Lord Strafford pleaded his own Cause better than Tully ever did those of his Clients.

90. Vol. xxii of the Prior Papers at Longleat consists of 'A Help to History or Annales, from anno 1459 to anno 1711 by Matthew Prior Esq.'

105. Ezéchiel Spanheim (1629–1710) came to London as the Prussian Ambassador in 1702. He was a member of the Royal Society and is buried in Westminster Abbey. He wrote *Dissertationes de praestantia et usu Numismatum antiquorum* (1664). P himself had a collection of coins and medals.

134. It is still not certain who wrote *The Whole Duty of Man* (1658) and the other works published as by the same author; the most frequent attribution is to Richard Allestree (1619–81). See *D.N.B.*, 'Pakington, Dorothy'.

135. Atterbury (see commentary on *Epitaph*, 1721), George Smalridge (1663–1719), Bishop of Bristol, and Francis Gastrell (1662–1725), Bishop of Chester, had all attended Westminster School.

140. In his 'Account of the Life and Writings of Mr Abraham Cowley', prefixed to the 1669 edition of Cowley's *Works* (sig. a2ʳ).

208. George Villiers, second Duke of Buckingham (1628–87).

209. Sir Fleetwood Shepherd. See P's two epistles to him (1689).

210. Richard Jones, first Earl of Ranelagh (1638?–1712).

214–16. Cf. *Dedication* (1708), ll. 38–41.

227. Bays. In *The Rehearsal*, IV. ii.

232. one Man. Cf. P's comment on the satirical writings of Dorset, in *Dedication* (1708), ll. 87–97.

252–3. Elsewhere, P recommends vocational training in these 'Arts of a Mechanical Consideration'. The passage quoted below is found in Drift's fair copy among P's notes on trade, finance, foreign policy, etc. (*L 23, 6*):

> Parents in [England] are mighty fond of Breeding their Children to be Schollars (as they call it) that is, indeed Divines, for not one in Ten that are bred at Our Universities apply themselves to any other Studdy than that of Theology. In order to this Our Youth is bred up in a Method of Studdy very bounded & narrow; Having first at Our Schooles only some Rudiments of Grammer and the knowledge of the Latin Tongue, with some Superficial Tincture of the Greek. From thence at Our Universities, their Studdying Logic Ethics & Metaphysics Enables 'em only to Dispute about Words, And leaves them generally Ignorant of Things.
>
> It would be more proffitable to the Nation that many of the Finer Genius's were turned to curious Arts & Manufactures, As working in Steel, Iron, Carving in Wood, Painting, Statuary, & those other arts by which Italy has gained so great Wealth & Reputation. Architecture should be likewise incouraged, which would produce more public Works as Churches, Town Halls, Bridges, Aqueducts, All which would be a greater incitement to Strangers to come & Visit Us.
>
> In Our public Schools Should be Taught to children (instead of troubling 'em with too much Grammer) the Principles of Arethmetic & Geometry, which indeed is properly the Grammer For the Children of a Trading Nation & which ought to produce Merchants & Seamen.

(586)   *Opinion*

MSS. *L 25*, 12 (D & P); *L 25*, 33 (D); *L 26*, 16 (D). (Index to *M*.)
Pub. *1907*, p. 190.
Text. *L 25* (D & P). Collated: *L 25* (D), *L 26*.

Opinion is so closely parallel in theme to *Alma* (1718) as to suggest that part of it, at least, may have been written at about the same time as the poem. There are two references to Louis XIV as dead, which show that the passages in which they occur were written after 1715 (ll. 142, 401), and another passage (l. 147) may be dated as after 3 April 1716. It is probable that Prior continued to work on the essay until his death, and never considered it finished. We include in the notes several prose fragments that are related to the essay and may have been written for it.

1. Cf. Pascal: 'L'imagination dispose de tout; elle fait la beauté, la justice, et le bonheur, qui est le tout du monde. Je voudrais de bon cœur voir le livre italien, dont je ne connais que le titre, qui vaut lui seul bien des livres: *Dell' opinione regina del mondo*. J'y souscris sans le connaître, sauf le mal, s'il y en a' (ii. 10; frag. 82).

26. *Divinæ particula auræ*. Horace, *Satires*, II. ii. 79.

29. *Nosce Te ipsum.* See note to *Lock and Montaigne* (1721, below), ll. 291–2.

39. Horace. *Ars Poetica*, ll. 161–78.

46. pritty Spanish Conceit. See note to *Alma*, i. 252–65. No Spanish source has been discovered. Since 'alma' is Spanish for *soul*, it is possible that P means this as a sly allusion to his own poem. He does refer (sometimes cryptically) to his poems in the prose dialogues, below.

59. Anger is a Short Frenzy. Cf. Horace, *Epistles*, I. ii. 62.

71. Predominant Passion. Cf. *Alma*, ii. 251–80. The concept is the same as Pope's 'ruling passion'; for the background, see Maynard Mack's Introduction to his edition of Pope's *Essay on Man*, 1950, p. xxxvi.

83–92. Cf. *Alma*, i. 487–504.

107–10. Corvino (not Cornaro) in Jonson's *Volpone*.

112. BAUDIUS's ANTHOLOGIA. The *Amores* published under the name of Dominicus Baudius in 1638 is an anthology of works dealing largely with the sordid amours of Baudius.

113. MORERI's Dictionary. P owned a copy of Louis Moréri's *Grand Dictionnaire Historique*, 6ᵉ éd., Utrecht, 1692.

117. Ovid, *Fasti*, vi. 5.

134. P may have in mind specifically the idealistic metaphysics of Bishop George Berkeley.

143–5. Charles Patin (1633–93), French physician and numismatist. During the three months' reign of the Emperor Otho (A.D. 69) no copper or brass coins were struck, but many forgeries are in circulation (J. G. Milne et al., *Coin Collecting*, 1950, p. 57).

147. See note to *Paulo Purganti* (1708), l. 114. Sloane was created baronet on 3 April 1716. His collections formed the nucleus of the British Museum.

149. FRAZER. Apparently James Fraser, who had been licenser of the press, 1688–92, and later had a 'noble library' at Chelsea College. He had a passion for rare books and frequented the sale of libraries (Macaulay, pp. 2299–2300; Edmund Bohun, *Diary and Autobiography*, 1853, pp. 83 n., 115).

157. Bartolommeo Bimbi (1648–1725), Florentine painter.

176. In Jonson's *Bartholomew Fair*.

177–88. P may have in mind the *Encomium Moriae* of Erasmus; cf. his imitation of a passage from it (1718). The commonplace book for 1720–1 contains a passage on the same theme (*L 29*, 113ᵛ–114):

Man is a Creature indued with reason. That reason is improved by Experience moved and Directed by Honor, it carries Him thrô the several Stations and Conditions of Life. Hence the Soldier is generous and Valiant the Lawyer Equitable and Merciful the Divine Abstemious in his Desires Laborious in the Exercise of his Duty and Exemplary in the Actions of his Life, the Subject is obedient to his Prince Honest to his Friend, and kind and humble to his Inferior. The Prince is true to his word, Just in the Execution of his Powers Protecting his People in Plenty, and persuading his Neighbors to Peace. He merits all the Titles the World gives him, It is by the Grace of God to the Nation that he rules, He is Father of His Country, and —— No such thing. Old Style all, and matters are quite Alter'd: This is Man as you see him printed in a Book. Contemplate Him and be acquainted with him in the World. He is an Amassed Complication of Passion and Error A customary Animal a Being that lives by Habitude or changes by Caprice, Puzzled at every thing, forseeing Nothing, Striving to extricate himself from the present Inconvenience—without reflecting what future pains it will cost him. Desiring to possess he knows not what and when he has it grows weary of it He knows not why. An idle thing in perpetual Motion, forgetting what he saw yesterday and Enquiring what he shal see to morrow. Not having strength of Mind enough to make his own Choice, but carryed away and determined by Plurality of Voices. Accomodating himself to all times, and finding Arguments to submit to any Reigning opinion. Happy if he can save appearances and live upon Expedients.

195. SOLOMON expresses it. Prov. xxix. 12.
208. QUARE. See note to *Alma*, iii. 265.
209. MATHAR. This is apparently the name which P now gives to the character he has been describing since l. 188. In *Wm* (133ᵛ–134ᵛ, 139, 145) there are rough drafts of three unpublished sketches that show P practising the composition of such 'characters' between 1690 and 1699:

[*A Coxcomb*]

Spends ten thousand pound in a garden and will not allow 50 pound a year to keep it in repair. He builds a palace but will not be at the charge of stopping a Window. He hires a house in the citty and furnishes it magnificently thô it be so scituated that the neighbours see him go to bed and rise, that they can almost read his letters as he writes them and see his Spadille when he plays at Ombre:
A Man may be a coxcomb and gett an estate without showing himself much to be one, he shelters himself under the formality of business and he conceals his Ignorance under the cover of a Cauteous prudence, every body consents in this that he is a laborious industrious thriving Man, which helps him to Something of a Character, but in Spending his Estate there appears the Man, his buildings are irregular and his pictures are signposts his liveries are rich & ill fancied his table is heap't up with a pyramide of Sweetmeats bought by the pound . . . and his wines are . . . a profusion of different flayvors in dirty glasses; the reason of this said a Woman of great quality and greater Sence is that he only spyes the Ignorance of others in the getting his Estate but in the spending he shows his Own to all the world else.

[*Shylon*]

Shylon is in raptures and weeps when you talk of the King, he is the first at the levy and stays the last at supper, on his Majesties birth day he invites half the town to a profuse feast, has his house illuminated and the greatest bonfire in the town before his door, he gives wine to the Mobb, and begins with a bumper out of the window vive le roy; but when any affair is debated in a house of commons where the giving his voice thô with all justice imaginable for his Masters interests may endanger his own Shylon is indisposed and absent, and if the King would borrow mony in the City upon any fund, and those that love his Majesty best hazard first, Shylon is his humble Subject and Servant, he has a house that must be finished, and children that must be bred, taxes are high and tenants dont pay.

[*Montus*]

Montus reads more then he reflects upon and reflects upon more then he makes use of: his knowledge is too rechearched and what would make him a president at

Gresham College sooner then a Minister of State, he knows the value of a Medal, the figure, the Exerge and the Æra, but is puzzled in the counting the change of a guiney and can not distinguish a brass half-crown: he describes a golden bridge that there is at Congo, but forgetts in his journey that their is a wooden one at Kingstowne, this Man has too much of other peoples knowledge and too little of his own.

226. John Keill (1671–1721), professor of astronomy and author of books on mathematics. P owned his Newtonian *Introductio ad Astronomiam* (1718).

257. EPICTETUS. *Encheiridion*, sec. 5.

278–82. Since *Alfrank* and *Pyso* seem to be names of fictitious characters, *the E: of G:* and *the D: of B:* are probably not intended to be identified as particular noblemen.

315–24. Cf. *Vicar of Bray and More* (1721, below). In his commonplace book for 1720–1, P applies this principle to the history of the Church (*L 29*, 105^v–106):

We use Arguments as they may best serve the present Occasion, and there are many Topics that may be thought right or wrong according to situation of the Disputant's mind and the Circumstances he is in, Authority as to religious Matters was thought so much the strongest by Tully that he confesses He had rather follow the opinion of the Preists and Augurs than of the Philosophers; and that He would always reverence those gods under whose protection the Roman Empire had flourished from the time that their Religion & republic were founded together; when the primitive Christians argued with the Gentiles they were to destroy these prejudices by producing reasonable Arguments to convince them of the Unity of the Godhead, and of the certainty of his perfections and Attributes: after a series of Ages Christianity or at least the greatest part of it is corrupted, We of the Reformation break from the Romish Communion and for so doing We urge those very Arguments taken from Reason & Philosophy which the Christians did against the Heathen, and vice versa the Church of Rome has recourse to Authority and Tradition which they strove Seventeen Hundred years since to confute: Several Sectaries Presbyterians, Anabaptists, Socinians, quakers fall off from the Church of England and to call them back we use Arguments taken from the Unity of the Catholic faith, the perpetuity of the Church, the Succession of Bishops nay even Infallibility it self in points necessary to Salvation, thô our best writers have employed all their best talents against the Papists if not in denying the Position of power of the Church & the Authority of tradition yet at least in extenuating the Validity and blunting the force of them. Ainsi va le monde.

363–6. Cf. *Lock and Montaigne* (1721, below), ll. 51–54.

367–8. 'We who are Jews by nature', Gal. ii. 15.

390. Tube. Telescope.

401–2. PROTOGENES and APELLES. See P's poem of that title (1718).

402–3. Kaspar Scioppius (1576–1649), German scholar and controversialist, attacked James I in *Ecclesiasticus auctoritati Jacobi regis oppositus* (1611).

Pierre Bayle (1657–1706) and Pierre Jurieu (1637–1713), French protestants who held professorships at Rotterdam. Their quarrels led to the dismissal of Bayle in 1693.

424. *Fænum habet in cornu.* Horace, *Satires*, I. iv. 34.

461. Lombard Street. The banking centre of London.

464. *Quos ultra . . . rectum.* Horace, *Satires,* I. i. 107. Cf. *Charles and Clenard* (1721 below), l. 155. In P's commonplace book for 1720–1 (*L 29*, 103), there is a similar comment:

> To what Horace has observed of the boundaries of Virtue and vice I would add that Every vertue has a vice very near it, a Kind of Deputy. Arrogance supplyes the place of Magnanimity, obstinacy comes almost up to Constancy, and Knavery and Subtilty often pass for Sagacity & wisdom, the saying of our Savior is very fine that We should be wise as Serpent[s] and innocent as Doves [Matt. x. 16]. We often doe the same thing thro' vanity or Decency that We ought to do by Honor or Duty.

(599)   *Charles and Clenard*

MSS. *L 21*, 147–8, 159 (P; notes for scattered passages); *L 25*, 63–82^v, 116 (D & P); *L 25*, 84 (D & P); *L 26*, 40 (D). (Index to *M*.)

Pub. *1907*, p. 207.

Text. *L 25* (84). Collated: *L 25* (63), *L 26*.

This is the first of Prior's four *Dialogues of the Dead* (as they are named on the general title-page of *L 26*). What evidence we have indicates that P was writing the dialogues concurrently during the last two or three years of his life and that he had not finished work on them at the time of his death. The few contemporary allusions they contain refer to circumstances existing in 1718 or later. The most definite of these is in *Lock and Montaigne,* ll. 815–17, where the 'News of the Day' refers to the events of April 1719. But that does not set a terminal date to P's composition even of this piece, for in *L 28*, 146, the verses *Intended for Lock* are inscribed 'Written at Down-Hall', i.e. in 1720 or 1721, and in P's commonplace book for those same years (*L 29*, 115^v–116), there is a rough draft of several speeches intended for *Cromwell and his Porter*. P does not mention the prose dialogues in his correspondence, and the letters that passed between his executors imply that they were known to few of his friends (Welbeck MSS., *Executors' Reports,* i. 146, 159). Pope saw them at some time after P's death, probably in 1723, and later commented that they were 'very good' (Spence, *Anecdotes,* ed. Singer, 1820, pp. 48–49).

For each of the first three dialogues there is an exceptionally complete series of manuscripts. First we have in *L 21* some preliminary notes in P's hand. Next we have in *L 25* a fairly complete draft of the dialogue in Drift's hurried hand, written on the left half of the page only, or on the versos only. This draft has extensive emendations by P, and also some insertions that Drift copied from P's rough drafts for separate passages (a few of which are bound into *L 25*). Then we have, also in *L 25*, Drift's copy of this revised version, with still further changes and additions in P's hand. Finally, we have in *L 26* the fair copy of this text that Drift made after P's death, in which he introduced many variations in detail and an occasional major error. It was from the posthumous transcripts in *L 26* that the dialogues were first printed in *1907*. It is clear, however, that the last copy which P revised presents the text as he approved it; and it is this that we take for our copy-text. We follow *L 26* only in giving consistent form to the titles. The scraps in *L 21* are too far removed from the final text to be collated, but a few rejected fragments of special interest are quoted in the notes.

P had projected several other dialogues: Ximenes and Wolsey, Wolsey and Cranmer, Luther and Loyola, Spenser and Camden, Jane Shore and the Queen of Edward IV (*L 21*, 145, 148ᵛ–149, 151, 155ᵛ–156), Virgil and Spenser (*L 29*, 46–47, 54–55). A few passages had been composed for some of these dialogues, but the only one that seems worth preserving is a speech intended for Jane Shore:

> Thou hadst him in his royal robes, I in his undress, and encountered him in my habit de Combat, but enough of that I may chance to offend your Pruderie: yet when I think of him and you together it puts me in Mind of the K: and Q: of Hearts, he with a gown trayling down to his heels and a ball & Cross in his hand & You with a stiff farthingal or what our Successors have turned into a hoop'd Pedicoat, and sweetly smelling a Nosegay.

. . . .

> The same passion that brought him from Lady Bona, ... of France to Katherine widow of . . . . . and mother of 5 Children for which he must provide, brought him yet from . . . . . to Jinny Shore the wife of a Goldsmith, nor encumber'd by any Children, but those whom as his vanity might have thought he had begott, his private command without any detremint to his Demoigns or his honor might have provided for. (*L 21*, 148ᵛ–149)

P knew the dialogues of the dead written by Lucian, Fontenelle (1683), and Fénelon (1712). His library contained Fontenelle's dialogues, and from one of them he took the French version of *Adriani Morientis* published with his own imitation in 1703; he had editions of Lucian in Greek, Latin, French, and English; and he made use of one of Fénelon's dialogues in a short passage in *Charles and Clenard* (ll. 492–5). Apart from this one instance of borrowing, however, P's dialogues have no specific indebtedness to these predecessors.

In *Charles and Clenard* the characters are Charles V (1500–58), Emperor of the Holy Roman Empire and King of Spain, and Nicolas Kleynaerts, called Clenardus or Clénard (1494?–1542), a priest who became professor of Latin, Greek, and Hebrew at the University of Louvain and later at Salamanca; he also served as tutor to Louis of Toledo, son of the Duke of Alba, and to Henry, brother of John III of Portugal. He studied Arabic with the hope that a knowledge of that language would aid in the peaceable conversion of the Moslems, and made a journey into Africa to that end. In 1542 he addressed to Charles V a request that the Arabic manuscripts in Spain be saved from destruction by the Inquisition. (See V. Chauvin and A. Roersch, 'Étude sur la vie et les travaux de Nicolas Clénard', *Mémoires Couronnés*, Académie Royale de Belgique, vol. lx, 1900–1.) P's library contained several editions of his *Institutiones Linguae Graecae*.

56. *Iliad*, I. 234.

70. *1 Henry IV*, IV. ii.

85. John of Leyden. Johann Buckholdt (*c.* 1508–35) led the Anabaptists of Münster in armed revolt, 1534. Massaniello. Tommaso Aniello (*c.* 1623–47), leader of a revolt in Naples, 1647.

132–3. The Peace of Augsburg (1555).

146–8. *The First Hymn of Callimachus* (1708), ll. 71–73.

154–5. See note to *Opinion*, l. 464.

222–5. Cf. Juvenal, *Satires*, x. 168–9.

243. In William Lily's *Brevissima Institutio, seu Ratio Grammatices* (Oxoniae, 1651, p. 17), this is l. 16 of Lily's mnemonic verses on 'Masculina excepta ex acutè crescentibus'.

287–91. Adrian Dedel (1459–1523) was successively a professor at Louvain, tutor to the young Charles, Regent of Spain, and Pope Adrian VI, 1522–3.

312–13. Plato says. *Phaedo*, 67.

347–8. Cf. Horace, *Odes*, IV. ix. 25–28.

381–3. The inscription on his temporary tomb in St. Peter's read: 'Adrianus VI. hic situs est, qui nihil sibi infelicius in vita duxit quam quod imperaret' (P. Bayle, *An Historical and Critical Dictionary*, London, 1710).

387–8. Jean-Éverard, Cardinal Nithard (1606–81), originally a Jesuit teacher, directed the government of Spain during the early years of Charles II's minority (1665–9).

392–5. In his commonplace book for 1720–1 (*L 29*, 114), P illustrates this point with reference to Louis XV, who became King of France in 1715 at the age of 5:

> There can not be a greater ridicule upon Monarchy than the manner in which the little King of France is taught to express himself, that having heard the advice of his Uncle the Duke of Orleans for the good of his Subjects, the Unity of the Church, the glory of his Monarchy, the tranquility of Europe &ca He accepts or recedes from the Constitution of the Pope, declares war against his Uncle the King of Spain &ca, makes treaties, which on the word and honor of a King he will execute. The person who thus hears, reflects and commands is a Child of Nine Years old, is Learning his Alphebete and soon wearied with his Esops fables impatient till he leaves his Counsellors and preceptors to play with his pages and whip his top: when I took Leave of him (then Dauphin) as Plenipotentiary of England he was instructed to give his Complements to the King of England, and immediately getting out of the Armed Chair which they had sett him in, and Knowing the Plenipotentiary to be Monsieur Prior, We lovingly went to Billiards: how long Some princes continue Children and how far may this reflexion be carryed?

427–9. Second Partition Treaty, 1699.

435–7. The question was whether the Doxology should read 'Glory be to the Father, *and* to the Son, *and* to the Holy Ghost' or '*in* (or *through*) the Son, . . .' This was part of the Trinitarian controversy which had been revived in 1712 by Samuel Clarke and was being hotly debated in 1718 and for some years after. See note to *The Conversation* (1720), l. 36.

479. A proverb: 'Chi sta bene non si muove.'

489. Grainville. Antoine Perrenot de Granvelle (1517–86).

492–5. Based on Fénelon's dialogue between 'Charles-Quint et un jeune moine de Saint-Just'.

541–2. A ballad based on the metrical romance of Sir Eglamore had been set to music. It is printed in Tom D'Urfey's *Songs compleat, pleasant and divertive*, 1719–20, iii. 293.

544–6. Dionysius the Younger, after being deposed as Tyrant of Syracuse (343 B.C.), went to Corinth, where he is said to have kept a school.

550. Virgil, *Aeneid*, vi. 448.

558–9. Quoted from Waller's *On St. James's Park*, ll. 95–96, where the reference is to Westminster Abbey, in which kings are both crowned and interred. (We are indebted to Professor A. B. Conron for pointing out this source.)

(615) *Lock and Montaigne*

MSS. *L 21*, 144, 149ᵛ–153, 156 (P; notes for scattered passages); *L 25*, 117 (D & P); *L 25*, 154 (D & P); *L 26*, 73 (D). (Index to *M*.)
Pub. *1907*, p. 223.
Text. *L 25* (117). Collated: *L 25* (154), *L 26*.

26–29. See Diogenes Laertius, *Lives*, vi. 26.

36. whole Duty of Man. See note to *Learning*, l. 134.

60. Apparently part of a jingle for remembering the principal parts of irregular verbs.

68–69. Attributed to Democritus (Diogenes Laertius, *Lives*, ix. 72) and to Heraclitus (Rabelais, *Pantagruel*, ch. xviii).

84–88. Locke, *Essay Concerning Human Understanding*, Bk. II, ch. iii, sec. 1.

88–92. Bk. I, ch. i, sec. 25.

97–100. Ch. I, sec. 27; ch. iii, sec. 12. Locke has 'Bay of Soldania'.

104–7, 113–19. Montaigne, iii. 572 (Bk. III, ch. xiii).

121–2. Locke, Bk. II, ch. vi.

128–34. Molière, *Le Bourgeois Gentilhomme*, III. iii.

186–7. In an exchange of pamphlets, 1696–9, Bishop Edward Stillingfleet condemned Locke's analysis of the understanding as excluding acceptance of the Christian mysteries such as the Trinity, and Locke denied that his work tended toward scepticism. Between 1690 and 1698, Robert South and William Sherlock were engaged in a renewal of the Socinian controversy.

202–4. See J. O. Halliwell, *The Nursery Rhymes of England*, 1886, p. 11.

228–32. Locke, Bk. II, ch. xxvii, sec. 7.

235. Bartholin. Either Kaspar Bartholin (1585–1629) or his son, Thomas (1616–80), both Danish physicians who wrote works on anatomy.

242–53. Locke, Bk. II, ch. xiii, sec. 8.

266–72. Locke, Bk. II, ch. xxvii, sec. 9. Locke quotes the story from Temple's 'Memoirs of what passed in Christendom from 1672 to 1679' (*Works*, 1814, ii. 284–6). Both Temple and Locke are noncommittal, but half convinced.

273–7. Locke, Bk. II, ch. xxxiii, sec. 16.

291. The maxim was attributed to Solon, one of the Seven Sages.

301. another wise Man. Solomon.

322–5. Berthold Schwartz competes with Roger Bacon for the honour of inventing gunpowder. Laurens Janszoon Coster (1370?–1440?) may have preceded Gutenberg in the use of movable cast-metal types. Anthony van Leeuwenhoek (1632–1723) was a manufacturer of microscopes as well as a microbiologist.

326–8. Thomas Tompion (1636–1713), famous clock- and watch-maker.

335–6. one of his Epistles. *Epîtres*, XI, 'A Mon Jardinier' (1695).

370–4. Montaigne's 'more Serious' simile is taken directly from Locke, Bk. II, ch. xxix, sec. 8, where it is explained more fully. The reference is to a curious sort of picture that was so drawn that it had to be viewed through a cylindrical mirror.

519–22. Pierre Chanet, *Traité de l'esprit de l'homme et de ses fonctions* (1649). P's source is probably a passage in 'A Vindication of Montaigne's Essays' prefixed to the third edition of Charles Cotton's translation of the *Essays*, 1700 (1870 reprint, p. 10): 'Chanet in his treatise of the operations of the understanding, quotes Montaigne's essays, as a work wherein judgment had no share, because, says he, every judicious man loves order, and there is nothing but confusion in that whole book.'

522. Malbranch. See note to *Alma*, iii. 354. The reference is to *De la Recherche de la Vérité*, Bk. II, Pt. III, ch. 3.

523. Joseph J. Scaliger (1540–1609) was reputed to have called Montaigne a 'hardi ignorant' (A. M. Boase, *The Fortunes of Montaigne*, 1935, p. 17).

533–6. Montaigne, i. 312 (Bk. I, ch. xxvi).

556. *Ipsa suis pollens opibus*. Lucretius, ii. 650.

557–62. See note to *Solomon* (1708), i. 502–11.

566–9. Arundel Collection. Brought together by Thomas Howard (1585?–1646), second Earl of Arundel.

The Duke of Bourbon led the Imperial troops at the sack of Rome, 1527. Irene was Byzantine Empress, A.D. 797–802. Regulus Memmius was governor of parts of Greece in the first century A.D.

571–80. Montaigne, i. 495–6 (Bk. I, ch. xlii).

594–6. iii. 337 (Bk. III, ch. ix).

600. Bocardo or Baralipton. Two of the moods of the scholastic syllogism.

603–4. Locke, 'Epistle to the Reader'.

605–13. Cf. Swift's interlude of the spider and the bee in the *Battle of the Books*, 1704.

633–4. *Phaedo*, 77; Eccl. i. 9.

653. See notes to *Alma*, i. 24, 245.

663–7. *De la Recherche de la Vérité*, Bk. II.

671. Locke, Bk. IV, ch. x, sec. 6 quotes *De Legibus*, II. vii.

678–84. Locke, Bk. III, ch. iv, sec. 8. The definition of motion (Dutch *beweeging*) is from Aristotle, *Metaph*. xi. 9.

702. Three Kings of Cologn. The Wise Men of the East, whose bones were said to be deposited in Cologne Cathedral.

714. Dialogue with your Cat. Montaigne, ii. 240 (Bk. II, ch. xii).

723. one of your Countrymen. We have been unable to identify this person.

745. Locke calls the brain 'the mind's presence-room', Bk. II, ch. iii, sec. I.

766. *Hamlet*, IV. iii.

815–17. Hostilities between France and Spain broke out in April 1719, over three months after the declaration of war by the Regent of France. In the same month some Spanish forces attempted to aid a Jacobite insurrection in Scotland.

821–3. Locke, Bk. II, ch. xi, sec. 7.

826–8. Ch. ix, secs. 13–14.

830–2. Sec. 5.

835–7. Ch. xxiii, sec. 22.

852–4. Montaigne, iii. 567–8 (Bk. III, ch. xiii).

870. Vortex. See note to *Alma* (1718), iii. 53–60.

(639)   *Intended for Lock*

MSS. *L 28*, 146 (D). (Index to *M*.)
Pub. *1907*, p. 323.
Text. *L 28*.

In the 'Contents' of *L 28*, Drift used the label 'Verses intended for Lock & Montaigne' both for this poem and for the preceding page of the manuscript, on which the following fragment appears:

> For Instance when You think you see a
> Fair Woman 'tis but her Idea
> If You her real Lipps salute
> Or but their shade will bear dispute.
> Look there say You, I see a horse
> Lord Sir how idly you discoarse.
> I see a horse, I'm sure that's true.
> I say the Devil a Horse see You

You see a horses Image lain
In Miniature upon your brain
But what you take for fourteen hand
Is less than half a grain of sand.
Things must be stated by their Nature
The Less can't comprehend the greater.
Now if your Groom would ne'r be Able
To gett old Crop into the stable
Unless pray Mind the door at least
Was something larger than the beast
The fellow sure would never be
Devoid of Sence to that degree
As to desire much less to try
To thrust his Nagg into your Eye.

(Our text is the most finished of Prior's rough drafts in *W*, 37–39. In *1907*, p. 322, Waller printed this fragment from Drift's transcript, *L 28*, 145, and gave it the title *Reality and Image*. The draft in *W* is labelled 'For Lock', but its position in the manuscript indicates that the verses were originally composed for *Alma*.)

(640) *Vicar of Bray and More*

MSS. *L 21*, 143, 160 (P; notes for scattered passages); *L 25*, 176 (D & P);
  L 25, 202 (D & P); *L 26*, 121 (D). (Index to *M*.)
Pub. *1907*, p. 247.
Text. *L 25* (176). Collated: *L 25* (202), *L 26*.

The legendary Vicar of Bray had become by the time of Thomas Fuller (1608–61) a symbol of prudent vacillation. Fuller reports that this nameless clergyman continued to hold his post in the Berkshire village of Bray during the reigns of Henry VIII, Edward VI, Mary, and Elizabeth, being twice a papist and twice a protestant. 'This vicar being taxed by one for being a turncoat and an inconstant changeling,—"Not so," said he; "for I always kept my principle, which is this, to live and die the vicar of Bray" ' (*History of the Worthies*, 1840, i. 113). Prior, who is more specific than Fuller concerning dates, says that the vicar kept his place from 1529 to 1586 (ll. 2–4) and died in the latter year at the age of 80 (l. 531), but this is mere embellishment of the legend. There seems to be no direct relation between this dialogue and the famous ballad about the vicar (W. Chappell, *Popular Music of the Olden Time*, 1859, ii. 653). In the ballad, which the *O.E.D.* dates *c.* 1720, the vicar's tenure at Bray extends from the reign of Charles I to that of George I.

An inaccurate version of six lines from P's verses beginning 'Your Conscience like a Firy Horse' (ll. 467–70, 477–8) was printed by John Nichols in the 'Advertisement' to his *Select Collection of Poems* (vol. i, 1780) as they were transmitted to him by 'the late recorder of Cambridge', who had seen a manuscript of the Dialogues. These lines were reprinted in *1892* (ii. 303), where they were given the title *Conscience*.

16–17. Bacon, in *De Augmentis*, IV. i, gives this version of the jest: 'More, at the very instant of death, when he had already laid his head on the fatal block, lifted it up a little, and gently drew aside his beard, which was somewhat long, saying, "this at least hath not offended the King" ' (translation from Bacon, *Works*, ed. J. Spedding, R. L. Ellis, and D. D. Heath, 1857–74, iv. 375).

55–57. Cf. Bacon's essay 'Of Death': 'It is as natural to die as to be born; and to a little infant, perhaps, the one is as painful as the other.'

67. Daughter Roper. Margaret, favourite daughter of More, the wife of William Roper.

87. one of . . . Wives. Anne Boleyn, executed the year after More's death.

88–90. Catherine Parr, Henry's sixth wife, is said to have differed with the king on a theological question and almost suffered arrest as a heretic in consequence.

91–92. *De Oratore*, I. i.

105–7. In P's commonplace book for 1720–1 (*L 29*, 110ᵛ), occur the following verses, which may have been intended for use at this point. Drift transcribed the verses in *L 28*, 155, under the title 'Fragments written at Down-Hall', and this text was published in *1907*, p. 324. We follow the text of *L 29*:

> For when your Judge becomes your Foe
> Think nor to give nor ward the blow.
> The danger prudently to shun,
> Forbear to plead and learn to run.
> What good can Culprit's staying do
> When Laws Explain'd by power pursue?
> Avails it ought what you can Say
> If all the bench resolves the Nay?
> When Truth outvoted comes too late
> What does She but prevaricate?
> The Circumstances change the Case
> Tis now no Tryal but a race.
> What signifies Achilles Speed
> But to be us'd in time of need?
> When angry Paris aim'd the dart
> Against the Heroes mortal part
> In stead of fighting had he fled
> His heel might have Secur'd his head.

118. *Merry Andrew* (1718) is based on this proverb.

120–4. These maxims are arranged like those in the books of 'Sententiae Pueriles', where the order depends on the number of words in the sentences, the shorter ones being given first.

177. See Acts xxiv. 25.

232–41. A brouillon of verses which appears with other dialogue material in *L 29, 54* (copy by Drift, f. 46), seems to have been written for the vicar to speak, perhaps in connexion with this passage:

> Who e'er forsakes old Mother Church
>   And of New doctrines makes profession
> Will find himself soon left in th' lurch
>   Or cited to the Quarter Session.
>
> I learn to think no precept strange
>   That Convocation can propose
> Nor ever wish nor seek for Change
>   Except in Mistresses and Cloaths.

These verses, and especially the last two lines, bear a close resemblance to an epigram by H. de Bueil, Marquis de Racan, in *Recueil des Plus Belles Epigrammes des Poëtes François* (Paris, 1698), ii. vii, which ends:

> Je vais où mon Pasteur me range,
> Et n'ay jamais aimé le change
> Que des femmes & des habits.

246–62. Cf. *To the Honourable Charles Montague* (1692) and note to *Solomon* (1708), iii. 223.

255–6. Cf. Horace, *Odes*, III. xxix. 29–30, quoted in *L 25* (202).

318. *Odes*, III. iii. 1–4.

320. Juvenal, *Satires*, viii. 80–83.

321–6. Among the 'Brouillons' in *L 29, 59* (transcribed by Drift on f. 49) there are six lines of verse that are similar in theme:

> Regards no Judges frown, nor Courtiers fawn
> Contemns the Knave tho' hid in furrs or Lawn
> Not covetous of Praise nor fearing blame
> With honour dyes, but will not live with Shame.
> Act Honestly however blam'd
> And rather dye than be ashamed.

334–8. Plato, *Gorgias*; Cicero, *De Finibus*, i. 49, *Tusculan Disputations*, Bk. I, *De Senectute*, chap. xix. Cf. *Alma*, iii. 600–9.

452–62. We are indebted to Professor J. Hutton for pointing out that the verses which P translates are in the *Greek Anthology*, x. 74.

467. P's rough draft of the fragment for *Alma* that we print in the notes to Canto iii, l. 9, of that poem shows that these verses in the dialogue were originally composed as a continuation of that fragment.

494. little Book. *Moriae Encomium* (1509). See P's imitation of a passage from it (1718).

521. Gilbert Burnet, *History of the Reformation*, vol. i (1679), Bk. I: 'He wrote, according to the way of the age, with much bitterness' (1829 ed., i. 64).

(655)   *Cromwell and his Porter*

MSS. *L 25*, 225 (D & P); *L 26*, 157 (D). (Index to *M*.)
Pub. *1907*, p. 262.
Text. *L 25*. Collated: *L 26*.

Prior did not invent Cromwell's mad porter, although he seems to have
been the first to make him a critic of his old master. We are indebted to
Professor Richard B. Vowles for calling to our attention two seventeenth-
century allusions to the porter: one in the Preface to Thomas D'Urfey's *Sir
Barnaby Whigg* (1681), the other in l. 82 of *A Satyr in Answer to the Satyr
Against Man* in *Poetical Recreations*, Pt. II (1688). In *Visits from the Shades* (Pt. II,
1705, pp. 129–41) there is a dialogue between 'Oliver's Porter and Mr.
B[isset]t the Enthusiast of St. C[atheri]ns', an attack on Whig clergymen.
A verse dialogue in *P.O.A.S.* iii (1704), 241–9, *Enter Oliver's Porter, Fiddler and
Poet in Bedlam*, represents the porter as ironically defending madness, and may
have suggested this use of the porter to P. P's theme is similar to that of
Sec. IX ('Digression on Madness') of Swift's *Tale of a Tub*, though P's tone
is very different. He may have found a general suggestion for his treatment
of Cromwell in Cowley's *A Discourse By way of Vision, Concerning the Government
of Oliver Cromwell*.

This is the shortest of P's dialogues, and a rough draft in the commonplace book for 1720 and 1721 (*L 29*, 115ᵛ-116) indicates that he may have
intended to expand it. However, since this passage cannot be inserted at any
point in the text of the other manuscripts, it is possible that it belongs to
a rejected earlier version:

for Cromwell Loquitur

Why if thou hadst not been mad thou woudst have found that there was a Necessity
for all that. The people are not to be led by Sence & reason but by passion and
appearance: as desirous as they were that their King should be murthered, and his
family banished they still wanted to See Some body clad with the ornaments they
used to revere and thô by the Instigation of My Self and my fellow Demogogues
I had brought them to hate the person of Charles Steuart I could not eradicate
from their Minds their desires to be governed by a Monarchy. Confusions arose in
our Counsells & clamor in the streets, and when I saw they must be ruled by one
man, who more proper for that employ then my Self: you see it was in my own defence
that I putt a ducal Crown as near a Kings as could be upon my cropt hair, covered
my clumsey shape with a purple mantle and made his Highness supply the place
of his Majesty, and you See my Successor acted his part so ungraciously that as
You observed just now they putt by poor Richard, and sett Charles again upon
the throne of his Ancestors.

P: The people theirfore doe not act by reason, but did You act any more by reason
than they did?

Crom: What dost thou call reason friend, I did every thing that could conduce
to the End I proposed.

P: The most unreasonable End that the maddest Imagination could suggest, to bring your Master's head to the block for some Seeming Mistakes in government, and not fear both your fellow conspirators who acted by your Inspiration [lines at bottom of fol. 115ᵛ trimmed off] in their turn for having openly violated the laws and utterly overthrown the constitution of your Country, and for the means by which this was to be brought about, good Lord bless Us all, dissenters and papists to destroy the Church, Independents & presbyterians to cutt each other's throats, armies to be kept up against the universal consent & liberty of the Nation, part of those Armies disbanded as Malcontents, and part purged, to opose their quondam brethren and fellow Souldiers, in short if there was ever any rule by which P[rince] and people should be governed in order to make each other happy, You and the Nation were equally Mad, You exposed to constant danger, Your Subjects to continued misery. Happy, if Providence had ordained a Madhouse bigg enough to receive you all, where bread & water and right contemplation might have brought Ye to your Witts again.

84–87. This alludes to the story that Cromwell one night conferred with Sir Richard Willis and John Thurloe, head of the secret service, concerning a plot to trap Charles II. Morland, Thurloe's secretary, pretended to be asleep at his desk. When Cromwell discovered his presence, he drew his poniard and threatened to kill him (*D.N.B.*, 'Sir Samuel Morland, 1625–1695').

106–8. The Irish seaport of Dundalk surrendered to Cromwell in Sept. 1649. Cromwell was Chancellor of Oxford University, 1651–7. St. Stephen's Chapel, Westminster, was at that time the seat of the House of Commons.

110. Westminster Hall. Then the chief law court of England.

151. A greater Philosopher. Epictetus; see *Opinion*, l. 257, and note.

234. Morefeilds. The new buildings for Bethlehem Hospital were erected in this district just outside the city walls, 1676.

Hodgdon. Hoddesdon, Herts., 17 miles north of London.

(663)   *Observations on Ovid's Metamorphoses*

MSS. *W*, 86 (P); *L 28*, 245 (D).
Pub. No publication known.
Text. *W*. Collated: *L 28*.

On the title-page of his rough draft (*W*, 86), Prior wrote, 'To be read over and revised. 1720/21'. It seems, however, that he had begun composition somewhat earlier, because mixed with the *Observations* in *W* is the rough draft for *Daphne and Apollo* (based on the *Metamorphoses*), which was written not later than 1715.

It was probably P's intention to develop his notes on Ovid into an essay at least as coherent as the *Observations on Homer* (1715), but in the state in which he left them they are too diffuse and disconnected to be printed as a whole. They constitute merely an unorganized series of comments that P set down in the order in which they occurred to him while he was re-reading the *Metamorphoses*. There are jottings on characters, incidents, philosophy, literary parallels, grammar, and points of style (especially propriety, tautology, similes, and *jeux de mots*), together with extensive quotations from Ovid's text. We print only about one-third of these notes, choosing the most extended and most interesting examples of each type of comment P made. We have retained P's opening and his conclusion in their original positions, but the other passages selected are rearranged in order to give greater coherence. After each quotation from the *Metamorphoses*, we have supplied the reference to book and line; we have not, however, emended the Latin as given by P.

 5. Nepos Cadmi. *Metamorphoses*, iii. 138.
  Autonœius heros. iii. 198.
  juvenis Hyantius. iii. 147.
 7. Mnemonides. v. 268, 280.
  Aonides. v. 333.
 15. Tirynthius heros. vii. 410.
 98–100. xii. 28–38.
 104. viii. 631–724. P used this episode in *The Ladle* (1703).
 108–9. Ceres . . . Fames. viii. 738–878.
 110. lying Spirit. 1 Kings xxii. 22; 2 Chron. xviii. 21.
 111–18. ix. 242–72.
 127. Hesione. xi. 211–15.
 128. Andromede. iv. 670–739.
 130. Polyphemus's complaint. xiii. 788–869.
 144. Thomas Sprat, *The Plague of Athens*, 1659. See commentary on *To the Bishop of Rochester* (1685).
 158. Dryope. ix. 331–93.
 161. Biblis. ix. 454–665.
 210. P proceeds to quote eighty-one more instances of the double use of words or word roots, like the play on *corpore*, *numen*, and *isto* in the line cited.
 228. xi. 475–582.
 235. Lapithes. xii. 210–536.
 239. Counter Scuffle. A coarse poem of this title, by Robert Speed, was published in 1623 and frequently reprinted.
 243. Drawcanser. Drawcansir in *The Rehearsal* (1671).
 281. See the conclusion of the *Metamorphoses*, xv. 875–9.

UNKNOWN DATE

(674)   *Epigram* ('When Nell')

MSS. *L 27*, 75 (D).
Pub. *1740*, p. 61.
Text. *L 27*. Collated: *1740*.

We present these poems according to date of publication, in the following groups: (1) forty-three poems first published in *1740*; (2) twenty-three of the twenty-four songs first published in *Lyric Poems 1741* (the one song that is dated has already been given); (3) one poem first published in *Evans 1779*; (4) ten poems first published in *1907*; (5) four poems never before published.

The first forty-three poems we give in the order in which they appeared in *1740*. Where there is a manuscript, however—as there is for almost half of them—we use it as our text rather than *1740*, for reasons explained in the Introduction, sec. VI.

B.M. Add. 31671, 33, contains a musical setting of this *Epigram*, dating from 1766–1813.

(674)   *Epigram* ('When Bibo')

MSS. *L 27*, 74 (D).
Pub. *1740*, p. 63.
Text. *L 27*. Collated: *1740*.

Set to music by John Travers in *Eighteen Canzonets 1745?*. The name 'Bibo' is used for a drunkard in *Alma* (1718), ii. 262.

(674)   *Epigram* ('O Death')

MSS. *L 27*, 72 (D).
Pub. *1740*, p. 64.
Text. *L 27*. Collated: *1740*.

(675)   *Epigram* ('Quoth Richard in jest')

MSS. *M*, 104 (D).
Pub. *1740*, p. 66.
Text. *M*. Collated: *1740*.

B.M. Add. 31671, 32, contains a musical setting dating from 1766–1813.

(675) *Cupid in Ambush*

MSS. None.
Pub. *1740*, p. 68.
Text. *1740*.

An imitation of Ovid, *Ars Amatoria*, i. 163–70.

(675) *Song* ('Hast my Nannette')

MSS. *M*, 80 (D); *L 27*, 68 (D).
Pub. *1740*, p. 70.
Text. *M*. Collated: *L 27*, *1740*.

Set to music by John Travers in *Eighteen Canzonets 1745?*. 'Nannette' also appears in *Cupid a Plowman*, below. It is possible that she represents a real person (Anne Durham or a French girl?); cf. Prior's reference in a letter to Bolingbroke, 13 May 1713—'Your huntress will be caught, if you have breath enough to follow her, and so will every huntress, from Atalanta and Diana, to Cloe and Nannette' (Bolingbroke, *Correspondence*, ed. G. Parke, 1798, iv, 108).

(676) *Written in Imitation of a Greek Epigram*

MSS. *M*, 91 (D).
Pub. *1740*, p. 73.
Text. *M*. Collated: *1740*.

Cf. *Greek Anthology*, ix. 72.

(676) *Epigram* ('Poor Hall')

MSS. *M*, 105 (D).
Pub. *1740*, p. 79.
Text. *M*. Collated: *1740*.

Set to music by John Travers in *Eighteen Canzonets 1745?*; B.M. *Add. 31671*, 33, contains a later musical setting, dating from 1766–1813.

(677) *Epigram* ('Prometheus forming')

MSS. *M*, 94 (D).
Pub. *1740*, p. 80.
Text. *M*. Collated: *1740*.

The contemporary application of this epigram still awaits satisfactory explanation.

1. Mr: D——. *1740* reads 'Mr DAY', which fits the rhyme.

6. H——. *1740* reads 'HARRY', which, again, fits the rhyme. Possibly the reference is to Henry St. John, Lord Bolingbroke, with whom Prior was on intimate terms 1710–15.

9. Squire Ne . . . . Possibly Sir Isaac Newton (1642–1727). *1740* reads 'WALLIS', i.e. John Wallis (1616–1703), mathematician. Although we can find no record of a specific attempt by either Newton or Wallis to 'prove all Poetry but Fable', the tendency of the scientists to contemn poetry as essentially false was apparent as early as Sprat's *History of the Royal Society* (1667).

(677)   *The Wandering Pilgrim*

MSS. None.
Pub. *1740*, p. 81.
Text. *1740*.

The present members of the Frankland family are unable to supply any clarification of this puzzling poem, and the parish registers of Coxwold, Yorkshire, tell nothing about Will Piggot except that he certainly did not die there. The Rev. R. L. H. Lloyd, Vicar of Coxwold, kindly informs us that until recently there were Piggots in the neighbouring village of Thirkleby, where Sir Thomas Frankland's estate was located, and that a Poor Men's Hospital was established at Coxwold in 1696. Mr. Lloyd suggests, therefore, that Will Piggot may have been one of Sir Thomas's household servants, who feared that he would be obliged to end his days in the poorhouse of a rival community unless his allowance was raised. The reference to his 'Old master' (l. 29) may indicate that Will had previously served Sir Thomas's father, Sir William Frankland, who died in 1697.

Sir Thomas Frankland (d. 1726) was Postmaster-General from 1690 to 1713. P carried on negotiations for him in 1698 and again in 1713 for the signing of a postal treaty with France (*H.M.C. Bath*, iii. 242; *1740 History*, pp. 402–3).

In style, this ballad is much like *The Viceroy* (1715); much of the humour, however, is unintelligible without more knowledge of the persons and circumstances than we have been able to recover. *Evans 1779* has the note, 'This merry petition was written to obtain the porter's place for Will Piggott'; but this statement probably rests on no authority other than the last stanza of the poem.

9. Rechabite. See Jer. xxxv. 2–19.

24. lin. Northern dialect for *to cease, to desist*. *O.E.D.* cites this line from P as a misuse for *to fail, to omit*.

39–40. See *Truth and Falshood* (1720).

(679)   *Fragment* ('Thus to the Muses')

MSS. *M*, 87 (D).
Pub. *1740*, p. 86.
Text. *M*. Collated: *1740*.

Probably suggested by an epigram in the *Greek Anthology*, ix. 39, as Professor James Hutton has pointed out to us. With the title *The Advice of Venus*, from *1740*, it was set to music by John Travers in *Eighteen Canzonets 1745?*.

(680)   *Cupid a Plowman*

MSS. *M*, 89 (D).
Pub. *1740*, p. 88.
Text. *M*. Collated: *1740*.

Moschus's Idyll VIII, *On Love Ploughing*, may be found in the *Greek Anthology*, xvi. 200, and elsewhere. For 'Nanet', see commentary on *Song* ('Hast my Nannette'), above.

(680)   *Epigram* ('O with what Woes')

MSS. *M*, 96 (D).
Pub. *1740*, p. 90.
Text. *M*. Collated: *1740*.

(680)   *Chast Florimel*

MSS. *M*, 71 (D).
Pub. *1740*, p. 92.
Text. *M*. Collated: *1740*.

For the name, see *Florimel* (1708), *Another* ('Ten Months after Florimel'), 1718, and *Alma* (1718), ii. 168.

(681)   *Partial Fame*

MSS. *M*, 73 (D).
Pub. *1740*, p. 95.
Text. *M*. Collated: *1740*.

(682)   *Song* ('Whither wou'd my Passion')

MSS. *M*, 77 (D).
Pub.   *1740*, p. 96.
Text. *M*. Collated: *1740*.

The assertion 'Set by Mr Purcel' in *1740* may, like several other titles in that volume, be erroneous. Ewing ('Musical Settings') was unable to find any record of a setting by either Henry or Daniel Purcell; nor have we been able to do so.

(682)   *Non Pareil*

MSS. None.
Pub.   *1740*, p. 97.
Text. *1740*.

(683)   *Upon Honour*

MSS. None. (Index to *M*.)
Pub.   *1740*, p. 100.
Text. *1740*.

8. SELDEN. John Selden (1584–1654), *Titles of Honour*, 1614.
ASHMOLE. Elias Ashmole (1617–92), *Institutions, Laws, and Ceremonies of the Order of the Garter*, 1672. In 1715 a new edition was published, with a continuation by T. Walker.

(684)   *Epigram* ('Phyllis You boast')

MSS. *M*, 101 (D).
Pub.   *1740*, p. 104.
Text. *M*. Collated: *1740*.

In *W*, 112, on a page containing the titles 'Observations on Homer' (1715) and 'progress of the Mind' (i.e. *Alma*, 1718), there is written in Prior's hand what seems to be an early draft of this poem:

> In vain thou boasts thou from deseas art free
>
> .   .   .   .
>
> Thou hast Incurable Antiquity.

Phyllis's Age (1718) is related to this poem in theme and in the use of the same name.

8. Blackmore. See note to *Paulo Purganti* (1708), l. 114.
10. Frey (p. 172) cites Villiers, *A Satyr on some Plays*: 'But Age, Beauty's incurable Disease.

(684) ## Epigram ('Luke Preach-ill')

MSS. *M*, 95 (D).
Pub. *1740*, p. 105.
Text. *M*. Collated: *1740*.

(684) ## Pontius and Pontia

MSS. None. (Index to *M*.)
Pub. *1740*, p. 107.
Text. *1740*.

Prior may have taken a hint from Martial, VI. xii.

(685) ## Epigram ('So good a Wife')

MSS. *M*, 103 (D).
Pub. *1740*, p. 109.
Text. *M*. Collated: *1740*.

Suggested by *Bonté de Cloris*, in *Les Epigrammes de Gombauld* (Paris, 1657),
p. 68:

> Son beau-frere est son favory.
> Par tout il la suit à la trace.
> Cloris ayma tant son mary,
> Qu'elle en aime toute la race.

The French epigram may also be found in *Recueil des plus belles pièces des Poètes François*, 1692 (1752 ed., iii. 84).

(686) ## To a Poet of Quality

MSS. *M*, 62 (D).
Pub. *1740*, p. 110.
Text. *M*. Collated: *1740*.

Lady Hinchinbroke (d. 1761) was Elizabeth, wife (m. 1707) of Edward
Richard Montagu (1692–1722), Viscount Hinchinbroke. Lord Hinchinbroke
was the only son of Edward Montagu (1670–1729), third Earl of Sandwich,
and Elizabeth, daughter of John Wilmot, second Earl of Rochester. Prior was
acquainted with Lady Sandwich as early as 1699, when she visited Paris,
and in Feb. 1720 she wrote an affectionate letter thanking him for his portrait
and praising his poems (*H.M.C. Bath*, iii. 353–4, 479). There seems to be no
record, however, of his acquaintance with Lady Hinchinbroke; nor have we
been able to identify the 'Poet of Quality'.

3. Sacharissa. Lady Dorothea Sidney, celebrated by Waller under this name.

Hortence. Presumably another lady celebrated by a poet.

6. Mamma. Her mother-in-law, Lady Sandwich, Rochester's daughter.

(686)   *Epigram* ('Lysander talks')

MSS. *M*, 93 (D).
Pub. *1740*, p. 111.
Text. *M*. Collated: *1740*.

Based on *Grand Parleur*, by Gombauld (*Les Epigrammes*, Paris, 1657, p. 49):

> Si l'on vous croit, bouche de rose,
> Lysandre parle bien; nul ne peut l'esgaler.
> Il devroit bien sçavoir parler;
> Il ne fait jamais autre chose.

Prior may have found Gombauld's poem in *Recueil des plus belles pièces des Poètes François*, 1692 (1752 ed., iii. 82).

(686)   *Truth Told at Last*

MSS. None.
Pub. *1740*, p. 120.
Text. *1740*.

The same names are used in *Pontius and Pontia*, above. This epigram was set to music by John Travers in *Eighteen Canzonets 1745?*.

(687)   *Riddle*

MSS. *W*, 26 (P); *L 28*, 163 (D). (Index to *M*.)
Pub. *1740*, p. 121.
Text. *W*. Collated: *L 28*, *1740*.

The answer would seem to be 'ice skates', made of iron and wood. Enigmas and their solutions appeared regularly in the *Gentleman's Journal*, the *Muses Mercury*, and other periodicals of the time; cf. Prior's *Enigma* (1693).

(687)   *Chanson Francoise*

MSS. *M*, 81 (D); *Lpo 18*, 212 (D); *B.M. Harl. 7316*, 44 (X); *B.M. Lansd. 852*, 57 (X).
Pub. *1740*, p. 123.
Text. *M*. Collated: *Lpo, Harl., Lansd., 1740*.

1740 gives the French original on the facing page:

Chanson Françoise

I.

Que fais tu Bergere dans ce beau verger
Tu ne songe gueres à me soulager?
Tu connois ma flamme, tu vois ma langueur,
Prens belle inhumaine pitié de mon cœur.

II.

Dequoy te plains tu malheureux Berger?
Que n'ay-je point fait pour te soulager?
J'ay quitté la plaine, mon troupeau, mon chien,
Prend on tant de peine quand on n'aime rien.

According to Frédéric Lachèvre, *Bibliographie des Recueils Collectifs de Poésies Publiés de 1597 à 1700* (Paris, 1901–5), iii. 710, these verses first appeared anonymously, with the title, *Gavotte*, in Bénigne de Bacilly, *Recueil des plus beaux vers qui ont esté mis en chant*, Pt. II, Paris, 1668.

Prior's translation was set to music by John Travers in *Eighteen Canzonets 1745?*. The table of contents in *1740* gives it the title, 'The CONSTANT SWAIN'.

(687)   *Human Life*

MSS. None.
Pub.   *1740*, p. 124.
Text. *1740*.

(688)   *Nelly's Picture*

MSS. None.
Pub.   *1740*, p. 144.
Text. *1740*.

It is hard to believe that Prior wrote this trite and artless song, unless as a burlesque. Several other undated poems for which *1740* is the only authority are strikingly inferior to most of P's work. We do not, however, feel justified in classifying these poems as 'doubtful' on the basis of style alone, and we have not been able to find any other basis for doubt.

(689)   *Prologue*

MSS. None.
Pub.   *1740*, p. 147.
Text. *1740*.

This poem was printed in *1740* with the title, *Prologue for Delia's Play*, and with a footnote identifying the play as Mrs. Manley's *The Royal Mischief*. With it were printed verses, said to be by the Duke of Buckinghamshire, which were addressed to Mrs. Manley as Delia and which had actually been prefixed to the 1696 edition of that tragedy. Prior's *Prologue*, however, was not published with *The Royal Mischief* and cannot apply to it. We have been unable to discover any drama of the period which fits the details here given concerning the authoress, characters, and plot. It is possible, as Mr. J. R. Allardyce Nicoll has kindly suggested to us, that the Prologue was intended for a privately produced play written by some young lady unknown to the stage.

7–8. Cf. *An English Padlock* (1704), ll. 78–79.

(689)   *Amaryllis*

MSS. None.
Pub. *1740*, p. 152.
Text. *1740*.

Based on Virgil's second eclogue, and perhaps also the third idyll of Theocritus.

(692)   *Upon Playing at Ombre*

MSS. None.
Pub. *1740*, p. 157.
Text. *1740*.

7. Matadores. The two black aces, always trumps. The poet is Ombre, playing against the two ladies. For the game, see G. Tillotson's edition of Pope's *The Rape of the Lock*, 1940, Appendix C.

(692)   *Cupid's Promise*

MSS. None.
Pub. *1740*, p. 159.
Text. *1740*.

1740 prints *Ode. Promesse de l'Amour* on the facing page:

I.

Hier, L'AMOUR *touché du Son*
Que rendoit ma Lire qu'il aime,
Me promit pour une Chanson,
Deux Baisers de sa Mere mesme.

II.

Non, luy dis-je, tu sçais mes Vœux,
　Tu connois quel penchant m'entraine,
Au lieu d'un j'en offre deux,
　Pour un seul Baiser de CLIMENE.

III.

Il me promit ce doux retour,
　Ma Lire en eut plus de Tendresse;
Mais vous, CLIMENE, *de l'Amour*
　Acquiterez-vous la Promesse?

We are indebted to Professor H. C. Lancaster of the Johns Hopkins University for informing us that the French poem is by Antoine Houdar de La Motte (1672–1731), and was first published in his *Odes* (Paris, 1709), pp. 289–90.

Prior's imitation was set to music by John Travers in *Eighteen Canzonets 1745?*.

(693)　　　　　　　　　*Dorinda*

MSS. None.
Pub. *1740*, p. 176.
Text. *1740*.

(695)　　　　　　　　*To Leonora*

MSS. None.
Pub. *1740*, p. 181.
Text. *1740*.

(696)　　　　　　*To Leonora. Encore*

MSS. None.
Pub. *1740*, p. 183.
Text. *1740*.

Set to music by John Travers in *Eighteen Canzonets 1745?*, and later by J. Mathews, *A Favorite Duett*, Bath [1800?].

(696)　　　　　　*On a Pretty Madwoman*

MSS. None.
Pub. *1740*, p. 184.
Text. *1740*.

(697)   *Absence*

MSS. None.
Pub.   *1740*, p. 186.
Text. *1740*.

(697)   *The New-Year's Gift*

MSS. None.
Pub.   *1740*, p. 187.
Text. *1740*.

Les Estreines (1701) uses the same figure.

(698)   *A Song* ('For God's-sake')

MSS. None.
Pub.   *1740*, p. 189.
Text. *1740*.

(699)   *Snuff*

MSS. None.
Pub.   *1740*, p. 190.
Text. *1740*.

In the table of contents in *1740*, this poem is marked with an asterisk to indicate that it was published in Prior's lifetime. We have not been able to discover any such publication. As explained in the Introduction, sec. V, it is possible that the asterisk was misplaced through a printer's error.

(699)   *To Celia*

MSS. None.
Pub.   *1740*, p. 191.
Text. *1740*.

(699)   *Upon a Friend*

MSS. None.
Pub.   *1740*, p. 192.
Text. *1740*.

(700)   'Strephonetta Why'

MSS. None.
Pub.   *Lyric Poems 1741*, p. 1.
       Collected: *1742*, Pt. I, p. 123.
Text. *1741.*

For a discussion of *Lyric Poems 1741* and the reasons for believing it authentic, see the Introduction. One of the twenty-four songs that it contains (*Les Estreines*) is dated 1701, and has been given under that date. The other twenty-three are here presented in the order in which they were first printed. We have expanded a few abbreviations and normalized stanzas engraved beneath the music.

The whole group of songs may well have been written at about the same time as the single dated one: the style and the marked 'Restoration' flavour of many of them suggest this. The settings all seem to have been composed long after Prior's death; twelve are by 'Mr. De Fesch', eight by 'Mr. Smith', two by 'Mr. C. R.', and two are anonymous. We are indebted to Ewing, 'Musical Settings', for information about these composers, given in the appropriate commentaries.

'Strephonetta Why' was set by Willem Defesch, a Flemish organist who came to England about 1731. He wrote two oratorios and numerous sonatas, concertos, and songs; he died about 1758.

(700)   *Parting with Flavia*

MSS. None.
Pub.   *Lyric Poems 1741*, p. 2.
       Collected: *1742*, Pt. I, p. 123.
Text. *1741.*

See the preceding commentary. *Parting with Flavia* was set by 'Mr. Smith', whom Ewing identifies as John Christopher Smith (1712–95), pupil, amanuensis, and friend of Handel. Smith wrote operas and oratorios, and composed the music for Garrick's adaptations of *A Midsummer Night's Dream* and *The Tempest*; his settings of Shakespeare's lyrics in these productions were long popular.

(702)   'Let perjur'd, fair, Aminta'

MSS. None.
Pub.   *Lyric Poems 1741*, p. 3.
       Collected: *1742*, Pt. I, p. 126.
Text. *1741.*

Set by 'Mr. De Fesch'. See commentary on *'Strephonetta Why'*, above.

(702)   ## To Phillis

MSS. None.
Pub. *Lyric Poems 1741*, p. 4.
     Collected: *1742*, Pt. I, p. 126.
Text. *1741*.

  Set by 'Mr. Smith'. See the commentary on *Parting with Flavia*, above.

(703)   ## 'Phillis this pious talk'

MSS. None.
Pub. *Lyric Poems 1741*, p. 5.
     Collected: *1742*, Pt. I, p. 127.
Text. *1741*.

  Set by 'Mr. De Fesch'; see commentary on *'Strephonetta Why'*, above.

(703)   ## 'Still, Dorinda'

MSS. None.
Pub. *Lyric Poems 1741*, p. 6.
     Collected: *1742*, Pt. I, p. 128.
Text. *1741*.

  Set by 'Mr. Smith'; see commentary on *Parting with Flavia*, above.

(705)   ## 'Is it, O Love'

MSS. None.
Pub. *Lyric Poems 1741*, p. 7.
     Collected: *1742*, Pt. I, p. 129.
Text. *1741*.

  Setting 'By Mr. De Fesch'. See commentary on *'Strephonetta Why'*, above.

(705)   ## A two part Song

MSS. None.
Pub. *Lyric Poems 1741*, p. 8; [Title as in text.] Single sheet without
     imprint.
     Collected: *1742*, Pt. I, p. 130.
Text. *1741*. Collated: *N.D.*

  Set by 'Mr. Smith'. See commentary on *Parting with Flavia*, above.
  The single sheet without imprint, listed above, is identical with *1741* in

title, text, and musical setting (ascribed to 'Mr. Smith'), but was made from a different plate. The B.M. *Catalogue of Printed Music* (ed. W. B. Squire, 1912), ii. 509 (s.v. 'Smith, John Christopher'), dates it '[London, 1735?]'. If this date is correct, the claim in the title of *1741* that none of the twenty-four songs had been printed is erroneous. We cannot, however, find any evidence that it antedates *1741*.

(706)   '*Morella, charming*'

MSS. None.
Pub.   *Lyric Poems 1741*, p. 9.
       Collected: *1742*, Pt. I, p. 131.
Text. *1741*.

   Set by Defesch; see commentary on '*Strephonetta Why*', above.

(706)   '*Since my words*'

MSS. None.
Pub.   *Lyric Poems 1741*, p. 10.
       Collected: *1742*, Pt. I, p. 131.
Text. *1741*.

   Set by Smith; see commentary on *Parting with Flavia*, above.

   15–16. Cf. Swift, *Ode to the Athenian Society* (1692), ll. 103, 109–10.

(707)   '*Love! inform*'

MSS. None.
Pub.   *Lyric Poems 1741*, p. 11.
       Collected: *1742*, Pt. I, p. 132.
Text. *1741*.

   Set by Defesch; see commentary on '*Strephonetta Why*', above.

(707)   '*Since Moggy*'

MSS. None.
Pub.   *Lyric Poems 1741*, p. 12.
       Collected: *1742*, Pt. I, p. 144.
Text. *1741*.

   The setting in *1741* is anonymous. In the *London Magazine*, xv (1746), 640, the song was published as *The Adieu to Moggy*, with an entirely different setting by 'S. F. H. E. S.'. This later setting was also published as a single sheet, without attribution or imprint; the B.M. *Catalogue of Printed Music* (ed. W. B. Squire, 1912), ii. 503, dates it '[1746?]'.

The use of *mun* for *must* and *Moggy* for *Molly* suggests rural dialect generally rather than that of any specific region.

(707)   *The Divided Heart*

MSS. None.
Pub. *Lyric Poems 1741*, p. 13.
      Collected: *1742*, Pt. I, p. 133.
Text. *1741.*

Set by Smith; see commentary on *Parting with Flavia*, above.

(709)   *'Some kind Angel'*

MSS. None.
Pub. *Lyric Poems 1741*, p. 14.
      Collected: *1742*, Pt. I, p. 145.
Text. *1741.*

The setting is anonymous.

(709)   *'Farewell Amynta'*

MSS. None.
Pub. *Lyric Poems 1741*, p. 15.
      Collected: *1742*, Pt. I, p. 135.
Text. *1741.*

Set by Defesch. See commentary on *'Strephonetta Why'*, above.

(710)   *'Nanny blushes'*

MSS. None.
Pub. *Lyric Poems 1741*, p. 17.
      Collected: *1742*, Pt. I, p. 137.
Text. *1741.*

Set by Defesch; see commentary on *'Strephonetta Why'*, above.

(711)   *'Since we your Husband'*

MSS. None.
Pub.   *Lyric Poems 1741*, p. 18.
     Collected: *1742*, Pt. I, p. 137.
Text. *1741*.

    Set by Smith; see commentary on *Parting with Flavia*, above.

(712)   *Advice to a Lady*

MSS. None.
Pub.   *Lyric Poems 1741*, p. 19.
     Collected: *1742*, Pt. I, p. 138.
Text. *1741*.

    The setting is by 'Mr. C. R.'; Ewing does not identify this composer, nor have we been able to.

(713)   *'Since, by ill Fate'*

MSS. None.
Pub.   *Lyric Poems 1741*, p. 20.
     Collected: *1742*, Pt. I, p. 140.
Text. *1741*.

    Set by Defesch; see commentary on *'Strephonetta Why'*, above.

(713)   *'Touch the Lyre'*

MSS. None.
Pub.   *Lyric Poems 1741*, p. 21.
     Collected: *1742*, Pt. I, p. 140.
Text. *1741*.

    Set by Defesch; see commentary on *'Strephonetta Why'*, above.

(713)   *'In vain alas!'*

MSS. None.
Pub.   *Lyric Poems 1741*, p. 22.
     Collected: *1742*, Pt. I, p. 141.
Text. *1741*.

    Set by Defesch; see commentary on *'Strephonetta Why'*, above.

(714)   *'Well—I will never'*

MSS. None.
Pub. *Lyric Poems 1741*, p. 23.
      Collected: *1742*, Pt. I, p. 142.
Text. *1741*.

Set by Defesch; see commentary on *'Strephonetta Why'*, above.

(715)   *'Chloe Beauty has'*

MSS. None.
Pub. *Lyric Poems 1741*, p. 24.
      Collected: *1742*, Pt. I, p. 143.
Text: *1741*.

Set by 'Mr. C. R.'; see commentary on *Advice to a Lady*, above. Cf. the song by George Granville, Lord Lansdowne (1667–1735), beginning, 'Cloe's the wonder of her sex . . .' in Anderson's *British Poets* (1793), vii. 717. Much of Lansdowne's verse seems imitative of Prior. He married in 1711 Lady Mary Villiers, to whom P wrote *To a Child of Quality* (1700).

(716)   *Verses in Lady How's Ovids Epistles*

MSS. *Lpo 18*, 161 (X); *B.M. Harl. 7316*, 12ᵛ (X; MS. owned and annotated by Edward Lord Harley).
Pub. *Evans 1779*, ii. 225.
Text. *Lpo*. Collated: *Harl*.

The poem is attributed to Prior in both the manuscripts listed above. 'Lady How' was probably Juliana (1665–1747), second wife of Scrope Howe, first Viscount Howe (1648–1713). She was the daughter of Lord Alington, and in 1698 married Sir Scrope (knighted 1663, made viscount 1701). Her daughter, Mary Howe, was appointed Maid of Honour to Princess Caroline in 1720, and was mentioned by Pope in several poems (*Works*, ed. W. Elwin and W. J. Courthope, 1871–89, iv. 447). We cannot, however, make this identification with any assurance, since there were several other Lady Howe's, and no record has survived to indicate which of them P was acquainted with. The List of Subscribers in *1718* includes 'The Honorable Lady Howe', as well as John Howe, Jr., and a Mrs. Howe.

The book alluded to may be *Ovid's Epistles*, 1680, described in the commentary on *A Satyr on the modern Translators* (1685).

(716) *Simile*

MSS. *W*, 51 (P); *L 28*, 157 (D; emend. by Pope). (Index to *M*.)
Pub. *1907*, p. 332.
Text. *W*. Collated: *L 28*.

This and the following nine poems were first published in *1907* from the Longleat manuscripts. Our text is in some instances substantially different because we reject the changes Pope made in the text of *L 28* and we use manuscripts not available to Waller. Sometimes we have been able to reconstruct Prior's intention from the rough drafts in his hand and extract a coherent work from what appears in *L 28* and *1907* as disjointed fragments.

For *Simile* P may have taken a hint from an *Enigma* (unsigned) published in the *Gentleman's Journal*, ii (1693), 238:

> *Of Fellows, neither good nor bad,*
> *A numerous Train I long have had:*
>
> *　　*　　*　　*
>
> *By me my Neighbours are improv'd,*
> *Yet I've no Pow'r when they're remov'd.* . . .

In the next issue (ii. 270–1), there is an answer 'by a Lady', beginning, '*Ne'er Cipher was decipher'd better,* | *Than the black Circle in your Letter*'. P's *Enigma* (1693) was published on the same page as this answer.

(716) *The Courtier*

MSS. *W*, 53 (P); *L 28*, 158 (D; emend. by Pope). (Index to *M*.)
Pub. *1907*, p. 332.
Text. *W*. Collated: *L 28*.

The Courtier seems to have been intended as a part of a larger composition; but it is complete in itself.

(717) *Narcissus*

MSS. *W*, 56 (P); *L 28*, 158 (D).
Pub. *1907*, p. 334.
Text. *W*. Collated: *L 28*.

Prior's preliminary draft in *W* shows how the epigram took shape:

> Thou lovest thy self
> And in that Love Hast no rival
> For nothing in the whole Creation
> But for thy self thou hast a passion.

Frey (p. 179) cites Horace, *Ars Poetica*, ll. 443–4, and La Fontaine, *Fables*,

I. xi, *L'Homme et son Image* (beginning, 'Un homme qui s'aimait sans avoir de rivaux') as possible sources.

(717)   *To Cloe*

MSS. *L 29*, 16 (X).
Pub. *1907*, p. 355.
Text. *L 29*.

(717)   *To a Painter*

MSS. *W*, 60 (P); *L 28*, 168 (D; emend. by Pope). (Index to *M*.)
Pub. *1907*, p. 337.
Text. *W*. Collated: *L 28*.

In *W* (and also in *L 28*) the poem is preceded by preliminary drafts of some interest:

> In foreign Lands my poetry stands dumb
> Thy pictures speak and act where ere they come.
>
> If thou paintst at Rome
> She speaks all tongues and always
>
> But narrow bounds the English Muse can boast
> Confin'd and fetter'd to her native Coast
> On foreign shores she sullen stands and dumb
> Larger her Sisters pace
>   at Paris and at Rome
> She speaks the tongue, and always is at home.

(718)   *Song* ('Thou arm'st thy Self')

MSS. *L 29*, 61ᵛ (P); *W*, 83 (P; ll. 3–8 only); *L 29*, 50 (D).
Pub. *1907*, p. 358.
Text. *L 29* (P). Collated: *W*, *L 29* (D).

Drift's transcript (printed in *1907*) makes the song appear incoherent and fragmentary, since it reproduces all Prior's drafts in the order in which they appear on the page. By studying P's original, we have been able to reconstruct what we believe to be the final version he had in mind.

(719)   *Song* ('Let us, my Dear')

MSS. *L 29*, 62 (D & P); *L 29*, 51 (D).
Pub. *1907*, p. 359.
Text. *L 29* (D & P). Collated: *L 29* (D).

Like the preceding song, this one was transcribed by Drift in the section of *L 29* headed: 'Transcript of Fragments in Prose & Verse, Written by Mr Prior. unfinished, Omitted in the Miscellanies. Folio.' Drift placed a marginal note in *L 29*, 51: 'If I remember right I take this to be the Brouillon of the Original Song I put into my Lords hands, with other lose Papers, and I think contain[in]g 4 Stanzas written in Drifts hand Dictated from this by Mr: Prior.' This finished manuscript has not survived; but by following the indications in Prior's draft we have educed a version that is probably close to what he finally intended.

(719)   *Invocation to Fortune*

MSS. *W*, 48 (P); *L 28*, 153ᵛ (D); *L 28*, 324 (D).
Pub. *1907*, p. 330.
Text. *W*. Collated: *L 28* (153ᵛ), *L 28* (324).

Waller, in *1907*, misinterpreted the markings in *L 28*, 153ᵛ, and gave these verses the title, 'Written under a Picture painted by Mr Howard', a phrase which applies to *The Lame and the Blind* (1720). We take the title from the table of contents to *L 28*; it does not occur with the verses in any of the manuscripts.

Drift's second transcript (*L 28*, 324) occurs at the end of his transcript of fragments for *Britanicus* (1721), and it is possible that the verses were written as a speech for that play. They are followed, however, by other material not related to *Britanicus*, so that no clear inference can be drawn from this position; neither of the other manuscripts is in a context that suggests any connexion with the play.

(720)   *Fragment* ('Thy King')

MSS. *W*, 28ᵛ (P); *L 28*, 132 (D; emend. by Pope).
Pub. *1907*, p. 318.
Text. *W*. Collated: *L 28*.

If this fragment refers to the political scene, it is probably a prophecy of what will happen if the standing army is dispersed and William III attacked and deprived of power by party violence. It suggests that William will go back to Holland (Belgia), and that will mean the end of the British monarchy and of her trade and empire; while Holland flourishes, England (especially the clergy) will decline. If this interpretation is correct, the piece was probably written 1697–1701, when Prior was stating the same theme in other poems.

On the other hand, all P's other pieces in blank verse are either translations or plays: the two hymns of Callimachus (1708, 1718), *Frederic* (1714),

Ronsard's Franciade and *Virgils Georgic 4* (both 1720), and *Ladislaus* and *Britanicus* (both 1721). One suspects, therefore, that this poem, too, may be a translation, or part of a play or narrative dealing with a fictitious situation.

(721)   *Fragment* ('O Dear to God and Man')

MSS. *L 29, 63* (P); *L 29, 52* (D).
Pub.   1907, p. 359.
Text. *L 29* (P). Collated: *L 29* (D).

If these couplets are addressed to a real king of England, they would fit James II or his son; but to ascribe such Jacobite sentiments to Prior contradicts all the known evidence. It seems likely that the fragment deals with a fictitious situation.

(721)   *Epigram* ('At Noble Mens table')

MSS. *W*, 44ᵛ (P).
Pub.   No publication known.
Text. *W*.

(722)   *The Normans Wish*

MSS. *M*, 92 (D).
Pub.   No publication known.
Text. *M*.

We are unable to explain the title. It is possible that Prior wrote 'The Womans Wish' and Drift misread it.

(722)   *Epigram* ('Tom's Sickness')

MSS. *M*, 98 (D).
Pub.   No publication known.
Text. *M*.

(722)   *Epigram* ('Rise not till Noon')

MSS. *M*, 99 (D).
Pub.   No publication known.
Text. *M*.

LATIN WORKS

For forty-three of the fifty Latin works in this section, the unique manuscript is Drift's fair copy in *L 28*, 326–99. For thirty-five of these Drift identifies his copy-text as the lost first volume of Prior's manuscript 'quarto miscellany' and gives page references indicating their original position among the English poems which that volume also contained. The transcripts, probably made after P's death, contain some absurd errors that show Drift did not understand Latin well enough to read accurately what must have been in the drafts from which he was copying. Often, familiarity with the characteristic ambiguities of P's hand has enabled us to restore the original. In our text of works published in *1740*, we accept its correction of Drift's misreadings.

Seven of the Latin works in *L 28* are here omitted as not by P. One poem, *Joannis Sylvii de Seipso Carmen* (*L 28*, 394), is by Pitcairne (see commentary to *Gualterus Danistonus*, 1710). The others have in their titles names of P's contemporaries at Westminster School or at Cambridge: *Ad Franc: Episc: Eliensem* (*Longland*), *L 28*, 344; *Piggot to Dr: Montagu*, *L 28*, 329; *Piggot to the Bishop of Oxford*, *L 28*, 328, 330; *Ad Dm: Montagu Carmen Gratulatorium. Green*, *L 28*, 357; *Ad Comitem Notinghamiae. Green*, *L 28*, 352; *Willis Ad Doctorem Montagu*, *L 28*, 327. Each is a complimentary petition for favour, presented by the boy named and ostensibly written by him. We do not know why P preserved these pieces; perhaps he used them as models, or perhaps he had some part in their composition.

We have arranged the Latin works according to date of composition in so far as possible, though many of the academic pieces cannot be dated precisely. Following the works definitely written in 1688, we give the academic pieces that have some connexion with St. John's and were therefore written 1683–8. After these we present the numerous academic exercises that may have been done either at Westminster School or at St. John's, following the order in which they originally stood in the lost quarto miscellany. The two other pieces that were contained in the lost quarto but that give no evidence of academic origin we place under 1690, the latest possible date for anything in that volume. See commentary on *To a Lady Sleeping* (1690).

1683

(723)   *On the Marriage*

MSS. None.
Pub. *Hymenæus Cantabrigiensis*. Cantabrigiæ: Ex Officina Johannis Hayes, celeberrimæ Academiæ Typographi. Ann. Dom. 1683 (Case 169), Sig. I1ʳ; *A Select Collection of Poems. . . . The Seventh Volume.* London:

Printed by and for J. Nichols, Red Lion Passage, Fleet-Street. MDCCLXXXI, p. 93.

Collected: *1793*, p. 386.

Text. *1683*.

The marriage of Princess Anne (later Queen Anne) to George, Prince of Denmark, 28 July 1683, was celebrated in a volume of congratulatory verse from Cambridge University. In some copies of the 1683 volume, this poem is followed by the signature '*A. Prior*, Coll. Div. Joh. Alumn.' Nichols's *Select Collection*, reprinting from one such copy, included a note by 'K' arguing that this was nevertheless written by Matthew Prior. The note was unnecessary: in other copies the poem is signed 'M. Prior', and there was at that time no 'A. Prior' among the sons of St. John's, either students or graduates (G. A. Aitken, 'Notes on the Bibliography of Matthew Prior', *Transactions of the Bibliographical Society*, xiv, 1915–17, 40). We follow the text of a copy with the correct signature; except for the wrong initial, the other setting shows no significant variants. This is P's earliest publication. As Nichols noted, it echoes Martial, *Epigrams*, IV. xiii.

(723)   *Ad Decanum Westmonasteriensem*

MSS.   *L 28*, 334 (D).

Pub.   No publication known.

Text.   *L 28*.

These hexameters celebrate the appointment of Dr. Thomas Sprat to succeed Bishop Dolben as Dean of Westminster, 21 Sept. 1683. They were probably written not long after that event, and certainly before July 1684, when Sprat was chosen Bishop of Rochester (see, below, Prior's poem on that occasion). The verses echo Virgil's pastoral poems, and especially *Eclogue I*.

1684

(725)   *Ad Comitem Dorcestriae*

MSS.   *L 28*, 333 (D).

Pub.   *1740*, p. 195.

Text.   *L 28*. Collated: *1740*.

Written to honour the Earl of Dorset on his forty-sixth birthday, 24 Jan. 1684. The humility with which Prior begs that his patron may accept this tribute perhaps reflects the break that had occurred the year before, when P chose to enter St. John's College, Cambridge, instead of Christ Church, Oxford (Eves, pp. 19, 23).

(726)   *In XXIX Diem Maij*

MSS. *L 28*, 336 (D).
Pub. No publication known.
Text. *L 28*.

     This pastoral celebrates 29 May as Charles II's birthday and the date of his return to London in 1660. It could not, therefore, have been written later than May 1684. Prior's chief model is Virgil's *Eclogue IV*.

(728)   *Ad Franc: Episc: Eliensem*

MSS. *L 28*, 344 (D).
Pub. *1740*, p. 206.
Text. *L 28*. Collated: *1740*.

     In *L 28* there are two pieces under this title. The first is a poem marked 'Longland', presumably to indicate that it was presented to Dr. Francis Turner by Isaac Longland, who was admitted to St. John's College, 27 March 1684 (*Alumni Cantabrigienses*, Cambridge, 1922–7). This poem was printed in *1740*, pp. 205–6, as if it were part of Prior's epistle.

     The new honour on which both pieces congratulate Bishop Turner is almost certainly his translation from Rochester to Ely, 16 July 1684. In 1685 P addressed two English poems to the bishop.

     2. V R. Vir Reverende.

(728)   *Reverendo in Christo Patri Thomae*

MSS. *L 28*, 340 (D).
Pub. *1740*, p. 202.
Text. *L 28*. Collated: *1740*.

     These elegiacs and the following epistle congratulate Dr. Sprat upon becoming Bishop of Rochester as well as Dean of Westminster (see above, *Ad Decanum Westmonasteriensem*). Although Sprat was not consecrated until 2 Nov. 1684, it was known by 11 July that he was to succeed Dr. Turner (Luttrell, i. 313).

(729)   *Epistola eodem tempore Missa*

MSS. *L 28*, 341 (D).
Pub. *1740*, p. 204.
Text. *L 28*. Collated: *1740*.

1685

(729)   *Supposito Hobbaeano statu naturae*

MSS.   *L 28*, 348 (D).
Pub.   No publication known.
Text.   *L 28*.

   This dated college exercise opposes Hobbes's theory that in the state of nature each man was at war with every other because all were given the right to all (*De Cive*, i. 10–12).

(730)   *Ad Regios Fratres*

MSS.   None.
Pub.   *Mœstissimæ ac Lætissimæ Academiæ Cantabrigiensis Affectus, Decedente Carolo II. Succedente Jacobo II. Regibus Augustissimis, Serenissimis Clementissimisque.* Cantabrigiæ, Ex Officina Joan. Hayes, Celeberrimæ Academiæ Typographi, 1684/5, Sig. T4ʳ.
      Collected: *1892*, ii. 301.
Text.   *1684/5*.

   These verses were Prior's signed contribution to the Cambridge volume published upon the death of Charles II and the accession of James II, 6 Feb. 1685. The collection was presented to the royal family on 25 March 1685 (C. H. Cooper, *Annals of Cambridge*, Cambridge, 1842–52, iii. 611).

(731)   *Theme. Scribimus indocti doctique*

MSS.   *L 28*, 358 (D).
Pub.   No publication known.
Text.   *L 28*.

   This humorous piece, which draws its title from Horace (*Epistles*, II. i. 117), refers to the publication of *Mœstissimæ ac Lætissimæ* (ll. 4–5); see the preceding commentary.

(731)   *Nobis Deus otia fecit*

MSS.   *L 28*, 353 (D).
Pub.   No publication known.
Text.   *L 28*.

   These hexameters take their title from Virgil (*Eclogues*, i. 6); in treatment, however, they echo Horace (*Odes*, II. xvi).

1687

(733)   *Fuit justum et injustum*

MSS. *L 28*, 365 (D).
Pub. No publication known.
Text. *L 28*.

The occasion for these hexameters is indicated in the title: the first congregation for degrees in 1687 (Ash Wednesday, 9 Feb.). As eleventh in the Cambridge *Ordo Senioritatis* for that year, Prior was among the bachelors 'quibus sua reservatur senioritas Comitiis prioribus' admitted to the B.A. degree at that time. P here denounces Hobbes's contention that there was neither justice nor injustice in the world until civil laws were written down and law courts established (*Leviathan*, ch. xiii; *De Cive*, ch. xviii).

1688

(734)   *For an Exhibition*

MSS. *L 28*, 368 (D).
Pub. No publication known.
Text. *L 28*.

This plea seems to have been addressed to Dr. Gower at some time between Prior's admission to the B.A. degree in 1687 and his election to a fellowship in April 1688. Its chief interest lies in the fairly specific references to P's early life.

6. V P R. Vir Plurime Reverende.

(735)   *Ad Socios Seniores*

MSS. *L 28*, 376. (D).
Pub. No publication known.
Text. *L 28*.

On 2 April 1688, the day before he subscribed to the oath as a Keyton Fellow (Eves, p. 38 n.), Prior addressed to the Senior Fellows of the college this statement of his desire to be worthy of their acceptance. He himself became a Senior Fellow on 3 Nov. 1707 (T. Baker, *History of the College of St. John the Evangelist*, Cambridge, 1869, i. 328).

(736)   *Ad Magistrum eodem die Epistola*

MSS.   *L 28*, 377 (D).
Pub.   No publication known.
Text.   *L 28*.

(737)   *In Scholâ Westmr:*

MSS.   *L 28*, 380 (D).
Pub.   No publication known.
Text.   *L 28*.

This speech, delivered at Westminster School a month after Prior became a Fellow of St. John's College, is based on the statement that Plutarch reports Julius Caesar to have made when he came to a little town as he was crossing the Alps (Plutarch, *Life of Caesar*, ch. xi; *Moralia*, iii. 225).

16. Gnatho. A parasite in Terence, *Eunuchus*.

(738)   *Ad Magistrum*

MSS.   *L 28*, 367 (D).
Pub.   No publication known.
Text.   *L 28*.

In this undated epistle, Prior thanks an unnamed Master for obtaining for him another good and gracious patron after having smiled upon his studies and having moulded his character. The piece stood in P's original volume of manuscripts between *Fuit justum et injustum*, written in Feb. 1687, and *For an Exhibition*, written before April 1688. It is, therefore, almost certainly addressed to Dr. Gower, perhaps in appreciation of his help in obtaining for P the position of tutor to the sons of the Earl of Exeter.

(738)   *Epistola ad Magistrum*

MSS.   *L 28*, 382 (D).
Pub.   No publication known.
Text.   *L 28*.

The original position of this epistle in the quarto volume and the allusion to the uncertainty and peril of the times suggest that it was composed late in 1688. Although it is Prior's first letter to Dr. Gower from Burleigh, his apologies make it clear that he has been there for some time as tutor to the Earl of Exeter's sons. Apparently he remained there at least until August of the following year (see *The Crest of the Arms of the Earl of Exeter*, Latin 1689).

6. V. P. Vir Plurime.

(739)   *Ad illustrissimam Dm: Margaritam*

MSS. *L 28*, 349 (D).
Pub. No publication known.
Text. *L 28*.

This poem and the three following are placed under 1688 because they relate to Prior's career at St. John's College. The present poem, honouring in Virgilian hexameters the Lady Margaret Beaufort, foundress of St. John's, is closely related to P's English poem, *Many Daughters have done well* (1688).

(740)   *Ad Dm: Gower*

MSS. *L 28*, 342 (D).
Pub. *1740*, p. 199.
Text. *L 28*. Collated: *1740*.

This letter of entreaty, like the following poem, is addressed to Dr. Humphrey Gower, Master of St. John's College, begging that Prior may receive pardon for his offence and may be restored to the table of his fellow students. P's breach of discipline is not specified; for those sections of the college statutes under which a student might be punished by being forbidden to eat in hall, see T. Baker, *History of the College of St. John the Evangelist*, Cambridge, 1869, ii. 1003–4.

3. V R. Vir Reverende.

(741)   *Carmen Deprecatorium*

MSS. *L 28*, 343 (D).
Pub. *1740*, p. 200.
Text. *L 28*. Collated: *1740*.

9. Cf. Juvenal, *Satires*, vii. 62; Horace, *Satires*, I. v. 12–13.

(741)   *Epistle to . . .*

MSS. *L 28*, 374 (D).
Pub. No publication known.
Text. *L 28*.

This epistle in hexameters was probably written to James Montagu, who together with his brother Charles had been Prior's close friend since child-hood. James, like the others, had gone from Westminster School to Cambridge, where he was admitted 26 June 1683 (W. W. R. Ball and J. A. Venn, *Admissions to Trinity College, Cambridge*, 1913, ii. 549). He left without his degree, however, to study law at the Middle Temple, whence he was called to the bar in 1689 (C. H. Hopwood, *Middle Temple Records*, 1905, iii. 1391). The reference to noble ancestry is appropriate because James's grandfather was the first Earl of Manchester. P's description of his day's activities—attending early chapel, reading Homer and Horace, drinking with his fellows—suggests his presence at St. John's at the time of composition.

26–27. See Horace, *Epistles*, I. ii. 1–4.

(742)   *Ad Doctorem Montague*

MSS. *L 28*, 360 (D).
Pub. No publication known.
Text. *L 28*.

This and the rest of the works under 1688 are academic pieces that may have been written at any time during Prior's years at school and college. Since we lack other evidence, we present them in the order in which they stood in the lost quarto miscellany. *Ad Doctorem Montague* is the only exception: we place it first because it is clearly associated with Westminster School.

This greeting to Dr. John Montagu, who was Master of Trinity College, Cambridge, 1683–99, seems to have been written for presentation upon one of his annual visits to Westminster School for the scholarship elections. It is similar to the pieces presented to him by Piggott and Green in 1684 and 1685 (see the general commentary on 'Latin Works'), but it lacks their appeals for personal favour. Although it is written from the viewpoint of one identified with Westminster, it would not be impossible for P to have read this at the public elections after he had already become a Cambridge student.

A Latin verse said to have been written by P at Westminster School is introduced on an odd sheet inserted into Sir James Montagu's *Memorandums* at Longleat, after Pt. I, p. 41:

Mr. Prior's Pentameter Verse spoken *ex tempore* to Dr. Busbey at Westminster School on his being threatened with Punishment for not having done his Exercise on the Subject of our Saviour's Miracle of turning the Water into Wine.

> Vidit & erubuit lympha pudica Deum.
> The modest Water saw it's God & blush'd.

The anecdote is probably apocryphal, however, for this Latin verse is alluded to in *The British Apollo* for 1 Dec. 1708, p. 3, as a famous monostich, 'said to owe it's Original to one School-boy of the Chautre-House'. P was apparently only one of several clever boys to whom it was attributed. A quatrain developing the same conceit was published in *Selecta Poemata Anglorum Latina* (Bathoniae, J. Salmon, 1774–6), i. 231.

23–32. This passage is identical with ll. 5–14 of the *Carmen Gratulatorium* (*L 28*, 357) addressed to Dr. Montagu by a John Green who was elected to Trinity College in 1685.

29–32. Dr. Montagu's father, Edward Montagu, as general at sea, brought to London the treasure captured from the Spanish West India fleet in 1656; there was a triumphal procession, and Parliament voted its thanks.

35–37. It was during the mastership of Montagu that Trinity completed construction of the new library designed by Sir Christopher Wren (G. M. Trevelyan, *Trinity College*, Cambridge, 1943, p. 48).

(743)   *Theme. Eheu fugaces Posthume, Posthume*

MSS.   *L 28*, 326 (D).
Pub.   No publication known.
Text.   *L 28*.

The subject (Horace, *Odes*, II. xiv. 1–2) is developed with some indebtedness to *Odes*, IV. vii.

(744)   *Theme. Minuti Semper et infirmi est Animi*

MSS.   *L 28*, 331 (D).
Pub.   No publication known.
Text.   *L 28*.

The theme is taken from Juvenal, *Satires*, xiii. 189–90.

(745)   *Dum bibimus*

MSS.   *L 28*, 332 (D).
Pub.   *1740*, p. 197.
Text.   *L 28*. Collated: *1740*.

The subject is taken from Juvenal (*Satires*, ix; ll. 128–9 are quoted as the title), but the poem also echoes Horace (e.g. *Odes*, II, xiv; IV, vii).

(745)   *Quicquid Vult, valde Vult*

MSS. None.
Pub.   *1740*, p. 208.
Text.   *1740*.

Although the title is taken from Cicero (*Epp. ad Atticum*, XIV, i), the poem is based on the story of Archimedes' continuing to concentrate on his mathematical calculations during the fall of Syracuse, in which he met his death (Plutarch, *Life of Marcellus*, ch. xix). Since there is no manuscript to indicate even an approximate date for this piece, it is here placed with other exercises of the same type.

(745) *Dulce Bellum inexpertis*

MSS. *L 28*, 339 (D).
Pub. No publication known.
Text. *L 28*.

The title is a proverb discussed at length by Erasmus (*Adagia*, IV. i. 1). The ultimate source is Pindar, Fragment 110. H. H. Hudson cites this as a typical subject for student themes (*The Epigram in the English Renaissance*, Princeton, 1947, p. 150).

(746) *Aliquando bonus dormitat Homerus*

MSS. *L 28*, 345 (D).
Pub. No publication known.
Text. *L 28*.

These elegiacs, which take their title from Horace (*Ars Poetica*, l. 359), criticize the indecorous behaviour of the Homeric gods, as do *Observations on Homer* (1715) and *Declamation*, below.

1. Μῆνιν ἄειδε θεά. *Iliad*, i. 1.
6. οὖλος ὄνειρος ἔχει. Cf. *Iliad*, ii. 6–8.

(746) *Tragaediae comaediis praeferantur*

MSS. *L 28*, 346 (D).
Pub. No publication known.
Text. *L 28*.

(748) *Theme. Paucos novit secura quies*

MSS. *L 28*, 351 (D).
Pub. No publication known.
Text. *L 28*.

The subject may have been suggested by Virgil, *Georgics*, ii. 467; the development recalls Juvenal, *Satires*, x.

(748) *Quod quisque vitet*

MSS. *L 28*, 355 (D).
Pub. No publication known.
Text. *L 28*.

Based on Horace, *Odes*, ii. xiii. 13–14.

(749) *Forma Viros neglecta decet*

MSS. *L 28*, 356 (D).
Pub. No publication known.
Text. *L 28*.

This racy satire on a theme from Ovid (*Ars Amatoria*, i. 509 ff.) dramatizes
a meeting with an effeminate fop named Cotilus (Martial, *Epigrams*, iii. 63).

  10. Curio. Manius Curius Dentatus (d. 270 B.C.), Roman hero.
  18. Othonis speculum. Cf. Juvenal, *Satires*, ii. 99–103.
  Abantis clypeus. Cf. *Aeneid*, iii. 286.

(750) *Non bene ibi imperatur*

MSS. *L 28*, 359 (D).
Pub. No publication known.
Text. *L 28*.

(750) *Declamation*

MSS. *L 28*, 362 (D).
Pub. No publication known.
Text. *L 28*.

  71. Anticyram. Anticyra, a town on the Corinthian gulf, was famous for
its hellebore, once considered a specific cure for insanity (Horace, *Satires*, ii.
iii. 83, 166).

(752) *Error Proprie et immediate*

MSS. *L 28*, 378 (D).
Pub. No publication known.
Text. *L 28*.

Prior takes the opposite view in *Epistle, to Lord* —— (1687), l. 123.

1689

(754)   *The Crest of the Arms of the Earl of Exeter*

MSS.   L *29*, 14 (P); L *28*, 390 (D); B.M. *Lansd. 852*, 85b (X, with a translation dated Dec. 1725).
Pub.   *1740*, p. 207.
Text.   L *29*. Collated: L *28*, *Lansd.*, *1740*.

Prior disregards Exeter's heraldic motto, 'Cor unum via una'. On 1 Aug. 1689 (the date given in L *28* and *1740*), P was probably still at Burleigh as tutor to the fifth earl's sons.

(754)   *Sent to Constantinople*

MSS.   L *28*, 386 (D).
Pub.   *1740*, p. 211.
Text.   L *28*. Collated: *1740*.

'Radulphus' is probably Bernard Randolph (1643–90?), a trader to the Levant, 1671–9, and a writer on the Morea and the islands in the Sea of Constantinople (*D.N.B.*, 'Edward Randolph, 1632–1703'). The British Consulate in Istanbul has not succeeded in finding the monument or any record of it.

According to the minutes of the Prerogative Court of Canterbury, which granted rights of administration on 20 May 1690, the father of the deceased was also named Robert Grove. We have not been able to identify either man, but they may have been related to one of the two Robert Grove's who were at this time connected with St. John's College, Cambridge—one as a Fellow and one as a student (*Alumni Cantabrigienses*, Cambridge, 1922–7).

1690

(756)   *Lamentatio Davidis*

MSS.   L *28*, 370 (D).
Pub.   No publication known.
Text.   L *28*.

This and the following work are dated 1690 on the basis of their original inclusion in the quarto miscellany. David's lament is found in 2 Sam. i; Prior expands it into an irregular ode.

(759) *Contra Astrologos*

MSS. *L 28*, 383 (D).
Pub. No publication known.
Text. *L 28*.

34. Aratus (315?–239 B.C.), author of *Phaenomena*, an astronomical poem.
66. Firmiano. Firmanus Tarutius (first century B.C.) cast the horoscope of Romulus in order to determine the date on which Rome was founded (Plutarch, *Life of Romulus*, ch. xii).

1692

(762) *Ad Virum Doctissimum, & Amicum Dominum Samuelem Shaw*

MSS. *L 28*, 388 (D).
Pub. *Disputatio Medica Inauguralis, De Ictero . . . Pro Gradu Doctoratus . . .* Samuel Shaw . . . Trajecti ad Rhenum, Ex Officinâ Francisci Halma, Academiæ Typographi, MDCXCII, Sig. B4ʳ.
     Collected: *1727*, p. 43.
Text. *1692*. Collated: *L 28*.

   These complimentary verses were addressed to Samuel Shaw for publication with his disputation on jaundice, which he presented for the degree of Doctor of Medicine from the University of Utrecht, 4 June 1692. Shaw had been at Cambridge when Prior was there and had gone to Leyden University as a medical student before entering Utrecht. He later wrote several works on the Latin language (R. W. Innes Smith, *English-Speaking Students of Medicine at the University of Leyden*, Edinburgh, 1932, p. 209). Also published with Shaw's thesis was a *Carmen* by William Emerson, a contemporary of P's at St. John's College and, in 1682, a medical student at Leyden. In the signature to P's poem as first published, he was styled 'A.M.' some eight years before he received that degree. A verse translation by 'Mr. Cooke' was printed with P's poem in *1727* and later collections.

(762) *Carolo de Berkely*

MSS. *L 28*, 389 (D).
Pub. *1740 History*, p. 11.
Text. *L 28*. Collated: *1740 History*.

   This letter to Charles Berkeley (1679–99), eldest son of Charles, Viscount

Dursley (later second Earl of Berkeley), was written at The Hague, where Prior was secretary to Lord Dursley. Although it is dated merely 4 Sept., the year must be 1692, since it was in the preceding December that Berkeley's aunt, Lady Theophila Lucy, sister of Lord Dursley and wife of Robert Nelson, made the visit at The Hague which P mentions (C. F. Secretan, *Memoirs of . . . Robert Nelson*, 1860, p. 46). Young Berkeley had been for eighteen months at a boarding school on the Continent where he studied Latin and French (see P's recommendation of him to Westminster School in 1694, *H.M.C. Bath*, iii. 22–23).

[Title.] Sam: Pam: Dit: Salutem plurimam dicit.

1695

(763)   *Inter Emblemata et Carmina*

MSS. *L 28*, 396 (D).
Pub.   No publication known.
Text. *L 28*.

The death of Mary II, 28 Dec. 1694, occasioned a flood of verses both in England and in the United Provinces; see commentary on *An Ode. Presented to the King, 1695*. In the present epigram Prior ridicules the poems (apparently illustrated) written by De Vrigny, an unidentified Frenchman.

1696

(763)   *To Lord Woodstock*

MSS. *L 28*, 395 (D).
Pub.   No publication known.
Text. *L 28*.

Prior writes from The Hague to answer a letter he has received from William Henry Bentinck, Lord Woodstock, the 14-year-old son of the first Earl of Portland.

1698

(764)   *In adventum Caesaris Mosci*

MSS. *L 28*, 397 (D).
Pub.   No publication known.
Text. *L 28*.

These elegiacs compliment Peter the Great, Czar of Muscovy, on his arrival in England in Jan. 1698. Prior had seen the czar at The Hague in Oct. 1697, but he may have failed to see him in England, for, at about the time of the czar's arrival, P left for Paris as Portland's secretary (Eves, p. 103).

1700

(764)　*Preamble to Baron Halifax's Patent*

MSS.　*P.R.O.*, *S.O. 7/130*, King's Bill (with royal sign manual, dated 10 Dec. 1700), copies of this in *P.R.O.*, *C. 82/2796* and *C. 66/3414*, No. 2.

Pub.　*The History of King William The Third* [by Abel Boyer]. London: A. Roper, F. Coggan, and Wm. Davis, iii (1703), 45. Never collected.

Text.　*P.R.O.* [King's Bill].

Although there is no positive evidence that Prior wrote this preamble, there is no reason to doubt the attribution made during P's lifetime by the author of *The Works and Life of the Right Honourable Charles, Late Earl of Halifax* (London: E. Curll . . ., J. Pemberton . . ., and J. Hooke . . . MDCCXV), pp. 61, 64. We can, of course, disregard the satirical assertion made in *The Second Part of The Mouse Grown a Rat* (1703), p. 4, that Montagu himself drew up this flattering document. P's letter to the Earl of Manchester on 10 Dec. 1700 shows that he approved of the honour paid his friend (*1740 History*, pp. 182–3).

1704

(765)　*Epitaphium Joannis Comitis Exoniae*

MSS.　*L 28*, 391 (D).

Pub.　*Monumenta Anglicana*, ed. J. Le Neve, iv (W. Bowyer, 1717), 1. Collected: *1740*, p. 214.

Text.　*L 28*. Collated: *1740*; *Monument* in St. Martin's Church, Stamford, Lincs., the text of which was kindly furnished by the Rev. Canon J. D. Day.

As the epitaph states, John Cecil, fifth Earl of Exeter, had his monument made in Italy before his death in 1700. It seems to have been kept in Rome until after the death of his wife, Anne, daughter of William Cavendish, third Earl of Devonshire, for the sculptor's signature is 'Petrus Stephanus Monnot Besantinus fecit Romae MDCCIV'. The epitaph was therefore composed between the countess's death in 1703 and its inscription on the stone in the following year.

1710

(766)   *Epitaph*

MSS.   *L 28*, 392 (D).

Pub.   *A Supplement to the Antiquities of St. Peter's, Westminster* [ed. Jodocus Crull]. London: J. Nutt, E. Curll, & J. Pemberton, 1713, p. 31. Never collected.

Text.   *L 28.* Collated: *Monument* in Westminster Abbey.

This epitaph for Admiral George Churchill, younger brother of the Duke of Marlborough, recounts his long career in the army and the navy. In 1704 Churchill had served as an intermediary in Prior's attempt to placate the Duchess of Marlborough (Strong, *Catalogue*, p. 109).

1719

(768)   *Epitaph on Charles Lord Halifax*

MSS.   *M*, 189 (D & A).

Pub.   *The Antiquities of St. Peter's . . . Westminster* [ed. Jodocus Crull], 3rd ed. London: E. Bell, &c., 1722, i. 122. Collected: *1740*, p. 217.

Text.   *M.* Collated: *1740, Monument* in Westminster Abbey.

On 27 Oct. 1719, over four years after the death of Charles Montagu, first Earl of Halifax, his brother, Sir James Montagu, requested Prior to compose the epitaph for his old friend (*H.M.C. Bath*, iii. 470). P complied although there had been some trouble between Charles and him in the years since P's complimentary preamble to Charles's patent as Baron Halifax in 1700 (Eves, pp. 171, 197, 202, 335–40).

59–61. According to the terms of the royal patents, Charles Montagu dying without male issue, his title as Baron Halifax was to go to his nephew, George Montagu, his title as earl becoming extinct. However, immediately after inheriting the barony, George Montagu was created Earl of Halifax, as he is here called.

1720

(770)   *Preamble to the Duke of Dorsets Patent*

MSS. *Welbeck Harley Papers*, xxxiv. 128b (D); *M*, 199 (D & A); *P.R.O.*, *S.O.* 7/177, King's Bill (with royal sign manual, dated 15 June 1720), copies of this in *P.R.O.*, *C. 83/19/1* and *C. 66/3538*, No. 11; sealed engrossment at Knole, a photograph of which is reproduced in C. J. Phillips, *History of the Sackville Family*, 1930, ii, facing p. 14.

Pub.   *1740*, p. 221.

Text. *Wh* [*Welbeck Harley Papers*]. Collated: *M*, *P.R.O.* [King's Bill], *1740*.

This preamble to the patent elevating Lionel Sackville to the title Duke of Dorset traces his lineage and compliments both him and his father, Prior's earliest patron (cf. *Dedication*, 1708 and *Postscript*, 1718). On 14 June 1720, P sent Lady Dorset a translation of the preamble (*L 14*, 284); on the 17th he sent to the Earl of Oxford a letter asking, 'How do you like my Preamble to my patron Dorset's patent?' and enclosed both the Latin text which we follow as having the greatest authorial approval and the following English translation, which may also be P's (*Welbeck Harley Papers*, xxxiv. 129):

Sackville We find to have been a Family in Normandy Ancient and Illustrious long before some of that Name came over into England, with William called the Conqueror. Their Posterity in a perpetual Series of great Actions have continued and improved the Glory of their Forefathers, and have accordingly been distinguished and belov'd by our Royal Predecessors, so that One of this Illustrious House was created a Baron of this Kingdom by King Richard the First, and Another (a long Series of Years intervening) by Queen Elizabeth, to whom he had the honor to be nearly related in blood, by the Name of Baron of Buckhurst. This Dignity being conferred on him in such a manner that he was rather re-established in his Ancient Title than advanced to a New one. The same Person a very little time after was promoted to a higher Degree of Peerage being made Earl of Dorset. The Family thus sufficiently Illustrious in their own Paternal Splendor received yet by their Alliance the Additional Honors of Baron Cranfield and Earl of Middlesex: These Titles were all Collected in the Person of Charles the late Earl of Dorset, and stand derived by Hereditary right to his Son, who has not only Sustained but increased the Glory of his Ancestors: Upon these Considerations and his many Services performed for Us, We have already given him the honor of the Garter, and as to the rank of his Nobility he being One of the First Earls, We have thought good to place him amongst the Dukes of this Kingdom, lest hereafter preferring others to that high Dignity we might seem to have forgot his Station and his merit, and thô with reason he might have Asked this great Title We of Our own Accord without his Asking have thought proper to confer it on him.

WORKS OF DOUBTFUL AUTHENTICITY

1684

(771) *Out of the Greek*

MSS. None.

Pub. *Choice Ayres and Songs*, 1684 (Day & Murrie, 68), Bk. V, p. 62; *Examen Poeticum*, 1693 (Case 172–3–a), p. 150.
Never collected.

Text. *1684*. Collated: *1693*.

This poem and the three that follow were attributed to Prior by Mr. F. R. D. Needham in *Times Literary Supplement*, xxix (1930), 458, on the authority of Lady Henrietta Harley. Mr. Needham reported that he had found the first three included in Lady Henrietta's 'List of my Priors Poems printed in Tonsons Miscellanys'; he added his attribution of the fourth because the subtitle describes it as 'By the Same Hand as the Former'. The small unbound notebook that contains this list, as well as copies of poems from the miscellanies, is now at the University of Nottingham in Box X. D. 52 of the Portland MSS. A photograph of the list, kindly sent to us by Mr. F. C. Tighe, reveals that it includes all four of the poems in question. Mr. Needham argued that P's closeness to the Harleys gives Lady Henrietta's attribution authority and that until there is some evidence to the contrary, the poems may be accepted as P's.

P's other poems in *1693* are all labelled 'By Mr. Prior', and these translations are so innocuous that it is hard to see why he would want them to remain anonymous. Apart from Lady Henrietta's note, there is nothing to connect them with P, and there is nothing in the style to suggest his work. For these reasons, we think it very unlikely that the poems are genuine; but we have found no definite evidence to disprove Lady Henrietta's attribution.

Mr. Needham was not aware that *Out of the Greek* was printed in 1684; if genuine, it would be P's first English poem to be published. Day and Murrie attribute it, conjecturally, to Robert Wolseley (1649–97), P's fellow diplomat; it may be significant that a poem by Wolseley immediately precedes the whole group in *1693*.

[Title.] Gilles Ménage (1613–92), French scholar and wit; his sayings were collected in *Menagiana*, 1693.

1693

(771)   *Out of the Italian*

MSS. None.
Pub. *Examen Poeticum,* 1693 (Case 172–3–a), p. 143.
      Never collected.
Text. *1693.*

   See the preceding commentary. Prior nowhere translates from the Italian, and there is nothing to indicate that he had more than a smattering of that language; he wrote to Lord Villiers in 1695: '. . . and I would buy me a Veneroni's Grammar and perfect my Italian if I had any assurance or promise that I should be your man for Florence' (*H.M.C. Bath,* iii. 59).

   [Title.] Count Fulvio Testi (1593–1646).

(773)   *Catullus. Epig. 19*

MSS. *B.M. Add. 28101,* 115 (X).
Pub. *Examen Poeticum,* 1693 (Case 172–3–a), p. 148.
      Never collected.
Text. *1693.*

   See commentary on *Out of the Greek,* above. In modern editions of Catullus this is xxii rather than xix. The translation is without attribution in *B.M. Add. 28101,* which is a late collection.

(774)   *Invitation into the Country*

MSS. None.
Pub. *Examen Poeticum,* 1693 (Case 172–3–a), p. 151.
      Never collected.
Text. *1693.*

   See commentary on *Out of the Greek,* above. In modern editions of Catullus this is xxxv rather than xxxiv.

1700

(775)   *On some Votes against the Lord S.*

MSS. *Bodl. Add. B. 105*, 27 (X).
Pub.   *P.O.A.S.* ii, 1703 (Case 211–2–a), p. 247.
       Never collected.
Text. *1703*. Collated: *Bodl.*

Printed anonymously in *P.O.A.S.*, and attributed to Prior only in the Bodleian manuscript listed above, where the title is: 'On the Report of my Ld. Somers being to be remov'd from his office of Ld. high Chancelour. By Mr. Prior.' This attribution was first pointed out by Eves (pp. 158–9), who also noted the parallel with P's letter to Manchester, 12 Feb. 1700:

> I must congratulate your Hapiness, that you are out of this Noise and Tumult, where we are tearing and destroying every Man his Neighbour. Tomorrow is the great Day when we expect that my Lord Chancellor will be fallen upon; though God knows what Crime he is guilty of, but that of being a very great Man, and a wise and upright Judge.   (*1740 History*, p. 164)

The verbal resemblance to the poem is not, however, close enough to be conclusive; the views expressed were, of course, common. The attribution in the Bodleian manuscript—a collection of verse copied chiefly from the miscellanies, made by an unknown collector—carries no particular authority. The evidence of P's authorship therefore is inadequate, though he may well have written the poem. If P did write it, his motives for failing to acknowledge it are obvious: he later, as an M.P., voted for the impeachment of Somers (April 1701).

John, Lord Somers (1651–1716), was Lord Chancellor from 1697 to 27 April 1700, when the king directed him to give up the seals because of the clamour in Parliament against him and the other Whig ministers. (Swift dedicated *A Tale of a Tub* to him in 1704.) The poem was probably written at about the same time as the letter quoted above.

In *L 29*, 56 (transcribed by Drift in *L 29*, 47; printed in *1907*, p. 357), there is a rough draft in P's hand for other verses on a similar theme:

> Now Eng. should obey and kings should reign.
> A less desert may gain a peoples trust
> But thou and Aristides were too Just
> And whilst thy Mind had everywhere its home
> They were most banisht who were nearest Rome.

(775)   *Prologue, By Sir John Falstaff*

MSS.   *U. Nott. Portland 1661*, iii. 370 (X).
Pub.   *Witt and Mirth: or, Pills to purge Melancholy*, 1700 (Day & Murrie, 188),
       Pt. II, pp. 313–14; *P.O.A.S.* ii, 1703 (Case 211–2–a), p. 218.
       Never collected.
Text. *1700.* Collated: *1703.*

First identified by Eves, p. 154, as being the prologue composed jointly
by Prior and the other Kit-Catters that P mentioned in a letter to Stanyan,
8 Jan. 1700:

> To-morrow night Batterton acts Falstaff, and to encourage that poor house the
> Kit Katters have taken one side-box, and the Knights of the Toast have taken the
> other. We have made up a Prologue for Sir John in favour of eating and drinking,
> and to rally your toasts, and I have on this occasion four lines upon Jacob. We will
> send you the whole Prologue when we have it together.
> N.B.—My Lord Dorset is at the head of us, and Lord Carbury is general of
> the enemy's forces, and that we dine at my Lord Dorset's, and go from thence in
> a body.   (*H.M.C. Bath,* iii. 394)

It appears that the prologue was soon after sent to Stanyan, who forwarded
it to Addison, who did not like it (Addison's *Letters*, ed. W. Graham, Oxford,
1941, p. 18). The alliance of the Kit-Catters and the Knights of the Toast to
support the play seems to have been intended as a reply to Jeremy Collier's
censure of the stage. For these two clubs, see R. J. Allen, *The Clubs of Augustan
London*, Cambridge, Mass., 1933, pp. 35–41.

This prologue fits the description in P's letter so well as to make it almost
certain that it is the one in question; but there do not seem to be 'four lines
upon Jacob' (i.e. Tonson?). It is patterned on Dryden's prologue to *Troilus
and Cressida*, 1679, 'Spoken by Mr. *Betterton*, Representing the Ghost of
Shakespear', which begins, '*See my lov'd* Britons, *see your* Shakespear *rise*, . . .'.

U. Nott. Portland (a manuscript miscellany deposited in the University of
Nottingham Library by the Duke of Portland) has four additional lines
between ll. 25 and 26:

> We Primitive Topers by a Toast meant Bread
> Our Ale we Drunk, and on our Toast we Fed
> But since these Modern Misteryes Intrude
> Brown George is Hocus Pocus Flesh and Blood.

The Portland miscellanies at Nottingham are not, like the Portland miscellanies at Longleat (*Lpo*), derived from the Harley family; since they are thus
without any special authority, we do not collate them. We are indebted to
Mr. F. C. Tighe and Professor V. de S. Pinto for use of their first-line indexes
to these manuscripts, and to Mr. G. E. Flack for sending photostats.

1703

(777)　　　　　　　*An Epitaph*

MSS.　*W*, 84 (P); *B.M. Harl. 6914*, 84 (X); *Harvard Eng. 629F*, 53 (X; a late collection).

Pub.　*Poetical Miscellanies: The Fifth Part*, 1704 (Case 172–5–a), p. 292. Never collected.

Text.　*W*. Collated: *Harl., 1704*.

See commentary on *Jinny the Just* (1708), to which this poem is closely related. *An Epitaph* is attributed to Dorset in *Harl.* and in *A New Miscellany*, 1730 (Case 361), and tentatively by Harris (*Dorset*, p. 236) and by William Kerr (*Restoration Verse 1660–1715*, 1930, p. 386), though Kerr also suggests the possibility of Prior's authorship ('It might be Prior's first sketch for this [*Jinny*], or the poem that suggested it to him'). Eves (p. 378) attributes it to P, on the basis of the Welbeck manuscript.

The manuscript evidence, however, is not conclusive. *An Epitaph, On the Countess of Dorchester*, and *On the Revolution of 1688* appear in *W* on a single sheet (84–85ᵛ), smaller than most sheets in the volume; they are written in P's 'fair copy' hand, which is distinct from the hand in which he composes. (None of them have titles in *W*.) *On the Countess of Dorchester* ('Tell me, Dorinda, why so gay') is definitely by Dorset and probably was written in 1680; *On the Revolution of 1688*—to be discussed in a moment—may be by Dorset. It appears, therefore, that P copied these three poems as if for a commonplace book; it is significant that Drift did not transcribe them, as he did virtually everything else in *W*. If, as seems likely, all three are by Dorset, P would have good reason for preserving them; see *Dedication* (1708), ll. 97–103.

The evidence for Dorset's authorship of the second of these poems, *On the Countess of Dorchester* (*W*, 84ᵛ), is conclusive; see Harris, *Dorset*, p. 82. The third, *On the Revolution of 1688* (*W*, 85), which begins, 'of a spleenitic Nation I sing', and was printed for the first time by Harris (*Dorset*, p. 152), has never been attributed to P. It is ascribed to Dorset in *B.M. Harl. 6914*, 83; in *B.M. Harl. 7316*, 24ᵛ, and *Harvard MS. Eng. 218.2* (Orrery Papers, ll. 1–8 only), it occurs without attribution. Harris (*Dorset*, p. 118 n.) thinks that Dorset did not write it because the poem—written about 1697—is a bitter satire on King William. This argument applies with equal force against P's authorship.

Since the other two poems are thus not P's, *An Epitaph* cannot safely be attributed to him on the basis of the copy in *W*, and there is no other basis for the attribution. There is no verbal resemblance to *Jinny the Just*, as there certainly would be if this were a rough draft for that poem; but the resemblance in theme and form makes it highly probable that *An Epitaph* was the prototype of *Jinny*.

We are greatly indebted to Professor Brice Harris for answering our inquiries about these poems and supplying useful information.

1704

(778)   *Epigram* ('Like a True Irish Marlin')

MSS.   *L 29, 57* (X); *L 29, 47* (D); *B.M. Harl. 6914, 80* (X); *B.M. Lansd. 852, 61* (X); *B.M. Add. 40060, 61ᵛ* (X).

Pub.   *The Roxburghe Ballads*, ed. J. W. Ebsworth, v (Hertford, 1885), 219 n. Collected: *1892*, ii. 304; *1907*, p. 357.

Text.   *L 29* (X). Collated: *L 29* (D), *Harl.*, *Lansd.*, *Add.*

Ascribed to Dorset in all the B.M. manuscripts listed above, and in Roxburghe (which prints from *Harl.*). First attributed to Prior by R. B. Johnson in *1892*, apparently through confusion; he calls it, 'Epigram. Alluded to in Pope's Correspondence with Lord Oxford', but it is not alluded to in that correspondence; it appears that Johnson interpreted the allusion to 'Epitaph on Jenny' (i.e. *Jinny the Just*) as referring to this poem. Waller prints the epigram from *L 29* without comment.

There is nothing to support the attribution to P except the occurrence of the poem in his manuscripts. As the preceding commentary has shown, P did in a few cases copy poems not his own in order to preserve them, and he was especially likely to do this with Dorset's poems. The transcript by Drift shows that he thought this epigram was P's; but Drift probably knew little of Dorset's poetry, and in at least one case transcribed verses that are definitely not P's (see *On a F . . t*, under Works Wrongly Attributed).

Harris, *Dorset*, p. 225, explains the occasion of the poem:

About the middle of October 1704 Dorset married Anne Roche, an Irishwoman who with her two sisters lived in Stable Yard, St. James. Employed by Dorset originally perhaps as housekeepers, the Roche sisters had for several years before the marriage managed his business. Anne, the third Lady Dorset, had at one time contracted to marry Sir John Dawes, it would seem, and had been disappointed. Among his papers Dorset left some verses on the affair. . . .

Although it is barely possible that P might have written this epigram on the occasion, it is extremely improbable; almost certainly, Dorset was the author.

1709

(778)   *The Mice*

MSS. None.
Pub.   *1740*, p. 28.
Text. *1740*.

The editors of *1740* undoubtedly found this epistle among the manuscripts they acquired from Drift. Since it is signed 'Matthew' and is concerned with a mouse named Matt, they probably felt no hesitation in publishing it as Prior's. It is now known, however, that it is Adrian Drift's family whose history is recounted here, and that the name subscribed is that of his brother, Matthew Drift (H. B. Wright, 'Biographical Allusions in Prior's "The Mice, A Tale" ', *Modern Language Notes*, liii, 1938, 498–501). This discovery casts serious doubt on the attribution to P, although it does not deny the possibility of his authorship. Matthew Drift is not known to have written verse, and the samples we have of Adrian's work are very different from the clever hudibrastics of this piece. These are much in the style of P, and in some places seem curiously inappropriate for a composition by either of the Drifts. It may be that P was paraphrasing a true letter from Matthew Drift or that he composed the epistle as a joke. Such a conjecture does not, however, explain the incongruous pentameter couplets, ll. 15–38. It seems likely that this passage was written by one of the Drifts; it has about the same quality as an unpublished epitaph on their sister Catharine that Adrian wrote into the back of his Prayer Book (*Md*).

In that Prayer Book Adrian Drift drew up a genealogical chart which supplements the facts concerning his family that are given in the article cited above, and thus further explains the allusions in the poem. When Matthew Drift, the elder, died in 1683, he left his widow with four children: Charles, Matthew, Catharine, and Adrian (who was then 7 years old). As Adrian says of his mother in the chart, her husband's memory 'being always dear to her, & the Welfare of her Children nearest her Heart, She chose to remain a Widow to the Day of her Death. Blest be her Memory for Ever.' Charles died in 1698; Catharine, who had married Walter Archer and had herself been widowed, died in 1703; and the mother died in the following year. Of the two sons who remained, the elder, Matthew, had attended Eton and King's College, Cambridge, had taken orders, and was already master of the grammar school at Lavenham, Suffolk; Adrian had become a clerk or secretary, apparently having accompanied Lord Villiers to the Congress of Ryswick, and by this time was clerk to the Board of Trade and Plantations.

Matthew Drift married Mary Pinchbeck of Lavenham, and on 4 Sept. 1708 she bore him a son who was named Adrian, after his uncle.

44. *Hudibras*, i. 23–24.
84. Portugueze. Snuff.

1712

(782)   *A Fable of the Widow and her Cat*

MSS. None.
Pub.   [Title as in text.] . . . Printed for John Morphew, near Stationers-Hall, 1712. [For other editions, see Swift, *Poems*, p. 151.]
       Collected: *1793*, p. 517.
Text. *1712*.

This poem has been fully edited by Sir Harold Williams, and we are unable to make any significant additions or corrections to his discussion of it. The poem—a satire on Marlborough's fall, published early in Jan. 1712—was first printed as probably Prior's in John Nichols's *Select Collection*, iv, 1780, 53; Nichols made the attribution on the basis of style, for he was aware that the earlier publications were all equivocal, ascribing it to 'either P or Swift' or to both together. All collected editions of P since Nichols have printed the poem, usually repeating Nichols's note, but not otherwise indicating its doubtful status; *1907* placed it in an appendix of 'Poems Attributed to Prior'.

Williams prints the poem as Swift's, 'with some hesitation'. It is possible that P had some part in its composition, but of this there is no clear evidence. See the discussion of *When the Cat's away*, under Works Wrongly Attributed.

(784)   *Epigram* ('I Stood, Sir')

MSS. None.
Pub.   *The Friendly and honest Advice of an Old Tory to the Vice-Chancellor of Cambridge*. London: Printed for S. Johnson, at Charing-Cross, MDCCLI, p. 23.
       Collected: *Evans 1779*, ii. 190.
Text. *1751*.

The anonymous author of the pamphlet ironically advises the Vice-Chancellor to increase his authority and dignity and gives an 'illustrious Example':

In the Year 1712 my old Friend *Mathew Prior*, who was then Fellow of *St. John's*, and who not long before had been employed by the Queen as her Pleni-potentiary at the Court of *France*, came to *Cambridge*; and the next Morning paid a Visit to the Master of his own College. The Master (whether Dr. *Gower*, or Dr. *Jenkins* I cannot now recollect) loved Mr. *Prior's* Principles, had a great Opinion of his Abilities, and a Respect for his Character in the World; but then he had a much greater Respect for himself. He knew his own Dignity *too well* to suffer a Fellow of his College to sit down in his Presence. He kept his Seat himself, and let the Queen's Ambassador stand. Such was the Temper not of a Vice-Chancellor, but of a *simple* Master of a College. I remember, by the Way, an extempore Epigram of *Matt's* on the Reception he had met with. We did not reckon in those Days, that he had a very happy Turn for an Epigram. But the Occasion was tempting; and he struck it off, as he was walking from *St John's* College to the *Rose*, where we dined together. It was addressed to the Master. [Then follows the epigram.]

This account could be true: Prior visited England late in 1712, shortly after being appointed Plenipotentiary; Dr. Robert Jenkin, a non-juror who finally took the oaths to Queen Anne, had succeeded Dr. Gower as master of St. John's in 1711. On the other hand, it is curious that the epigram, if genuine, is not mentioned elsewhere. We have not been able to identify the author of the pamphlet; and without this information, we have no basis for judging its authority.

1714

(784)   *Epigram* ('To Richmond and Peterburgh')

MSS. *L 29*, 31 (X); *B.M. Harl. 7316*, 91 (X).
Pub. *Evans 1779*, ii. 227.
Text. *L 29*. Collated: *Harl.*

In both manuscripts the epigram is headed 'Mr. Prior'. There is no way of telling whether this is intended as a title or as an attribution; Evans took it to be the latter, since he printed the epigram (from *Harl.*) as Prior's in *1779*, without questioning it. In both manuscripts, the epigram is followed, after a space, by a couplet:

> This in the days of good King George I writ
> When Ambrose Philipps had a place for Wit.
> A. Pope.

The couplet is of special interest because it relates to the composition of the *Dunciad*; Pope wrote to Swift on 15 Oct. 1725 (*Correspondence*, ed. G. Sherburn, Oxford, 1956, ii. 332; the manuscript is in *Lpo 13*, 106):

I'm sorry poor Philips is not promoted in this age; for certainly if his reward be of the next, he is of all Poets the most miserable. I'm also sorry for another reason; if they don't promote him they'l spoil a very good conclusion of one of my Satyrs, where having endeavour'd to correct the Taste of the town in wit and Criticisme, I end thus.

> But what avails to lay down rules for Sense?
> In ——'s Reign these fruitless lines were writ,
> When Ambrose Philips was preferr'd for wit!

James Sutherland, in his edition of the *Dunciad* (1943, pp. ix–x), quotes this letter and comments: 'In view of later developments, it is reasonable to see in this nameless satire in which Pope had endeavoured "to correct the taste of the town in wit and criticism" the germ of the poem that afterwards became the *Dunciad*.' The lines appear in the 1729 *Dunciad* (iii. 321–2):

> B** sole Judge of Architecture sit,
> And Namby Pamby be prefer'd for Wit!

and in the 1743 version (iii. 325–6):

> On Poets' Tombs see Benson's titles writ!
> Lo! Ambrose Philips is prefer'd for Wit!

Although the couplet is thus unquestionably Pope's, the spacing in both manuscripts is such that it is impossible to be certain that the couplet refers to the epigram. The hands in both manuscripts are secretarial, and we are unable to identify either. Unfortunately, Lord Harley did not annotate this page in *Harl*. It is clear, at any rate, that the epigram cannot safely be accepted as P's.

The occasion of the epigram is described in a letter from P to Bolingbroke, Paris, 25 Sept. 1714, bound in the volume at Longleat with Sir James Montagu's *Memorandums* (for which see commentary to *The Hind and the Panther Transvers'd*, 1687), Pt. II, pp. 80–82:

I send your Lordsp. the copy of a Letter No. (1) which I wrote to you the 13th of August. The Letter I wrote in my own hand Mr Drift copy'd it made it up & I delivered it to my Ld. Peterborow Mr. Drift being by & seeing me do so. There is nothing more in it than reffering you to what his Excellence cou'd inform you as he found the state of things here but it serves to justifie my exactness in Corresponding with your Lordsp. & to prove that I have omitted no occasion to inform you in what manner I continue to do my Duty.

There is another omission my Lord more essential: that is the Duke of Richmond neglecting to give you mine of the 9th of August N.S. the Copy of which & papers reffered to therein I send you inclosed No. 2. Your Lordsp. sees the Points Containd therein of great Moment, & such as ought to be laid before their Excellency's. There was likewise a Letter to the Duke of Shrewsbury a copy of which I now likewise send to his Grace & two Packets. . . . I can only say that as the Duke of Richmond required with great earnestness that he might be charged with any thing I might have to write to your Lordsp. & as he was to go 40 hours before the Post & said he wou'd see you & the Duke of Shrewsbury immediately upon his arrival at London I cou'd not possibly foresee any miscarriage or delay, this is Plain, this is truth. Your Lordsp. will judge of my surprize & represent the Fact to the Lord Justices.

If P wrote the epigram, he did so presumably at about this time. If Pope wrote it, the date may be later.

We are indebted to Mr. James William Johnson and to Professors George Sherburn and John Butt for answering inquiries and assisting us with this problem.

1. Richmond. Charles Lennox, first Duke of Richmond (1672–1723).
    Peterburgh. Charles Mordaunt, third Earl of Peterborough (1658–1735).
4. Knights of the Post. See note to *The Thief and the Cordelier* (1718), l. 8, for the double meaning.

1715

(784)   'Mais cette voix'

MSS. None.
Pub. *Prefaces, Biographical and Critical, to the Works of the English Poets*. By Samuel Johnson. Volume the Sixth. London: Printed by J. Nichols: . . . M DCC LXXXI, 'Prior', p. 38.
     Collected: *1835*, vol. i, p. xviii; *1892*, ii. 303.
Text. *1781*.

Dr. Johnson says (*Lives*, ii. 198), 'In a gay French company, where every one sung a little song or stanza, of which the burden was *Bannisons la Mélancholie*, when it came to his turn to sing, after the performance of a young lady that sat next him, he produced these extempory lines: . . .' (then follows the poem).

Since we have not discovered Johnson's source, nor any earlier mention of the poem, we do not feel justified in accepting it as authentic. If genuine, it was presumably written before Prior left France for the last time in 1715.

1716

(785)   Song in Prison

MSS. None.
Pub. *European Magazine*, xliii (1803), 11.
     Collected: *1892*, ii. 384.
Text. *1803*.

This poem was contributed to the *European Magazine* by Joseph Moser (1748–1819), together with an account of its oral transmission to him by a relative who learned it from Prior when she was a child. Although Moser does not name this relative, it seems probable from his narrative that she was his aunt, Mrs. George Michael Moser, who was the daughter of Claude Guynier, the painter. Moser confesses that he can 'only recollect a few verses of it, and those perhaps not quite correct'. For this reason, we are obliged to place the fragmentary text that he gives among the 'doubtful' works, although we do not doubt that it represents the remains of a half-forgotten poem composed by P in 1715 or 1716. The strongest evidence of Moser's honesty is that nothing in the verses themselves is incompatible with what we now know of the situation, although Moser's copious annotations show several instances of his misunderstanding. (See H. B. Wright, 'Matthew Prior's Cloe and Lisetta', *M.P.* xxxvi, 1938, 17–19.)

As a parliamentary prisoner, P was confined in the home of John Hollingshead, the messenger, from the time of his examination by the Secret Committee, 16 June 1715, until Parliament was prorogued, 26 June 1716. During the day, neither P nor Hollingshead was permitted to 'stir out of doors'; but 'every evening . . . for a great part of the time' P was, by order of the Speaker, allowed to take a walk for his health in the custody of Mr. Wybergh, the serjeant at arms (*Calendar of Treasury Papers*, 1714–19, pp. 374–5, 454). According to this song, one of their regular walks was from Hollingshead's house in Brownlow Street to the tavern kept by John Cox and his wife, Elizabeth Cox, in Long Acre, which was just two streets away. Betty, who there served P (and teased him), later became his mistress (see commentary on *The Question*, 1718).

3–4. P's relations with his 'jailer' were evidently cordial. P described John Hollingshead as 'by Birth a Gentleman, and a very good natur'd Man', and they continued to be friends throughout the poet's life.

10. news. The hoped-for news of P's release.

33–34. Moser explains: 'The poet had, while leaning upon the bar, observed to [Betty] that the lemons were small. She replied, that they were, on that account, more tart and juicy; he therefore ordered a dozen to be squeezed, which were charged; but he having had the precaution to count the peels, and finding only eleven had been used, gives her a hint of the trick that she had played him.'

40. Nan. Probably Anne Durham; see commentary on *To Mr. Howard* (1708).

1717

(787)   *The Old Gentry*

MSS. None.
Pub. *Poems on Several Occasions*, 1717 (Case 260–2–a), p. 58.
        Never collected.
Text. *1717.*

The authorship of this poem has been extensively debated by Norman Ault and A. E. Case: see Ault's Introduction to *Pope's Own Miscellany*, 1935; Case's review, *M.P.* xxxiv (1937), 305–13; Ault's reply to the review, *M.P.* xxxv (1937), 179–87; Case's reply to Ault, *M.P.* xxxv (1937), 187–91. Ault argues that it is by Pope; Case contends that the evidence for attributing it to Pope is insufficient. He does not attempt to prove that the poem is Prior's; his thesis is that it is more likely to be P's than Pope's, but that the evidence does not support any definite attribution. We agree with this conclusion. See the commentary on *The Old Gentry* (1721), which is unquestionably by P and is based on the present poem; Pope, in going over P's manuscripts, inserted the title and first stanza from the present poem in the poem of 1721.

As Ault points out, the poem is a paraphrase of a French poem sometimes attributed to Mme de Coulanges. We quote it from Bouhours, *Pensées Ingénieuses*, 1692 (a volume in P's library), where it is described as a madrigal 'sur la Noblesse':

> D'Adam nous sommes tous enfans,
>   La preuve en est connuë;
> Et que tous nos premiers parens
>   Ont mené la charruë.
>
> Mais las de cultiver enfin
>   Leur terre labourée:
> L'un a détellé le matin,
>   L'autre l'apresdisnée.

2. *Wh—ston*. See note to *Alma* (1718), iii. 369. Whiston succeeded Newton as Lucasian professor of mathematics at Cambridge, but was expelled from the University in 1710 because of his Arian views. In 1711 he published *Primitive Christianity Revived*, and in 1715 started a society for reviving primitive Christianity according to his heretical tenets.

1718

(787)   *Upon Lady Katherine H—de's first appearing*

MSS.   *B.M. Sloane 4456*, 148ᵛ (X); *B.M. Add. 23904*, 107 (X); *Worcester Col.* (George Clarke's hand).

Pub.   *Upon Lady Katherine H—de's first appearing at the Play-House in Drury-Lane*. By M——w P——r, Esq; Sold by W. Graves, in Pater-noster-Row; and W. Chetwood, at Cato's Head in Russel-Court, near the Play-house. 1718. (Price Two-pence.); *The Female Phaeton*. By Mr. Prior. Printed for E. Curll, and sold by T. Warner in Pater-noster-row. (Price Twopence.) N.B. The copy, before publish'd, has not one Stanza printed right. N.D. [1718]; *The Court Miscellany*, 1719 (Case 308–1), p. 18; *Three Poems*, . . . London: Printed for E. Curll in Fleet-street. MDCCXX, p. 12; *A New Miscellany*, 1720 (Case 315), p. 219. Collected: *1722*, p. 5.

Text.   *1718*. Collated: *N.D.*

The first (W. Graves) edition appeared on 8 April 1718 (adv. *Daily Courant*), and was followed immediately by Curll's edition (adv. *St. James's Evening Post*, 8–10 April). In both these and in Curll's *Court Miscellany*, the poem is attributed to Prior. On the other hand, it is attributed to 'Mr. Harcourt' in Hammond's *A New Miscellany* and Curll's *Three Poems*, as well as by George Clarke in his commonplace book. The two B.M. manuscripts ascribe it to P; but they are late collections without authority. In *1722 Memoirs*, Curll says: 'The two Copies of Verses upon Lady KATHERIN HYDE, have been mistakenly applied by some Persons to another Hand; tho' whoever will in the least but impartially consider, they must allow, that the Easy Turn, and Epigrammatick Point, in those performances, could be the Produce of no other, than Mr. PRIOR's peculiar Pen. . . .' And in *1722* (where the poem is, of course, printed as P's), he adds the following note: 'Lady KATHERINE HYDE: To whom, this, and the following Copy [*The Judgment of Venus*] was sent, by the late Honourable *Simon Harcourt*, Esq;.' In *A New Miscellany*, 1720, p. 277, appears *To Mr. Harcourt, Occasioned by reading his Judgment of Venus. Sent from Cambridge*, beginning:

> HARCOURT! so pleasing are thy Lays,
> So Charming is thy Lyre;
> That some have robb'd Thee of thy Praise,
> And falsly call'd Thee *Prior*.

In it, the present poem, as well as *The Judgment of Venus*, is attributed to Harcourt. On the other hand, in *The Grove*, 1721 (Case 319), p. 280, a poem by Dr. Sewell says:

> Dear SIM, by Wits extolled by Wits cry'd down,
> Each Way become the Proverb of the Town
> To KITTY's Favour with Success aspire,
> The Second Place by Merit you acquire,
> But HE who wrote the VERSES, must be PRIOR.

From all this, it is clear that P's contemporaries did not know whether he or Harcourt wrote the poem. The attributions to Harcourt by Hammond and George Clarke carry more weight than those to P; for Curll—though he wavered occasionally—was the person who most industriously ascribed the poem to P (in addition to the publications mentioned, he advertised a third edition of the broadside in the *Post Boy*, 26–28 Feb. 1719). Simon Harcourt (1684-1720) was a friend of P's (see his letter of 1717 in *H.M.C. Bath*, iii. 449); he was secretary to the Brothers' Club and an intimate of the Tory wits; Pope wrote his epitaph. The verse of his that is preserved in the *Harcourt Papers* (ed. E. W. Harcourt, Oxford, 1880), ii. 161–5, is not distinguished. One cannot say, however, that this verse is so bad or so different from the poems in question as to make it unlikely that Harcourt could have written them.

Apart from the evidence summarized, there are two strong reasons for believing that P did not write the poem. The first is that in *L 28*, 74–128, there are included the printed sheets from *1722* of all the poems in that collection except this one and *The Judgment of Venus*; the inference is clear that Drift (and, presumably, Harley) believed these poems not to be P's. The second is P's *Answer to the Female Phaeton* (1718), which, if taken literally, is conclusive. It is possible, however, to argue (as does Eves, p. 392) that P intended to deny authorship in order 'to let whatever praise the little poems merited go to Harcourt', or to explain the denial in other ways. We therefore admit the remote possibility of P's authorship.

The poem was set to music by Charles Dieupart in 1731 and by Thomas Arne in 1757; a Latin translation appears in *B.M. Sloane 4456, 149*.

1. *Kitty*. Lady Katherine Hyde (1700–77); she married in 1720 Charles Douglas, third Duke of Queensberry, and was the patron of Gay and friend of Swift. See Austin Dobson, 'Prior's "Kitty" ', in *Eighteenth Century Vignettes*, first series, 1892.

13. Lady *Jenny*. Her elder sister, Lady Jane; on 27 Nov. 1718 she married William Capel, third Earl of Essex.

1720

(789) *The Judgment of Venus*

MSS. None.
Pub. *A New Miscellany*, 1720 (Case 315), p. 222; *Three Poems, . . .* London: Printed for E. Curll in Fleetstreet. MDCCXX, p. 15.
Collected: *1722*, p. 7.
Text. *1720 [Miscellany]*.

Much of the evidence cited in the preceding commentary applies also to this companion poem. It is attributed to Harcourt in *A New Miscellany* and *Three Poems*, and is almost certainly by him. It was first ascribed to Prior by Curll in *1722*, and the ascription has gained the weight of tradition because virtually all subsequent editions have printed it as his.

5. ' To the Picture of Lady RANELAUGH' (*1722*).
13. '*Picture of the Lady* SALISBURY' (*1722*).
17. '*Lady* JANE DOUGLAS, *Sister to the Duke of Douglas*' (*1722*).

1721

(790)   *Couplets*

MSS.   (1) *B.M. Add. 23076*, V. 21, B.M. 19b (Vertue Notebooks).
       (2) *Pierpont Morgan Lib., Original Portraits Drawn by Robert White, Sir James Thornhill, George Vertue, &c.*, p. 41 (X).
Pub.   (1) *Anecdotes of Painting in England; . . . Collected by the late Mr. George Vertue; And now digested and published from his original MSS.* By Mr. Horace Walpole . . . Volume the Fourth and last. Strawberry-Hill: Printed by Thomas Kirgate, MDCCLXXI, p. 50; *European Magazine*, Dec. 1793, p. 450.
       (2) *European Magazine*, Dec. 1793, p. 450.
       Collected (1 and 2): *1892*, ii. 389.
Text. (1) *B.M.* Collated: *1771, 1793*.
       (2) *Morg.* Collated: *1793*.

(1) Vertue, in his account of Charles Christian Reisen, says: 'as he was continually jokeing upon others. so every one endevourd to return his due. & his face being of a swarthy complexion his chin inclining to lenght enough. it gave a handle to many to be witty on his *mazzard* by drawing of it. on many occasions. amongst the rest upon a sketch that Sr. James Thornhill drew Mr Prior being in Company at the Noble Lords (Harley.) before mention'd. writt under it . . .' (then follows the couplet). (Printed in *Vertue Note Books*, iii. 25; Walpole Society, vol. xxix, 1933–4, Oxford 1934.) Reisen (1680–1725) was an engraver of gems and seals and an art collector; the first Earl of Oxford was his patron, and Sir James Thornhill was one of his executors.

(2) The Morgan MS. is written in pencil on a portrait labelled, 'Timothy Thomas, Chaplain to Ld. Oxford, Drawn by Sir J. Thornhill. N.B. the verses are Matthew Prior's, and his own handwriting.' This statement must mean that the verses on the original portrait are in Prior's hand; those on this copy are not.

The account in the *European Magazine*, by an anonymous contributor, is as follows:

Matthew Prior

in the latter part of his life resided at Down Hall, and amused himself, with a select party of friends, at any kind of nonsense that occurred. Sir James Thornhill was often of the party, and in the evening, between dinner and supper, used to make drawings of some of Mr. Prior's guests. Prior used to write verses under them. Under the head of Mr. Timothy Thomas, Chaplain to Lord Oxford, Prior wrote—[then follows Couplet 1].

Under Christian, the Seal-Engraver's Head, Prior wrote—[then follows Couplet 2].

An ingenious and elegant Collector has many of these portraits, with the verses under them in Prior's handwriting.

Mr. F. R. D. Needham informs us that not Timothy Thomas, but his brother William, was Lord Oxford's chaplain; Timothy belonged to the Westminster School circle of wits and minor poets, and translated Pope's *Essay on Man* into Latin.

Since P saw much of Thornhill, Christian, and the other 'virtuosi' 1719–21 (*H.M.C. Bath*, iii. 477, 482, 498–500), it seems likely that the couplets are genuine, but we have been unable to verify the existence of the original portraits with the verses in P's hand.

INDEX OF FIRST LINES OF VERSE

An asterisk * *indicates a variant line cited in the critical apparatus.*
A question mark ? *indicates a work of Doubtful Authenticity.*
Square brackets [ ] *indicate a work Wrongly Attributed to Prior.*

INDEX OF SHORT TITLES
USED FOR CROSS-REFERENCE

A question mark ? indicates a work of Doubtful Authenticity.
Square brackets [ ] indicate a work Wrongly Attributed to Prior.